5.

STIRLING UNIVERSITY LIBRARY
BOOK NUMBER   VOL COPY

| 1 | 2 | 6 | 8 | 6 | 2 | - | 1 | 1 |

D1757663

Stirling University Library (01786) 467220

12686211

Loans - ALL READERS - return or renew on the date
stamped at latest.

Library books not in immediate use should be on OUR
SHELVES NOT YOURS.

Recordings of use - please initial

DISPLAY		2 7 MAY 2005
3 1 MAY 1985	CANCELLED	2 0 JUL 2010
	29 MAY	
1 7 SEP 1985 CANCELLED	CANCELLED 1990 C	
1 6 SEP 1985 CANCELLED		
	0 1 MAY 1995 CANCELLED	
	CANCELLED	WITHDRAWN
1 9 DEC 1997 CANCELLED		from
		STIRLING UNIVERSITY LIBRARY

B
8 . 8
FEA

THE ORIGINS AND GROWTH OF COMMUNICATION

Lynne Feagans
Catherine Garvey
Roberta Golinkoff
with
Mark T. Greenberg
Carol Harding
and
John N. Bohannon

WITHDRAWN

from

STIRLING UNIVERSITY LIBRARY

2/85

 ABLEX PUBLISHING CORPORATION
Norwood, New Jersey 07648

Copyright © 1984 by Ablex Publishing Corporation

All rights reserved. No part of this publication may
be reproduced, stored in a retrieval system, or
transmitted, in any form or by any means, electronic,
mechanical, photocopying, microfilming, recording,
or otherwise, without permission of the publisher.

Printed in the United States of America.

Library of Congress Cataloging in Publication Data
Main entry under title:

The Origins and growth of communication.

  Includes indexes.
    1. Communication—Psychological aspects—Congresses.
2. Interpersonal communication—Congresses.   3. Infant
psychology—Congresses.   4. Children—Language—Congresses.   5. Child development—Congresses.   6. Conversation—Congresses.   I. Feagans, Lynne.   II. Garvey,
Catherine, 1930–   .   III. Golinkoff, Roberta M.
HM258.064 1983   302.2   83-10041
ISBN 0-89391-164-X

Ablex Publishing Corporation
355 Chestnut Street
Norwood, New Jersey 07648

Contents

Preface

In the summer of 1979 a group of scholars interested in the origins and growth of communication spent a month together at an institute of this topic sponsored by SRCD and Carnegie Corporation. As an outgrowth of this experience the participants and faculty of the institute agreed to continue the pursuit of the ideas which stemmed from the institute and to collaborate on important theoretical and data based papers which dealt with the important issues at the institute. This resulted in periodic gatherings of some of us at academic meetings and much correspondence among the group. This continued interaction on topics generated from the institute eventually led to the funding of an SRCD study group supported by Carnegie Corporation which would gather the fruitful products of collaboration into a book which would capture at least some of the ideas from the original institute.

In November 1981 a subgroup of the original institute met in Chapel Hill, North Carolina to review submitted chapters for possible inclusion in the book. Through the hard work of editing and communicating with authors, the subgroup produced the collection of papers included in this book. This subgroup was composed of the following scholars: Roger Bakeman, John N. Bohannon, Philip Dale, Lynne Feagans, Catherine Garvey, Roberta Golinkoff, Mark Greenberg, Carol Harding, Catherine Snow, and Daniel Stern.

In addition gratitude is due to the many staff members at the Frank Porter Graham Child Development Center who spent many hours typing and editing the manuscript and co-ordinating the many activities of the study group. They are Mary Ann Kimball, Debbie Jeffreys and Gina Walker.

A special thanks must go to Barbara Finberg at the Carnegie Corporation who, from the beginning, saw the institute as a contribution to our knowledge about communication and who supported the continuing interaction of the group over these several years so that this book could become a reality.

List of Contributors

Dr. Roger Bakeman
Associate Professor of Psychology
*Professor of Psychology (beginning in
    September)
Psychology Department
Georgia State University
Atlanta, Georgia 30332

Dr. Elaine Baker
Research Student
Psychology Department
University of Manchester
Manchester, England M13 9PL

Dr. David Baldwin
Psychology Department and Regional Primate
    Research Center
University of Washington NI-25
Seattle, Washington 98195

Dr. John Neil Bohannon, III
Associate Professor of Psychology
School of Psychology
Georgia Institute of Technology
Atlanta, Georgia 30332

Dr. Joseph Byrne
Consultant in Infant & Child Development
Department of Psychology
Izaak Walton Killam Hospital for Children
Post Office Box 3070
Halifax, Nova Scotia
Canada, B3J 3G9

Dr. Thomas Carr
Associate Professor of Psychology
School of Psychology
Michigan State University
East Lansing, Michigan 48823

Dr. Anne Dunlea
Lecturer
Department of Linguistics, GFS301
University of Southern California
Los Angeles, California 90089-1693

Dr. Judy Dunn
Senior Research Fellow
Medical Research Council Unit on
    Development and Integration of Behavior
University of Cambridge
Madingley, Cambridge
England, CB3 8AA

Dr. Mary Ann Evans
Assistant Professor
Department of Psychology
University of Guelph
Guelph, Ontario, Canada N1G-2W1

Dr. Lynne Feagans
Research Associate Professor
Frank Porter Graham Child Development
    Center
Highway 54 Bypass West
Chapel Hill, North Carolina 27514

Dr. Anne Fernald
Post Doctoral Fellow
Department of Psychology
University of Denver
Denver, Colorado 80210

Dr. Catherine Garvey
Professor of Psychology
Department of Psychology
University of Maine at Orono
301 Little Hall
Orono, Maine 04469

Dr. Roberta Michnick Golinkoff
Associate Professor
Educational Studies and Psychology
University of Delaware
Willard Hall Education Building
Room 213
Newark, Delaware 19711

Dr. Mark T. Greenberg
Associate Professor of Psychology
Department of Psychology
University of Washington
Seattle, Washington 98195

Dr. Carol Harding
Assistant Professor
Foundations of Education
Loyola University
820 N. Michigan Ave.
Chicago, Illinois 60611

Dr. Alan Hayes
Lecturer
The Fred and Eleanor Schonell Educational
    Research Centre
University of Queensland
St. Lucia, Queensland
Australia 4067

Dr. Kathy Hirsh-Pasek
Visiting Assistant Professor
Psychology Department
Swarthmore College
Swarthmore, Pennsylvania 19081

Dr. Peter Lloyd
Lecturer
Psychology Department
University of Manchester
Manchester, England M13 9PL

Dr. Cindy Miller
Assistant Professor
Department of Psychology
University of Western Ontario
London, Ontario
Canada N6A 5C2

Dr. Anat Ninio
Associate Professor
Department of Psychology
Hebrew University of Jerusalem
Jerusalem, Israel 91905

Dr. Ann Pace
Assistant Professor
Department of Psychology
University of Missouri
Columbia, Missouri 65201

Dr. Richard Scoville
Assistant Professor
Virginia Polytechnical Institute
Blacksburg, Virginia 24061

Dr. Catherine E. Snow
Associate Professor
Graduate School of Education
Harvard University
703 Larsen Hall
Appian Way
Cambridge, Massachusetts 02138

Dr. Susan Sonnenshein
Assistant Professor
Department of Psychology
University of Maryland
Catonsville, Maryland 21228

Dr. Polly Wheeler
Lecturer in Psychology
Northeastern University
Boston, Massachusetts 02115

Dr. Pat Zukow
Adjunct Assistant Professor
Department of Psychology
University of California
Los Angeles, California 90024

Introduction: The Origins and Growth of Communication

Catherine Garvey

Human communication, even in the first few years of life, is a broad and complex topic. A number of different disciplines have contributed to the rapidly expanding body of knowledge, of research techniques, and of theoretical perspectives that currently influence the study of communication. With the dual objectives of promoting interdisciplinary exchange and of making this body of knowledge available to young specialists in the area of human development, the Society for Research in Child Development sponsored a Summer Institute in 1979, entitled The Origins and Growth of Communication. This month-long Institute, which was funded by the Carnegie Corporation, brought together several resident faculty members, all of whom had taken part in planning the Institute, as well as a number of visiting faculty members and a group of thirty fellows. (A list of the Institute faculty is found at the end of this chapter.) Since that time, a majority of the fellows and faculty have maintained the lines of communication formed during the Institute. The present volume collects the work of a number of the fellows, and both fellows and faculty members have collaborated in the editorial work.

The conceptual framework for the Institute was based on the view that communication is of central importance to the development of the individual and to the structure of the interactions, relationships, groups, and communities that comprise the environment of human growth. Communication can best be understood within the social networks from which it arises and to which it further contributes. An emphasis on the social contextedness of communication was further reflected in the keynote address, "Early Relationships," presented by Robert Hinde, which elaborated his earlier statements (Hinde, 1976) of this approach.

Although the fellows and faculty represented a diversity of perspectives, special-izations, and backgrounds, they discovered a number of common substantive and methodological concerns. Among the themes that repeatedly emerged in the lec-tures, discussions, and informal conversations were the following: the use of natu-ralistic observation to complement or validate more highly controlled investigation; the importance of interindividual influences and techniques for assessing such influ-ences; problems in determining appropriate units and levels of analysis of commu-nicative behavior; and the effects of observer characteristics and the interactions between observer and the subject observed. These shared concerns as well as the topical content of the Institute have led not only to the continuing communication among the participants, but also to the preparation of this volume. Presentation of the body of the proposal which served as a blueprint for the work of the participants will provide the most informative introduction to this book.

BACKGROUND TO THE STUDY OF COMMUNICATION AND RATIONALE FOR THE INSTITUTE

An interdisciplinary approach to the study of human communication is both neces-sary and inevitable. The topic includes the various means by which human beings influence one another, coordinate their activities, create and maintain social order, and produce and transmit information across time and space. These processes have been investigated at micro- and macrolevels of analysis, and the various means on which these processes depend have been studied from a variety of scientific per-spectives. Among those disciplines that have contributed to our knowledge of human communication are sociology, psychology, psychiatry, ethology, linguis-tics, philosophy, biology, anthropology, and the communication sciences. Within each discipline, specialized fields of inquiry have been directly concerned with aspects of communication. Not all these subfields have directly addressed the ques-tion of *development*. Their representation in the Institute was justified, however, by the fact that (a) they offer useful research and analysis techniques that can be applied to the study of children's communication, or (b) they provide information on the characteristics of adult communication of which we must determine the ontogeny. Thus, for example, techniques developed in animal ethology have been adapted to the study of children's interpersonal behavior (Blurton-Jones, 1972; Strayer & Strayer, 1976). Descriptions of the dynamics of more mature conversa-tion (Sacks, Schegloff, & Jefferson, 1974) have enriched investigations of how interacting mothers and infants coordinate their alternating contributions and how these mechanisms may develop from the prelinguistic period and through the period of language acquisition (Snow, 1977). Recent advances in the philosophy of lan-guage (Grice, 1975; Searle, 1969) have found immediate application in the study of children's developing competence in social uses of language (Bates, 1976; Dore, 1975; Garvey, 1975). Social psychological theories of the way in which human beings organize their social world and classify and interpret its dimensions and events (Heider, 1958; Schutz, 1962) have directly influenced empirical (Sedlak,

1974) and conceptual (Cook-Gumperz, 1975; Ryan, 1974) studies of the so-cial–cognitive bases of children's communication. More formal systems of linguistic analysis (Halliday, 1967) have provided frameworks for the study of the structure of discourse in child–adult interaction situations (Sinclair & Coulthard, 1975). Other subfields have included, almost from their inception, direct investigation of children's communication as, for example, sociolinguistics (Ervin-Tripp, 1969; Slobin, 1967) and ecological psychology (Barker, 1963). Thus, the position taken in designing this Institute was that a foundation of knowledge concerning human communication exists; some areas of investigation focused directly on developmental questions while others offered techniques and approaches that have great potential for application to the study of the growth of communication. The Institute in bringing these several perspectives together facilitated more comprehensive and more adequate investigations of the roles of communication in child development.

CONTENT OF THE INSTITUTE

Six topic areas, or courses, were included. From a chronological perspective, we began with the communicative abilities and behavior of the newborn infant, moved through the period of language acquisition and the elaboration of communicative skills, and ended with a characterization of the capabilities of the child ready to enter elementary school. From a thematic perspective, many of the important issues were introduced in the first week and subsequently reexamined from different points of view. These included the interrelations of verbal and nonverbal behavior and their relations to the context of situation and setting; the interactional framework of communication, including establishment of joint attention and the alternation and integration of turns at acting; the effects of the child's maturation on his own and his partners' contributions to social interactions; the problem of delimiting units of coherent episodes of behavior; and the problem of analyzing the data of sequenced and/or hierarchically structured, interactive behavior. The relatively neglected topic of the role of affect in communication was also introduced in the first week. Although the methodology is listed as an independent topic area, it was an integral part of each course. One day for each of the five remaining topic areas was devoted specifically to work with the methodological problems of greatest concern to that area and to the specific techniques available for description and analysis of the different aspects of communication. Each topic area is briefly described below, with indication of the specific aims of the course and some of the major research questions that were included. The organizers and resident faculty and number of days allotted for each course are listed with each topic area.

I. The Origins of Communication in the First Year of Life (4 days)

Language, both its production and comprehension, has been the central topic of most attempts to understand the origins and growth of human communication. This focus has understandably resulted from language's unique place within the communicative systems of our species. Because language proper does not begin until roughly the second year of life, on grounds of biological "readiness," the period preceding this onset, namely the first year of life, has received relatively less study as an important epoch in which communicative systems develop.

In spite of this, it is commonly observed that parents and infants, almost from the first day of life, do indeed communicate and appear to do so quite effectively. In this early phase, communication is achieved through facial expressions, gaze behaviors, gesture, posture, and vocal (nonverbal) behaviors on both the infant's and the adult's part. What is more, normal as well as abnormal communicative patterns in the "prelinguistic" modes can be intuitively discerned and objectively identified (Schaffer, 1977).

One of the more striking features of the early communicative process is that it is largely involved with the transmission of information about affective states and states of general arousal (Emde, Gaensbauer, & Harmon, 1976; Sroufe & Waters, 1976). It also functions largely to modulate the flow of the dyadic interaction in the sense of providing the signals to initiate, maintain, readjust, terminate, and avoid the communicative process itself.

There are two central research questions in this first phase of communication. First, what is the nature of normal and abnormal communicative systems that emerge during this early period? And second, how and to what extent does the infant's knowledge and experience of these earliest communicative systems act as an indispensable foundation and framework within which his later linguistic development proceeds? The thrust of the topics which comprised this section is directed toward these questions. The course was organized around four major subjects.

The first subject was devoted to an examination of the behavior with which mothers and infants begin to communicate. These included the infant's developing repertoire of communicative behaviors, including sucking, vocalization, gaze, facial expression, gesture and posture, and the mother's changing repertoire of infant-directed behavior. The central foci of this subject will be on different methodologies of collecting, describing, and analyzing the behaviors in these separate channels; on conceptualizing and studying the integrated use of behaviors in different modalities; and on the changes in these behaviors and patterns of cross-modal behavior over the first year of life. A major issue was the developmental continuities and discontinuities in modalities of communication during this period.

The second subject was the conceptualization and study of the interactive process itself. Among the various conceptual frameworks that were proposed are the S-R paradigms, ethological models, mutual regulation, and "reciprocity." These were discussed along with the methodologies best suited to, or required by, the different positions. The behavioral repertoires and capabilities discussed the preceding day were reexamined as structures within alternative interactive frameworks and new work on potentially important interactive mechanisms such as "imitation" were introduced. A major issue was the variation in the goals of the early interactive process as viewed from cross-cultural perspectives.

The third subject was the role of affect in organizing mother–infant communication. Affect is, perhaps, the most central "organizer" of the early communicative process and one that requires far more study than it has received to date. The behavioral and physiological aspects of affect were examined, and the expression of affect in its social and cognitive context was discussed. The objective of this section was to provide a developmental view of the organization of affect; the first two subjects of this course were recast in terms of the affective organization of the interactive process.

The fourth subject concerned clinical applications of the study of the early communicative process. Two major aspects of the problems of applying basic developmental data to relevant clinical issues were explored. The first concerned the process of deriving clinical cues and tools at the necessarily more molar level from studies and observations at the more molecular level. The second issue was that of the clinical application of knowledge of the early communicative process to work with "high-risk" newborn infants. These issues are of obvious importance. Although rarely addressed explicitly, they deserved detailed examination in this course and their consideration will set the stage for discussion of comparable application and "translation" problems arising in subsequent courses in this Institute.

Workshops composed of small groups of participants and a faculty member were conducted each day. Raw data (TV tapes and 16 mm films) were available for the workshops and provided longitudinal developmental data and cross-sectional data from groups that differed along some important dimension (e.g., culture, normality). Laboratory workshops with these materials provided participants with (a) experience in scoring with several different techniques and at various levels of analysis, (b) practice in analyzing data appropriate to scoring technique and level of abstraction of data scored, and (c) direct contact with data discussed at a more abstract level in the morning lectures. Small groups of participants reconvened later each day to discuss the outcomes of these work sessions which, taken together, comprised a delimited mini-experiment. Discussions of the various findings at different levels of analysis provided material for the methodology section of the final day of that week. Organizer and Instructor: Daniel Stern.

II. Development of Linguistic Communication (3 days)

With the onset of language, the child acquires a major new means for communicating. The acquisition of language viewed as the development of a linguistic code has been an important focus of psycholinguistic research. The field has expanded from its original concern with the formal, syntactic structure of language and the problems of inducing the grammatical rules, or grammars, of the developing system (McNeill, 1970) to investigation of semantic development (Clark, 1973). Questions of the relationship of language acquisition and cognitive development have further enriched this field (Bloom, Lightbown, & Hood, 1975; Brown, 1973). A still more recent contribution to an understanding of the processes and substance of first language acquisition is the reintroduction of questions of the functions of speech and of the pragmatic aspects of communication (Bates, 1976; Greenfield & Smith, 1976; Halliday, 1975). Two important advantages are achieved by relating the emergence of language to cognitive development on the one hand and, on the other, to the communicative functions it serves for the child in his daily activities. The first is that cognition provides a basis on which to trace the precursors of specific linguistic developments; the second is that the goals and settings of language in use may be used to account for variation in utterance form across communicative situations. The latter point has been stressed by Ervin-Tripp and Mitchell-Kernan (1977): "If it is the case that the development of formal structures is in part at the service of changes in communicative intent, then to study formal development without attention to function leaves change unmotivated" (p. 6). The objective of this course was to provide a view of linguistic development that takes into account the interactive setting and interpersonal activities in which language first appears and to relate this perspective to the cognitive changes that take place in this period.

This section of the Institute examined the linguistic aspects of communication during the language acquisition period and was organized around three subjects. Following a review of the infant's capabilities in Stages 4 and 5 of the sensorimotor period and an introduction of major theoretical views of the emergence of language, the first subject of discussion was the intentional use of nonlinguistic and prelinguistic vocalizations. The influence of the theory of speech acts (Austin, 1962; Searle, 1969) on work in this area was considered at this point and reexamined in later courses, as well. Important issues were the questions of continuity in development; the theoretical problem of intentionality across this period and the problem of empirical validation of preverbal pragmatic intentions (Bruner, 1975); and the role of intonation and prosody in prelinguistic communication.

The second subject was the passage into single-word speech. Important issues were determination of the concepts and functions the child expresses in one-word speech, and the role of presupposition and nonlinguistic context in the production of one-word utterances. Also discussed were the determinants of what is expressed in speech; the changing relations and balance that exist between gesture, context, and what is linguistically encoded; and the extent to which linguistic structure and communicative context influence comprehension.

The third subject was the development of two-word speech (and beyond) and the acquisition of linguistic conventions for expressing intentions, structuring conversations, and executing verbal routines. Major issues were the children's use of communicative strategies, the relation of comprehension and production of speech acts (of which directives have been the most widely studied); individual differences in use of linguistic resources; the developmental changes in use of cohesive devices in conversation (e.g., anaphora, conjunction, ellipsis); the onset of metalinguistic awareness (Gleitman, Gleitman, & Shipley, 1972) and the "ability to talk about whole speech acts or coordinates of a given speech act" (Bates, 1976).

The methodology and problems of "rich interpretation" were discussed throughout this course. Another theme relevant to each of these three days was the repeated finding that different children may employ rather different strategies in the course of their linguistic development. The parallel achievements in cognitive development over the period of language acquisition were related to each day's subject. Information on communicative development in deaf children born to hearing parents (Feldman, Goldin-Meadow, & Gleitman, 1976) was included to help in distinguishing communication from language production per se.

Workshops in this course included analysis of audio- and videotaped data of child–adult and child–child interactions; techniques for comparing levels of linguistic development, for studying the relation and co-occurrence of verbal and nonverbal gestures, and for classifying prelinguistic vocalizations; and methods for experimental elicitation of child judgments and linguistic responses topics for small-group study and laboratory exercises. Organizer and Instructor: Roberta Golinkoff.

III. Psychological and Social Dimensions of the Expansion of Communication (4 days)

With the onset of language, the beginnings of symbolic representation, and other emerging intellectual, locomotor, and manipulative achievements, the communicative capabilities of the child increase as to the opportunities and demands he encounters. The preschool child can be viewed as an active and interactive member of a changing and expanding set of interpersonal contacts and relationships in which both interactions and communication become increasingly complex and varied. At the same time, the underlying social–cognitive skills and concepts of social events, of self, and of others must undergo change and reorganization. In order to provide a framework for a more comprehensive understanding of this period, three areas of social–psychological functioning, heretofore relatively isolated as research topics, were brought together: cognitive and social–cognitive development, changes in social behavior, and communicative development. It is the case that although major theoretical formulations (Piaget, Vygotsky, Mead, Sullivan, Werner, and Kaplan) of this period have been advanced, empirical investigation on the relations between social cognition and interpersonal behavior or communication has been primarily limited until quite recently to a few research paradigms such as referential communication (reviewed by Glucksberg, Krauss, & Higgins, 1975) or attempts to distinguish and clarify the various processes of perspective-taking (reviewed by Shantz, 1975) and to relate these to aspects of moral development.

This section of the Institute was organized into four subjects. The first reviewed the above-mentioned theoretical positions on preschool social and cognitive development as well as the perspectives contributed by ethology. A summary of the literature on cognitive development, including reasoning, attentional, and memory processes, provided a basis for discussion of social cognition as it related to interactions and communication. The second subject was the preschooler's conceptions of others as assessed in the perspective-taking and person-perception literature. Major issues were the nature of the developing knowledge of others' psychological or emotional states and processes (DeVries, 1970; Flavell, 1974) and of interactions and relations among others and between the child himself and others (Livesley & Bromley, 1973; Marvin & Greenberg, unpublished). Information on children's concepts of what others know and think, how others feel and react, the intentions and motives of others' action, and their conceptualization of social events and "streams of behavior" must be based in part on work with older children and on work now in progress with preschoolers. This information was subsequently related to the picture that emerges from the study of children's spontaneous interpersonal interactions.

The third subject was the spontaneous communication and social interaction of children. It emphasized developmental changes in the structure of preschoolers' interactions with parents and other adults (Lamb, 1976; Marvin, 1977; Ross & Goldman, 1977) and with peers (Eckerman, Whatley, & Kutz, 1975; Strayer & Strayer, 1976) and in communicative techniques used to initiate, maintain, and terminate these interactions (Goldman & Ross, in press; Gottman & Parkhurst, 1977; Mueller & Lucas, 1975). An attempt was made to present research that represented the wide variety of children's social activities now being studied, including private play, nursery school contacts, and interactions with familiar and unfamiliar adults and children of different ages. Research in this area, which is expanding at a particularly high rate, addresses the issue of the differentiation of interactive behavior on dimensions of task, setting, and participants. One of the major issues is the nature of the social knowledge that such covariation of behavior and situation implies.

The fourth subject concerned the relations among social cognition and social and communicative development. Studies that have independently measured at least two of these aspects (Spivack & Shure, 1974; Shantz, 1977) were discussed, and the methodological and empirical continuities/discontinuities in the development of social acts and meaning systems (Kuczaj, 1975) were examined. Major issues are the conceptual relationship of the three aspects (Bates, Benigni, Bretherton, Camaioni, & Volterra, 1977) and the question of whether specific types of social interaction are the ontogenetic "source" of specific social cognitive and communication skills or vice versa, and the possibility of developing a single descriptive/conceptual system for the analysis of both cognitive and interactive processes.

Throughout this course certain research issues recurred. Among these were methodological and conceptual questions of the measurement of social–cognitive development as a continuous ability or as a discontinuous stage/level phenomenon; measurement of social behavior in terms of quantitative features or qualitative categories; and possible explanations of the often-noted discrepancies between experimentally derived assessments of social competencies and the performances consistently observed in naturalistic observation.

Several workshops were planned. At least two were devoted to laboratory work in analysis of recorded materials. Of these, one focused on the problems of inferring social–cognitive competencies from videotaped records of ongoing interactions of preschoolers with adults or other children; in the other, analyses were made of ritualized play and pretend play—both rich sources of data on the organization of skilled social behavior. Two workshop-discussion groups were formed to examine techniques currently in use in experimental investigations of children's social–cognitive competencies, including elicitation procedures, selection of response measures, and the conceptual–logical analysis of the componential structure of experimental tasks. The uses of alternative methods of investigation of social–cognitive development (e.g., the longitudinal "case study" method) were evaluated in these workshops. Organizers: Carolyn Shantz and Robert Marvin; Instructor: Robert Marvin.

IV. Ethnological, Anthropological, and Sociological Approaches to Communication (3 days)

Social speaking can be viewed as a skilled activity in its own right as well as an extremely sensitive index of social discriminations. Through the language acquisition period, the child also learns the uses to which language can be put (Halliday, 1973); techniques for creating joint conversational events (Keenan, 1974); and the ways in which speech form is adapted to types of interactional events and their specifically contexted variants. Considering the functional and contextual variability of speech and other aspects of communicative behavior, it is essential to employ analytic and conceptual frameworks that permit comparisons of aspects of communicative competence across time and across social settings and culture areas.

Cross-cultural studies have had a significant impact on many areas of investigation: the study of cognition, of patterns of language acquisition, of primary socialization, and of the role of play in human development—to name only a few. Ethnographic analyses of natural conversation (Hymes, 1972), and in particular the organizing frameworks employed in the ethnography of speaking, the study of communicative competence, and conversational analysis, underlie a substantial body of empirical findings. These approaches view talk as a social activity. Though they diverge on a number of issues, all have emphasized three concepts as vital to the study of communication: (a) the importance of the context of situation, (b) the covariation of the function and structure of speech, and (c) the fact that speech and other social behavior is structured by rules of various types and orders (Ervin-Tripp, 1972). Whether comparisons are made across cultures or subcultures, or across situations or time within a single community, researchers cannot afford to neglect the components of situation, the functional aspects of speech, and the patterning of communicative events that shape, constrain, or direct children's performances and interpretative abilities.

It was the objective of this course to review major theoretical positions (Goffman, Hymes, Garfinkel, Cicourel, and Habermas), representative techniques for data collection, and procedures for description and analysis in the ethnography of communication and in sociolinguistics, and to summarize the results of current research and work-in-progress. The course was organized around three subjects.

The first subject concerned the analysis of situation and the major approaches

(Hymes, Labov, Crystal, and Davy) to covariation of communicative behavior and dimensions of situation. The concepts of speech situation, event, and act and their respective classification systems were discussed, as well as the perennially controversial issue of the status of "rule" in the study of social behavior systems. A focal point for many of these issues was the notion of register and the basic and extended functions of a given register. The phenomenon known as Baby Talk, one of a set of "simplified" registers, has been documented in numerous cultures and has been investigated in some detail (Snow & Ferguson, 1977). It was of particular interest not only as an example of the interaction of dimensions of situation, function, and speech forms, but also as a register that children themselves begin to acquire at an early age (Sachs & Devin, 1976) and can use with considerable skill in make-believe role enactment.

The second subject was the development of conversation and the functional differentiation and elaboration of such activities as persuading and directing others, narrating, teaching, and simply conversing. Verbal interaction, or speech exchanges, entail skill in regulating speaker participation; in establishing topics and adjusting the flow of new and given information (Keenan & Schieffelin, 1976); and in structuring the event or encounter. Research in conversational analysis has focused on the placement and form of recurrent patterns of exchanges; on the acquisition of routines and ritual sequences; on such functional systems as aggravation, mitigation, or politeness; and on the conversational uses to which certain response strategies are put (e.g., repetition, dependent questions). Major subtopics are the order of acquisition and utilization of cohesive devices in conversation and the several relations (e.g., redundancy, complementarity, contrast) and developmental change in the relations between verbal and nonverbal modalities. An important theoretical issue was the evidence for rival hypotheses concerning the causal relations between the child's expanding experience of language functions and the acquisition of linguistic structure—do new forms first serve old functions, or do the functions impel the acquisition of new forms and structures?

The third subject examined current cross-cultural work on the development of communication. Ethnographic and anthropological approaches to the study of communicative competence reveal critical problems in the collection, analysis, and interpretation of natural speech samples—problems that are often obscured (but no less present) in work in cultural settings and groups in which the investigator is a member. In this section, we considered problems of observing, selecting or identifying variables, and recording and classifying the data of natural speech that arise in field work. Some models of structural ethnographic analysis of adult data were reviewed (Frake, Gumperz), and the more recent cross-cultural work on children's talk (by Schieffelin, Whiting & Lubin, Kernan, and Watson) and the implications of this work for an understanding of communication were discussed.

Workshops in this topic area included practice with the more widely used systems of notation for indicating paralinguistic and prosodic features of conversational exchanges; comparison of available structural analyses of at least one type of speech event (e.g., ritual insults or narratives); and discussion of alternative coding systems for at least one type of strategic interaction such as persuasion episodes. The work was based on audio and video records of children's spontaneous interactions. Organizer and Instructor: Courtney Cazden.

V. Problems in the Analysis of Discourse (2 days)

A natural continuation of the preceding topic area is a consideration of the problems that arise in the study of any type of face-to-face verbal interaction. Since discourse is a product of the conjunction of language and interaction, its study can depart from a focus on either of the conjuncts or from questions concerning the social or psychological processes that make the conjunction possible. Previous sections of the Institute reflected these various perspectives. In this section we discussed some of the major issues that arise in the analysis of discourse, with particular attention to those that relate directly to the empirical investigation of children's interactive speech. The topic of this section was the translation of the available discourse-analytic theory and practice into developmental studies of children's conversational interactions. The subjects were (a) units and structures, (b) sequencing and cohesion, and (c) general principles of interpretation.

A basic question was the nature of the units of discourse and their composition. Neither the linguistic units of clause or sentence nor the speech unit of utterance is adequate to an analysis of the transactions of discourse. The unit, speech act, is widely used; but in empirical work its constituent structure and the criteria employed in identification of a token, or instance, rarely conform to the structure and criteria proposed in theoretical work (Sadock, 1974; Searle, 1975). Most researchers, however, acknowledge the existence of three aspects of the basic unit of discourse: what is said (form properties); what is meant (meaning properties); and what is done (functional properties). None of these aspects is analytically simple. The basic unit (be it speech act, move, or turn) occurs in, and must be analyzed with regard to, its textual and interactional environment. Beyond the basic unit and up to the level of the speech event (e.g., interview, lesson), higher order units are postulated, their relationships reflecting a hierarchical structure (Sinclair & Coulthard, 1975). Most theoretical and empirical work to date has focused on the level of the speech exchange, composed of an act and the response to that act. A comprehensive account of what has transpired in an exchange would, minimally, present its linguistic, propositional, paralinguistic, kinesic, textual, and contextual features and would show how these relate to the participants' understanding of the exchange (Labov & Fanshel, 1977). From the point of view of the listener, different types of information are used in arriving at an interpretation of a message token. The relative contribution of the various sources of information to a working interpretation of what was said/meant/done does not necessarily remain constant across exchanges. Further, the relative contributions must be expected to change with the developing competence of the child speaker–listener. (The work of Shatz, Gleitman, Blank, and Friedlander suggests that children do make changing use of text, context, and gesture in making sense of adults' speech.)

A second question was that of sequencing. What are the organizing principles that lead to the orderly sequencing of acts (Mohan, 1974), turns at speaking (Sacks et al., 1974), or moves (Merritt, 1976) in a transaction? Descriptive and empirical analyses of text (Clarke, 1975; Gunter, 1974; Halliday & Hasan, 1976) suggest a high level of redundancy in the marking of cohesion—in form, meaning, and functional aspects of discourse. At the same time, such characteristics as formal ellipsis or stylistic "indirectness" result in breaks of different kinds in the thread of discourse which must be joined by inferential work on the part of the participants *and* analysts (Clark, 1976; Grice, 1975). Proposals concerning the bases for conversational sequencing and the empirical support for these hypotheses will be discussed along with their current applications to child discourse.

Attempts to arrive at general principles of discourse structure or function *or* to specify parameters or developing competence in discourse must assign observed behavior (tokens) to classes or categories (types). The bases for these assignments vary not only with the level of analysis and the specific research question asked, but also with the assumptions of the investigator concerning the interpretation of the behavioral data. The third subject was a comparison of several approaches to the interpretation of the raw data of discourse and a discussion of the assumptions they make, in respect particularly to the validity of the classification procedures. Representative analyses (from the work of Halliday, Goffman, Sacks, Labov) and their rationales provided material for discussion. Major issues were those of the uniqueness of any classification and whether a determinate classification can represent participants' interpretative procedures. Finally, we compared several classification schemes for analysis of a functionally defined discourse category that is the focus of current research across several disciplines, for example, clarification sequences, as they have been studied by Corsaro, Stokes, Ervin-Tripp, Garvey, Cherry, Holtzman, and Shatz. Organizer and Instructor: Catherine Garvey.

VI. Methodology and Analysis (4 days, 1 day each week)

The Institute was designed to foster an interdisciplinary outlook, not only on substantive issues but also in respect to procedures and methodology. In this section, we hoped to demonstrate how elements of current disciplines can coalesce in new and meaningful ways to promote "a substantial science of naturalistic developmental processes" (McCall, 1977). To a large extent, the requisite conceptual and methodological elements exist, albeit distributed over several disciplines. This course explored McCall's proposals for bringing together naturalistic description, longitudinal designs, multivariate data, and developmental concerns with developmental processes as they occur in natural environments.

A major objective was to encourage critical and knowledgeable use of the many techniques available for studying human communication. Typically, new methodologies arise when a researcher pursuing a substantive concern finds no appropriate techniques available in his area and must develop new ones or adapt techniques developed in other areas to his specific problems. Accordingly, the emphasis was on the necessary fit between problem, data, and technique; methodological issues, alternative approaches, and critical appraisal of both accepted and innovative procedures were coordinated with the several topic areas. The specific aims of this course included (a) presentation of the best possible examples of current methodological practice with regard to design, data collection, analysis, and interpretation, and (b) systematic analysis of alternative techniques, their underlying assumptions, and the limitations they place on interpretation. Given the general concerns of the Institute, a major focus was on techniques that reduce the observed streams of behavior to analyzable and interpretable results. At the same time, the problems inherent in reduction—in the use of code and category systems and the sometimes "hidden" assumptions in reduction techniques—were considered in relation to specific types of interactional data.

Presentations by guest faculty centered on three subjects. The first was the rationale, history, and recent resurgence of naturalistic observation. Although experimental studies have been dominant over the past 20 years, earlier observational work was often methodologically sound. A critical overview of the work done in the 1920s and 1930s (and some from the 1940s and 1950s) can provide historical perspective on the uses and limitations of naturalistic observation in contemporary investigations. Longitudinal designs also have a substantial history and a unique potential that deserve review and reevaluation.

The second subject was the contribution of ethology, in particular in the observation and "unitizing" of complex, interactive behavior in natural settings. A major issue was the extent to which verbal behavior or complexes of verbal and nonverbal behavior are amenable to analysis by existing ethological techniques. New techniques for the study of classes of nonverbal behavior and their patterning and function were also discussed.

The third subject was the conceptual and technical problems of data collection and analysis. The emphasis was on the data of complex and sequential interactions. Problems in the translation of data analytic strategies and techniques across substantive disciplines was a major issue.

Integration of substantive, conceptual, and methodological topics was achieved by arranging for some overlapping participation of visiting faculty in the topical courses and workshops and those in the methodology discussions. More formal presentations alternated with workshop/discussion sessions keyed to the specific topics and, when possible, to problems which arose in the research of the student participants themselves. Organizer and Instructor: Roger Bakeman.

The plan for the Institute as set forth in the proposal was, admittedly, somewhat ambitious for a convocation lasting only four weeks. The content selected, however, was the very minimum required to demonstrate the multidimensionality of communication and to serve as a basis for discussion of the developmental issue of the relations between socialization and communication—between becoming a person in a social world and exchanging messages with others.

Catherine Garvey

Director, Institute on the
Origins and Growth of Communication
June–July, 1979

Faculty of the Interdisciplinary Institute on the Origins and Growth of Communication

---

Keynote Speaker: Robert Hinde, University of Cambridge, England

1. The Origins of Communication in the First Year of Life

Daniel Stern, Cornell University Medical Center (Section Organizer)
T. Berry Brazelton, Harvard Medical School
Judy Dunn, University of Cambridge, England
Susan Goldberg, The Hospital for Sick Children, Toronto
Melvin Konner, Harvard University
Edward Tronick, Children's Hospital Medical Center, Boston

2. The Development of Linguistic Communication

Roberta Golinkoff, University of Delaware (Section Organizer)
Elizabeth Bates, University of Colorado
Philip Dale, University of Washington at Seattle
Patricia Greenfield, University of California at Los Angeles

3. Psychological and Social Dimensions of Communication

Robert Marvin, University of Virginia (Section Organizer)
Robert Cairns, University of North Carolina
William Damon, Clark University
Edward Mueller, Boston University
Kenneth Rubin, University of Waterloo, Canada

4. Ethological, Anthropological, and Sociological Approaches to Communication

Courtney Cazden, Harvard University (Section Organizer)
Ester Goody, University of Cambridge, England
David Lubin, Harvard University
Bambi Schieffelin, University of Pennsylvania
Beatrice Whiting, Harvard University

5. The Analysis of Discourse

Catherine Garvey, The Johns Hopkins University (Section Organizer)
Jenny Cook-Gumperz, University of California at Berkeley
Erving Goffman, University of Pennsylvania

6. Research Methods

Roger Bakeman, Georgia State University (Section Organizer)
John Gottman, University of Illinois at Champaign/Urbana

REFERENCES

Austin, J. L. *How to do things with words.* Oxford: Oxford University Press, 1962.

Barker, R. G. (Ed.). *The stream of behavior.* New York: Appleton, 1963.

Bates, E. *Language and context: The acquisition of pragmatics.* New York: Academic Press, 1976.

Bates, E., Benigni, L., Bretherton, I., Camaioni, L., & Volterra, V. From gesture to the first word: On cognitive and social prerequisites. In M. Lewis & L. A. Rosenblum (Eds.), *Friendship and peer relations.* New York: Wiley, 1977.

Bloom, L. M., Lightbown, P., & Hood, L. Structure and variation in child language. *Monographs of the Society for Research in Child Development,* 1975, *40*(Serial No. 160).

Blurton-Jones, N. (Ed.). *Ethological studies of child behavior.* London: Cambridge University Press, 1972.

Brown, R. *A first language: The early stages.* Cambridge, MA: Harvard University Press, 1973.

Bruner, J. The ontogenesis of speech acts. *Journal of Child Language,* 1975, *2*, 1–19.

Clark, E. V. What's in a word? On the child's acquisition of semantics in his first language. In T. E. Moore (Ed.), *Cognitive development and the acquisition of language.* New York: Academic Press, 1973.

Clark, H. Inferences in comprehension. In D. LaBerge & S. J. Samuels (Eds.), *Perception and comprehension.* Hillsdale, NJ: Erlbaum, 1976.

Clarke, D. D. The use and recognition of sequential structure in dialogue. *British Journal of Social Clinical Psychology,* 1975, *14*, 333–339.

Cook-Gumperz, J. The child as practical reasoner. In M. Sanches & B. Blount (Eds.), *Sociocultural dimensions of language use.* New York: Academic Press, 1975.

DeVries, R. The development of role-taking as reflected by the behavior of bright, average, and retarded children in a social guessing game. *Child Development,* 1970, 41, 759–770.

Dore, J. Holophrases, speech acts and language universals. *Journal of Child Language,* 1975, *2*, 21–40.

Eckerman, C., Whatley, J., & Kutz, S. Growth of social play with peers during the second year of life. *Developmental Psychology,* 1975, *11*, 42–49.

Emde, R., Gaensbauer, T., & Harmon, R. Emotional expression in infancy: A biobehavioral study. *Psychological Issues Monograph Series,* 1976, *10*, 1–37.

Ervin-Tripp, S. M. Sociolinguistics. In L. Berkowitz (Ed.), *Advances in experimental social psychology* (Vol. 4). New York: Academic Press, 1969.

Ervin-Tripp, S. On sociolinguistic rules: Alternation and co-occurrence. In J. J. Gumperz & D. Hymes (Eds.), *Directions in sociolinguistics: The ethnography of communication.* New York: Holt, Rinehart & Winston, 1972.

Ervin-Tripp, S., & Mitchell-Kernan, C. (Eds.). *Child discourse.* New York: Academic Press, 1977.

Feldman, H., Goldin-Meadow, S., & Gleitman, L. R. On describing a self-generated sign system: A study of deaf children of hearing parents. In A. Locke (Ed.), *Action, gesture, and symbol: The emergence of language.* London: Academic Press, 1976.

Flavell, J. H. The development of inferences about others. In Mischel, W. (Ed.), *Understanding other persons.* Oxford: Blackwell, Basil, Mott, 1974.

Garvey, C. Requests and responses in children's speech. *Journal of Child Language,* 1975, *2*, 41–64.

Gleitman, L. R., Gleitman, H., & Shipley, E. The emergence of the child as grammarian. *Cognition,* 1972, *1*, 137–164.

Glucksberg, S., Krauss, R., & Higgins, E. The development of referential communication skills. In F. D. Horowitz (Ed.), *Review of child development research* (Vol. 4). Chicago: University of Chicago Press, 1975.

Goldman, B., & Ross, H. Social skills in action: An analysis of early peer games. In J. Glick & A. Clarke-Steward (Eds.), *Social and cognitive development: The development of social understanding.* New York: Gardner Press, in press.

Gottman, J. H., & Parkhurst, J. T. Developing may not always be improving: A developmental study of children's best friendships. Paper presented at the biennial meeting of the Society for Research in Child Development, New Orleans, March, 1977.

Greenfield, P. N., & Smith, J. H. *The structure of communication in early language development.* New York: Academic Press, 1976.

Grice, H. P. Logic and conversation. In P. Cole & J. L. Morgan (Eds.), *Syntax and semantics* (Vol. 3): *Speech acts.* New York: Seminar Press, 1975.

Gunter, R. *Sentences in dialog.* Columbia, SC: Hornbeam Press, 1974.

Halliday, M. A. K. Notes on transitivity and theme in English. *Journal of Linguistics,* 1967, *3,* 37–81.

Halliday, M. A. K. *Explorations in the functions of language.* London: Edward Arnold, 1973.

Halliday, M. A. K. Learning how to mean. In E. Lenneberg & E. Lenneberg (Eds.), *Foundations of language development: A multidisciplinary approach.* New York: Academic Press, 1975.

Halliday, M. A. K., & Hasan, R. *Cohesion in English.* London: Longman Group Limited, 1976.

Heider, F. *The psychology of interpersonal relations.* New York: Wiley, 1958.

Hinde, R. A. On describing relationships. *Journal of Child Psychology and Psychiatry,* 1976, *17,* 1–19.

Hymes, D. H. Models of the interaction of language and social life. In J. J. Gumperz & D. Hymes (Eds.), *Directions in sociolinguistics.* New York: Holt, Rinehart & Winston, 1972.

Keenan, E. O. Conversational competence in children. *Journal of Child Language,* 1974, *1,* 163–183.

Keenan, E. O., & Schieffelin, B. Topic as a discourse notion: A study of topic in the conversations of children and adults. In C. Li (Ed.), *Subject and topic.* New York: Academic Press, 1976.

Kuczaj, S. On the acquisition of a semantic system. *Journal of Verbal Learning and Verbal Behavior,* 1975, *12,* 211–221.

Labov, W., & Fanshel, D. *Therapeutic discourse.* New York: Academic Press, 1977.

Lamb, M. E. *The role of the father in child development.* New York: Wiley, 1976.

Livesley, W. J., & Bromley, D. B. *Person perception in childhood and adolescence.* London: Wiley, 1973.

Marvin, R. S., & Greenberg, M. T. Preschoolers' changing conceptions of their mothers: A social-cognitive study of mother-child attachment. Unpub. manuscript submitted for publication.

Marvin, R. S. An ethological-cognitive model for the attenuation of mother-child attachment behavior. In T. M. Alloway, L. Krames, & P. Pliner (Eds.), *Advances in the study of communication and affect* (Vol. 3): *Attachment behavior.* New York: Plenum Press, 1977.

McCall, R. B. Challenges to a science of developmental psychology. *Child Development,* 1977, *48,* 333–344.

McNeill, D. *The acquisition of language: The study of developmental psycholinguistics.* New York: Harper & Row, 1970.

Merritt, M. On questions following questions in service encounters. *Language in Society,* 1976, *5,* 315–357.

Mohan, B. Do sequencing rules exist? *Semiotica,* 1974, *12,* 75–96.

Mueller, E., & Lucas, T. A developmental analysis of peer interaction among toddlers. In M. Lewis & L. A. Rosenblum (Eds.), *Friendship and peer relations.* New York: Wiley, 1975.

Ross, H. S., & Goldman, B. D. Establishing new social relations in infancy. In T. M. Alloway, L. Krames, & P. Pliner (Eds.), *Advances in the study of communication and affect* (Vol. 3): *Attachment behavior.* New York: Plenum Press, 1977.

Ryan, J. Early language development: Towards a communicational analysis. In M. P. M. Richards (Ed.), *The integration of a child into a social world.* London: Cambridge University Press, 1974.

Sachs, J., & Devin, J. Young children's use of age-appropriate speech styles. *Journal of Child Language,* 1976, *3,* 81–98.

Sacks, M., Schegloff, E., & Jefferson, G. A simplest systematics for the organization of turn taking for conversation. *Language,* 1974, *50,* 696–735.

Sadock, J. M. *Towards a linguistic theory of speech acts.* New York: Academic Press, 1974.

Schaffer, H. R. (Ed.). *Studies in mother-infant interaction.* London: Academic Press, 1977.

Schutz, A. [*Collected papers I: The problem of social reality*] (M. Natason, Ed. and intro). The Hague: Nijhoff, 1962.

Searle, J. *Speech acts: An essay in the philosophy of language.* Cambridge: Cambridge University Press, 1969.

Searle, J. A taxonomy of illocutionary acts. In K. Gunderson (Ed.), *Language, mind and thought.* Minneapolis: University of Minnesota Press, 1975.

Sedlak, A. J. An investigation of the development of the child's understanding and evaluation of the actions of others. Unpublished doctoral dissertation, Rutgers, 1974.

Shantz, C. The development of social cognition. In M. Hetherington (Ed.), *Review of child development research V.* Chicago: University of Chicago Press, 1975.

Shantz, M. Children in conversation: The relationship between cognitive processes and the development of communication skills. Paper presented at the biennial meetings of the Society for Research in Child Development, New Orleans, March 1977.

Sinclair, J. McH., & Coulthard, R. M. *Towards an analysis of discourse.* London: Oxford University Press, 1975.

Slobin, D. I. *A field manual for cross-cultural study of the acquisition of communicative competence.* Berkeley: University of California Press, 1967.

Snow, C. E. The development of conversation between mothers and babies. *Journal of Child Language,* 1977, *4,* 1–22.

Snow, C. E., & Ferguson, C. A. (Eds.). *Talking to children.* Cambridge: Cambridge University Press, 1977.

Spivak, G., & Shure, M. *Social adjustment of young children.* San Francisco: Jossey-Bass, 1974.

Sroufe, L. A., & Waters, E. The ontogenesis of smiling and laughter: A perspective on the organization of development in infancy. *Psychological Review,* 1976, *83,* 173–189.

Strayer, F. F., & Strayer, J. An ethological analysis of social agonism and dominance among preschool children. *Child Development,* 1976, *47,* 980–989.

SECTION I

AFFECTIVE BEGINNINGS AND EARLY RELATIONSHIPS

Introduction

Mark T. Greenberg

The recognition that affective experience, perception, and communication are inextricably linked in early development has rapidly changed the perspective of developmental psychologists studying infant processes. The parochial division of infant researchers as those who only study perception, affect, social interaction, or learning has created impediments to a wholistic understanding of how infants experience their animate and inanimate environments. For example, the fact that studies of perceptual recognition are often accomplished by assessing affective reactions has pointed to the need for a more integrated study of social, cognitive, and affective development in early infancy. The chapters in this section attempt to build such an integration by examining the interrelationships of perception, affect, and cognition in the context of early child-caregiver interaction.

In Chapter 1, Fernald explores the interface between the perceptual features of caregiver's speech to the young infant, and the infant's perceptual and affective reactions. While much is known regarding the psycholinguistic aspects of "Motherese," there has been little investigation of the perceptual aspects of this style or its salience for the infant. Fernald draws on diverse sources to propose explanations of the why and how of infant interest in this ubiquitous sensory input. Most importantly, given the theme of this volume, Fernald presents an integrative explanation of how the affective and perceptual salience of motherese combine to create a social context for the early growth of communication and meaning.

The issue of stability and change is the "bread and butter" of developmental psychology. The effects of multiple levels of causal factors interacting in the complex, transactional system of early dyadic interaction provides a challenging and difficult context in which to predict developmental growth. How does care-giver–child interaction, occurring at a nonlinguistic level and primarily mediated by emotion, affect later infant competencies and characteristics? Baldwin, in Chapter 2, addresses this complex inquiry by providing a systematic, comprehensive model for research on the effects of early interaction. Baldwin delineates the commonalities and variances across primates in these early interactions and proposes that the opportunity for controlled observations in nonhuman primates can allow one to more fully test hypotheses regarding early experience. Baldwin elaborates the model in a nonreductionist manner by discussing the use of outcome measures from a variety of domains. This contribution is particularly valuable for its balanced presentation of the value as well as difficulties and assumptions inherent in interpretation of inter- and intraspecies variation.

In Chapter 3, Miller reviews and integrates our knowledge on the infant's developing social cognitions in the domains of voice, speech, and face perception. Miller explores the polar hypotheses of ethologists and environmentalists regarding the process by which infants are uniquely drawn to the human face and voice. Drawing on a transactional model of development, Miller illustrates the dialectical nature of our understanding in which both seemingly opposing hypotheses play an important role. By documenting the commonalities and differences in the process and growth of understanding of voices, speech, and faces, Miller provides a beginning for an integrative conceptualization of the manner in which infants learn from, and communication with their caregivers.

Finally, Miller and Byrne review a variety of literatures on the perception and role of timing and sequence in the ontogeny of communication. Taking a novel approach, the authors emphasize the critical nature of perception of time and sequence for the infant's ability to assimilate and begin to attach meaning to its surroundings. In doing so, Miller and Byrne demystify processes such as synchrony and reciprocity by beginning to formally examine one of their critical defining properties. Thus, such comprehension may be viewed as a processing skill following a developmental path that is manifest both in and between modalities as the infant interprets his/her early social interactions.

CHAPTER 1

The Perceptual and Affective Salience of Mothers' Speech to Infants

Anne Fernald

INTRODUCTION

When adults speak to infants, they use higher pitch and relatively smooth, simple, and highly modulated intonation contours, as compared to normal adult conversation (Fernald & Simon, in press; Stern, Spieker, Barnett, & MacKain, in press). The exaggerated pitch patterns of this "motherese" speech register have been observed in the speech of adults to infants and young children in several languages (Ferguson, 1964), and may constitute a universal human caretaking behavior. In this chapter I shall argue that the characteristic intonation contours of motherese are highly salient auditory stimuli for the infant and play an important role in the development of meaning.

An arbitrary relationship between sound and meaning is a general property of human language. With the exception of onomatopoetic words, and certain hand signs in manual languages, which share a more or less "analog" acoustic or visual correspondance to their referents, there is no necessary connection between a word and its meaning, as evidenced by the many different signs to be found for any particular referent among the languages of the world. The gradual mastery of such abstract sound–meaning relationships is one of the central accomplishments of language acquisition. I shall argue here, however, that the infants' early experience with language builds upon relationships between sound and meaning that are not arbitrary.

This nonarbitrariness has a biological as well as an experiential basis, resulting from the salience of maternal speech for the infant on several levels, including the peripheral and central auditory systems and autonomic–arousal systems. The infant's heightened sensitivities to certain acoustic characteristics of the motherese speech register suggest perceptual predispositions for listening to maternal vocalizations. Similarly, the infant's autonomic, somatic, and behavioral responsiveness to particular auditory dimensions characteristic of maternal intonation, and the intimate and universal involvement of intonation in the communication of emotion, suggest an affective basis for the potency of maternal speech as an auditory stimulus for the infant. Thus, the special status of the human voice for the infant is multiply determined. Early responses to maternal speech are shaped by perceptual and affective predispositions, as well as by experience—both the prenatal auditory experience presumably contributing to the newborn's ability to recognize the mother's voice (DeCaspar & Fifer, 1980), and postnatal auditory experience with the highly intonated motherese speech patterns used extensively by adults in caretaking and in social interaction with the infant.

But what about meaning? Is the early communication between mother and infant "meaningful" in any sense that is continuous with the later linguistic use of meaning? I will suggest the mothers' vocalizations do convey meaning to their prelinguistic infants. These meanings are affective in nature, since affect is the primary content of early mother–infant social exchange. And they are to some extent idiosyncratic, in that they lack a culturally conventionalized form. However, within a particular mother–infant dyad a kind of ritualization of vocalization occurs, such that certain shared meanings can be said to take on a conventional form within a very limited social domain (cf. Ratner & Bruner, 1978).

This chapter will focus on developing these views of the relation of sound and meaning in early infancy. First, research on the nature of maternal vocalizations to infants, and the interactional situations in which they typically occur, will be reviewed. In the next two sections, evidence will be presented to support the claim that certain perceptual and affective predispositions underlie the infant's initial responsiveness to maternal speech. The final section will concern the development of meaning, in light of the assertion that these early perceptual and affective predispositions provide a biological, and in that sense nonarbitrary, basis for the association of particular vocalizations with the affective meanings that develop between mother and infant in the first months of life.

THE PROSODIC ORGANIZATION
OF MOTHER'S SPEECH TO INFANTS

The language spoken by adults to infants is syntactically, semantically, and phonologically simplified, when compared to the language spoken among adults. The linguistic modifications characteristic of "motherese" have been extensively documented (see Snow, 1977, for a review). However, while the use of high pitch and exaggerated intonation in adult speech to children has been anecdotally reported in several languages (Ferguson, 1964), the prosodic organization of motherese has only recently been systematically investigated.

In a study of the prosody of the speech to newborns, Fernald and Simon (in press) acoustically analyzed the intonation contours of 24 German-speaking mothers. It was found that when addressing their infants, mothers spoke with higher pitch, wider pitch excursions, shorter utterances, and longer pauses than when addressing an adult. As shown in Figure 1, the pitch contours of motherese are relatively simple in form, resembling musical glissandi (i.e., they are characterised by a high degree of pitch continuity), compared to the more complex and variable pitch patterns of normal adult conversation. Such expanded intonation contours were found to be typical of the infant-directed speech of both primaparous and multi-parous mothers, who differed greatly in the extent of their previous experience with infants. Fernald and Simon found that 77% of the utterances addressed by German mothers to their newborns conformed to a limited set of motherese prosodic patterns that occured only rarely in normal adult speech (i.e., they consisted either of characteristic expanded intonation contours, or they were whispered).

This radical modification of normal adult intonation patterns was also found in a longitudinal study of American English motherese by Stern, Spieker, Barnett, and MacKain (in press), who analyzed age-related changes in the prosodic features of speech to infants at 0, 4, 12, and 24 months. Stern et al. found that the extent of pitch contouring and repetition was greatest at 4 months, during the period in infancy when face-to-face interaction is most intense. Since the mother's perceived goal during face-to-face interaction with a 4-month-old infant is primarily to engage and maintain the infant's attention, and to modulate the infant's arousal level, Stern et al. suggest that the exaggerated pitch contours typical of motherese may be particularly effective in achieving this goal.

The hypothesis that motherese pitch contours are functionally related to the interactional context between mother and infant was further explored in a study by Stern, Spieker, and MacKain (1982). Two types of pitch contours were found to be used consistently by mothers of infants 2–6 months old, in specific interactional and motivational contexts. When the infant was looking away, and the mother attempted to regain eye contact, she typically used a high, rising pitch contour. However, when the infant was gazing and smiling at the mother, and her goal was to maintain the infant's eye contact and positive affect, then she typically used a "bell-shaped" or "sinusoidal" pitch contour. The finding that mothers made consistent use of particular intonation contours in particular interactional contexts suggests that the pitch contours of motherese may function as meaningful units in early communication with the infant, an hypothesis that will be explored in later sections of this chapter.

The three acoustic studies of motherese described above, along with anecdotal observations of speech to children in several other languages (Ferguson, 1964), all point to exaggerated pitch modulation as a highly characteristic feature of the motherese speech register. Are infants, indeed, more responsive to the exaggerated

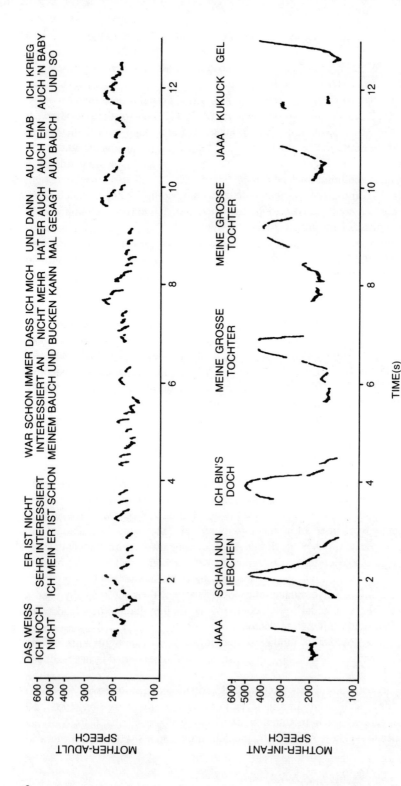

Figure 1.

The fundamental frequency contours of speech by a single mother directed at another adult (top) and at her own infant (bottom). The frequency (Hz) is plotted on the ordinate and time (sec) on the abcissa. This is a native German speaker and the text is shown above the frequency contours.

intonation of motherese than to normal adult intonation? Using an operant auditory preference procedure, in which a head-turn to one side triggered a recorded sample of natural infant-directed speech, while a head-turn to the opposite side triggered an equivalent sample of adult-directed speech, Fernald (1982) found that 4-month-old infants preferred to listen to motherese. However, since motherese differs from adult-directed speech along several linguistic and acoustic dimensions, this infant preference for motherese could be determined by any of a number of factors, including lexical usage, pitch contours, amplitude patterns, and rhythm. In subsequent experiments designed to clarify this question, the motherese and normal adult speech samples used as auditory reinforcers in the first experiment were low-pass filtered to remove all segmental content, while still retaining the pitch contour characteristics of the natural speech. Infants showed a strong preference for the pitch contours of motherese, even without linguistic content. Furthermore, it was found that infant preference for motherese was influenced much more by its pitch characteristics than by its amplitude or durational characteristics (Fernald, 1982).

In summary, the intonation of motherese, characterized by exaggerated pitch level and range, slow rhythm and tempo, and relatively smooth and simple pitch contours, appears to be attractive to infants. Why should this be so? In the following sections I shall argue that this infant preference can be at least partially understood in terms of certain perceptual, attentional, and affective predispositions that the infant brings to the task of learning language.

THE PERCEPTUAL SALIENCE OF MOTHERS' SPEECH TO INFANTS

Perceptual Predispositions and Species-Specific Communication

In 1872, in *The Expression of the Emotions in Animals and Man,* Darwin suggested that "when male animals utter sounds in order to please the females, they would naturally employ those which are sweet to the ears of the species" (Darwin, 1955, p. 91). Darwin's metaphorical statement, extended beyond courtship calls to a wide variety of animal sounds, has found confirmation in a number of behavioral and neurophysiological investigations of species-specific responses to conspecific vocalizations. Rhesus monkeys reared in social isolation respond appropriately to several species-typical rhesus calls, but not to the calls of other species (Ploog, 1979). Such findings suggest a strong genetic component to this perceptual bias, although prenatal auditory experience has also been implicated in the ability of the young of some species to recognize conspecific calls (Gottlieb, 1979). On a neurophysiological level, Wollberg and Newman (1972) have shown that single cells in the auditory cortex of squirrel monkeys are selectively responsive to particular conspecific calls, further evidence of the high degree of specificity involved in the perception of species-specific vocalizations in animal communication.

The question of the role of innate perceptual predispositions adapted for human communication has been pursued from various directions. Highly specific mechanisms have been proposed, such as phonetic "feature detectors," to account for the ability of young infants to make phonetic discriminations in a categorical fashion (Eimas, 1975). Other arguments for the innate basis of human communication skills have been made that are considerably more global, ranging from Lenneberg's (1967) nativist assertions about the biological bases of language, to Trevarthan's (1979) claim that what is innate is "intersubjectivity," the intuitive understanding of other minds that orients the infant to the social world and provides the essential foundation for human communication. Thus, the proposals for innate predispositions underlying human communication that have received the greatest attention so far have either focused on mechanisms that are highly specific to language, such as feature detectors for decoding speech at the segmental level (Eimas, 1975), or innate syntactic structures (Chomsky, 1980), or they have focused on nonspecific communicative predispositions, such as "intersubjectivity" (Trevarthan, 1979).

As diverse as they are, these various approaches to the question of what is innately specified in human communication share an emphasis on the *differences* between the ontogenies of human and animal communication skills. While these differences must undoubtedly be respected, it seems that important continuities have been overlooked. As with all other animal species, the perceptual and expressive capabilities of human beings have been adapted for successful communication with conspecifics. The communication of mother and young depends on complementary adaptation, or what Gottlieb has called "a selection for the entire developmental mainfold, including both the organic and normally occurring stimulative features of ontogeny" (Gottlieb, 1980, p. 584). To be effective, the communicative signals of the mother must be well matched to the perceptual capabilities and limitations of the young.

The perceptual predispositions of human infants to be discussed here are not language-specific; rather, they are general properties of the developing auditory system that result in the selective orientation of the infant to certain kinds of human vocalizations. I shall argue that such maternal vocalizations are, in Darwin's words, "sweet to the ears of the species," in that they are highly appropriate to the developing perceptual and affective capabilities of the infant, and thus facilitate successful mother–infant interaction and the development of communication. In particular, the expanded pitch range, high degree of pitch continuity, and tonal and temporal coherence of motherese intonation contours contribute to their perceptual prepotency for the infant, relative to other auditory stimuli.

Motherese and Infant Auditory Sensitivity

One auditory dimension along motherese which pitch contours may be perceptually more prominent for the infant is loudness. Perceived loudness can vary not only as a function of intensity, but also as a function of frequency. For example, a pure tone will be heard to grow gradually louder as its frequency, is increased from 200 Hz to 500 Hz, although the amplitude of the signal is constant. This increase in perceived loudness is a direct consequence of the sensitivity of the human auditory system to sounds at different frequencies. At threshold, a 200 Hz pure tone must be about 10dB more intense than a 500 Hz tone to be audible, since auditory sensitivity is greater at the higher frequency (Watson, Franks, & Hood, 1972). Recent studies of infant pure-tone thresholds (Schneider, Trehub, & Bull, 1979; Sinnot, Pisoni, & Aslin, in press) reveal that while infant auditory thresholds are generally elevated, compared to those of adults, the shape of the sensitivity function is roughly comparable. That is, infants are also relatively more sensitive to higher frequencies then to lower frequencies in the region of 100–2000 Hz. While care must be taken in generalizing from pure tone auditory thresholds to sensitivity for complex, suprathreshold signals such as speech, it is likely that a pitch contour with a peak at 500 Hz will be subjectively louder for the infant than a comparable pitch contour of the same duration and intensity with a peak at 200 Hz.

The greater subjective loudness of pitch contours with a high fundamental frequency, such as mothers typically use when speaking to infants, could have significant implications for infant auditory processing in naturally noisy environments. By moving her vocalizations up into a higher pitch range, the mother effectively increases the intensity of the signal, thus enhancing the signal-to-noise ratio for the infant. Schneider et al. (1979) report that the auditory sensitivity of 6-month-old infants is more severely impaired in the presence of background noise than is the case for older infants or adults, suggesting that infants may be unable to perceive certain signals that are audible to adults in a normally noisy environment. The effectiveness of maternal vocalizations in maintaining infant attention may thus depend, in part, on achieving an appropriate signal-to-noise ratio, so that the mother's voice "stands out" for the infant against background noises and other sounds. In maternal intonation, the extreme modulation of pitch, which is in itself a compelling acoustic attribute, has the additional effect of modulating loudness, resulting in vocalizations that are potentially both spectrally and dynamically more salient to the infant than are vocalizations in the normal adult prosodic range.

Motherese Pitch Contours as Salient Auditory Patterns

The tonal structure of maternal pitch contours is another prosodic characteristic that could contribute to the acoustic salience of motherese for the infant. Considered as auditory patterns, the intonation contours of mothers' speech possess several acoustic characteristics that can be related to such classical Gestalt principles as good continuation, simplicity, proximity, and common fate. The Gestalt principles have traditionally been applied to the study of simple visual patterns, as heuristic rules for explaining how elements of the optic array are segregated into the "figure" and "ground" (Wertheimer, 1923). The figure/ground problem is no less important for the auditory system than for the visual system, since at any point in time, the waveform we hear is likely to represent acoustic information combined from several different sources. However, we generally perceive this complex acoustic input as separate sounds emanating from separate sources, a fact requiring explanation in terms of auditory processes responsible for "parsing" the spectrum.

The work of Bregman and his colleagues on "auditory streaming" has elucidated some of the stimulus factors leading to the segregation of acoustic components (see Bregman, 1978). When pure tones from a high range of frequencies alternate rapidly with tones from a range of frequencies about an octave and half lower, the listener perceives this tone sequence as splitting into two separate streams (Bregman & Campbell, 1971). One stream is heard as a pattern of low frequency tones, while the other stream consists of high frequency tones, and no pattern relating the two streams is evident. However, stream segregation can be greatly reduced by connecting the successive tones by frequency glides, so that the frequency transitions between high and low tones are gradual and smooth rather than abrupt and discontinuous (Bregman & Dannenbring, 1973).

Bregman (1978) argues that certain innate auditory processing heuristics, which obey Gestalt principles, operate to parse the acoustic input. His basic assumption is that listeners are "built to pay attention to sources, not to acoustic components" (Bregman, 1978, p. 74). This highly adaptive perceptual tendency accounts for the formation of separate auditory streams. In the natural auditory environment, sudden, large discontinuities in the frequency of successive tones often indicate a change in the source of the sound, while smooth and regular frequency transitions generally reflect a single sound source. Thus, a tone sequence that exhibits a high degree of pitch continuity, or "good continuation," will tend to be identified as coming from a single sound source.

The pitch contours of mothers' speech are typically long, smooth glissandi, where abrupt pitch transitions rarely occur. They are simple in form and separated from one another by substantial pauses. As auditory patterns, they would appear to qualify as "good Gestalten," compared to the relatively complex pitch patterns of normal adult intonation. This high degree of pitch continuity in motherese may help the infant to track the voice of a particular speaker, an essential skill in the comprehension of spoken language. Even for adults, the prosodic contours of speech are important in allowing the listener to attend more readily to one voice among many (Nooteboom, Brokx, & deRooij, 1976). However, the adult can also use higher order heuristics, such as syntactic and semantic continuity, in addition to the innate auditory parsing heuristics suggested by Bregman. Obviously, the infant does not have this option, and must rely initially on the acoustic, rather than linguistic, organization of the speech stream in selectively attending to a particular voice.

Another important difference between infant and adult listening abilities must be mentioned here. If tracking a single sound source were the only problem, then speech spoken in a monotone would seem to be an ideal form of auditory stimulation for the infant, since a monotone would both maximize pitch continuity and minimize pitch variability. However, several competing requirements must be met in maintaining the infant's attention. As mentioned earlier, infant listening may be particularly vulnerable to the effects of masking from background noise, such as other voices in the infant's natural environment. It was suggested that maternal intonation serves to enhance the audibility of speech by increasing the signal-to-noise ratio. At the same time, mothers move their pitch up into a frequency region well above that of normal adult conversation, and thus not as easily masked by background voices. Speech spoken in a low monotone, on the other hand, would be more readily masked by competing background conversation. But what about a high-pitched monotone? Speech addressed to the infant in a high-pitched monotone might appear to solve the auditory figure/ground problem for the infant, in that it would both provide a coherent auditory stream, necessary for tracking the sound source, and it would reduce the effects of masking by background conversation, by moving into a higher frequency range. However, while perhaps satisfying certain perceptual criteria for optimizing the separation between figure and ground for the infant, a high-pitched monotone would fail to engage the infant's attention for very long. In the auditory as well as the visual domain, infants are in general less responsive to monotonous stimulation than to stimuli characterized by contrast and change (Kagan, 1970). The exaggerated intonation of mothers' speech, with its greatly expanded pitch range and high degree of pitch continuity, thus maximizes both perceptual contrast, necessary for engaging and maintaining infant attention, and perceptual coherence, facilitating the task of following the voice of a single speaker.

Another Gestalt characteristic of maternal pitch contours that may contribute to their salience as auditory patterns for the infant is the simplicity of their melodic form. As described earlier, the intonation contours of speech addressed to infants are typically much simpler in their patterns of pitch movement than the intonation contours of adult conversation. That is, in adult–adult utterances there are generally multiple shifts in the direction of pitch movement within a single utterance, while mother–infant utterances are characterized by more or less monotonically rising or falling pitch contours, or by bell-shaped or sinusoidal pitch contours with only one or two major changes in the direction of pitch movement. Research on the recognition of auditory patterns by adult listeners has shown that even within a set of simple tone sequences, certain configurations constitute "better" auditory figures than do others. In studies using three- (Divenyi & Hirsh, 1974) and four-tone (Nickerson & Freeman, 1974) sequences, listeners' memory for those sequences in which the frequencies were arranged in either a strictly ascending or descending order was much better than for other orders. If figural properties of such simple auditory patterns affect adult recognition performance, then they are probably even more influential in infant perception, where memory constraints are so much greater. It seems likely that the melodic simplicity of maternal pitch contours makes them easier auditory patterns for the infant to remember than the relatively more complex and variable intonation contours of adult speech.

Intonation Contours and Holistic Auditory Processing

Another argument for the special perceptual status of the simple, melodic pitch contours of motherese rests on the level of neurological maturation in the infant's developing auditory system. The young infant relies primarily on subcortical auditory processes (Whitaker, 1976) which are adequate for the "holistic" analysis of certain acoustic signals. The development of auditory processes that are more "analytic" in nature, those ultimately specialized for decoding speech, depends on later cortical maturation. Thus, in the early months, the infant auditory system may be better equipped to process relatively simple auditory patterns such as the melodic pitch patterns of motherese than the more complex auditory patterns of normal adult speech. In developing this argument, I will first discuss evidence for a holistic processing mode in the perception of melodies and other auditory sequences by adult listeners. Then I will propose that such holistic pattern recognition constitutes a prelinguistic auditory processing mode, for which the exaggerated pitch contours of mothers' speech may be a particularly appropriate form of acoustic stimulation.

A number of studies of adult auditory perception have drawn a distinction between the processing of the more global, configurational features of auditory patterns on the one hand, and the processing of individual elements within an auditory pattern on the other. Research on the perception of musical melodies provides one example. In a study of memory for simple melodies, Dowling and Fujitani (1971) found that listeners relied much more on melodic contour (i.e., the sequence of ups and downs in the melody) than on exact interval size, concluding that memory for pitch contour is central to memory for melody. Infants, too, appear to perceive the psychological similarity of melodic phrases having the same contour, but transposed into different keys (Chang & Trehub, 1977). It is interesting to note that in mothers' speech, the repetition of pitch contours, often "transposed" to different pitch levels, frequently occurs (Fernald & Simon, in press), contributing to the musical quality of maternal intonation. As in music, this melodic repetition in speech to infants may serve to provide both auditory predictability and variation at the same time.

Warren (1976) makes a distinction between holistic and analytic processing modes, in some sense analogous to Dowling's (1978) distinction between the processing of contours and intervals. Warren's "Holistic Pattern Recognition" involves global recognition of complex acoustic sequences, independent of the identification of constituent sounds. This holistic processing mode allows for same/different discrimination of two auditory patterns, as well as recognition of a particular pattern. The analytic mode of processing, however, is required to identify the individual elements in a sequence of sounds, which involves attaching distinctive verbal labels to successive items. Thus, according to Warren, the identification of serial order depends on analytic processing, which is mediated by verbal symbols, while the identification of overall temporal patterns of sounds is based on holistic processing, which does not require categorization of component sounds.

The analytic processing mode, Warren (1976) claims, is limited to humans. Nonhumans, such as monkeys (Dewson & Cowey, 1969), are incapable of temporal order judgments of any complexity, presumably because of limitations on their ability to store and retrieve symbols representing individual sounds. Holistic pattern recognition, on the contrary, appears to be a phylogenetically prelinguistic ability, when we consider the auditory–vocal communication systems of nonhuman primates. The species-specific vocalization of primates consist of continuous, graded acoustic signals, unlike the discrete and rapidly changing acoustic signals of human speech (Bastian, 1965). That is, the information in primate vocalizations is not conveyed by complex spectral and temporal variations, as in speech, but rather by graded shifts in frequency and intensity. Thus, the auditory processing of conspecific vocalizations by primates involves extracting information about the acoustic pattern as a whole, and not as a sequence of discrete elements. Such a communication system, consisting of a limited repertoire of species-specific vocalizations, is semantically limited, since signals are processed as unanalyzed wholes, and are not recombined to generate new meanings. However, such graded auditory signals are highly effective in conveying emotional information, as will be discussed later.

Recent speech perception research with both nonhuman animals and human infants suggests that holistic pattern recognition may be an ontogenetically, as well as phylogenetically, prelinguistic ability. Kuhl and Miller (1978) have shown that chinchillas can discriminate speech sounds, presumably as temporal compounds, or holistic patterns, in Warren's (1976) sense. Similarly, infant discrimination of speech sound categories is thought to rely on holistic auditory processing capabilities which are not specific to human speech, but which are characteristic of mammalian auditory systems in general (Jusczyk, 1982; Jusczyk, Pisoni, Walley, & Murray, 1980).

An ontogenetically early reliance on holistic pattern recognition is further suggested by the immaturity of the infant auditory system. In human infants, the prethalamic auditory pathways are relatively well developed during the prenatal period. However, myelination of the postthalamic auditory pathways requires a long period of postnatal development. According to LeCours (1975), myelogenesis of the auditory cortex is not complete until around the age of five. Thus, auditory processing in the young infant is mediated primarily by subcortical neuronal connections. In research with animals, there is evidence to suggest that the holistic processing of auditory signals is integrated at lower levels within the central nervous system. For example, Walker and Hales (1972), recording neuronal discharges in the cat, found that complex acoustic patterns, such as spoken words, were discriminated at the level of subcortical auditory nucleii. Although Warren (1976) does not associate the processing mode he calls "Holistic Pattern Recognition" with any particular level of the auditory pathway, it seems plausible, in light of such neurophysiological findings, that subcortical neuronal connections are involved in the analysis of global, configurational properties of auditory stimuli.

While the contribution of subcortical structures to linguistic processing in humans is not well understood (Whitaker, 1976), Chaucard (1963) has suggested that the subcortical limbic/hypothalamic system plays a considerable role in the production and reception of affective messages. In lower primates, the production of species-specific vocalizations, which are primarily affective in nature, is largely under the control of the limbic system (Ploog, 1979), as are the cries and early vocalizations of the human infant (Lamendella, 1977). Subcortical pathways are also thought to be involved in the recognition of graded acoustic signals, for both humans and lower animals (Lamendella, 1977). In human communication, the intonation or prosody of speech is in some sense analogous to the graded vocalizations of primates, in that pitch and intensity are physically continuous prosodic variables. The exaggerated intonation contours of mothers' speech to infants may provide a particularly appropriate form of acoustic stimulation at the level of auditory processing available to the infant. The expanded pitch range and enhanced pitch continuity of motherese intonation contours, as well as the often rhythmic regularity with which these contours are repeated, would seem to make such vocalizations maximally distinctive and accessible to the infant's more holistic auditory analysis capabilities.

Auditory Stimulation and Intersensory Facilitation in Infancy

In the preceding sections I have suggested that the characteristic intonation contours of motherese may be highly salient auditory stimuli for the infant. However, the effects of this perceptual salience are not necessarily limited to the auditory domain. Perceptual processing in other sensory modalities may also be facilitated for the infant by motherese, because of the special status of auditory signals in human information processing. Unlike visual stimuli, auditory signals have an automatic alerting capacity that summons attention. Posner (1978) has shown with adults that auditory stimuli produce rapid and automatic changes in the activation level of the central processing system, resulting in clear intersensory facilitation. If subjects are required to process visual stimuli, their response is faster when an auditory signal is presented simultaneous with, or even slightly after, the imperative visual event. Posner attributes this facilitation to the effects of auditory signals on the state of alertness.

Several studies with infants have also demonstrated intersensory facilitation resulting from auditory stimulation. Mendelsohn and Haith (1976), investigating the relation between vision and auditon in newborns, found that in a blank field, sound caused the infants to maintain better eye control, to scan more economically, and to be wider-eyed than in silence. Mendelsohn and Haith conclude that sound helps the newborn to organize visual activity. This conclusion is supported by a series of experiments with older infants (Culp, 1975; Paden, 1975; Self, 1975) which showed that after infants had habituated to a visual stimulus, the addition of auditory stimulation served to recover visual fixation. These results, too, suggest that auditory events affect the way in which an infant gathers information about the visual world.

If, as suggested here, mothers' speech is a particularly salient form of auditory stimulation for the infant, it seems possible that intersensory facilitation might be greater in response to motherese pitch contours than to other acoustic stimuli. Do infants, in fact, alert more strongly to motherese than to other sounds? This question has been addressed only indirectly, and with inconclusive results. Paden (1975) found that infants showed recovery of visual fixation when music was presented as an auditory signal, and Culp (1975), using a variation of the same visual dishabituation technique, found the same effect in response to the mother's voice. Since the results of these two experiments cannot be directly compared, due to differences in design and procedure, the relative effectiveness of mothers' speech and music in eliciting infant visual behavior cannot be determined.

A more direct comparison was made by Mendelsohn and Haith (1976), who investigated the effects of two different auditory stimuli—a sequence of tones and a male voice reading a poem—on newborn scanning behavior. Although Mendelsohn and Haith found that both the voice and tone sequence resulted in intersensory facilitation, these results do not really address the hypothesis that motherese and other sounds are differentially effective. For one thing, the recording of a male voice reading a poem was probably not representative of the speech register typically addressed to newborns, where utterances are often monosyllabic, and pitch contours are simple in form and separated by long pauses. Another consideration is that in each of the studies investigating the relation of audition and vision in infancy, the experimental situation was perceptually relatively impoverished, compared with the natural environments in which infants generally find themselves. For example, in the Mendelsohn and Haith study, infants scanned a blank visual field or simple lines and gratings in silence and in the presence of sound. Under these circumstances, it seems likely that *any* sound would have a maximal alerting effect, as the results of the study suggest. The infant's natural environment, in contrast, is full of competing sights and sounds, so that the alerting power of an auditory signal may depend primarily on its salience relative to other background noises and visual events. In this context, the high pitch and exaggerated intonation contours of motherese may have a perceptual advantage, for the many reasons proposed earlier.

While the greater effectiveness of motherese in alerting the infant to visual events has yet to be demonstrated experimentally, a study by Culp and Boyd (1975) suggests that intonation is indeed more powerful than other acoustic parameters of speech in its effect on infant visual behavior. Infants in this study responded more strongly to variation in intonation than to variation in verbal content. This finding is strongly supported by behavioral observations of mother–infant social interaction, where exaggerated pitch modulation appears to be a common, and effective, strategy used by adults to attract the visual attention of the infant. Stern, Spieker and MacKain (1982) describe the characteristic high-rising pitch contour used consistently by mothers to elicit eye contact when the infant has looked away. Mothers playing with older infants are also consistent in their use of high pitch to call the infant's attention to new objects and events in the world (Fernald and Mazzie, 1983).

Summary

In this section, I have proposed that the intonation contours of motherese are perceptually prepotent for the infant. This prepotency does not consist of a specific neural attunement to particular species-typical vocalizations, as found in certain animal species (Wollberg & Newman, 1972), but rather consists of a more general perceptual and attentional "advantage" at several different levels of auditory processing. At a sensory level, the higher pitch and harmonics of motherese may optimize auditory processing because of the infant's relatively greater sensitivity to frequencies within this range. At a more central level, the pitch contours of motherese consist of auditory patterns that may be more easily processed and remembered by the infant, when compared with the more complex and variable prosodic patterns of normal adult speech. The relatively simple motherese contours would also appear to be well matched to the more holistic processing capabilities of the infant's immature auditory system. Finally, the high pitch and exaggerated pitch modulation of motherese may be attributes of auditory signals that are particularly alerting to the infant, summoning attention and facilitating intersensory perceptual processing.

Thus, the prepotency of mothers' speech for the infant may result, in part, from the combined effects of these different perceptual and attentional "filters." However, since these perceptual and attentional biases are all general characteristics of the human auditory system, shared presumably by both infants and adults, it is misleading to conclude that the infant is specifically preadapted to respond to motherese. Rather, the adaptation is complementary, involving both the ability and motivation of the caretaker to provide appropriate stimulation for the infant, as well as the infant's perceptual and attentional predispositions. In Gottlieb's (1980) words, once again, what has been selected for is "the entire developmental manifold" in which the characteristics of auditory stimulation provided by the adult are particularly appropriate to the needs and capabilities of the young.

THE AFFECTIVE SALIENCE OF MOTHERESE FOR THE INFANT

The salience of motherese for the infant may result not only from perceptual predispositions to attend to, and to process, certain sounds more readily and effectively than others, but also from the infant's selective affective responsiveness to certain attributes of auditory signals. The earliest indices of affective responsiveness in infants are considered to include autonomic and somatic responses, such as heart rate and body movement, as well as behavioral measures such as facial expression and vocalization. Such affective responsiveness to maternal vocalizations may be largely shaped by experience, a process which perhaps begins even prenatally (cf. DeCasper & Fifer, 1980). However, as Papoušek and Papoušek (1981) have argued, the intonation contours of motherese may also directly activate the infant's orienting responses or defensive behaviors, eliciting signs of pleasure or distress, which suggests that the salience of motherese on an affective level has a biological, as well as an experiential, basis.

Autonomic and Behavioral Responsiveness of Infants to Auditory Stimuli

The selective responsiveness of human infants to particular dimensions of auditory stimuli has been documented in several studies. Fetal heart rate changes reliably in response to sound (Grimwade, Walker, Bartlett, Gordon, & Wood, 1971), although no data are yet available on differential fetal response to auditory signals as a function of frequency and intensity. In newborns, however, such differential effects of frequency, intensity, bandwidth, and rise-time have been established, using a variety of autonomic and behavioral response measures. While some studies have used these infant response measures primarily as indices of auditory discrimination (Stratton & Connolly, 1973), others have emphasized the adaptive nature of the infant's differential response to auditory stimuli. For example, Levarie and Rudolph (1978), investigating newborn response to a pure tone and a noise presented at the same 85 dB intensity level, found that infants responded to noise, but not tone, with eye blink and/or startle. The authors conclude not only that infants could discriminate between these two auditory signals, but also that they were disturbed by the noise sound because it was an unpleasant stimulus.

This affective quality of the newborn's response to sound has been investigated in a long series of studies by Eisenberg (1976). Eisenberg's observations indicate that young infants respond very differently to "constant" signals, such as pure tones and noise bands, than to "patterned" signals, such as tone sequences and speech sounds. Very little overt behavior is evoked by constant auditory stimuli, whereas patterned auditory stimuli consistently elicit arousal or orienting behaviors, often accompanied by facial expression and vocalization. Eisenberg (1979) suggests that "stimulus significance" is a primary determinant of infant responsiveness to sound. Infants are predisposed to respond positively to certain kinds of sensory stimuli, in this case patterned auditory signals, which have survival value for the infant. Since the most common source of patterned auditory stimulation in the infant's immediate environment is the human voice, the infant's affective predispositions for this form of stimulation have obvious implications for the development of social responsiveness. Thus, Eisenberg's explanation for the affective prepotency of certain ecologically significant auditory signals for the infant parallels the argument made in the preceding section for the perceptual prepotency of motherese.

While much more evidence is needed to substantiate the claim that the acoustic characteristics of motherese are indeed those to which the infant selectively responds, certain findings point in this direction. In a study of newborn heart rate and eye opening in response to auditory stimulation, Kearsley (1973) found that specific combinations of frequency, bandwidth, intensity, and rise-time appeared to be optimal stimuli for eliciting orienting and defensive behavior. Kearsley compared the response of newborns to narrow-band noise centered at different frequencies, including two in the range of fundamental frequencies typical of normal female speech (250 Hz) and motherese (500 Hz). While it is not clear from Kearsley's report whether these differences were significant, the 500 Hz sound elicited both more eye opening and greater cardiac deceleration than the 250 Hz sound, two responses characteristic of orienting behavior. This finding is consistent with naturalistic observations of mother–infant interaction, where mothers frequently use high, rising pitch contours in the vicinity of 500 Hz to get the infant's attention (Stern et al., 1982).

Another naturalistic observation that has found experimental support involves the mother's use of low-frequency vocalizations. Papoušek and Papoušek (1981) report that mothers commonly use low, falling pitch contours when soothing a distressed infant. In a study of the effects of low frequency (150 Hz) and high frequency (500 Hz) tones on highly aroused infants, the low frequency tones were found to be more effective in soothing the infants (Birns, Blank, Bridger, & Escalona, 1965). The greater effectiveness of low frequency sounds in calming distressed infants has also been reported by Bench (1969). Here again, these findings suggest that the effectiveness of certain characteristic motherese pitch contours, in both arousing and soothing infants, is at least partly a consequence of biological predispositions of the infant to respond affectively in particular ways to particular kinds of sounds.

Acoustic Correlates of Emotional Expression

In all languages, intonation can serve, among other functions, to convey emotional tone. Bolinger (1964) relates this universal expressive function of intonation to an association between emotional tension and tension in the vocal cords, which automatically raises pitch. Several studies of intonational cues in normal adult conversation (Scherer, 1979) have shown that high pitch and expanded pitch range are acoustic concomitants of positive affect, signaling happiness and pleasantness, as well as vitality and surprise, to adult listeners. While these findings need further cross-linguistic validation, similar relationships between intonation and emotional expression have been documented in several languages. For example, Fonagy and Magdics (1972), in a study of Hungarian intonation, found that both joy and tenderness are expressed with increased pitch range, consistent with Scherer's (1979) findings for German and English.

Such cross-linguistic findings suggest, however indirectly, that the prosodic expression of positive affect may be to some extent biologically determined. Such constraints on the expression of emotion imply nothing about the perception of emotional tone, which is undoubtedly strongly influenced by experience. However, it is interesting to note that in mothers' speech to infants, certain acoustic attributes such as pitch level and pitch range, which are known to convey positive emotional information, are exaggerated well beyond the range of normal adult speech, perhaps providing particularly prominent affective cues for the infant.

The Special Relationship of Affect and Audition

Auditory and visual development differ in many ways, but two rather simple and obvious differences between auditory and visual experience seem to be particularly relevant to both perceptual development and the development of communication. First, like the rest of us, infants do not have ear-lids. While we can generally regulate incoming visual stimulation by closing or averting the eyes, there is no such peripheral mechanism for regulating auditory stimulation. And second, patterned auditory stimulation is not always accessible to the infant. Except in total darkness, there is almost always a variety of patterned visual stimulation available in the infant's natural environment. This is not the case with sound. The most ubiquitous (and presumably the richest) source of patterned auditory stimulation for infants is the human voice. However, the infant cannot regulate this source of stimulation merely by orienting the receptors, as is possible with visual stimuli. While the infant's own sucking noises, and eventually cooing and babbling, provide a source of self-produced sound, vocalizations are infrequent in the early weeks, and crying is not, at first, under voluntary control. Thus, the young infant must rely primarily on caretakers to provide appropriately patterned auditory stimulation, since initially only limited sound production is under the infant's control.

In his insightful book, *Rules That Babies Look By,* Marshall Haith (1980) proposes that the visual activity of newborns obeys a set of biological constraints, or "rules," for seeking visual information in the environment. For example, if awake and alert, infants open their eyes. If they find light but no edges, they engage in a broad, uncontrolled search. If they find an edge, they look near the edge and try to cross it, scanning broadly near areas of low contour, and narrowly near areas of high contour. According to Haith, these "rules" represent behaviors which function to maximize cortical firing in the visual system, during a period of rapid perceptual development.

As in other animal species, the visual–neural pathways of the human infant require adequate activation for maintenance and growth. Research on other immature mammalian visual systems has shown that early selective deprivation can result in irreversible loss of visual function. For example, kittens reared for the first two months in a visual environment consisting only of vertical stripes emerge with permanent deficits in their ability to discriminate stripes with other orientations (Blakemore & Cooper, 1970), and also with deficits in binocular vision (Blasdel, Mitchell, Muir, & Pettigrew, 1977). Such findings lend credibility to Haith's claim that the organization of visual activity in human newborns is highly adaptive. According to Haith, the infant is innately wired to seek out constantly the most informative portions of the visual environment, thus providing the immature visual system with stimulation urgently needed for normal perceptual development (i.e., the human infant is equipped with an innate "agenda" for seeking and regulating visual stimulation during a critical period of development).

Is the infant also innately endowed with means to acquire auditory stimulation during this period? The effects of early auditory deprivation have not been extensively investigated, although the few studies in this area (e.g., Tees, 1967) report effects analogous to those of visual deprivation. For example, rats exposed daily to one or two sound patterns for the first four months of life show selective neurophysiological effects of early exposure, and reduced sensitivity to other sound patterns (Clopton & Winfield, 1976). While in human infants, the period of neural plasticity in the auditory system is probably considerably longer than in the visual system (cf. LeCours, 1975), it still seems reasonable to assume that adequate patterned stimulation in the early months is important for normal auditory development, as it is for visual development. If this is the case, then an extrapolation from Haith's arguments would suggest that human infants are also innately equipped with an "agenda" for providing themselves, however unintentionally, with adequate patterned auditory stimulation, just as they seek out patterned visual stimulation.

The innate stimulus-seeking behaviors which keep the infant in contact with visual stimulation are intrinsic to the visual system (i.e., eye opening and scanning). Clearly, no such stimulus-seeking behaviors are intrinsic to, or even possible within, the auditory system. The implication of this important difference is that the infant must rely on very different strategies to obtain visual and auditory stimulation from the environment. In seeking visual stimulation, the infant is to some extent self-sufficient, needing only to orient the eyes in a world of ever-present visual richness. In contrast, to obtain auditory stimulation, the infant must rely primarily on caretakers, signaling in such a way as to elicit vocalizations. These infant signals are affective in nature, signs of distress, and pleasure that motivate the caretaker to engage in social interaction. Thus, from the very beginning, affect is necessarily involved in regulating auditory experience, since the mother's vocalizations, a significant source of appropriately patterned auditory stimulation for the infant, are elicited most effectively by affective signs. If there are, indeed, innate "rules that babies listen by," analogous to Haith's (1980) "rules that babies look by," serving to provide the infant with adequate early auditory stimulation, then these rules must go beyond the auditory system itself and take affect into account, since it is through affect that the infant elicits the most engaging and informative sounds of all, the sounds of the human voice.

The adaptive role of infant affective signals as a means of eliciting adult vocalizations is crucial not only from the perspective of auditory development, but also from the perspective of the development of communication. It was suggested above that the effectiveness of motherese in communication with infants reflects a complementary adaptation, involving not only the infant's selective responsiveness to certain kinds of auditory stimuli, but also the ability and motivation of the adult to provide the infant with such appropriate stimulation. If the intonation contours of motherese constitute auditory stimuli that are, indeed, particularly well matched to the perceptual needs and capabilities of the infant, what is it that motivates adults to modify their normal intonation patterns in such a way? The infant's affective and attentional responses, such as crying, smiling, body movement, orienting and gaze aversion, are potent elicitors of maternal behaviors, including motherese (Papoušek & Papoušek, 1977; Stern, 1977). Furthermore, the infant's affective signals serve as feedback for the adult, indicating, among other things, whether the adult's vocalizations are pleasant or unpleasant for the infant, and motivating the adult to repeat vocalizations that are effective in communicating with the infant. Thus the infant is endowed not only with selective perceptual biases, but also with selective affective responses, which function both to elicit and to reward appropriate vocalizations from the adult.

Summary

The general claim that has been made here is that the salience of motherese may derive from the infant's affective, as well as perceptual, responsiveness to certain dimensions of auditory signals. Three different kinds of evidence were offered in support of this claim. First, several studies show that infants selectively respond to auditory signals with signs of positive and negative affect, as reflected in autonomic and somatic responses, and other behaviors indicating arousal, as well as orienting and defensive reactions. Second, cross-linguistic studies show that certain intonational patterns are consistently correlated with the expression of positive emotion, including such highly characteristic features of motherese as expanded pitch range and pitch level. Both of these kinds of evidence, from infant psychoacoustic studies and from cross-linguistic studies of intonation, are consistent with the idea that the infant's affective responsiveness to motherese is, as least to some extent, biologically determined.

The third line of argument presented in this section focused on the special relationship of affect and auditory stimulation. Unlike the visual system, where the infant can, to some extent, directly control stimulus input by eye opening and gaze direction, the control of auditory stimulation for the infant is intrinsically less direct. While the motherese speech register addressed by adults to infants provides a rich, and perhaps developmentally essential, source of patterned auditory stimulation, the infant's access to this source is largely dependent on the caretaker's motivation. Infant affective signals appear to be highly effective in eliciting and reinforcing adult vocalizations, and are probably critical in motivating adults to address infants with the high pitch and exaggerated intonation characteristic of motherese.

MOTHERS' SPEECH AND THE DEVELOPMENT OF MEANING

In the first year of life, according to Halliday (1975), infants are "learning how to mean." Before mastering any words, the child gradually becomes capable of expressing a wide range of meanings, at first through the use of intonation contours, used consistently in particular functional contexts. Halliday describes the early "meaning potential" developed by the child in terms of the goals or purposes achieved by the infant through the use of vocal sound. For example, from an early age, vocalizations are used by the infant to regulate the behavior of others, to express meanings that might be glossed as "Do that," or "Do that again." This functionalist approach to the study of language development emphasizes the continuity between the child's earliest efforts to express intentions holistically, by means of intonation contours accompanied by gesture and facial expression, and the child's later use of a lexical mode to express meanings.

What about the infant's developing ability to *perceive* meaning? If the infant's first expression of meaning is through intonation, as Halliday (1975), Dore (1975), and others have suggested, then it seems important to consider the role of intonation in the development of comprehension as well. While recent research on the development of receptive language capabilities does not address this question, focusing primarily on word comprehension (Huttenlocher, 1974), several earlier studies have suggested that infants are responsive to meaning conveyed by prosodic contours long before they respond to the segmental content of utterances. In *Infant Speech,* Lewis (1936) proposed that the affective content of adult speech to infants, expressed through intonation contours, is central to the development of meaning. The human voice, according to Lewis, is never a neutral stimulus for the infant, whose response to adult speech in the early months "is due partly to the affective character of the speech in itself, and partly to the presence of the human speaker to whom the child responds by smiling—again either as a primary or a learnt reaction" (Lewis, 1936, p. 52). This view is consistent with the arguments presented here, that the infant's responsiveness to mother's speech is determined both by perceptual and affective preferences for certain forms of auditory stimulation, and by the association of maternal vocalizations with meaningful experience.

Lewis (1936) asserts that "the primary affective character of heard speech" (p. 120) is accessible to the infant through the intonation contours of adult speech, and that this early responsiveness to intonation contour provides a basis for the child's later responsiveness to segments and words. This view, analogous to that of Halliday (1975), suggests considerable continuity of the development of the child's ability to perceive meaning in adult vocalizations, at first, in the prelinguistic period, through prosody, and then gradually in terms of linguistic content.

Does this continuity in the development of comprehension imply that the infant perceives the intonation contours of motherese as meaningful? If meaning is understood to consist of a list of basic properties of a referent—a traditional conceptualization of word meaning in psycholinguistics and philosophy—then maternal pitch contours could hardly qualify as meaningful. A much broader conceptualization of meaning is necessary, one that can accomodate affective associations, intentions, and motivations, as well as referential functions. In animal communication, for example, as Menzel and Johnson (1976) point out, the meaning of a particular signal lies not in the signal itself, but in the total context of communication. What meaning does a sudden sound in the leaves have to an animal walking through the forest? That sudden sound, or any of a number of different visual or olfactory stimuli occurring in the same situation, may have the same pragmatic meaning— "Watch out, something is there"—causing the animal to freeze in its tracks or flee. Thus, there is no one-to-one correspondence between a sign and its pragmatic meaning. Similarly, the same sign can have multiple meanings, depending on the context, even in human language. Menzel and Johnson give the example of the word "snake," which may have different meanings if you are talking with a priest as opposed to a biologist, or if someone shouts "Snake!" just as you put your hand in the water. Meaning in this sense is clearly not limited to the representation of semantic features, but rather incorporates the affective and pragmatic significance for the organism of things and events in the world. In this sense, I will argue that the intonation contours of mothers' speech convey meaning to the infant.

In their daily life together, the mother vocalizes to her infant in ways that appear to be relatively consistent across interactional situations, using high, rising pitch to engage and arouse the infant (Stern, Spieker, & MacKain, 1982), and low, falling contours to soothe the distressed infant (Papoušek & Papoušek, 1981). The mother's words may vary, but her pitch contours are highly consistent and frequently repeated (Fernald & Simon, in press). These motherese vocalizations are, of course, accompanied by, and become associated with, many other behaviors, including facial expressions, gestures, and body movements, that are also involved in accomplishing the mother's goal of arousing or soothing the infant. Through these vocalizations, in association with other appropriate maternal behaviors, the mother conveys her emotions and intentions to the child. Just as the child "learns how to mean" by expressing intentions through intonation and gesture (Halliday, 1975), the infant learns how to perceive meaning by responding to the mother's intentions and affective states, also expressed through intonation and gesture.

While considerable research is needed to substantiate these claims, I will conclude by proposing several ways in which the vocalizations of mothers' speech acquire meaning for the prelinguistic infant. First, as described in earlier sections, considered as auditory stimuli, the pitch contours of motherese are perceptually and affectively highly salient to the infant. In this sense, the association of particular types of vocalization with particular affective meanings has a nonarbitrary, biological basis. Second, through repeated experience with the mother's vocalizations and other behaviors, and their effects on the infant, the child comes to associate particular prosodic contours with positive and negative affective outcomes. These affective meanings resemble what Stechler and Carpenter (1967) have called "sensory-affective schemata" (i.e., internal representations that are mediated not by sensorimotor feedback, in the Piagetian sense, but rather by affective experience). Third, while meaning could conceivably "coalesce" around any stimulus event which consistently occurred in the infant's experience, the intonation contours of motherese are particularly suitable to convey affective meanings. Because of their discreteness and high acoustic salience, and perhaps also because of a human predisposition to attach meaning to human vocalizations, the mother's pitch contours readily become "signs" in the infant's prelinguistic communication system. And finally, while the intonation meanings shared by mother and infant lack a culturally conventional form, they may become ritualized within a particular mother-infant dyad. Ratner and Bruner (1978) describe the ritualized use of pitch contours in mothers' games with infants, suggesting that the experience of sharing such private meanings between mother and infant is an important foundation for the child's later use of culturally shared verbal forms.

The infant's developing ability to make sense of adult speech is influenced by many factors, including biological constraints on perceptual processing, affective predispositions to respond to sound in certain ways, and the child's increasingly complex and differentiated associations of vocalizations and experience. In this light, the exaggerated intonation of motherese would seem to be a particularly adaptive means of communication with the infant, and may make an important contribution to language development, enabling the young infant, from an early age, to experience meaning in the sound of human speech.

REFERENCES

Bastian, J. Primate signaling systems and human languages. In I. Devore (Ed.), *Primate behavior: Field studies of monkeys and apes.* New York: Holt, Rinehart & Winston, 1965.

Bench, J. Some effects of audio-frequency stimulation on the crying baby. *The Journal of Auditory Research,* 1969, *9,* 122–128.

Birns, B., Blank, M., Bridger, W. H., & Escalona, S. K. Behavioral inhibition in neonates produced by auditory stimuli. *Child Development,* 1965, *36,* 639–345.

Blakemore, C., & Cooper, G. F. Development of the brain depends on the visual environment. *Nature,* 1970, *228,* 477–478.

Blasdel, G. G., Mitchell, D. E., Muir, D. W., & Pettigrew, J. D. A physiological and behavioral study in cats of the effect of early visual experience with contours of a single orientation. *Journal of Physiology,* 1977, *265,* 615–636.

Bolinger, D. L. Intonation as a universal. In *Proceedings IX International Conference on Linguistics in Cambridge, Massachusetts, 1962.* The Hague: Mouton, 1964.

Bregman, A. S. The formation of auditory streams. In J. Requin (Ed.), *Attention and Performance VII.* Hillsdale, NJ: Erlbaum, 1978.

Bregman, A. S., & Campbell, J. Primary auditory stream segregation and perception of order in rapid sequences of tones. *Journal of Experimental Psychology,* 1971, *89,* 244–249.

Bregman, A. S., & Dannenbring, G. L. The effect of continuity on auditory stream segregation. *Perception and Psychophysics,* 1973, *13,* 308–312.

Chang, H. W., & Trehub, S. E. Auditory processing of relational information by young infants. *Journal of Experimental Psychology,* 1977, *24,* 324–331.

Chaucard, P. Emission and reception of sounds at the level of the central nervous system in vertebrates. In R. G. Busnel (Ed.), *Acoustic behavior of animals.* Amsterdam: Elsevier, 1963.

Chomsky, N. On cognitive structures and their development: A reply to Piaget. In M. Piattelli-Palmavini (Ed.), *Language and learning.* Cambridge, MA: Harvard University Press, 1980.

Clopton, B. M., & Winfield, J. A. Effect of early exposure to patterned sound on unit activity in rat inferior colliculus. *Journal of Neurophysiology,* 1976, *39,* 1081–1089.

Culp, R. E. The use of the mother's voice to control infant attending behavior. In F. D. Horowitz (Ed.), *Monographs of the Society for Research in Child Development,* 1975 (Serial No. 158).

Culp, R. E., & Boyd, E. F. Visual fixation and the effect of voice quality and content differences in 2-month-old infants. In F. D. Horowitz (Ed.), *Monographs of the Society for Research in Child Development,* 1975 (Serial No. 158).

Darwin, C. *The expression of the emotions in animals and man.* New York: Philosophical Library, 1955.

DeCasper, A. J., & Fifer, W. P. Of human bonding: New borns prefer their mothers' voices. *Science,* 1980, *208,* 1174–1176.

Dewson, J. H., & Cowey, A. Discrimination of auditory sequences by monkeys. *Nature,* 1969, *222,* 695–697.

Divenyi, P. A., & Hirsh, I. J. Identification of temporal order in three-tone sequences. *Journal of the Acoustical Society of America,* 1974, *56,* 144–151.

Divenyi, P. L., & Hirsh, I. J. Some figural properties of auditory patterns. *Journal of the Acoustical Society of America,* 1978, *65,* 1369–1385.

Dore, J. Holophrases, speech acts, and language universals. *Journal of Child Language,* 1975, *2,* 21–70.

Dowling, W. J. Scale and contour: Two components of a theory of memory for melodies. *Psychological Review,* 1978, *4,* 341–354.

Dowling, W. J., & Fujitani, D. S. Contour, interval, and pitch recognition in memory for melodies. *Journal of Acoustical Society of America*, 1971, *49*, 524–531.

Eimas, P. D. Speech perception in early infancy. In L. B. Cohen, & P. Salapatek (Eds.), *Infant perception: From sensation to cognition* (Vol. 2). New York: Academic Press, 1975.

Eisenberg, R. B. *Auditory competence in early life: The roots of communicative behavior.* Baltimore: University Park Press, 1976.

Eisenberg, R. B. Stimulus significance as a determinant of infant responses to sound. In E. B. Thoman (Ed.), *Origins of the infant's social responsiveness.* Hillsdale, NJ: Erlbaum, 1979.

Ferguson, C. A. Baby talk in six languages. *American Anthropologist*, 1964, *66*, 103–114.

Fernald, A. *Acoustic determinants of infant preference for "motherese".* Unpub doctoral dissertation, Univ. of Oregon, 1982.

Fernald, A., & Mazzie, C. Pitch-marking of new and old information in mothers' speech. Paper presented at the meeting of The Society for Research in Child Development, Detroit, April 1983.

Fernald, A. & Simon, T. Expanded intonation contours in mothers' speech to newborns. *Developmental Psychology*, in press.

Fonagy, I., & Magdics, K. Emotional patterns in intonation and music. In D. Bolinger (Ed.), *Intonation.* Baltimore, MD: Penguin, 1972.

Gottlieb, G. Development of species identification in ducklings: V. Perceptual differentiation in the embryo. *Journal of Comparative and Physiological Psychology*, 1979, *93*, 831–854.

Gottlieb, G. Development of species identification in ducklings: VI specific embryonic experience required to maintain species-typical perception in Peking ducklings. *Journal of Comparative and Physiological Psychology*, 1980, *94*, 579–587.

Grimwade, J. C., Walker, D. W., Bartlett, M., Gordon, S., & Wood, C. Human fetal heart rate change and movement in response to sound and vibration. *American Journal of Obstetrics and Gynecology*, 1971, *109*, 86–90.

Haith, M. M. *Rules that babies look by.* Hillsdale, NJ: Erlbaum, 1980.

Halliday, M. A. K. *Learning how to mean—Explorations in the development of language.* London: Edward Arnold, 1975.

Huttenlocher, J. The origins of language comprehension. In E. Solso (Ed.), *Theories in cognitive psychology.* Hillsdale, NJ: Erlbaum, 1974.

Jusczyk, P. W. Auditory versus phonetic coding of speech signals during infancy. In J. Mehler, M. Garrett, & E. Walker (Eds.), *Perspectives in mental representation: Experimental and theoretical studies of cognitive processes and capacities.* Hillsdale, NJ: Erlbaum, 1982.

Jusczyk, P. W., Pisoni, D. B., Walley, A., & Murray, J. Discrimination of relative onset time of two-component tones by infants. *Journal of the Acoustical Society of America*, 1980, *67*, 262–270.

Kagan, J. The determinants of attention in the infant. *American Scientist*, May, 1970.

Kearsley, R. B. The newborn response to auditory stimulation: A demonstration of orienting and defensive behavior. *Child Development*, 1973, *44*, 582–590.

Kuhl, P., & Miller, J. D. Speech perception by the chinchilla: Identification functions for synthetic VOT stimuli. *Journal of the Acoustical Society of America*, 1978, *63*, 905–917.

Lamendella, J. T. The limbic system in human communication. In H. Whitaker & H. Whitaker (Eds.), *Studies in neurolinguistics* (Vol. 3). New York: Academic Press, 1977.

LeCours, A. R. Myelogenetic correlates of the development of speech and language. In E. H. Lenneberg & E. Lenneberg (Eds.), *Foundations of language development* (Vol. 1). New York: Academic Press, 1975.

Lenneberg, E. H. *Biological foundations of language.* New York Wiley, 1967.

Levarie, S., & Rudolph, N. Can newborn infants distinguish between zone and noise? *Perceptual and Motor Skills*, 1978, *47*, 1123–1126.

Lewis, M. M. *Infant speech: A study of the beginnings of language.* London: Routledge & Kegan Paul, 1936.

Mendelsohn, M. J., & Haith, M. M. The relation between audition and vision in the human newborns. *Monographs of the Society for Research in Child Development*, 1976, *41*.

Menzel, W. E., & Johnson, M. K. Communication and cognitive organization in humans and other animals. In S. R. Harnad, H. D. Steklis, & J. Lancaster (Eds.), *Origins and evolution of language and speech*. New York: New York Academy of Sciences, 1976.

Nickerson, R. S., & Freeman, B. Discrimination of the order of the components of repeating tone sequences: Effects of frequency separation and extensive practice. *Perception and Psychophysics*, 1974, *16*, 471–477.

Nooteboom, S. G., Brokx, J. P. L., & deRooij, J. J. Contributions of prosody to speech perception. *IPO Annual Progress Report*, 1976, *11*, 34–54.

Paden, L. The effects of variations of auditory stimulation (music) and interspersed stimulus procedures on visual attending behavior in infants. In F. D. Horowitz (Ed.), *Monographs of the Society for Research in Child Development*, 1975 (Serial No. 158).

Papousek, H., & Papousek, M. Mothering and the cognitive head-start: Psychobiological considerations. In H. R. Schaffer (Ed.), *Studies in mother-infant interaction*. London: Academic Press, 1977.

Papousek, M., & Papousek, H. Musical elements in the infant's vocalizations: Their significance for communication, cognition, and creativity. In L. Lipsitt (Ed.), *Advances in infancy research* (Vol. 1.). New Brunswick, NJ: Ablex, 1981.

Ploog, D. Phonation, emotion, cognition with reference to the brain mechanisms involved. *Brain and mind*. Amsterdam: Excerpta Medica, 1979.

Posner, M. I. *Chronometric explorations of mind*. Hillsdale, NJ: Erlbaum, 1978.

Ratner, N., & Bruner, J. Games, social exchange and the acquisition of language. *Journal of Child Language*, 1978, *5*, 391–401.

Scherer, K. Acoustic concommitants of emotional dimensions: Judging affect from synthesized tone sequences. In S. Weitz (Ed.), *Nonverbal communication*. New York: Oxford University Press, 1979.

Schneider, B. A., Trehub, S. E., & Bull, D. The development of basic auditory process in infants. *Canadian Journal of Psychology*, 1979, *33*, 306–319.

Self, P. A. Control of infant visual attending by auditory and interspersed stimulation. In F. D. Horowitz (Ed.), *Monographs of the Society for Research in Child Development*, 1975 (Serial No. 158).

Sinnott, J. M., Pisoni, D. B., & Aslin, R. N. A comparison of pure tone auditory thresholds in human infants and adults. *Infant Behavior and Development*, in press.

Snow, C. E. Mother's speech research: From input to interaction. In C. E. Snow & C. A. Ferguson (Eds.), *Talking to children: Language input and acquisition*. Cambridge: Cambridge University Press, 1977.

Stechler, G., & Carpenter, G. A viewpoint on early affective development. In J. Hellmuth (Ed.), *The exceptional infant* (Vol. I). Seattle: Special Child Publications, 1967.

Stern, D. *The first relationship: Mother and infant*. Cambridge, MA: Harvard University Press, 1977.

Stern, D. N., Spiker, S. & MacKain, K. Intonation as signals in maternal speech to pre-linguistic infants. *Developmental Psychology*, 1982, *18*, 727–735.

Stern, D. N., Spieker, S., Barnett, R. K., & MacKain K. The prosody of maternal speech: Infant age and context related changes. *Journal of Child Language*, in press.

Stratton, P. M., & Connolly, K. Discrimination by newborns of the intensity, frequency and temporal characteristics of auditory stimuli. *British Journal of Psychology*, 1973, *64*, 219–232.

Tees, R. C. Effects of early auditory restriction in the rat on adult pattern discrimination. *Journal of Comparative Physiological Psychology*, 1967, *63*, 389–393.

Trevarthan, C. Communication and cooperation in early infancy: A description of primary intersubjectivity. In M. Bullowa (Ed.), *Before speech: The beginning of interpersonal communication*. Cambridge: Cambridge University Press, 1979.

Walker, J. L., & Hales, E. S. Neuronal coding at subcortical auditory nuclei. *Physiology and Behavior*, 1972, *8*, 1099–1106.

Warren, R. M. Auditory perception and speech evolution. In S. R. Harnad, H. D. Steklis, & J. Lancaster (Eds.), *Origins and evolution of language and speech*. New York: New York Academy of Sciences, 1976.

Watson, C. S., Franks, J. R., & Hood, D. C. Detection of tones in the absence of external masking noise. I. Effects of signal intensity and signal frequency. *Journal of the Acoustical Society of America*, 1972, *52*, 633–643.

Wertheimer, M. Untersuchungen zur Lehre von der Gestalt, II. *Psychologische Forschung*, 1923, *4*, 301–350.

Whitaker, H. A. Neurobiology of language. In E. C. Carterette & M. P. Friedman (Eds.), *Handbook of perception* (Vol. 7). New York: Academic Press, 1976.

Wollberg, Z., & Newman, J. D. Auditory cortex of squirrel monkey: Response patterns of single cells to species-specific vocalizations. *Science*, 1972, *175*, 212–214.

CHAPTER 2

Assessing Significance in Early Dyadic Interactions: A Comparative Perspective*

David V. Baldwin

In a broad sense, communication consists of information shared between individuals. A communicative interaction embodies the essence of sociality and can be defined as the encoding, transmission, and decoding of discernible (i.e., relatively brief) signals, requiring internal processing as reflected by subsequent probabilistic behavioral responses (Green & Marler, 1979). A communicative signal thus reduces uncertainty in predicting the recipients' subsequent behavior (Gottman, 1979a). Children (Goldin-Meadow & Feldman, 1977) and animals (Green & Marler, 1979) commonly use relatively simple signals in conjunction with intimate social knowledge of a familiar interactant in their communication.

With respect to early mother–infant interactions, Thoman (1980; Thoman & Freese, 1980) has argued that observed subtle and sometimes simultaneous behaviors constitute a communicative system from birth; in her view, potentially all behaviors within these interactions may have communicative significance. For example, the manner in which a mother departs from (Papoušek & Papoušek, 1975), speaks to (Stern, Spieker & Mackain, 1982), or touches her infant contains nonlinguistic information which may modify the perceived meaning of those interactions for the infant. Early mother–infant interactions thus can be seen as communicating through nonlinguistic signals and stimulation in a variety of sensory modes.

*Preparation of this chapter was supported by NIH grant HD 08633 from the NICHD Mental Retardation branch, and by grant RR 00166 from the Division of Research Resources to the Regional Primate Research Center at the University of Washington. The author thanks Roger Bakeman, Mark Greenberg, Virginia Gunderson, James Moriarity, Jim Sackett, and Karyl Swartz for their comments on various early drafts.

It may be largely affective information that the mother and her infant communicate in their early interactions; the nonlinguistic system has been closely identified with expression of emotional or affective information among human adults (Ekman, Friesen, & Ellsworth, 1972). When studying these early dyadic relationships, then, cross-cultural or nonhuman primate studies of nonlinguistic social communication may have as much relevance as linguistic rules of verbal communication. Even after linguistic communication develops, it joins nonlinguistic communication rather than replaces that behavioral system.

Stern (1977) notes that initially the infant has limited opportunities to learn that there is any way to "be" with another person except through those characteristic interactions experienced with the primary caregiver. Yet early interactions within the human dyad appear to reflect individual differences in mothers and in infants. For example, Bakeman & Brown (1977) found variations in the patterns of dyadic interaction reflecting maternal parity and infant sex differences. Their approach, which emphasizes the categorical structure of mother–infant "behavioral dialogues" rather than the specific behaviors, provides a means of assessing the significance early experience may have for subsequent development. If early dyadic experiences can somehow alter later behavior, one mechanism may be the internalization of communicated information in infant memory. Such internal information might influence responses on later recall. Nonetheless, one question that has not been much addressed by communication research is: What difference, if any, does variance in early mother-infant communication make in subsequent infant development?

The purpose of this chapter is to consider that question and describe an approach to research which may prove useful in answering it. This approach is not limited to studying communication, and in fact might reveal that interactive variance independent of differences in early communicative patterns influences later outcome measures, or even that no measured differences affect them. The approach is longitudinal, since the dyads must be observed over time for effects on infant development to be seen (Wohlwill, 1973). It is also comparative, with the rationale that additional information can be gained about dyadic influences on the early socialization process by observing diverse types of mothers and their infants in interaction. Some aspects of the communicative interactions within these diverse dyads may differ, providing the infants with different experiences which might affect subsequent measures of infant development or the dyadic relationship.

This chapter will describe a comparative framework for research, and then consider the dyad in some human and nonhuman primates, including mother and infant variables which may alter their interactions and relationship. A consideration of external factors which can affect primate dyads, and the problems such extrinsic influences pose for research in this area, will follow. In light of such complicating problems, the chapter next discusses one approach to observing behavioral dialogues and suggests behavioral and physical criteria which might be used to evaluate consequences for infant development. Thus, these criteria point toward outcome measures or dependent variables which assess the significance of variance in early interactions, including communicative patterns, for subsequent infant development. Conclusions are drawn in summation.

A COMPARATIVE FRAMEWORK

From a biological perspective, some characteristics seen in human mother–infant pairs are common across many species, particularly within the primate order. Primate mothers give birth to one infant (except marmosets, which typically have twins). The maternal role includes feeding, transporting, and protecting her infant. The primate infant is relatively immature (Gould, 1977), requires active parenting from its caregiver, and is relatively open to environmental influences over a long period of time. In fact, increased parenting and socialization may have co-evolved with and compensated for dependent offspring (Kurth, 1976). The mother–infant attachment bond, a relatively long period of socialization, and emphasis on learning to survive in a variety of complex environments (Jerison, 1973) can be seen as responses to evolutionary pressures among most primate species (Mason, 1979b). Moreover, the structural milieu surrounding the dyad may have reinforced primate communicative competence. The social organization of most nonhuman primates can be characterized as comprising long-term mother–infant bonds living among overlapping generations within relatively stable groups, in which group members play a variety of social roles (e.g., daughter and mother) across recurring reproductive cycles during their lifetimes. Green and Marler (1979) argue that such circumstances facilitate the use of prior experience and contextual cues in communication, and the development of subtle communicative signals, by providing opportunities for experienced individuals to anticipate prospective courses of their interactions as they are repeatedly rehearsed.

Striking parallels have been found between primate species in some sensory and memory capabilities. Individual differences in vision among humans and among macaques are larger than the average differences between them (Teller & Boothe, 1980). Like humans, adult pigtail macaques (*Macaca nemestrina*) are capable of prolonged retention of visual detail (Overman & Doty, 1980); rhesus (*Macaca mulatta*) and human serial position curves were similar when their recognition memory was tested for serially presented items (Sands & Wright, 1980). Moreover, maturation of some sensory and cognitive abilities that are fundamental to communicative behaviors and socialization also follows similar patterns across species. For example, the development of visual contrast sensitivity and acuity in pigtail macaques appears comparable to, but proceeds approximately four times faster than, visual development in human infants (Teller & Boothe, 1980). When infant pigtail monkeys acquire object permanence, they progress through a sequence of stages which parallel those passed by human infants, again about four times faster (Williams, 1979). Parallels in the development of these perceptual and cognitive processes are important since across species the primate infant learns to survive largely from information communicated by the mother and learned through observation or environmental exploration.

There are additional commonalities. Human and nonhuman primates have adapted, evolved, and continue to live in diverse habitats and physical environments. Such diversity, and the effectiveness of movable surrogate and dog mothers as attachment figures in rhesus (Mason, 1979a), suggest that species-typical rearing conditions are as difficult to define for monkeys as for humans. Riesen (1974) notes that some processes within the primate mother–infant relationship, such as development of affiliation in the dyad or maturation of the infant, are similar across different environments and species. Indeed, researchers studying macaque mother–infant interactions in the field (Berman, 1980; Kaufmann, 1966) have noted the similarity of their observations with reports of mother–infant pairs in laboratory settings (Hansen, 1966; Hinde, Rowell, & Spencer-Booth, 1964).

A comparative developmental psychologist thus has some interest in the interactions between mother and infant, as well as in studying similarities and differences in communicative behaviors used between and within species. Observation of communicative postural and gestural expressions in various old world macaque species, the cross-cultural study of human social interaction, and identification of functionally equivalent communicative behaviors spanning verbal and nonverbal modes (Eibl-Eibesfeldt, 1979) all provide potential avenues for comparative research in this area. Nonlinguistic communication appears to have some level of generality between cultures and across several primate species. Chevalier-Skolnikoff (1974) examined maturation of communication in stumptail (*Macaca arctoides*) macaque infants, and Hinde and Rowell (1962) described the principal postures and facial expressions seen in social communication among rhesus monkeys. Generally comparable expressions are seen in other old world primates (Hooff, 1962). Homologous gestural and postural signals in humans have been identified which appear to have communicative significance across cultures (Deutsch, 1979; Ekman & Oster, 1979; Goldenthal, Johnston, & Kraut, 1981; Gunderson & Lockard, 1980; Lockard, Allen, Schiele, & Wiemer, 1978).

In humans, nonlinguistic communication appears to play a prominent role in early interactions between mothers and their infants. Stern, Spieker, and MacKain (1982) report maternal use of intonation contour for communicative effect in interactions with infants, signals which capitalize on infant perception of rhythm (Demany, McKenzie, & Vurpillot, 1977). Papoušek and Papoušek (1977, 1979) microanalyzed films of mother–infant interactions and found evidence of short, frequent, and automatic parental responses including facial displays, slower speech, restricted vocabulary, and higher and more variable pitch. A typical greeting response on making visual contact with the infant consisted of raised eyebrows, a slight head movement, widely opened eyes and slightly opened mouth followed by smile or vocalization. Over time, adult behaviors selectively imitated emerging patterns of infant behavior, especially facial expressions and vocalizations.

Nonlinguistic communication may also include nonverbal vocalizations expressing emotional or affective content. For example, Goffman (1979) describes several instances of response cries given by (usually) solitary humans and defines them as animal-like displays exclaimed in certain situations to inform others of the crier's internal state. They include the pain cry, threat startle, revulsion sounds, and the spill cry. Citing evidence that the emotional component of communicated information is mediated by the phylogenetically old limbic system and its connections to the brain stem, Ploog (1977) concludes that conservative phylogenetic traits, to a large extent common among primates, influence this affective, nonlinguistic communication system. He believes that comparative studies among primates offer the best possibility to investigate emotional and communicative behavior at its biological roots.

The comparative approach need not be limited to research on nonlinguistic communication. To the extent that language is a gradually evolved biological process, its various perceptual, physiological, and cognitive substrates may exist in nonhuman primates (Zoloth & Green, 1979) and other animals (Kuhl, 1978, 1979). Thus, precursors of verbal communication, as well as nonlinguistic communicative behaviors, may be found across phylogenetically similar species and some such responses and sensitivities shown by very young human infants may provide the basis for further social development. Marler (1970, 1975, 1979) has written extensively on some general parallels, in fact, between song learning in certain birds and the development of speech perception and production in human infants. These parallels include evidence that such learning results in local dialects, that all species members share some species-specific universal characteristics and respond selectively to species-specific sounds during learning, and that such learning occurs most efficiently during early sensitive periods without need of social or food reinforcement. Further, the young progress from highly variable to more stereotyped sounds during development. Hearing is important both to monitor own vocalizations and to receive relevant communicative sounds, and neural control is similarly lateralized across species. Such broad similarities suggest a degree of homology in the organization of communicative ontogeny extending across quite dissimilar species. Perhaps insights into the origins of communication will be aided by research to further delineate the boundaries of cross-cultural and cross-species similarities of communicative behaviors, including comparisons of developmental process, potential roles of tactile or other sensory systems, and universal perceptual sensitivities.

The comparative paradigm also brings two specific contributions to this area of developmental research apart from observational methods and analyses (Barnett, 1975). The first is to provide new hypotheses by expanding the possibilities for interpretation of data. Cultural and social conventions are perhaps too easily attributed causal influence over initial sensitivities that may determine subsequent behaviors. Comparative information can illustrate the danger of defining attributes as uniquely human when only human data are known and thus may help counter such anthropocentric bias. For example, some comparative research has focused on the capacities of nonhuman animals, including monkeys and chinchillas, to perceive speech-sound categories. Kuhl and Miller (1975) found that chinchillas break a synthetic speech continuum as would an English-speaking adult (e.g., at the point where we would hear a change from /da/ to /ta/). Morse and Snowden (1975) report that rhesus monkeys similarly discriminate other between-category pairs of sounds more easily than within-category pairs differing by the same absolute degree. These data are consistent with the notion that apparent discontinuities perceived by humans in speech-sound contrasts may stem from characteristics common across all mammalian auditory systems; speech-sound contrasts may thus exploit natural perceptual discontinuities (Kuhl, 1978, 1979).

Another contribution of the comparative paradigm stems from its emphasis on diverse kinds of subjects differing in known ways. Comparisons provide additional information about the general process being studied, particularly when made using common criteria or within a single experimental design. In principle, comparisons need not be made only between subjects of different species; it may be equally valuable to compare subjects from different cultures, historical periods, subgroups within a given culture, or from different risk groups if they can be defined in advance. With respect to longitudinal research focused on the possible consequences of early dyadic social interactions for later infant development, deliberate selection of diversity in maternal and neonatal characteristics increases the likelihood of uncovering variance among the observed dyads. For example, dyads could be selected and grouped according to maternal experience, infant competence, or other relevant attributes. Both verbal and nonlinguistic communication patterns between mother and infant may differ considerably between dyads at high and low risk for poor neonatal outcome, although invariance of interactions under such conditions might also prove informative. The relative influence of communicative and noncommunicative dyadic influences on later infant development may vary with risk and can be assessed with appropriate outcome measures. Let us now consider the primate dyad in more detail.

THE DYAD

Discussions of human parent–infant interactions have often focused on the closeness with which the mother attends and tries to "read" infant behavioral signals (Bullowa, 1979; Field, Dempsey, Hallock, & Shuman, 1978; Taylor, 1979). Individual differences in parental responsiveness and ability to interpret infant state, and in the infant's competence to send clear and unambiguous behavioral cues, are thought to affect the unfolding relationship between parent and infant (Goldberg, 1977). The initial period of care after birth may be a difficult time of stress in which missteps are inevitable; it encompasses a period of rapid change in infant behaviors, during which both caregiver and infant must learn to read their partner and communicate simultaneously. Numerous differences in either a mother or her infant may affect the course of their developing relationship. Moreover, the ontogeny of infant communicative behavior during the first year is partially correlated with maternal characteristics (Hardy-Brown, Plomin, & DeFries, 1981). Osofsky (1976), for example, found consistent relationships between neonatal and maternal behavior in which more alert and responsive infants had more responsive and sensitive mothers, consistencies which held up over two observational situations before hospital discharge.

Similarly, individual nonhuman primates differ in activity and maternal behavior;

their infants also show various levels of exploratory behavior and activity. Simpson and Howe (1980) clustered behavioral measures into relatively independent categories which they believe most efficiently characterize rhesus mother–infant dyads. The behavior classes are: maternal restrain, prevent nursing, infant play, infant vocalization, and infant alone. These, plus maternal leaving of male infants and maternal grooming of female infants, form a set of categories which capture a large portion of the individual dyadic differences they observed. Moreover, maternal and infant characteristics may be partially correlated in macaques as they are among humans (Suomi, Kraemer, Baysinger, & DeLizio, 1981). Stevenson-Hinde and colleagues (Stevenson-Hinde & Simpson, 1981; Stevenson-Hinde, Stillwell-Barnes, & Zunz, 1980; Stevenson-Hinde & Zunz, 1978) have reported subjective ratings of individual monkeys. They found that "confident" and "sociable" mothers had similarly rated yearling infants, but that "excitable" mothers had infants who were not rated "confident." Measures of maternal approach, leave, and restrict were correlated with females rated "excitable," while "confident" ratings were negatively correlated with maternal rejection and leaving of female infants.

Risk and Early Interactions

A number of factors have been identified which may influence maternal caretaking behavior in humans. These include maternal education, mental and physical health, personality variables, parity and spacing of births, stress, early bonding with the infant, and socioeconomic status. Maternal age is not generally considered an important factor, although mothers younger than 16 years have seldom been observed and would obviously differ from most older mothers on other characteristics. Factors such as those described are often confounded, complicating discovery of their relative contributions to maternal competence. Furthermore, human studies do not make clear to what extent variables affecting bonding or maternal attitudes are learned from the mother's own early experiences with her mother.

In nonhuman primates, there is evidence that maternal behavior is open to modification by earlier experiences. Seay (1966) found strikingly similar rhesus maternal and infant behavior across categories of maternal cradle, restrain/retrieve, and infant ventral and nipple contact when he observed primiparous and multiparous mothers with their infants. On the other hand, rhesus mothers who were themselves deprived of mothering and peer contact when they were infants have been shown to be inadequate with their first infants (Harlow, Harlow, Dodsworth, & Arling, 1966; Seay, Alexander, & Harlow, 1964), although maternal skills improve with subsequent births (Ruppenthal, Arling, Harlow, Sackett, and Suomi, 1976). Seay (1966) argued that adequate social behavior may develop from multiple experiential bases. He believes this accounts for the similarity of maternal behavior among primiparous and multiparous monkey mothers, the apparent learning effect seen in mothers deprived of conspecific contacts as infants, and the nearly adequate social behavior of surrogate-reared monkeys who have contact with peers during infancy.

Additionally, differences in the human infant may potentially impact upon the course of mother–infant interactions. Apart from prematurity or low birthweight, infant physical characteristics, mental retardation, and temperament may affect the developing relationship including the potential for infant abuse (Friedrich & Boriskin, 1976). Dyadic interactions could further be influenced by prenatal experiences, sensory deficits, or developmental delays which affect infant signal reception and communicative behaviors. Thoman, Becker, & Freese (1978) describe individual differences in three infants who were developmentally delayed after the first year. When their earlier interactions were compared with other observed infants, the three had received higher proportions of maternal caregiving, but less social interaction such as looking and stimulation. Low birthweight and premature infants are less active, less responsive, and neurologically less able to clearly signal their physiological state. Premature birth has been found to influence the early mother–infant relationship, with mothers being more likely to initiate or continue interactions and premature infants less likely to assume an active role as they develop (Bakeman & Brown, 1980a). Goldberg, Brachfeld and DiVitto (1980) note that parents of prematures receive meager rewards from interactions with their infants compared with parents of fullterm infants, and thus claim that prematurity alters the course of subsequent dyadic interactions.

Individual variation observed in macaque dyadic interactions may also reflect infant differences and can remain stable for several months (Hinde & Spencer-Booth, 1971; Reite & Short, 1980). Hinde and Simpson (1975) have described rhesus mother–infant interactions in terms of qualities such as maternal control and warmth; they suggest that the mothers may like to see their infants move. Other laboratory experiments with rhesus macaques reveal that mother monkeys are less able to accept and rear infants delivered by C-section than by normal vaginal deliveries; this may be especially true of laboratory-reared mothers (Meier, 1965). On the other hand, infants born by C-section behave differently at birth. Like premature human infants, they are quieter and less active, and they make fewer avoidance responses to noxious stimulation (Meier, 1964). These differences may persist for some months after birth (Meier & Garcia-Rodriques, 1966) in monkey infants reared in laboratory nurseries.

Risk may be defined as potential vulnerability to deviant outcome. Human dyads considered to be at high risk for poor neonatal outcome include those with perinatal complications, in which the mother is of lower socioeconomic status, young, or with an infant who may be low birthweight or premature. The characteristics mentioned are often confounded. Observing interactions of high-risk dyads, Field (1980) reported that both the high-risk infant and its mother tend to be either hypo- or hyperactive. From the infant's perspective, either a hypoactive or a hyperactive mother will be less contingently responsive to social initiations. Field's data indicate that mothers who were initially more active and less sensitive to infant signals were also overprotective and more controlling in interactions observed two years after birth.

There are both species (Sackett, Ruppenthal, Fahrenbruch, Holm, & Greenough,

1981) and individual differences in infant vulnerability to social isolation rearing in macaques. Epidemiological and experimental data from a breeding colony of pigtail monkeys suggest that particular female (and male) individuals predictably produce specific types of pregnancy outcomes, such as spontaneous abortion, neonatal death, premature or low-birthweight infants (Sackett & Holm, 1980). Surviving infants of high-risk breeders are physically less mature at term and develop more slowly after birth when reared in a laboratory nursery. When performance of high- and low-risk offspring was compared on learning set (concept formation) tasks several months after birth, low-risk infants performed better. On the other hand, set-breaking (inhibition of learned behavior) performance was affected by maternal stress during pregnancy (Sackett, 1981). These pregnancy outcomes are predicted well for breeders at extremes of risk by a variety of prenatal (and preconceptual) factors comparable to those reported for humans (Sackett, Holm, & Landesman-Dwyer, 1975), and possibly related to factors producing differential risk for deviant offspring development. Thus, broad parallels across primate species in vulnerability to factors producing abnormal development, and common features of primate mother and infant roles, suggest that monkeys may serve as useful models for humans in the study of early dyadic interaction and infant development.

Pigtail macaque mothers, differing with respect to risk for poor neonatal outcome, may give birth to infants which differ predictably in competence at birth. It seems plausible to suggest that monkeys from these different risk groups might also show diverse patterns in their maternal caretaking behavior from the moment of birth. Further, these differences may be reflected in subsequent infant development and may suggest their sources: maternal factors, infant readiness, or interactional patterns which may develop as a function of the particular individuals in each dyad. But such differences can be completely overwhelmed by influences external to the dyad and beyond the control of either the mother or the researcher. Many factors influence both mother–infant interactions and infant development. In studies where extrinsic influences are uncontrolled or unobserved, they may obscure the effects of antecedent variables within the dyad (Sackett, Sameroff, Cairns, & Suomi, 1981). For example, if an hypothetical monkey mother rejects her infant much of the time, permitting only enough contact for adequate nursing, the infant might respond by exploration of the surrounding environment and with more play with peers at an earlier than usual age. Such influences are not always obvious or invariant, however. After play has developed, maternal interference which disturbs infant resting may actually lessen the amount of peer play (Jonge, Dienske, Luxemburg, & Ribbens, 1981).

Peer Play

In general, infant maturation influences the sequence and to some extent the timing of play development (Harlow, 1969), while social context determines play frequency (Meier & Devanney, 1974). Reviewing the socializing functions of play for the infant, Poirier and Smith (1974) emphasize that play improves muscular coordination and provides the basis for an adult dominance hierarchy, facilitating the integration of younger primates into the group. But they argue that the most important function of play is in teaching social behaviors appropriate to communicate the individual's role within its group.

Kenney, Mason, and Hill (1979) have reported that lipsmacking and grimacing (facial expressions of friendliness and fear) develop sooner and are displayed more frequently and more appropriately by rhesus monkeys reared with visual exposure to conspecifics and people than in macaques reared without such exposure. Similarly, Anderson and Mason (1974) observed more complex social interactions in yearlings reared with mother and age mates than in socially deprived monkeys. Experienced macaques interacted in larger subgroups with a more complex response structure; only they appeared to recognize the status relations of other group members. Returning to our hypothetical macaque mother, we may find that her infant— as a result of greatly increased play—shows no behavioral patterns which might plausibly stem from maternal rejection. In fact, this infant may be unusually socially competent with peers as a result of increased peer play.

Experimental attempts to rehabilitate rhesus monkeys reared in isolation provide dramatic evidence of the powerful communicative and socializing effects of play in macaques. Monkeys isolated from birth for 12 months were allowed 8 hours/week access to much younger socially normal conspecifics who typically display nonaggressive, clinging, and playful behaviors. Over several months, development of play behaviors was observed in the normal monkeys and some social recovery was apparent in the isolates (Novak & Harlow, 1975). At 3 years of age (near sexual maturity), and after additional extensive exposure to same-age socially normal monkeys, these isolates displayed appropriate social behavior to peers with relatively few remaining behavioral differences (Novak, 1979; see also Gluck, 1979).

Taken together, these observations imply that peer play is an important, perhaps necessary, component in the normal development of social behavior in primates and may partially compensate for the total absence of maternal care in rhesus. These results seem consistent with data on the importance of play in human development (Bruner, Jolly, & Sylva, 1976; Tizard & Harvey, 1977), with maturational change in playful behavior during infancy (Gustafson, Green, & West, 1979) and similarities in play behaviors among children of diverse cultures (e.g., Oudenhoven, 1979), and with the view that socialization is associated with cognitive development in children (Doise, Mugny, & Perret-Clermont, 1975). That extensive play experience may offset differences which unusual or inadequate mother–infant interactions might produce in subsequent development is both adaptive and fortunate for the monkey infant; it may have implications for intervention with neglected or abused human children (Horenstein, 1977) as well. Unfortunately for researchers hoping to relate differences in mother–infant interactions to subsequent development, extensive play experience may also offset measurable differences that atypical mother–infant interactions might produce in the infant.

Surrounding Environment

Aspects of the dyadic relationship including communication and socialization have been discussed almost as if the pair were isolated from the larger society or surrounding cultural expectations. For some purposes this is the best approach to take. It simplifies discovery of fundamental processes in the dyad and probably reduces confusion. Some processes, such as development of affiliation within the dyad or maturational change in the infant, appear largely independent of ecological or demographic influence (Berman, 1980; Kaufmann, 1966; Riesen, 1974). Other environmental conditions, such as weather and time of day, may (like age and sex) influence group behavior similarly even across primate species displaying distinctive activity profiles (Bernstein, 1971, 1980). In contrast, the influences of social structure are particularly complex and difficult to measure; they can result in striking qualitative differences in caretaking practices affecting behavioral development in unpredictable ways (Altmann & Altmann, 1979). Comparisons across a variety of studies afford an opportunity to understand such extrinsic influences. This approach may be necessary in human studies as well, to provide insight into mechanisms and effective interventions, or if results are to be generalized across socioeconomic groups or cultures. Such broader influences must be considered in a comparative account of primate socialization where some commonality of process is apparent across species.

A number of researchers have directed efforts toward the study of socialization in nonhuman primates and the development of social behavior. Important works include Altmann (1980), Berman (1980), Hansen (1966), Harlow and Harlow (1965), Hinde et al. (1964), Hinde and Spencer-Booth (1967), Kaufmann (1966), and Sackett (1970). This broad area has been recently reviewed by Sackett, Gunderson, & Baldwin (1982), and by Swartz and Rosenblum (1981).

Altmann (1980) has noted from her observations of yellow baboon (*Papio cynocephalus*) dyads at the Amboseli National Park, Kenya, that the baboon infant may learn it can be away from its mother at particular times, dependent on the mother's activity. Altmann believes this may be one of the earliest forms of socialization, as it reinforces infant attention to the mother and may provide the social sensitivity on which later integration into the group depends. Failure to attend to the mother or other group members in the field can have fatal consequences. Most feral-living primates depend on the group for protection against predators and attend to the alpha male for direction (Chance, 1967; Chance & Jolly, 1970). Among the savanna-living baboons at Amboseli, Altmann observed 90% concordance between the predominant activity of the focal subject and the remainder of the group. It was only in the first few days after a birth that this figure was lowered by decreased maternal feeding and increased social attention by some group members toward the new infant.

In vervet (*Cercopithecus aethiops*) monkeys also living at Amboseli, infants apparently learn appropriate alarm responses from observing their mother or other adult group members. Seyfarth, Cheney, and Marler (1980) report evidence from controlled field experiments that vervet monkeys give alarm calls on sight of various predators (i.e., baboon, eagle, leopard, or snake), which differ in intensity and acoustic structure depending on the type of predator. Adult members of the group hearing the alarm respond appropriately for each predator type depending on their vulnerability to attack. For example, the most commonly observed response to eagle alarms was to look up or run out of the tree, while the most common response to python alarms was to look down or approach the snake. As compared with adults, infants gave alarm calls to a wider variety of species, but even infants restricted calls to categorically appropriate stimuli; they gave eagle alarms only to birds, for example. Playback of taped alarms elicited appropriate avoidance behaviors from adults, but infants did better when they were near their mothers and playback increased the time they spent looking at their mothers (Seyfarth & Cheney, 1980).

In the field, maternal rank is associated with reproductive success. Dominant maternal genealogies grow at a faster rate in rhesus than lower-ranking genealogies (Sade, Cushing, Cushing, Dunaif, Figueroa, Kaplan, Lauer, Rhodes & Schneider, 1976). Drickamer (1974) found that infants born to higher-ranking rhesus mothers had a greater survival rate, that high-ranking females reproduced more frequently, and that their daughters reproduced successfully at a young age than daughters of lower-ranking females. Moreover, Altmann (1980) reports individual differences in rearing style associated with maternal dominance, and independent of infant sex, which may facilitate this reproductive advantage. Dominant baboon mothers were more laissez-faire, while subordinate mothers were more restrictive of their infants. Glance rate, a measure of maternal nervousness, was also positively associated with restrictive mothering behavior. Restrictive mothers retained contact with their infants about as much as permissive mothers did with infants who were one month younger. The laissez-faire maternal style resulted in increased infant exposure to infection and death over the short term, but may provide a long-term reproductive advantage because surviving infants became independent of the mother at younger ages. In fact, the average one-month acceleration of independence among permissively reared infants would have been greater except for their increased illness, since baboon mothers respond with increased care when their infants weaken. Perhaps these mothers adopt the rearing style most appropriate to their position within the group. Thus, it is not clear whether such different rearing practices cause, or are only correlated with, differential reproductive advantage. Among humans, socioeconomic status is also associated with reproductive success (Rush, 1980), infant mortality (Adamchak, 1979), maternal interactive behavior (Zegiob & Forehand, 1975), and the infant's experiences after birth (Kilbride, Johnson, & Streissguth, 1977; Sameroff & Chandler, 1975).

Since feral-living primate females generally leave group members and give birth at night (Jolly, 1972), returning to the group before it moves off next morning, parturition and perinatal dyadic interactions have been seldom seen in the field. Altmann (1980) observed increased attractiveness of the baboon infant for group members lasting five months from birth. She noted that resulting stressful interactions provide the infant's earliest associations of maternal fear responses with agonistic behaviors involving specific individuals in the group; thus, such experiences may strongly influence the infant's subsequent dominance rank. Further, behavior of other group members varies in response to the new mother's dominance rank in the group. Dominant mothers are less affected by the increased attention than are subordinate mothers who may risk losing their infant (Hrdy, 1976) to a stronger interested female. Captive group housing may be particularly difficult for all but the most dominant monkey mothers just after they give birth. In rhesus macaques, group members also show increased attention to the new dyad at the same time the mother evinces decreased affinity for other group members (Hinde & Proctor, 1977).

In fact, maternal rank during infancy is strongly related to the dominance rank later attained by offspring in several primate species (Hausfater, 1975; Koford, 1963; Koyama, 1967; Sade, 1967) and it determines infant experiences (Gouzoules, 1975) and choice of playmates (Caine & Mitchell, 1979) in most monkeys, though apparently not in bonnet (*Macaca radiata*) macaques who have a very different social organization (Rosenblum & Kaufman, 1967). Among humans, Strayer (1980) reports evidence that preschool children form their own dominance hierarchies among nursery school classmates, probably largely independent of parental status except as such status may determine choice of nursery school.

In comparative terms, both dominance and socioeconomic status may be thought of as relative positions in the competition for scarce resources within a given environment. An individual's standing in any hierarchy can depend on the measures used and may fluctuate over time. Still, the confounding of external influences, such as socioeconomic status in humans and dominance status in group-living nonhuman primates, complicates efforts toward separating how interactions within dyads of various risk may differ from how the circumstances of these dyads obviously vary. If we are to answer the question originally posed, external influences affecting either dyadic interactions or infant development must be removed from the effects of differential dyadic communication patterns per se.

ASSESSMENT OF BEHAVIOR AND OUTCOME

One example of a behavioral observation system has already been mentioned. Bakeman and Brown (1977) present a closely reasoned method for assessing the style of human mother–infant interactions by focusing on the sequential analysis of behavior classes. They view interaction as a behavioral dialogue encompassing not just vocalizations but all "communicative acts" that the mother and infant perform. Sequentially analyzed (e.g., Bakeman, 1978; Gottman, 1979a; Sackett, 1979), these interactions can then be described in terms of cause and effect. Contingent response probabilities are used to measure how patterned or predictable the interactions were as a whole, as well as the total time spent by either partner in particular categories of behaviors such as joint activity, independent infant or maternal activity. The behavior dialogic approach successfully revealed human dyadic interaction differences due to infant sex, prematurity, and maternal parity, suggesting that this method is valid (Bakeman & Brown, 1977, 1980a).

The same approach might be used to analyze the structure of dyadic interaction in nonhuman primates. An observational scoring system designed to reveal important behavioral dialogues between monkey mothers and their neonates would include measures of physical contact, direction of maternal and infant visual attention, and other maternal and infant behaviors. Dyads might be compared with respect to contact, activity level, proportion of maternal attention directed toward the infant, and infant attention directed toward its mother or on her nipple, as well as contingently occurring maternal or infant activities. The interactions of dyads from various selected risk groups might reveal different structural patterns, including patterns of communicative behaviors, which may accompany different developmental courses. However, a caution need be noted: In any study where behavior is observed, but particularly where the subjects are of another species, the possibility exists that behaviors and communicative acts conspicuous to the observer are not so intended or perceived by the interactants. Reducing observer inference and judgments may lessen the problem, but where this disparity is great the observed interactions may not predict subsequent differences on outcome measures.

On the other hand, one major advantage of laboratory research using nonhuman subjects is that the researcher can control variables which in human or feral populations may be poorly specified or confounded with the variables under study. There is less "noise" in competition with dyadic communication under these conditions. Captive monkeys live in environments that do not differ greatly from one subject to the next and their contact with conspecifics and human experimenters can be monitored and carefully controlled. Newborn macaques can be reared by their mothers in individual housing to insure that they do not play with peers or interact with other monkeys before outcome measures are taken. The first 30 days after birth are considered a neonatal period for macaque infants, and typically they are just beginning to leave their mother for extended exploration of their home cages in the final week of observation. Subsequent outcome measures would provide a means of assessing some effects on infant development of differences in prior mother–infant interactions, including communication, before those effects are offset by contact with peer and adult conspecifics.

In comparable research with humans, however, serious problems can arise when subjects are selected or volunteer for observation of interactions. Extrinsic environmental influences are not easily controlled. Variations in family structure, which may be confounded with risk, have been associated with differential offspring development (Kellam, Ensminger, & Turner, 1977) and family interactions (Kimball, Stewart, Conger, & Burgess, 1980). Moreover, individuals who might be at high risk for displaying negative and socially undesirable behaviors toward their children are likely to be unknown to the experimenters, difficult to identify, and reluctant to volunteer for observation of their characteristic interactions. They may also be disproportionately likely to drop out during a longitudinal study unless continuing support can be provided. Also, subjects observed outside their familiar home surroundings are likely to show some differential behaviors not characteristic of their interactions at home (Belsky, 1980; Gottman, 1979b pp. 237–248). There is evidence that heightened self-awareness or the awareness of being observed may alter behaviors displayed (Wicklund, 1979; Zegiob, Arnold, & Forehand, 1975), perhaps especially among high-risk subjects. Other information suggests that such effects may influence behavior even without the subject's knowledge. Nisbett and Wilson (1977) review evidence that human subjects are sometimes unaware of the existence of a stimulus that influenced their response, unaware of the response, and unaware that the stimulus affected their response.

The biases mentioned above probably operate unequally on the behavior of high- and low-risk subjects. Even though compared groups of dyads might show some behavioral differences despite such methodological problems, the observed interactions may not be truly representative of those behavioral interactions in which the infant is typically involved when unobserved. Subsequent development, as reflected by outcome measures, thus is likely to be less closely associated with the observed interactions than with those characteristic but unobserved interactions which normally influence the infants' development.

These and other problems complicate the study of antecedent dyadic influences on subsequent development. Bakeman and Brown (1980b) report results from a careful longitudinal study in which the behavioral interactions of 21 premature and 22 term infants were observed with their mothers during feedings, and the infants' subsequent social and mental development was assessed at 3 years of age. Unfortunately, although the behavioral measures distinguished preterm from term infants' dyadic interactions, they generally did not predict outcome on the social and cognitive measures. Aside from the possibility that human mother–infant interaction data might not predict infant behaviors at 3 years, reasons suggested by the authors for the lack of predictability include weak effects due to few observations or small sample size, possible constraint on interactions in the observed feeding situations, differential social worker contacts made by parents of preterm subjects during the study, and the problem of poor measures. Conceivably, additional reasons may include differential refusal to participate in the study by fathers of term infants, constraint on observed interactions from awareness or situation biases other than feeding, extrinsic environmental influences (including peer play) affecting infant development, and various combinations of the above possibilities.

Complications such as these suggest that observation of interactional differences between analogous high- or low-risk groups of mother–infant monkey dyads may actually reveal more differences and better predictability of infant outcome than similar observation of comparable human pairs. But field studies face equivalent problems of confounding variables among group-living primates. The infant's playful experiences with peers may independently influence its development, for example, and interaction within the observed dyad might well be affected by the primate mother's relationship with other group members. There may also be a question here of ecological or demographic variables affecting the dyadic relationship and infant development in ways not initially apparent to the human observer (Altmann &

Altmann, 1979). Comparable problems arise, and may even be exaggerated, in laboratory observation of confined groups of unrelated monkeys (Berman, 1980; McGinnis, 1980). The challenge is to understand the diversity of possible influences and to compare results across studies, species, and times.

Physical Growth as Outcome

As mentioned earlier, a problem often confronted by developmental researchers concerns the selection of suitable outcome criteria. For example, predictively valid measures of human intelligence may not be available for several years after birth (McCall, 1979; Scarr-Salapatek, 1976). Similar difficulties may surround the use of social competence measures for outcome; they can be time consuming, situation dependent, and unstable (see Beckwith, 1979). Additionally, some measures of social competence with peers may be largely independent of affection toward adults (Harlow & Harlow, 1965). Implausible results from outcome measures thus may elude satisfactory interpretation until more is known about primate developmental processes. On the other hand, assessing the relative significance of different maternal styles may be little more than subjective conjecture in the absence of clear outcome criteria. Though true even for human studies, this is particularly obvious where subjects are of another species. Ideally, outcome measures would yield dichotomous or distinct categories into which the subjects could be classified. Two possible outcome criteria will be suggested here with the caution that neither is guaranteed.

In infancy studies, one outcome criterion for which early mother–infant interactions might be predictive is infant physical growth, on the grounds that growth is a primary task of infant development which may be slowed by disturbance in maternal care. Failure to thrive by some apparently healthy infants (English, 1978) represents an extreme example of this enigmatic relationship. Aside from its reliability and inexpensive data collection, growth may be variously and repeatedly measured, providing continual outcome measures in relation to appropriate norms.

Broadly defined, health includes social, emotional, and psychological well-being, in addition to the more restrictive absence of physical disease. Physical growth, as an indirect indicator of health (Tanner, 1976), may provide useful outcome measures related to antecedent maternal behavior, risk, or other variables. For example, Pollitt, Gilmore, and Valcarcel (1978) report that four specific human maternal and infant behaviors observed during feeding accounted for 32% of the variance in neonatal weight gain in their sample. Rosa (1976) notes that important social aspects of child care which may influence growth include family economic structure, maternal health, cohabitation after childbirth, family spacing, and sanitation or medical care practices.

Psychosocial factors may also affect growth of children through their parents' and their own learned choice of diet. In the early postpartum period, the most common such choice is between breast and bottle feeding the infant. This decision changes the frequency of feeding and affects the character of these early interactions (Dunn & Richards, 1977); it also may influence infant growth through differential protection against outside infection (Donnet & Stanfield, 1977; Head, 1977). Individual differences in the taste or nutritional composition of breast milk, varying perhaps with maternal diet or milk production ability, might explain some additional variance in the growth of breast-fed infants. Many variables thus can affect infant growth both after and before birth. Prominent among them are parental genetic factors, the infant's constitution, nutrition, and disease.

Psychosocial deprivation is a common pathological cause of growth retardation among children in industrialized countries (Savage, 1977). Some researchers have reported that maternal visual gaze directed toward the infant shortly after birth reflected the only difference observed between infants without organic problems, later judged failure to thrive, and normally growing infants. Vietze, Falsey, O'Connor, Sandler, Sherrod, and Altemeier (1980) noted some overlap between mothers in the two groups, but speculated that maternal visual gaze may reflect early interest in the baby or maternal bonding to the infant. An alternative mechanism by which psychosocial factors might influence growth is through noncommunicative sensory stimulation. Perhaps the stimulation of different senses characteristic of nonlinguistic interaction acts independently to facilitate neonatal neurological or physical development. It might be hypothesized that patterned sensory stimulation could facilitate growth apart from its communicative content. Barnard (1981) and Korner (1980) describe separate intervention programs for use with premature newborns which provide temporally patterned movement, sound, and tactile-kinesthetic stimulation.

Among infant monkeys, growth can be assessed by weight gain, x-ray, and anthropometric measures (Fahrenbruch, Burbacher, & Sackett, 1979). Samples of mother's breast milk can be obtained and analyzed for protein and triglyceride (fat) content. If the milk of individual monkey mothers differs greatly in content, and if variation in milk content is an important determinant of infant growth, then differences on growth outcome measures should be associated with maternal milk composition. Certainly, maternal behaviors which inhibit nursing or maternal competition with the infant for milk might be inversely associated with growth. Independently, maternal communicative behaviors (such as the manner of infant grooming and contingent infant responses) may be associated with differences in growth. The influence of stimulation apart from communicative content, as in maternal and infant activity levels, might also be evaluated. It may be that differential infant growth is associated with risk independently of the other variables. Still, the relative influence of risk, stimulation, diet, and communication variables on infant growth may be tentatively assessed, where external factors cannot offset dyadic influences on the subsequent outcome measures.

A separate possible outcome criterion may more closely reflect the relationship between mother and infant on an affective level and the development of attachment through communication patterns within the dyad (Ainsworth, 1979; Main, 1981).

Let us now consider studies of separation and especially the subsequent reunion behaviors of human and monkey mother–infant pairs.

Reunion Response as Outcome

Perhaps the best known and most widely studied behavioral application of nonhuman primates as models for humans is their use in studies of mother–infant separation, sparked by clinical reports that children separated from their mothers sometimes evidenced severe consequences (Ainsworth, 1962; Bowlby, 1960; Spitz, 1946). Since controlled research was impossible with children, some primate researchers separated infant monkeys from their mothers to study the reported phenomenon more closely (Seay, Hansen, Harlow, 1962; Jensen & Tolman, 1962).

Bowlby (1969, 1973) described as protest, despair, and detachment three behavioral phases which may be observed in young children separated from their mothers. He observed that following prolonged separation, some children showed signs of detachment, indifference, or hostility toward their mothers upon reunion. To date, however, no published study has reported evidence of behavior resembling detachment in any monkey species (Mineka & Suomi, 1978; Swartz & Rosenblum, 1981). Instead, macaque studies typically report increased attachment and contact between mother and infant extending for some time after reunion, before behavior returns to baseline levels (Hinde, Spencer-Booth, & Bruce, 1966; Jensen & Tolman, 1962; Kaufman & Rosenblum, 1969; Seay & Harlow, 1965; Spencer-Booth & Hinde, 1971). Primate researchers have generally concluded that the nonhuman primate model for separation behavior includes close parallels of protest and probably despair phases, without showing aloof behavior toward its mother following reunion. In fact, Seay and Harlow (1965) suggest that detachment might require greater symbolic or psychological defense mechanisms than exist in rhesus. Hence, some researchers turned toward further study of separation behaviors, such as peer separations or repeated separations, and often ignored reunion responses of the monkey subjects.

Continued research on separation responses in several macaque species has revealed that the consequences of separating an infant or young monkey from its mother or attachment object are complex and depend on the precise circumstances of separation procedures (Hinde, Leighton-Shapiro, & McGinnis, 1978; Hinde & McGinnis, 1977; Mineka & Suomi, 1978). While it is difficult to summarize these complexities briefly, it is known that species, separation environment and duration, prior mother–infant relationship and infant experience, availability of substitute care, and perhaps infant age and sex all can affect the infant's response to separation from its mother (see Mineka & Suomi, 1978; Swartz & Rosenblum, 1981, for reviews). Moreover, widely different and discrepant individual responses to separation have been reported even in studies using similar procedures, leading some to suggest that the nonhuman primate is not a suitable model for human depression

(Lewis, McKinney, Young, & Kraemer, 1976). Suomi and Harlow (1977), noting that known and unknown variables uncontrolled across the many studies may be responsible for such differences among both human and nonhuman primates, conclude that maternal separation in monkeys probably provides an excellent model for maternal separation in human infants (see also Rosenblum & Plimpton, 1981).

Reunion responses of separated monkeys may be similarly complex. Age, sex, species, preseparation history, duration and repetition of separations, and separation and reunion environments have all been observed to affect an infant's response to reunion (Mineka & Suomi, 1978), but these variables have not been systematically studied. Most reports of reunion behavior in monkeys describe studies performed in laboratory group-living situations. In some of these experiments, the mothers' social relations with group members were found to have an important influence on mother–infant interactions following reunion (McGinnis, 1980).

Failure to observe aloofness from the mother on reunion may have resulted, in part, from the fact that the monkeys lived in captive groups, where conspecifics or human observers represented a perceived threat to the reunited infant or its mother. In such situations, infant aloofness might well be suppressed in favor of attachment to the mother, since monkeys seek physical contact with their mothers when frightened (Harlow & Harlow, 1965; Patterson, Bonvillian, Reynolds, & Maccoby, 1975). Moreover, Singh (1977) has reported from a field experiment that the need to be vigilant for predators diminished depressive responses after separation from peers when the separated infant remained in its normal environment (and the peers were removed). Berman (1980) analyzed data taken on 52 rhesus mother–infant pairs in a captive colony at Madingley, England, between 1961 and 1974 and found that mothers became less restrictive toward their infants over the years. The absence of aloof infant behavior on reunion with its group-living mother may stem partly from the social structure of these groups (see also McGinnis, 1980). This suggests that individual housing of young monkey dyads might provide a more appropriate laboratory model for reunions in contemporary human dyadic relationships than do captive group-living pairs.

Should infant monkeys show dichotomous reunion responses under some standard set of procedural conditions, the response could afford a sensitive behavioral outcome measure related to antecedent infant, maternal, or relationship characteristics. Such a measure might aid in objectively assessing the relative contributions of risk and other dyadic variables. Conceivably, differential reunion responses might be independent of antecedent infant, maternal, or dyadic characteristics. On the other hand, temperament or maturity may be associated with an infant's interpretation of the separation from its mother, since maturation largely determines development of cognitive operations such as object permanence in infant monkeys (Williams, 1979). Alternatively, maternal factors, prior mother–infant communication, or other interactions might also influence and predict macaque reunion responses, as some data suggest with human dyads (Main, 1981). Moreover, aloof behavior by some monkeys after reunion with the mother may extend the usefulness of nonhuman primates as models to the detachment component of Bowlby's (1969, 1973) reunion response. Since the detachment response cannot be experimentally investigated with human subjects, nonhuman primates might be used to test or provide hypotheses as to the nature of this response among human children.

SUMMATION

What difference does variance in early dyadic communication, per se, make in subsequent infant development? The variety and relative power of external influences on human dyadic interaction and on infant development confound experimental efforts to resolve the question with which this chapter began. If that question merits an answer, resolution may come from research on other primate species serving as models for humans on the strength of biological and behavioral similarities in the dyadic relationship. Having begun with a comparative perspective, we end with a potential model of early mother–infant interactions. Generalization of results across species inevitably requires some faith (Harlow, Gluck, & Suomi, 1972). But where results appear plausible and contrary evidence cannot be obtained, a nonhuman primate model can at least contribute hypotheses to its human relatives.

From a comparative perspective, close examination of the influence dyadic communication may have on infant development reveals a diversity of environmental and demographic effects on behavior matched only by the diversity of environments in which both human and nonhuman primates have adapted, evolved, and thrived. Uncovering the influences of these various extrinsic factors on the dyadic relationship requires not only that a wide variety of subjects, but a wide variety of research approaches be employed, so that experiments can resolve questions in one group or species where they cannot be performed on another, so systematic effects can be separated from random influences. It is not a question of field or laboratory studies of nonhuman primates, nor of home or laboratory observation of human dyads in feeding or nonfeeding interactions, but rather of all relevant approaches being brought to bear to unravel important influences on a very complex communicative system, a system which has survived and adapted through many more environmental variations than any researchers have yet observed.

REFERENCES

Adamchak, D. J. Emerging trends in the relationship between infant mortality and socioeconomic status. *Social Biology* 1979, *26*, 16–19.

Ainsworth, M. D. The effects of maternal deprivation: A review of findings and controversy in the context of research strategy. In *Deprivation of maternal care: A reassessment of its effects*. Geneva: World Health Organization, Public Health Papers #14, 1962.

Ainsworth, M. S. Attachment as related to mother–infant interaction. *Advances in the Study of Behavior,* 1979, *9*, 2–51.

Altmann, J. *Baboon mothers and infants*. Cambridge, MA: Harvard University Press, 1980.

Altmann, S. A., & Altmann, J. Demographic constraints on behavior and social organization. In I.

Bernstein & E. Smith (Eds.), *Primate ecology and human origins: Ecological influences on social organization*. New York: Garland STPM Press, 1979.

Anderson, C. O., & Mason, W. Early experience and complexity of social organization in groups of young rhesus monkeys (*Macaca mulatta*). *Journal of Comparative and Physiological Psychology*, 1974, *87*, 681–690.

Bakeman, R. Untangling streams of behavior: Sequential analyses of observational data. In G. Sackett (Ed.), *Observing behavior* (Vol. 2): *Data collection and analysis methods*. Baltimore, MD: University Park Press, 1978.

Bakeman, R., & Brown J. Behavioral dialogues: An approach to the assessment of mother-infant interaction. *Child Development*, 1977, *48*, 195–203.

Bakeman, R., & Brown, J. Analyzing behavioral sequences: Differences between preterm and full-term infant-mother dyads during the first months of life. *Exceptional Infant*, 1980, *4*, 271–299. (a)

Bakeman, R., & Brown, J. Early interaction: Consequences for social and mental development at three years. *Child Development*, 1980, *51*, 437–447. (b)

Barnard, K. E. A program of temporally patterned movement and sound stimulation for premature infants. In V. Smeriglio (Ed.), *Newborns and parents: Parent-infant contact and newborn sensory stimulation*. Hillsdale, NJ: Erlbaum, 1981.

Barnett, S. A. Ethology and development. *Psychological Medicine*, 1975, *5*, 323–326.

Beckwith, L. Prediction of emotional and social behavior. In J. Osofsky (Ed.), *Handbook of infant development*. New York: Wiley, 1979.

Belsky, J. Mother-infant interaction at home and in the laboratory: A comparative study. *Journal of Genetic Psychology*, 1980, *137*, 37–47.

Berman, C. M. Mother-infant relationships among free-ranging rhesus monkeys on Cayo Santiago: A comparison with captive pairs. *Animal Behavior*, 1980, *28*, 860–873.

Bernstein, I. S. Activity profiles of primate groups. In A. Schrier, H. Harlow, & F. Stollnitz (Eds.), *Behavior of nonhuman primates* (Vol. 3). New York: Academic Press, 1971.

Bernstein, I. S. Activity patterns in a stumptail macaque group (*Macaca arctoides*). *Folia Primatologica*, 1980, *33*, 20–45.

Bowlby, J. Separation anxiety. *International Journal of Psycho-analysis*, 1960, *41*, 89–113.

Bowlby, J. *Attachment*. New York: Basic Books, 1969.

Bowlby, J. *Separation*. New York: Basic Books, 1973.

Bruner, J. S., Jolly, A., & Sylva, K. *Play—Its role in development and evolution*. New York: Basic Books, 1976.

Bullowa, M. (Ed.) *Before speech: The beginning of interpersonal communication*. New York: Cambridge University Press, 1979.

Caine, N., & Mitchell, G. The relationship between maternal rank and companion choice in immature macaques (*Macaca mulatta* and *M. Radiata*). *Primates*, 1979, *20*, 583–590.

Chance, M. R. A. Attention structure as the basis of primate rank orders. *Man*, 1967, *2*, 503–518.

Chance, M. R., & Jolly, C. *Social groups of monkeys, apes, and men*. New York: Dutton Press, 1970.

Chevalier-Skolnikoff, S. The ontogeny of communication in the stumptail macaque. *Contributions to Primatology*, 1974, *2*, 1–174.

Demany, L., McKenzie, B., & Vurpillot, E. Rhythm perception in early infancy. *Nature*, 1977, *266*, 718–719.

Deutsch, R. D. On the isomorphic structure of endings: An example from everyday face-to-face interaction and Balinese legong dance. *Ethology and Sociobiology*, 1979, *1*, 41–57.

Doise, W., Mugny, G., & Perret-Clermont, A. Social interaction and the development of cognitive operations. *European Journal of Social Psychology*, 1975, *5*, 367–383.

Donnet, M. L., & Stanfield, J. A survey of infant nutrition, growth and development in Glasgow. *Nutrition and Metabolism*, 1977, (Supplement #1), 220–222.

Drickamer, L. C. A ten-year summary of reproductive data for free-ranging *Macaca mulatta*. *Folia Primatologica*, 1974, *21*, 61–80.

Dunn, J. B., & Richards, M. Observations on the developing relationship between mother and baby in the neonatal period. In H. Schaffer (Ed.), *Studies in mother–infant interaction*. New York: Academic Press, 1977.

Eibl-Eibesfeldt, I. Human ethology: Concepts and implications for the sciences of man. *Behavioral and Brain Sciences*, 1979, *2*, 1–57.

Ekman, P., Friesen, W., & Ellsworth, P. *Emotion in the human face*. New York: Pergamon Press, 1972.

Ekman, P., & Oster, H. Facial expressions of emotion. *Annual Review of Psychology*, 1979, *30*, 527–554.

English, P. C. Failure to thrive without organic reason. *Pediatric Annals*, 1978, *7*, 774–781.

Fahrenbruch, C. E., Burbacher, T., & Sackett, G. Assessment of skeletal growth and maturation of premature and term *Macaca nemestrina*. In G. Ruppenthal & D. Reese (Eds.), *Nursery care of nonhuman primates*. New York: Plenum Press, 1979.

Field, T. M. Interactions of high-risk infants: Quantitative and qualitative differences. *Exceptional Infant*, 1980, *4*, 120–143.

Field, T. M., Dempsey, J., Hallock, N., & Shuman, H. The mother's assessment of the behavior of her infant. *Infant Behavior and Development*, 1978, *1*, 156–167.

Friedrich, W. N., & Boriskin, B. The role of the child in abuse: A review of the literature. *American Journal of Orthopsychiatry*, 1976, *46*, 580–590.

Gluck, J. P. The intellectual consequences of early social restriction in rhesus monkeys (*Macaca mulatta*). In G. Ruppenthal & D. Reese (Eds.), *Nursery care of nonhuman primates*. New York: Plenum Press, 1979.

Goffman, E. Response cries. In M. von Cranach, K. Foppa, W. Lepenis, & D. Ploog (Eds.), *Human ethology*. New York: Cambridge University Press, 1979.

Goldberg, S. Social competence in infancy: A model of parent-infant interaction. *Merrill-Palmer Quarterly*, 1977, *23*, 163–177.

Goldberg, S., Brachfeld, S., & DiVitto, B. Feeding, fussing, and play: Parent-infant interaction in the first year as a function of prematurity and perinatal medical problems. In T. Field, S. Goldberg, D. Stern, & A. Sostek (Eds.), *High-risk infants and children*. New York: Academic Press, 1980.

Goldenthal, P., Johnston, R., & Kraut, R. Smiling, appeasement, and the silent bared-teeth display. *Ethology and Sociobiology*, 1981, *2*, 127–133.

Goldin-Meadow, S., & Feldman, H. The development of language-like communication without a language model. *Science*, 1977, *197*, 401–403.

Gottman, J. M. Detecting cyclicity in social interaction. *Psychological Bulletin*, 1979, *86*, 338–348. (a)

Gottman, J. M. *Marital interaction: Experimental investigations*. New York: Academic Press, 1979. (b)

Gould, S. J. *Ontogeny and phylogeny*. Cambridge, MA: The Belknap Press of Harvard University Press, 1977.

Gouzoules, H. Maternal rank and early social interactions of infant stumptail macaques, *Macaca arctoides*. *Primates*, 1975, *16*, 405–418.

Green, S., & Marler, P. The analysis of animal communication. In P. Marler & J. Vanderbergh (Eds.), *Handbook of behavioral neurobiology:* Volume 3, *Social behavior and communication*. New York: Plenum Press, 1979.

Gunderson, V. M., & Lockard, J. Human postural signals as intention movements to depart: African data. *Animal Behaviour*, 1980, *28*, 966–967.

Gustafson, G. E., Green, J., & West, M. The infants' changing role in mother-infant games: The growth of social skills. *Infant Behavior and Development*, 1979, *2*, 301–308.

Hansen, E. W. The development of maternal and infant behavior in the rhesus monkey. *Behaviour*, 1966, *27*, 107–149.

Hardy-Brown, K., Plomin, R., & DeFries, J. Genetic and environmental influences on the rate of communication development in the first year of life. *Developmental Psychology*, 1981, *17*, 704–717.

Harlow, H. F. Age-mate or peer affectional systems. *Advances in the Study of Behavior*, 1969, *2*, 333–383.

Harlow, H. F., Gluck, J., & Suomi, S. Generalization of behavioral data between nonhuman and human animals. *American Psychologist*, 1972, *27*, 709–716.

Harlow, H. F., & Harlow, M. The affectional systems. In A. Schrier, H. Harlow, & F. Stollnitz (Eds.), *Behavior of nonhuman primates* (Vol. 2). New York: Academic Press, 1965.

Harlow, H. F., Harlow, M., Dodsworth, R., & Arling, G. Maternal behavior of rhesus monkeys deprived of mothering and peer associations in infancy. *Proceedings of the American Philosophical Society*, 1966, *110*, 58–66.

Hausfater, G. Dominance and reproduction in baboons: A quantitative analysis. *Contributions to Primatology*, 1975, *7*, 1–150.

Head, J. R. Immunobiology of lactation. *Seminars in Perinatology*, 1977, *1*, 195–210.

Hinde, R. A., Leighton-Shapiro, M., & McGinnis, L. Effects of various types of separation experience on rhesus monkeys 5 months later. *Journal of Child Psychology and Psychiatry*, 1978, *19*, 199–211.

Hinde, R. A., & McGinnis, L. Some factors influencing the effects of temporary mother-infant separation—some experiments with rhesus monkeys. *Psychological Medicine*, 1977, *7*, 197–212.

Hinde, R. A., & Proctor, L. Changes in the relationships of captive rhesus monkeys on giving birth. *Behaviour*, 1977, *61*, 304–321.

Hinde, R. A., & Rowell, T. Communication by postures and facial expressions in the rhesus monkey (*Macaca mulatta*). *Proceedings of the Zoological Society of London*, 1962, *138*, 1–21.

Hinde, R. A., Rowell, T., Spencer-Booth, Y. Behaviour of socially living rhesus monkeys in their first six months. *Proceedings of the Zoological Society* (London), 1964, *143*, 609–649.

Hinde, R. A., & Simpson, M. Qualities of mother-infant relationships in monkeys. *CIBA Foundation Symposium*, 1975, *33*, 39–67.

Hinde, R. A., & Spencer-Booth, Y. The behaviour of socially living rhesus monkeys in their first two and half years. *Animal Behaviour*, 1967, *15*, 169–196.

Hinde, R. A., & Spencer-Booth, Y. Towards understanding individual differences in rhesus mother-infant interaction. *Animal Behaviour*, 1971, *19*, 165–173.

Hinde, R. A., Spencer-Booth, Y., & Bruce, M. Effects of 6-day maternal deprivation on rhesus monkey infants. *Nature*, 1966, *210*, 1021–1023.

Hooff, J. van. Facial expressions in higher primates. *Symposium of the Zoological Society of London*, 1962, *8*, 97–125.

Horenstein, D. The dynamics and treatment of child abuse: Can primate research provide the answers? *Journal of Clinical Psychology*, 1977, *33*, 563–565.

Hrdy, S. B. Care and exploitation of nonhuman primate infants by conspecifics other than the mother. *Advances in the Study of Behavior*, 1976, *6*, 101–158.

Jensen, G. D. & Tolman, C. Mother-infant relationship in the monkey *Macaca nemestrina:* The effect of brief separation and mother–infant specificity. *Journal of Comparative and Physiological Psychology*, 1962, *55*, 131–136.

Jerison, H. *Evolution of the brain and intelligence*. New York: Academic Press, 1973.

Jolly, A. Hour of birth in primates and man. *Folia Primatologica*, 1972, *18*, 108–121.

Jonge, G. de, Dienske, H., Luxemburg, E., & Ribbens, L. How rhesus monkey infants budget their time between mothers and peers. *Animal Behaviour*, 1981, *29*, 598–609.

Kaufman, I. C., & Rosenblum, L. Effects of separation from mother on the emotional behavior of infant monkeys. *Annals of the New York Academy of Science*, 1969, *159*, 681–695.

Kaufmann, J. H. Behavior of infant rhesus monkeys and their mothers in a free-ranging band. *Zoologica*, 1966, *51*, 17–32.

Kellam, S. G., Ensminger, M., & Turner, R. Family structure and the mental health of children. *Archives of General Psychiatry*, 1977, *34*, 1012–1022.

Kenney, M. D., Mason, W., & Hill, S. Effects of age, objects, and visual experience on affective responses of rhesus monkeys to strangers. *Developmental Psychology*, 1979, *15*, 176–184.

Kilbride, H. W., Johnson, D., & Streissguth, A. Social class, birth order, and newborn experience. *Child Development*, 1977, *49*, 1686–1688.

Kimball, W. H., Stewart, R., Conger, R., & Burgess, R. A comparison of family interaction in single-versus two-parent abusive, neglectful, and control families. In T. Field, S. Goldberg, D. Stern, & A. Sostek (Eds.), *High-risk infants and children.* New York: Academic Press, 1980.

Koford, C. B. Rank of mothers and sons in bands of rhesus monkeys. *Science*, 1963, *141*, 356–357.

Korner, A. F. Maternal deprivation: Compensatory stimulation for the prematurely born infant. In R. Bell & W. Smotherman (Eds.), *Maternal influences and early behavior.* New York: SP Medical & Scientific Books, 1980.

Koyama, N. On dominance rank and kinship of a wild Japanese monkey troop in Arashiyama. *Primates*, 1967, *8*, 189–216.

Kuhl, P. K. Predispositions for the perception of speech–sound categories: A species-specific phenomenon? In F. D. Minifie & L. Lloyd (Eds.), *Communicative and cognitive abilites—early behavioral assessment.* Baltimore: University Park Press, 1978.

Kuhl, P. K. Models and mechanisms in speech perception: Species comparisons provide further contributions. *Brain, Behavior and Evolution*, 1979, *16*, 374–408.

Kuhl, P. K., & Miller, J. Speech perception by the chinchilla: Voiced-voiceless distinction in alveolar plosive consonants. *Science*, 1975, *190*, 69–72.

Kurth, G. Neencephalization, hominization and behavior. *Journal of Human Evolution*, 1976, *5*, 501–509.

Lewis, J. K., McKinney, W., Young, L., & Kraemer, G. Mother–infant separation in rhesus monkeys as a model for human depression: A reconsideration. *Archives of General Psychiatry*, 1976, *33*, 699–705.

Lockard, J. S., Allen, D., Schiele, B., & Wiemer, M. Human postural signals: Stance, weight-shifts and social distance as intention movements to depart. *Animal Behaviour*, 1978, *26*, 219–224.

Main, M. Avoidance in the service of attachment: A working paper. In K. Immelmann, G. Barlow, L. Petrinavich, & M. Main (Eds.), *Behavioral development.* New York: Cambridge University Press, 1981.

Marler, P. A comparative approach to vocal learning: Song development in white-crowned sparrows. *Journal of Comparative and Physiological Psychology*, 1970, *71*, 1–25.

Marler, P. On the origin of speech from animal sounds. In J. Kavanagh & J. Cutting (Eds.), *The role of speech in language.* Cambridge, MA: MIT Press, 1975.

Marler, P. Development of auditory perception in relation to vocal behavior. In M. von Cranach, K. Foppa, W. Lepenis, & D. Ploog (Eds.), *Human ethology.* New York: Cambridge University Press, 1979.

Mason, W. Maternal attributes and primate cognitive development. In M. von Cranach, K. Foppa, W. Lepenis, D. Ploog (Eds.), *Human ethology.* New York: Cambridge University Press, 1979. (a)

Mason, W. Ontogeny of social behavior. In P. Marler & J. Vanderbergh (Eds.), *Handbook of behavioral neurobiology* (Vol. 3): *Social behavior and communication.* New York: Plenum Press, 1979. (b)

McCall, R. B. The development of intellectual functioning in infancy and the prediction of later IQ. In J. Osofsky (Ed.), *Handbook of infant development.* New York: Wiley, 1979.

McGinnis, L. M. Maternal separation studies in children and nonhuman primates. In R. Bell & W. Smotherman (Eds.), *Maternal influences and early behavior.* New York: SP Medical & Scientific Books, 1980.

Meier, G. W. Behavior of infant monkeys: Differences attributable to mode of birth. *Science*, 1964, *143*, 968–970.

Meier, G. W. Maternal behavior of feral- and laboratory-reared monkeys following the surgical delivery of their infants. *Nature*, 1965, *206*, 492–493.

Meier, G. W., & Devanney, V. D. The ontogeny of play within a society: Preliminary analysis. *American Zoologist*, 1974, *14*, 289–294.

Meier, G. W., & Garcia-Rodrigues, C. Development of conditioned behaviors in the infant rhesus monkey. *Psychological Reports*, 1966, *19*, 1159–1169.

Mineka, S., & Suomi, S. Social separation in monkeys. *Psychological Bulletin*, 1978, *85*, 1376–1400.

Morse, P. A., & Snowden, C. An investigation of categorical speech discrimination by rhesus monkeys. *Perception & Psychophysics*, 1975, *17*, 9–16.

Nisbett, R., & Wilson, T. Telling more than we can know: Verbal reports on mental processes. *Psychological Review,* 1977, *84,* 231–259.

Novak, M. A. Social recovery of monkeys isolated for the first year of life: II. Long-term assessment. *Developmental Psychology,* 1979, *15,* 50–61.

Novak, M. A., & Harlow, H. Social recovery of monkeys isolated for the first year of life: I. Rehabilitation and therapy. *Developmental Psychology,* 1975, *11,* 453–465.

Osofsky, J. D. Neonatal characteristics and mother-infant interaction in two observational situations. *Child Development,* 1976, *47,* 1138–1147.

Oudenhoven, N. van. *Common Afghan street games.* Lisse, Switzerland: Swets & Zeitlinger B. V., 1979.

Overman, W. H., & Doty, R. Prolonged visual memory in macaques and man. *Neuroscience,* 1980, *5,* 1825–1831.

Papoušek, H., & Papoušek, M. Cognitive aspects of preverbal social interaction between human infants and adults. *CIBA Foundation Symposium,* 1975, *33,* 242–270.

Papoušek, H., & Papoušek, M. Mothering and cognitive headstart: Psychobiological considerations. In H. Schaffer (Ed.), *Studies in mother-infant interaction.* New York: Academic Press, 1977.

Papoušek, H., & Papoušek, M. Early ontogeny of human social interaction: Its biological roots and social dimensions. In M. von Cranach, K. Foppa, W. Lepenies, & D. Ploog, (Eds.), *Human ethology.* New York: Cambridge University Press, 1979.

Patterson, F. G., Bonvillian, J., Reynolds, P., & Maccoby, E. Mother and peer attachment under conditions of fear in rhesus monkeys (*Macaca mulatta*). *Primates,* 1975, *16,* 75–81.

Ploog, D. Social behavior and brain function in man and his relatives. *Klinische Wochenschrift,* 1977, *55,* 857–867.

Poirier, F. E., & Smith, E. Socializing functions of primate play. *American Zoologist,* 1974, *14,* 275–287.

Pol itt, E., Gilmore, M., & Valcarcel, M. Early mother-infant interaction and somatic growth. *Early Human Development,* 1978, *1,* 325–336.

Reite, M., & Short, R. A biobehavioral developmental profile for the pigtailed monkey. *Developmental Psychobiology,* 1980, *13,* 243–235.

Riesen, A. H. Comparative perspectives in behavior study. *Journal of Human Evolution,* 1974, *3,* 433–434.

Rosa, F. W. The family unit in health programmes. In G. Beaton & J. Bengoa, (Eds.), *Nutrition in preventive medicine.* Geneva: World Health Organization, 1976.

Rosenblum, L. A., & Kaufman, C. Laboratory observations of early mother-infant relations in pigtail and bonnet macaques. In S. Altmann (Ed.), *Social communication among primates.* Chicago: University of Chicago Press, 1967.

Rosenblum, L. A., & Plimpton, E. The infant's effort to cope with separation. In M. Lewis & L. Rosenblum (Eds.), *The uncommon child.* New York: Plenum Press, 1981.

Ruppenthal, G. C., Arling, G., Harlow, H., Sackett, G., & Suomi, S. A ten-year perspective of motherless-mother monkey behavior. *Journal of Abnormal Psychology,* 1976, *85,* 341–349.

Rush, D. Cigarette smoking, nutrition, social status, and prenatal loss: Their interactive relationships. In I. Porter & E. Hook, (Eds.), *Human embryonic and fetal death.* New York: Academic Press, 1980.

Sackett, G. P. Unlearned responses, differential rearing experiences, and the development of social attachments by rhesus monkeys. *Advances in Primate Behavior,* 1970, *1,* 111–140.

Sackett, G. P. The lag sequential analysis of contingency and cyclicity in behavioral interaction research. In J. Osofsky, (Ed.), *Handbook of infant development.* New York: Wiley, 1979.

Sackett, G. P. A nonhuman primate model for studying causes and effects of poor pregnancy outcomes. In S. L. Friedman & M. Sigman (Eds.), *Preterm birth and psychological development.* New York: Academic Press, 1981.

Sackett, G. P., Gunderson, V., & Baldwin, D. Studying the ontogeny of primate behavior. In J. L. Fobes & J. King (Eds.), *Primate behavior.* New York: Academic Press, 1982.

Sackett, G. P., & Holm, R. Effects of parental characteristics and prenatal factors on pregnancy outcomes of pigtail macaques. In R. Bell & W. Smotherman (Eds.), *Maternal influences and early behavior*. New York: SP Medical & Scientific Books, 1980.

Sackett, G. P., Holm, R., & Landesman-Dwyer, S. Vulnerability for abnormal development: Pregnancy outcomes and sex differences in macaque monkeys. In N. Ellis (Ed.), *Abberant development in infancy: Human and animal studies*. New York: Halstead Press, 1975.

Sackett, G. P., Ruppenthal, G., Fahrenbruch, C., Holm, R., & Greenough, W. Social isolation rearing effects in monkeys vary with genotype. *Developmental Psychology*, 1981, *17*, 313–318.

Sackett, G. P., Sameroff, A., Cairns, R., & Suomi, S. Continuity in behavioral development: Theoretical and empirical issues. In K. Immelmann, G. Barlow, L. Petrinovich, & M. Main (Eds.), *Behavioral development*. New York: Cambridge University Press, 1981.

Sade, D. S. Determinants of dominance in a group of free-ranging rhesus monkeys. In S. Altmann (Ed.), *Social communication among primates*. Chicago: University of Chicago Press, 1967.

Sade, D. S., Cushing, K., Cushing, P., Dunaif, J., Figueroa, A., Kaplan, J., Lauer, C., Rhodes, D., & Schneider, J. Population dynamics in relation to social structure on Cayo Santiago. *Yearbook of Physical Anthropology*, 1976, *20*, 253–262.

Sameroff, A. J., & Chandler, M. Reproductive risk and the continuum of caretaking casualty. *Review of Child Development Research*, 1975, *4*, 187–244.

Sands, S. F., & Wright, A. Serial probe recognition performance by a rhesus monkey and a human with 10- and 20-item lists. *Journal of Experimental Psychology: Animal Behavior Processes*, 1980, *6*, 386–396.

Savage, D. C. The problem of retarded growth. *The Practitioner*, 1977, *218*, 513–520.

Scarr-Salapatek, S. An evolutionary perspective on infant intelligence: Species patterns and individual variation. In M. Lewis (Ed.), *Origins of intelligence: Infancy and early childhood*. New York: Plenum Press, 1976.

Seay, B. Maternal behavior in primiparous and multiparous rhesus monkeys. *Folia Primatologica*, 1966, *4*, 146–168.

Seay, B. M., Alexander, B., & Harlow, H. Maternal behavior of socially deprived rhesus monkeys. *Journal of Abnormal and Social Psychology*, 1964, *69*, 345–354.

Seay, B., Hansen, E., & Harlow, H. Mother-infant separation in monkeys. *Journal of Child Psychology and Psychiatry*, 1962, *3*, 123–132.

Seay, B. M., & Harlow, H. Maternal separation in the rhesus monkey. *Journal of Nervous and Mental Disease*, 1965, *140*, 434–441.

Seyfarth, R. M., & Cheney, D. The ontogeny of vervet monkey alarm calling behavior: A preliminary report. *Zeitschrift fur Tierpsychologie*, 1980, *54*, 37–56.

Seyfarth, R. M., Cheney, D., & Marler, P. Vervet monkey alarm calls: Semantic communication in a free-ranging primate. *Animal Behaviour*, 1980, *28*, 1070–1094.

Simpson, M. J., & Howe, S. The interpretation of individual differences in rhesus monkey infants. *Behaviour*, 1980, *72*, 127–155.

Singh, S. D. Effects of infant-infant separation of young monkeys in a free-ranging natural environment. *Primates*, 1977, *18*, 205–214.

Spencer-Booth, Y., & Hinde, R. Effects of 6 days separation from mother on 18- to 32-week old rhesus monkeys. *Animal Behaviour*, 1971, *19*, 174–191.

Spitz, R. A. Anaclitic depression. *Psychoanalytic Study of the Child*, 1946, *2*, 313–347.

Stern, D. *The first relationship: Infant and mother*. Cambridge, MA: Harvard University Press, 1977.

Stern, D. N., Spieker, S., & MacKain, K. Intonation contours as signals in maternal speech to prelinguistic infants. *Developmental Psychology*, 1982, *18*, 727–735.

Stevenson-Hinde, J., & Simpson, M. Mothers' characteristics, interactions, and infants' characteristics. *Child Development*, 1981, *52*, 1246–1254.

Stevenson-Hinde, J., Stillwell-Barnes, R., & Zunz, M. Subjective assessment of rhesus monkeys over four successive years. *Primates*, 1980, *21*, 66–82.

Stevenson-Hinde, J., & Zunz, M. Subjective assessment of individual rhesus monkeys. *Primates*, 1978, *19*, 473–482.

Strayer, F. F. Social ecology of the preschool peer group. *Minnesota Symposia on Child Psychology,* 1980, *13,* 165–196.

Suomi, S. J., & Harlow, H. Production and alleviation of depressive behaviors in monkeys. In J. Maser & M. Seligman (Eds.), *Psychopathology: Experimental models.* San Francisco: Freeman, 1977.

Suomi, S. J., Kraemer, G., Baysinger, G., & DeLizio, R. Inherited and experiential factors associated with individual differences in anxious behavior displayed by rhesus monkeys. In D. F. Klein & J. Raskin (Eds.), *Anxiety: New research and changing concepts.* New York: Raven Press, 1981.

Swartz, K. B., & Rosenblum, L. The social context of parental behavior: A perspective on primate socialization. In D. Gubernick & P. Klopfer (Eds.), *Parental care in mammals.* New York: Plenum Press, 1981.

Tanner, J. M. Growth as a monitor of nutritional status. *Proceedings of the Nutrition Society,* 1976, *35,* 369–375.

Taylor, P. M. (Ed.). Parent-infant relationships. *Seminars in Perinatology,* 1979, *3,* 1–105.

Teller, D. Y., & Boothe, R. Development of vision in infant primates. *Transactions of the Opthalmological Societies of the United Kingdom,* 1980, *99,* 333–337.

Thoman, E. Disruption and asynchrony in early parent-infant interaction. *Exceptional Infant,* 1980, *4,* 91–119.

Thoman, E. B., Becker, P., & Freese, M. Individual patterns of mother-infant interaction. In G. Sackett (Ed.), *Observing behavior* (Vol. 1): *Theory and applications in mental retardation.* Baltimore: University Park Press, 1978.

Thoman, E. B., & Freese, M. A model for the study of early mother-infant communication. In R. Bell & W. Smotherman (Eds.), *Maternal influences and early behaviors.* New York: SP Medical & Scientific Books, 1980.

Tizard, B., & Harvey, D. *Biology of play.* Philadelphia: Lippincott, 1977.

Vietze, P., Falsey, S., O'Connor, S., Sandler, H., Sherrod, K., & Altemeier, W. Newborn behavioral and interactional characteristics of nonorganic failure-to-thrive infants. In T. Fields, S. Goldberg, D. Stern, & A. Sostek (Eds.), *High-risk infants and children.* New York: Academic Press, 1980.

Wicklund, R. A. The influence of self-awareness of human behavior. *American Scientist,* 1979, *67,* 187–193.

Williams, A. E. A longitudinal study of object concept development in pigtail macaques (*Macaca nemestrina*). (Doctoral dissertation, University of Washington, 1979). *Dissertation Abstracts International,* 1979, *40*(5), p. 2868-B. (University Microfilms no. 7927889).

Wohlwill, J. F. *The study of behavioral development.* New York: Academic Press, 1973.

Zegoib, L. E., Arnold, S., & Forehand, R. An examination of observer effects in parent-child interactions. *Child Development,* 1975, *46,* 509–512.

Zegoib, L. E., & Forehand, R. Maternal interactive behavior as a function of race, socioeconomic status, and sex of the child. *Child Development,* 1975, *46,* 564–568.

Zoloth, S., & Green, S. Monkey vocalizations and human speech: Parallels in perception? *Brain, Behavior and Evolution,* 1979, *16,* 430–442.

CHAPTER 3

Social and Linguistic Perception in Infancy: Factors Related to the Development of Communication

Cynthia L. Miller

During the period of infancy, development is rapid and complex. Nowhere, perhaps, is this more dramatic than in the development of communication skills. Usually by the end of the first year, not only is the infant using meaningful linguistic forms, that is, words (DeVilliers & DeVilliers, 1978), but also seems to have a relatively mature appreciation of the function of language and communication, and has become an adept social/communicative partner, taking turns, giving and receiving messages, etc. (Schaffer, 1979). It is clear that the infant is learning a great deal about language and communication during this "prelinguistic" period.

Although most students of infant development would agree that development during this period is the result of complex and dynamic transactions between the infant and her environment (Sameroff & Chandler, 1975), this belief has not translated well into empirical research. Rather than examining directly these transactions, investigators of language development during the first year have more frequently chosen to focus their research efforts on one or the other side of the transactional equation (i.e., either the organism or the environment). As a consequence, two relatively distinct and independent lines of research have developed, neither of which speak very directly to the other. On the one hand, there exists a very large literature which describes an impressive array of perceptual skills relevant to the perception of speech and language (cf. Morse & Cowan, in press, for a review of this literature). At the same time, an equally large literature has focused on describing in more naturalistic settings the nature of the input (both social and linguistic) that the young infant receives from the environment (cf. Schaffer, 1979).

Although both approaches are useful, they are ultimately limited in their ability to account adequately for the development of language and communication. By focusing on the infant, laboratory research on infant speech perception may be inadequate to describe how the infant might respond to language samples within a naturalistic social interaction. Similarly, descriptive observational research is typically conducted and interpreted from an "adult's eye" view, thus showing little regard for how the *infant* might be receiving, processing, and learning from this input.

It is to this latter issue that the present chapter is addressed. Its primary purpose is to describe the developmental course of the infant's perception of selected social and linguistic events. Underlying this discussion is the assumption that any description of organism–environment transactions must include an understanding of the dual role of natire endowment and environment input in the organization of perceptual development. More specifically, by examining the specific types of perceptual skills available to the newborn in approaching social/linguistic situations and the way in which these skills change over the first several months, we should find ourselves in a better position to understand (a) how the infant is experiencing these events at various points in development, and (b) how those events might have contributed to that development.

The second purpose of the chapter is to attempt something of a marriage between two somewhat distinct research areas. Over the last several years, infancy researchers, particularly those interested in language development, have emphasized the important linkage between social behavior and language behavior (Lewis & Cherry, 1977). Especially during the period of infancy, the two are considered virtually synonymous. However, this linkage has not yet been extended to the study of perceptual development. For example, the perception of social objects (e.g., face perception) is not typically included in discussions of the development of communication (Schaffer, 1979; Morse & Cowan, in press). Thus, in this chapter, in addition to infant speech perception, I will also summarize briefly some of the research concerned with the perception of these social stimuli (i.e., faces and voices). The discussion of face and voice perception attempts to elucidate something akin to "person perception" or "social cognition" during the early period of infancy.

In recent years, it has become increasingly popular to view the process of infant development within an ethological perspective (Bowlby, 1969; Freedman, 1974). According to this viewpoint, the human infant is seen as phylogenetically "prepared" (Seligman, 1970) for the development of language and for social intercourse in general. With respect to infant perception, the implications of this theory are (a) that social and linguistic stimuli are prepotent in that the infant from birth will "prefer" (i.e., exhibit greater attention to) social and linguistic stimuli over nonsocial and nonlinguistic stimuli, and (b) that these initial attentional preferences will result in perceptual and conceptual precocity in processing social/linguistic as compared with nonsocial/nonlinguistic stimuli. Because this theoretical perspective offers us a useful organizational scheme within which to view the development of infant perception, the research reviewed herein will be discussed with respect to these specific predictions.

INFANT SPEECH PERCEPTION

Within the ten years that have elapsed since the publication of the now-classic study of infant speech perception (Eimas, Siqueland, Jusczyk, & Vigorito, 1971), research in this area has proliferated so rapidly that a recent review of this literature sports 175 references (Morse & Cowan, in press). Generally speaking, this research has revealed the very young infant to be remarkably well equipped for processing and discriminating most of the major acoustic cues that characterize speech and language. At birth, the auditory apparatus is highly developed (Hecox, 1975), and at least by 2 months of age (and probably sooner) infants are able to discriminate many of the acoustic cues that are represented in the language (cf. Morse & Cowan, in press). For example, these young infants can discriminate segmental constituents such as vowel stimuli (Swoboda, Kass, Morse, & Leavitt, 1978; Swoboda, Morse, & Leavitt, 1976; Trehub, 1973; Trehub & Rabinovitch, 1972), and most consonants (Eimas, 1974; Eimas et al., 1971; Miller, 1974; Miller & Morse, 1976; Miller, Morse, & Dorman, 1977), as well as suprasegmental features, such as intonation patterns (Morse, 1972; Kaplan, 1969; Sullivan and Horowitz, in press) and stress (Jusczyk & Thompson, 1978; Spring & Dale, 1977). Furthermore, even at a very early age, infants appear to be constrained in their discrimination abilities by phonetic labels (Eimas et al., 1971; Miller & Morse, 1976). Together with evidence of early hemispheric specialization for speech (Glanville, Best, & Levenson, 1977; Molfese, 1977), these very early perceptual skills seem to implicate an innate propensity for the processing of speech and language.

Although these apparently innate features of the auditory system may facilitate the infant's response to and perception of speech stimuli, the extent to which they are specifically "linguistic" is a matter of some controversy. With respect to this question, the bulk of evidence suggests that early infant speech perception may not represent a "special" (i.e., linguistic) mode of processing at all, but rather reflects more *general* psychoacoustic properties of the auditory system (Kuhl, 1979). This conclusion has emerged from two related sources of data. First, in studies of infant discrimination of complex *nonspeech* stimuli, it has been observed that the infant's discrimination of many of these stimuli follows patterns of perceptual discontinuity similar to that observed for speech stimuli (Jusczyk, Rosner, Cutting, Foard, & Smith, 1977). Second, both rhesus monkeys and chinchillas have been found to exhibit patterns of speech perception remarkably similar to (and previously thought to be unique to) both infant and adult human listeners (Kuhl & Miller, 1975; Morse & Snowdon, 1975; Sinnott, Beecher, Moody, & Stebbins, 1976). The clear indication, then, is that these patterns of perceptual behavior are not unique to speech, nor are they even unique to human listeners. Thus, rather than positing specific linguistic knowledge, we might more reasonably consider the phylogenetic contribution to speech perception to be a more general system of psychoacoustic/psychophysical boundaries that can be applied equally to both linguistic and nonlinguistic auditory stimuli (Kuhl, 1979). That the specific linguistic/phonetic categories of human languages tend to fall within these boundaries would seem to facilitate the processes of speech perception and language acquisition.

What then is the role of development and of environmental input in producing a mature language receiver, one who responds to speech as a linguistic event? Since one of the tasks of development for the infant is to organize perceptually the particular phonological system of his/her to-be-acquired language, one developmental question of interest is the nature and extent of the flexibility of these initial perceptual propensities. There is a developing literature on cross-language perception which has begun to suggest ways in which the infant's language-learning environment might interact with these early skills in the development of higher-level speech perception. Although these data are not entirely consistent, they do suggest that experience with a particular language serves both to refine and to expand these "innate" perceptual categories. For example, some contrasts that are readily discriminable to young infants are quite difficult for adults whose native language does not differentiate the pair as phonemically contrastive (Eimas, 1975; Trehub, 1976; Werker, Gilbert, Humphrey, & Tees, 1981). Similarly, some contrasts that are phonetically distinctive in the native language are discriminated categorically (i.e., according to phonetic categories) only *after* experience with that language (Eilers, Gavin, & Wilson, 1979; Streeter, 1976). Thus, these cross-language studies seem to suggest that the language-learning environment may reinforce and thus maintain some discrimination skills and perceptual categories, while extinguishing others that are not functional (and indeed may be dysfunctional).

In addition to the discrimination of inter- and intracultural phonetic contrasts, development (i.e., experience with a linguistic environment) has been implicated for other aspects of language reception as well. Studies by Eilers and Minifie (1975) and Eilers, Wilson, and Moore (1977) have shown developmental changes in the discrimination of some fricative consonants between 3 and 12 months of age. In addition, in a series of important and innovative studies, Kuhl and her colleagues (Holmberg, Morgan, & Kuhl, 1977; Kuhl, 1980) have shown that by 7 months of age, infants exhibit phonetic constancy for some vowels and consonants. That is, these infants are able to ignore irrelevant acoustic and contextual variations and to respond to speech stimuli solely on the basis of their phonetic labels. It is not yet clear whether younger infants do this also, but it is likely that they do not (but see Kuhl, 1977).

Perhaps the most indicting criticism of the bulk of research on infant speech perception is its focus on the single (often synthetic) syllable. We do not speak, nor do we listen, in single syllables. Thus, it is of interest to investigate also the infant's processing of multisyllabic utterances (and eventually, more complex aspects of running speech). Although research in this area has not been extensive, it does appear that development plays an important role here as well. Trehub (1973), for example, failed to observe discrimination within trisyllables in 4- to 17-weeks-olds, whereas Goodsitt, Morse, Cowan, and VerHoeve (1981) have shown that 7-month-olds perform multisyllabic discriminations quite well. Since differences in procedural parameters and/or the stimuli employed might have accounted for the differences between two studies, clear statements about development are premature. These studies do, however, highlight the need for more extensive and systematic research in this area.

Taken together, all of these studies of infant speech perception suggest that, although the young infant seems to be endowed, either at birth or soon thereafter, with a high degree of sensitivity for speech and language, much of the more linguistically relevant knowledge develops throughout the first year in conjunction with extensive experience with the linguistic and social environment. Although we have learned much in the past decade about how this development might proceed, large gaps in our knowledge still exist. Our most immediate concerns lie in three general areas. First, much more research will be needed to delineate more specifically the psychoacoustic underpinnings of very early speech perception from a phylogenetic point of view. Currently, we can only speculate what these might be (Kuhl, 1979). Second, from an ontogenetic point of view, it is important that we begin to investigate more directly the development of multisyllabic speech perception, which will include the perception of running speech, of word segmentation, and of word recognition (Morse & Cowan, in press). Finally, as we learn more about the specific character of the infant's linguistic environment (e.g., "motherese," Newport, 1977), research on infant speech perception must continue to address itself to the perception of these more naturalistic speech samples (Fernald, 1981; Fernald & Kuhl, 1981).

SOCIAL COGNITION: FACES AND VOICES

In this section, research will be reviewed that has been concerned with the infant's perception of selected social stimuli (i.e., human faces and human voices). The literature that has been tapped is often somewhat diverse and thus the studies examined are not always as cohesive as we might like. The review is also selective in the sense that in many cases, only representative studies have been noted, and only those perceptual skills that would seem relevant to communication are discussed. For a more exhaustive treatment of some of the specific issues discussed here, the reader is referred to Lamb and Sherrod (1981).

The major goal of this section is to examine the phylogenetic and ontogenetic status of face and voice perception during the first several months of life. Considering that the infant is inherently a social being, and that for the infant, social interaction and communication might be viewed as one and the same event (Lewis & Cherry, 1977), it is appealing to consider social stimuli as somehow special in the infant's perceptual world. Thus, as noted earlier, this research will be viewed within the framework provided by ethological theory. For organizational purposes, the literature on face perception and on voice perception will be discussed within the context of four basic questions:

1. Does the neonate respond preferentially to social over nonsocial stimuli, and what are the featural bases of this response?
2. What is the nature and developmental course of the infant's response to familiar vs. unfamiliar social stimuli?
3. Can we detect areas of precocity in the infant's perception of social as compared with nonsocial stimuli?

4. How might we describe the infant's perception of features of social stimuli that might be considered clearly communicative (e.g., affect)?

Face Perception

The notion that human faces are phylogenetically prepotent to the young infant, although still embraced by some (Freedman, 1974), has been largely disavowed in recent years. Within the past 20–25 years, numerous studies have been conducted designed to delineate the specific features of visual stimuli to which neonates and young infants are most responsive. Generally speaking, the bulk of this research has demonstrated that the stimulus features that govern infant attention to social patterned stimuli (i.e., faces) are the same as those governing attention to nonsocial patterned stimuli. These include such features as complexity (Brennan, Ames, & Moore, 1966; Greenberg, 1971; Greenberg, O'Donnell, & Crawford, 1973), contour density (Karmel, 1969), symmetry (Bornstein, Gross & Ferdinandsen, 1980; Fisher, Ferdinandsen, & Bornstein, 1981), and movement (Nelson & Horowitz, 1980). Consequently, when presented with a choice of two stimuli varying equally along these dimensions, no preferences are observed in infants 2 months of age and younger (Hershenson, 1964; Maurer & Barrera, 1981).

A second challenge to the view of face perception as phylogenetically "prepared" exists in research that has investigated infant scanning patterns and visual acuity. Specifically, the evidence suggests that, prior to about 2 months of age, infants do not attend to internal features of patterned stimuli (including faces), but rather tend to scan only external borders (Maurer & Salapatek, 1976). One possible explanation for this apparent disinterest in internal facial features is that these features may not be very informative. A recent study by Souther and Banks (1979), in which filters based on the infant's contrast sensitivity function were applied to a series of photographs of faces, suggests that internal facial features may present little more than a faint blur to these young infants.

After two months, however, there are large and rapid strides in the infant's perceptual abilities with respect to faces. That the human face has achieved some sort of "special" status is seen by a variety of observations of precocious discrimination of facelike as compared with nonfacelike stimuli. For example, 5-month-olds discriminate two faces more readily when they are presented in the upright orientation than when they are rotated 180° (Fagan, 1972). In addition, they prefer "real" faces (i.e., photographs) over simple line drawings, mannequins, distorted faces, and faces with scrambled features (Haaf & Bell, 1967; Haaf & Brown, 1976; Kagan, 1967; Kagan, Henker, Hen-Tov, & Lewis, 1966; Lewis, 1969). More recent evidence suggests that infants as young as 2 months prefer schematic faces in which the features are positioned correctly over those with scrambled features (Maurer & Barrera, 1981), although others (Haaf & Bell, 1967; Haaf & Brown, 1976) have not observed similar responding prior to about 4 months of age. Ignoring for the moment these age differences (which are most likely attributable to procedural differences), these studies all suggest that very soon after infants begin to scan systematically internal features of patterned stimuli (Maurer & Salapatek, 1976), they appear to recognize the human face (both photographed and schematized) as a familiar set of invariantly positioned features. This understanding will be important to higher level knowledge of faces, such as the discrimination and recognition of specific persons, the perception of facial expressions, and various related classificatory skills.

In view of the prominent role ethological theory has occupied in theoretical accounts of infancy (Freedman, 1974), and in particular mother–infant attachment (Bowlby, 1969), it is surprising that so little research has been conducted investigating the development of the infant's visual recognition of her mother. Although there are a few reports of mother recognition with face–voice pairings, only three studies have investigated the infant's recognition of her mother based solely upon visual cues (Barrera & Maurer, 1978, 1981b; Bigelow, 1977). In the first of these studies, Bigelow (1977) demonstrated that *visual* discrimination of mother from stranger did not occur before 13 weeks of age, although 5-week-olds seemed able to discriminate mother from stranger when both auditory and visual cues were available. Subsequently, Barrera & Maurer (1981b) also reported mother–stranger discrimination (as well as preferential looking to mother) in 3-month-olds, despite an unsuccessful first attempt (Barrera & Maurer, 1978).

With respect to the discrimination of *unfamiliar* persons, the evidence is somewhat less clear. Most of this research has reported little or no evidence of face discrimination prior to about 5 months of age (Cohen, DeLoache, & Pearl, 1977; Fagan, 1972, 1976). Arguing that these negative results for younger infants might be attributed to procedural insensitivity, Barrera and Maurer (1981a) recently reported more positive evidence of unfamiliar face discrimination in 3-month olds. Moreover, this discrimination was evident whether the faces of the two strangers were similar or dissimilar to each other (as judged by adult raters). Thus, it appears that, with appropriately sensitive measures, infants as young as 3 months of age can not only discriminate a photograph of mother from the photograph of a stranger, but can distinguish between the faces of unfamiliar persons as well. At a somewhat later point in development (probably around 7 months), these infants are also recognizing invariances in particular faces; for example, they can generalize knowledge of one face across several poses (Cohen et al., 1977), and discriminate categorically male from female faces (Cornell, 1974).

One of the more recent developments in the study of infant face discrimination has been research investigating the development of infant recognition of facial expressions denoting affect. Affect, of course, is a very powerful source of information in human communication systems, and might be particularly so during the period of infancy (Sroufe, 1979). There are two sources of data that address this particular aspect of infant face perception. First, Maurer and Salapatek (1976) and Caron, Caron, Caldwell, and Weiss (1973) have reported that once infants begin to fixate and to scan internal facial features, the most preferred feature(s) within this configuration are the eyes. One would presume that this preferential attention to eyes is due in large part to the infant's more general attraction to high-contrast stimuli (Mendelson & Haith, 1976). However, for whatever reason, eyes provide a very rich source of affective/communicative signals, and thus this attraction to the eyes can be seen as an important learning experience for these infants. The second line of research in this area addresses more directly the question of infant discrimination of facial expression. Several studies now have demonstrated such discrimination in 3-month-olds (Barrera & Maurer, 1981c; Browne, Rosenfeld, & Horowitz, 1977) and in 4- to 6-month-olds (Browne et al., 1977; LaBarbera, Izard, Vietze, & Parisi, 1976). For example, 3-month-olds discriminate a smiling from a frowning face (Barrera & Maurer, 1981c, but see also Browne et al., 1977, for conflicting data), and a "surprised" expression from a "happy" expression (Browne et al., 1977). Moreover, this discrimination is evident whether the expressions are posed by the infant's mother or by a stranger (Barrera & Maurer, 1981c). Finally, there is also suggestive evidence that by 7 months, infants can generalize across persons expressions such as "happy" vs. "fear" (Nelson, Morse, & Leavitt, 1979).

Unfortunately, the literature on facial expression discrimination is far from complete and/or clear. For example, although Barrera and Baurer (1981c) did observe smile/frown discrimination in 3-month-olds, Browne et al. (1977) did not. In addition, the results of the Nelson et al. (1979) study were complicated by order effects, leaving the question of generalization across persons somewhat unclear. In both of these cases, modifications in procedural parameters have been implicated in the ambiguity (Barrera & Maurer, 1981c; Nelson et al., 1979). Finally, only a very few of the many affective facial expressions employed in communication have been investigated in these studies (e.g., happy, sad, surprise, fear). Thus, although it is encouraging that this type of research has begun, it appears that extensive parametric research is still badly needed. Such research should explore more systematically these methodological questions, as well as the more substantive issues of generalization across persons posing the same expression, of the discriminability and/or salience of different expressions (Barrera & Maurer, 1981c; Nelson et al., 1979), and especially of the featural bases upon which these discriminations are made.

In summarizing these findings with respect to phylogenetic and ontogenetic questions, the following inferences can be made. First, it does not appear that the human face *qua* human face is a prepotent stimulus to the newborn infant. Rather, as noted in the discussion of the perception of speech and language, the visual system appears to be organized to respond in a similar way to both social and nonsocial stimuli. At the same time, however, this organization seems to favor those particular features that characterize the human face. That is, attention in the very young infant appears to be particularly attracted by such features as complexity (Brennan et al., 1966; Greenberg, 1971; Greenberg et al., 1973), some "optimal" number of light–dark contrasts (Karmel, 1969; Mendelson & Haith, 1976), symmetry (Bornstein et al., 1980; Fisher et al., 1981), and movement (Nelson & Horowitz, 1980), thus making the face a particularly salient stimulus. Although within the first two months, the face does not appear to be particularly interesting (Maurer & Salapatek, 1976) or informative (Souther & Banks, 1979) to the infant, after this time, development is rapid, such that by three months or so, infants are exhibiting discrimination between faces and nonfaces (Maurer & Barrera, 1981), between different familiar and unfamiliar faces (Barrera & Maurer, 1981a, 1981b), and between different emotional expressions on the same face (Barrera & Maurer, 1981c; Browne et al., 1977). Further, these discriminations appear to be specific to face as compared with nonface stimuli (Fagan, 1972). This apparent precocity in the perception of faces might be attributed to any one of a number of environmental circumstances, but is most likely the result of a combination of factors related to the infant's experiences with the human face, such as its frequency of occurrence, its particular configuration of attention eliciting properties, and its association with positive affect.

Voice Perception

The developmental course of voice perception seems to follow a pattern similar to that observed for the perception of faces. Unfortunately, research on infant voice perception is considerably more limited than that for faces, and we have no literature that even approaches the sophistication of the face perception literature with respect to the identification of particular features that capture and maintain the infant's attention. However, as is the case with faces (and despite earlier suggestions to the contrary, e.g., Eisenberg, Griffin, Coursin, & Hunter, 1964; Hutt, Hutt, Lenard, Bernuth, & Muntjewerff, 1966), there seems to be little evidence that, all other factors considered, the human newborn is more responsive to human voices than to other nonsocial auditory stimuli. In fact, relative to white noise, the human voice is not a particularly effective consoling agent until around 3 months of age (Kopp, 1970). However, again as with faces, we would assume voices to be especially frequent events in the infant's life, and thus, some preference for voices over other auditory stimuli soon appears. By 3 months of age, human voices are most effective pacifiers, while nonsocial auditory stimuli seem to have lost much of their effectiveness (Kopp, 1970).

The paucity of research on infant voice perception is surprising (and somewhat depressing) when we consider that the perception of voices might well be the primary interface between social and linguistic perception. In one sense, the human voice is a social stimulus, emanating from a social object. Thus, part of learning to recognize and of developing a relationship with one's primary social object (mother/caretaker), as well as significant others, must certainly include voice recognition. At the same time, however, the voice is also an important source of linguistic information. The particular acoustic form that any given utterance will take depends almost entirely upon the size and shape of the vocal tract producing the utterance (Lieberman, 1975). Systematic differences among vocal tracts (e.g., male vs. female) produce concomitant acoustic differences in particular phonemes and combinations of phonemes (Fant, 1973; Peterson & Barney, 1952). Thus, the infant's perceptual organization and interpretation of that linguistic input appears to be tied to the ability to discriminate, to recognize, and even to categorize these different voices.

The research on infant voice perception can be described along the same lines as the research on face perception (i.e., recognition of mother, discrimination among unfamiliar voices, and the development of classification skills). As suggested above, development in voice perception seems to follow a roughly similar course as does face perception, except that at the present time, voice perception appears to be somewhat more precocious than face perception. For example, there are now several studies that suggest that the infant recognizes his/her mother's voice somewhat earlier than recognizing the mother's face (DeCasper & Fifer, 1980; Mehler, Bertoncini, Barriere, & Jassik-Gershenfeld, 1978; Mills & Melhuish, 1974). In a series of very similar studies, Mills and Melhuish (1974) and Mehler et al. (1978) have suggested that the recognition of mother's voice may occur as early as 3 to 5 weeks of age, while DeCasper and Fifer (1980) report that this recognition occurs as early as the first few days after birth. All three of these studies have employed somewhat different versions of a "preference" paradigm, in which auditory stimuli are presented to the infant contingent upon high-amplitude sucking. In this situation, infants have been observed to suck more in the presence of the mother's voice than in the presence of a stranger's voice, suggesting, in addition to discrimination between mother and stranger, that infants seem to *prefer* to listen to their mothers' voices. This evidence of such early voice recognition can be contrasted with the infant's recognition of her mother's *face,* which has not been observed prior to 3 months of age (Barrera & Maurer, 1981b).

Research investigating the infant's ability to discriminate between two or more unfamiliar voices is more limited, but also suggests somewhat advanced development relative to face perception. Most of the studies conducted have explored discrimination between mother and a female stranger. For example, Boyd (1975) reported mother–stranger discrimination in 7- to 10-week-olds, and although this study did not address directly the question of mother recognition, it did suggest that infants could discriminate between two female voices. In addition, in the studies referred to earlier (DeCasper & Fifer, 1980; Mehler et al., 1978; Mills & Melhuish, 1974), a *preference* for mother's voice certainly implies discrimination as well. Although a smaller number of studies have investigated specifically the discrimination of unfamiliar voices, there is evidence that at least by 2 months of age, infants can discriminate among different female voices (Miller, in press), among different male voices (Miller, in press), and between a male and a female voice (Kaplan, 1969; Miller, in press). Finally, under some conditions, these young infants also discriminate between two different samples of the same unfamiliar voice (Culp & Boyd, 1975; Culp & Gallas, 1975). Once again, we may compare these data with the face perception research which suggests that parallel abilities with respect to faces may not appear before 3 months (Barrera & Maurer, 1981a, 1981c; Cohen et al., 1977; Fagan, 1972, 1976).

In studies that can be seen as roughly analogous to the research on infant discrimination of facial expression, there are at least two suggestions that very young infants (i.e., within the first 2 months) are beginning to respond to properties of voices that seem to convey affective information. For example, in their investigation of the infant's discrimination between two samples of the same voice, Culp and Boyd (1975) observed such discrimination only when speakers were instructed to vary the "emotional tone" of their voices ("harsh" vs. "soft") and not when the linguistic content alone was varied. Unfortunately, this study lacks the appropriate control conditions required to make a very strong statement about this finding. However, additional support for this notion can be found in the Mehler et al. (1978) study of mother recognition. In this study, the infant's recognition of his/her mother's voice occurred only under "normally intonated" conditions. Mother–stranger discrimination did not obtain when monotonic speech patterns were presented. The implications of this latter finding are quite intriguing. First, the data suggest that such early recognition of mother's voice may not reflect a generalized recognition as much as it does recognition of some particular idiosyncracy of the way in which a mother generally talks to her infant. Second, and perhaps more interestingly, they suggest that whatever features characterize these "normally intonated" speech patterns might be among the first and/or most salient features to which an infant attends when listening to voices. In any event, since affective communication plays such a prominent role in mother–infant interaction (Sroufe, 1979), it is important that we begin to investigate more directly the role of voice cues and suprasegmental information in the development of infant perception of affect. Particularly informative will be research investigating the specific features of human voices that are salient to infants, especially affective information, such as intonation and stress.

The final question to be considered with respect to voice perception concerns the extent to which infants can *categorize* voices (e.g., male vs. female). It is of interest to ask this question for several reasons. First, as suggested earlier, accurate decoding of linguistic input appears to be related to an appreciation of the characteristics of the source of that input (Lieberman, 1975). Perhaps the largest source of systematic anatomical, and consequently output, variation is the gender of the speaker, that is, male vs. female (Fant, 1973; Peterson & Barney, 1952). Rand (1971), for example, has shown that speaker gender has systematic effects on the identifications and category boundaries that adult listeners assign to a [bae-dae-gae] continuum. Thus, for the infant, such sophisticated perceptual abilities as phonetic constancy (Kuhl, 1980) might suggest that the infant does have some appreciation for these sources of output variation. Second, voice classification is important for more general aspects of social/communicative development as well, as it reflects the infant's growing awareness of social objects and categories.

My colleagues and I have recently completed a series of studies investigating the development of voice categorization (male vs. female) in infants. In the first set of studies, we demonstrated that 7-month-old infants appear to have developed some appreciation for these gender characteristics of voices (Miller, Younger, & Morse, 1982). Using an operant head-turning procedure (Eilers et al., 1977), infants successfully learned to produce a head turn in the presence of one voice category (e.g., several female voices saying "hi") and to inhibit head turns in the presence of members of the other voice category. Subsequently, it was demonstrated that performance on this task could not be attributed to rote memorization of the specific category tokens, nor was it simply a high-pitch vs. low-pitch discrimination (Miller et al., 1982). More recently, I have demonstrated that the ability to classify voices in this way is a *developmental* accomplishment (Miller, in press). In this study, the voice classification of 2- and 6-month-old infants was investigated, using a multiple-token habituation-dishabituation procedure. Within each age group, infants received either a between-category shift condition (e.g., shift from female voice tokens to male voice tokens), a within-category shift condition (e.g., shift from one set of female voice tokens to another set of female voices), or a control condition (no stimulus shift). The results revealed that 2-month-old infants discriminated both the between-category and the within-category shifts, whereas 6-month-olds exhibited discrimination of only the between-category shift. These results suggested that, although 2-month-olds were either insensitive to or unimpressed by male vs. female category boundaries, by 6 months infants appeared to be constrained in their discrimination by these categories (Miller, in press).

These latter results (i.e., age changes in voice classification) are important for several reasons. Perhaps the most relevant to the present discussion are the implications for the infant's processing of speech and language. It has been argued (Miller et al., 1982; Miller, in press) that the ability to form stimulus categories in infancy reflects the infant's ability to "normalize" or to ignore irrelevant information, thereby permitting more efficient processing of relevant information (note that in this context, "relevant" and "irrelevant" may be defined solely by the task demands, and not by any absolute sense). Further, with specific reference to voice classification, the classification of these voices according to speaker gender may allow the infant to organize linguistic information (e.g., phonetic categories) more efficiently. Thus, the data from the Miller (in press) study suggest that, inasmuch as 2-month olds appear to respond to specific qualities of individual voices, the ability to organize linguistic input from several sources would appear also to be limited in these infants. On the other hand, 6-month olds seem able to approach language reception from a qualitatively more organized and more mature perspective.

Unfortunately, the research literature describing infant voice perception is considerably smaller and less theoretical in approach than those for speech perception and face perception. Within this literature, for example, there is no systematic analysis of the specific properties of human voices that mediate infant attention, and very little developmental work. Thus, it is difficult to summarize this research within a phylogenetic/ontogenetic perspective as has been done with speech and face perception. The following, then, is a preliminary and speculative attempt at such an analysis. We can hope that in the next 5–10 years, the gaps that are evident here will be closed. First, it appears as if human voices are no more salient than similarly complex auditory stimuli to the newborn infant (Kopp, 1970). Although recognition of mother's voice appears to occur quite early in life (DeCasper & Fifer, 1980; Mehler et al., 1978; Mills & Melhuish, 1974), it is possible that this "recognition" is specific to idiosyncracies of the mother's voice that may have little relevance to voice perception in the larger sense. At least by 2 months, however, infants discriminate quite well among unfamiliar voices (Miller, in press), and thus attention to voice quality may be something that is learned quite early. Infants appear also to be learning something about "emotional tone" during this period (Culp & Boyd, 1975; Mehler et al., 1978), but this possibility can be inferred only indirectly from the available research. More direct and extensive investigation of this question remains for future research. Finally, sometime between 2 and 6 months of age, infants are learning to attend to more general qualities of voices, and are beginning to classify voices according to speaker gender (Miller, in press). This developing ability seems to have important implications for the infant's ability to process speech and language, as well as for the development of social/person perception.

SUMMARY AND CONCLUSIONS

In recent years, two general world views have dominated our thinking about infant development. First, ethological theory has provided us with a useful framework within which to view the character of the behavioral and perceptual repertoire of the newly born infant. According to this view, the human infant is seen as almost entirely dependent upon the ministrations of adult conspecifics for survival (Bowlby, 1969; Freedman, 1974). Because of this initial helplessness, evolution has endowed the infant with certain skills that will faciliate the elicitation and maintenance of these adult behaviors (Bowlby, 1969; Freedman, 1974). If we assume that the defining qualities of human existence are social intercourse and intraspecific communication, it then follows that this phylogenetic "gift" to the human newborn consists of skills that are specifically designed for the development of social and communicative skills (Freedman, 1974). With respect to the infant's perceptual repertoire, this theory thus predicts (a) that social and linguistic stimuli will be preferred to nonsocial and nonlinguistic stimuli, and (b) that higher level perceptual processes (e.g., recognition, discrimination, classification) will be relatively more advanced to social/linguistic as compared to nonsocial/nonlinguistic stimuli. Thus, one of the purposes of this chapter has been to examine the research on infant social and linguistic perception within this organizational framework. In summarizing the contributions of three research areas (i.e., infant speech perception, face perception, and voice perception), it was seen that the first of these hypotheses is not generally supported by the available evidence. That is to say, newborns (i.e., younger than 2 months) do not seem to prefer faces over nonfaces (Hershenson, 1964; Maurer & Barrera, 1981) or voices over nonvoices (Kopp, 1970), and they exhibit similar perceptual responses to both speech and nonspeech stimuli (Jusczyuk et al., 1977). At the same time, however, it does appear that the infant's perceptual apparatus, both auditory and visual, is organized in such a way that makes these social and linguistic stimuli very salient. For example, although the neonatal visual system appears not to respond to "faceness" per se, it does seem to respond preferentially to particular visual dimensions (e.g., contrast, symmetry) that are prominent in faces (Bornstein, 1980; Brennan et al., 1966; Karmel, 1969; Nelson & Horowitz, 1980). From an evolutionary point of view, this tendency towards "constrained flexibility" would seem to be advantageous. In addition, these initial attentional preferences, in combination with a supportive environment, appear to result in behavior that does support the second hypothesis, that is that development in the perception of social/linguistic stimuli is precocious relative to that for nonsocial/nonlinguistic stimuli (Fagan, 1972, 1976). Thus, the available evidence seems to suggest that evolution does favor the development of social/communicative skills to the extent that it has provided the infant with the attentional preferences that may facilitate the processes of social cognition and language acquisition. There does appear to be a significant role for environmental input within this process, however, (i.e., the initial perceptual apparatus is not rigidly fixed).

The second view, one that has been embraced by most contemporary developmental psychologists, is the transactional model of development (Sameroff & Chandler, 1975). In essence, this perspective rejects both the early view of the infant as a passive recipient of environmental input (Watson, 1926) upon whom the environment acts, as well as the view that describes development entirely as a maturational process, independent of the environment. Instead, it has been suggested that infant behavior is both a cause and an effect in interaction with the environment. Within the mother–infant dyad, for example, the infant's own behavioral repertoire is both influenced by and a modifier of the mother's behavior. On a somewhat broader scale, this view extends to the infant's existence within the larger environment as well. That is to say, infant behavior (including perception) transacts in complex ways with the environment, again both as an influence of and as a modifier of that environment. Further, these transactions are dynamic and in constant flux. Developmentally speaking, then, this viewpoint suggests that the initial perceptual propensities exhibited by the newborn are (a) designed to exploit those environmental events the infant is likely to encounter more frequently (i.e., speech, faces, and voices), and (b) modified as a function of interacting with and responding to those stimuli. Thus, it is not particularly surprising, given the frequency with which the young infant encounters and interacts with social and linguistic stimuli, that by 2 to 3 months of age, the infant is exhibiting precocious perception of those stimuli relative to others less frequent in the infant's life (such as scrambled faces and checkerboards).

The research reviewed herein suggests that at various points in development, the infant enters a communicative situation with differential abilities to extract meaning from and to influence that interaction. This suggestion has at least two implications for the nature of dyadic interaction at various levels of development. First, we would expect different forms of social stimulation to be effective at different developmental levels. For the newborn, who is probably not preferentially attentive to faces, all visual stimuli with areas of high contrast will probably be equally effective. In addition, if one desired to maintain a high level of attention in the newborn during a face-to-face interaction, one might move one's entire head, since this newborn is probably scanning borders, and thus, movement of the entire stimulus is necessary to maintain some optimal level of novelty. For a 4-month old, who is attending both to "faceness" and to internal features of stimuli, perturbation of one's mouth and eyes during interaction is likely to be sufficient to maintain this infant's attention. A second implication of this research for mother/caretaker–infant interactional research is that we can no longer assume that "a maternal behavior is a maternal behavior is a maternal behavior." Rather, we would expect that the same maternal behavior (e.g., exaggerated movements of the mouth and eyes) would be differentially salient to the newborn and the 4-month old, and further that these two infants would present to the caretaker different feedback regarding the effectiveness of this stimulation. Finally, if we accept this view, then we must also question the value of our current assumptions of ecological validity in this observational research. If we consider the infant's perceptual apparatus to be an important component in these interactions, then we can no longer assume that a particular event is ecologically valid simply by virtue of its having been observed to occur within a naturalistic setting. Instead, we must define the infant's ecology from the perspective of the infant's perceptions, rather than from our own.

This latter argument then leads us to the question, what precisely is the infant's ecology, and how is it different at different stages of development? The research conducted so far has given us a brief glimpse into what that ecology might be for the infant. However, much remains to be learned. If we approach this issue from a transactional perspective, then several immediate research questions arise. First, it is necessary that we investigate more directly the relationship between infant perception and environmental input, at all stages of development. In the area of infant speech perception, for example, there is much we still need to learn about the infant's response to speech (e.g., perception within multisyllables, words, word recognition, and prosodic and paralinguistic features of running speech, to mention only a few). Combined with a more extensive description of the infant's linguistic input, as well as with naturalistic observations of the infant's response to that input within the social context, this research should contribute to a better understanding of the transactional events occurring in these exchanges.

Similarly, much remains to be learned about the beginning of social cognition in early infancy. The studies investigating infant face perception in the laboratory are quite numerous; however, we know very little about the salience of, and the response to, human faces in more naturalistic interactional situations. The data that do exist appear to be somewhat conflicting. For example, whereas Kaufmann and Kaufmann (1980) report what they interpret to be greater attention to moving faces (as would be more typical in a social situation) than to stationary faces, Field (1979) observed cardiac accelerations (i.e., defensive responses) to the *most* "naturalistic" (animate mother's face) and cardiac decelerations (i.e., attention) to the *least* naturalistic (inanimate doll's face) of the stimuli she employed. Thus, the nature of the infant's response to her mother's face during interaction is still unclear. In addition to these perceptual questions, there is no descriptive work that has documented the nature of the infant's *experience* with faces (e.g., the number of different faces encountered over a period of time). Thus, although we assume that the developmental changes that have been observed in face perception are influenced by the infant's experiences with faces, this remains only an assumption without the appropriate documentation. The same types of convergent analyses are also needed in the study of infant voice perception. Before such work can or should begin, however, we also need a considerably more extensive and systematic laboratory analysis of the development of voice perception (e.g., the properties of voices that are salient to infants) and the processes underlying voice recognition, discrimination, and generalization.

Finally, the ultimate question we should be asking is, what are the implications of all of this for the infant's developing ability to communicate effectively and deliberately? At all other stages of development, social cognition is seen as intimately tied to effective communication (Glucksberg, Krauss, & Higgins, 1975; Shatz & Gelman, 1973). Yet only recently have we even recognized that such a process might be important in infancy (Lamb & Sherrod, 1981). This recognition must now translate itself into empirical research.

REFERENCES

Barrera, M. E., & Maurer, D. Recognition of mother's photographed face by three-month-old infants. Paper presented at the International Conference on Infant Studies, Providence, March, 1978.

Barrera, M. E., & Maurer, D. Discrimination of strangers by the three-month old. *Child Development*, 1981, *52*, 558–563. (a)

Barrera, M. E., & Maurer, D. Recognition of mother's photographed face by the three-month-old infant. *Child Development*, 1981, *52*, 714–716. (b)

Barrera, M. E., & Maurer, D. The perception of facial expressions by the three-month old. *Child Development*, 1981, *52*, 203–206. (c)

Bigelow, A. Infants' recognition of their mothers. Paper presented at the biennial meeting of the Society for Research in Child Development, New Orleans, March 1977.

Bornstein, M. H., Gross, C. G., & Ferdinandsen, K. Perception of symmetry in infancy. Paper presented to the International Conference on Infant Studies, New Haven, CT, 1980.

Bowlby, J. *Attachment*. New York: Basic Books, 1969.

Boyd, E. F. Visual fixation and voice discrimination in 2-month-old infants. In F. D. Horowitz (Ed.), Visual attention, auditory stimulation, and language discrimination in young infants. *Monographs of the Society for Research in Child Development*, 1975, *39*(5–6), 63–77.

Brennan, W. M., Ames, N. W., & Moore, R. W. Age differences in infants' attention to patterns of different complexities. *Science*, 1966, *151*, 354–356.

Browne, G. Y., Rosenfeld, H. M., & Horowitz, F. D. Infant discrimination of facial expressions. *Child Development*, 1977, *48*, 555–562.

Caron, A. J., Caron, R. F., Caldwell, R. C., & Weiss, S. Infant perception of the structural properties of the face. *Developmental Psychology*, 1973, *9*, 385–399.

Cohen, L. B., DeLoache, J. S., & Pearl, R. An examination of interference effects in infants' memory for faces. *Child Development*, 1977, *48*, 88–96.

Cornell, E. H. Infants' discrimination of faces following redundant presentations. *Journal of Experimental Child Psychology*, 1974, *18*, 98–106.

Culp, R., & Boyd, E. Visual fixation and the effect of voice quality and content differences in 2-month-old infants. In F. D. Horowitz (Ed.), Visual attention, auditory stimulation, and language discrimination in young infants. *Monographs of the Society for Research in Child Development*, 1975, *39*, 78–91.

Culp, R., & Gallas, H. Discrimination of male voice quality by 8- and 9-week-old infants. Paper presented at the biennial meeting of the Society for Research in Child Development, Denver, CO, 1975.

DeCasper, A., & Fifer, W. Of human bonding: Newborns prefer their mother's voices. *Science,* 1980, *208,* 1174–1176.

DeVilliers, J. G., & DeVilliers, P. A. *Language and acquisition.* Cambridge: Harvard University Press, 1978.

Eilers, R. E., Gavin, W., & Wilson, W. R. Linguistic experience and phonemic perception in infancy: A cross-linguistic study. *Child Development,* 1979, *50,* 14–18.

Eilers, R., & Minifie, F. Fricative discrimination in early infancy. *Journal of Speech and Hearing Research,* 1975, *18,* 158–167.

Eilers, R., Wilson, W., & Moore, J. Developmental changes in speech discrimination in infants. *Journal of Speech and Hearing Research,* 1977, *20,* 766–780.

Eimas, P. D. Auditory and linguistic processing of cues for place of articulation by infants. *Perception and Psychophysics,* 1974, *16,* 513–521.

Eimas, P. D. Speech perception in infancy. In L. Cohen & P. Salapatek (Eds.), *Infant perception: From sensation to cognition* (Vol. 2). New York: Academic Press, 1975.

Eimas, P. D., Siqueland, E. R., Jusczyk, P., & Vigorito, J. Speech perception in infants. *Science,* 1971, *171,* 303–306.

Eisenberg, R. B., Griffin, E. J., Coursin, D. B., & Hunter, M. S. Auditory behavior in the human neonate: A preliminary report. *Journal of Speech and Hearing Research,* 1964, *7,* 245–269.

Fagan, J. F. Infants' recognition memory for faces. *Journal of Experimental Child Psychology,* 1972, *14,* 453–456.

Fagan, J. F. Infants' recognition of invariant features of faces. *Child Development,* 1976, *47,* 627–638.

Fant, G. *Speech sounds and features.* Cambridge, MA: MIT Press, 1973.

Fernald, A. 4-month-olds prefer to listen to "motherese." Paper presented at the biennial meetings of the Society for Research in Child Development, Boston, 1981.

Fernald, A., & Kuhl, P. K. Fundamental frequency as an acoustic determinant of infant preference for motherese. Paper presented at the biennial meeting of the Society for Research in Child Development, Boston, 1981.

Field, T. M. Visual and cardiac responses to animate and inanimate faces by young term and preterm infants. *Child Development,* 1979, *50,* 188–194.

Fisher, C. B., Ferdinandsen, K., & Bornstein, M. H. The role of symmetry in infant form discrimination. *Child Development,* 1981, *52,* 457–462.

Freedman, D. G. *Human infancy: An evolutionary perspective.* Hillsdale, NJ: Erlbaum, 1974.

Glanville, B., Best, C., & Levenson, R. A cardiac measure of cerebral asymmetries in infant auditory perception. *Developmental Psychology,* 1977, *13,* 54–59.

Goodsitt, J., Morse, P., Cowan, N., & VerHoeve, J. Infant speech perception in a multisyllabic world. Paper presented at the biennial meeting of the Society for Research in Child Development, Boston, 1981.

Glucksberg, S., Krauss, R. M., & Higgins, E. T. The development of referential communication skills. In F. D. Horowitz, E. M. Heterington, S. Scarr-Salapatek, & G. Siegel (Eds.), *Review of child development research* (Vol. 4). Chicago: University of Chicago Press, 1975.

Greensberg, D. J. Accelerating visual complexity levels in the human infant. *Child Development,* 1971, *42,* 905–918.

Greenberg, D. J., O'Donnell, W. J., & Crawford, D. Complexity levels, habituation, and individual differences in early infancy. *Child Development,* 1973, *44,* 569.

Haaf, R. A., & Bell, R. Q. The facial dimension in visual discrimination by human infants. *Child Development,* 1967, *38,* 893–899.

Haaf, R., & Brown, C. Infants' response to face-like patterns: Developmental changes between 10 and 15 weeks of age. *Journal of Experimental Child Psychology,* 1976, *22,* 155–160.

Hecox, K. Electrophysiological correlates of human auditory development. In L. B. Cohen & P.

Salapatek (Eds.), *Infant perception: From sensation to cognition* (Vol. 2). New York: Academic Press, 1975.

Hershenson, M. Visual discrimination in the human newborn. *Journal of Comparative and Physiological Psychology*, 1964, *58*, 270–276.

Holmberg, T., Morgan, K., & Kuhl, P. Speech perception in early infancy: Discrimination of fricative contrasts. *Journal of the Acoustical Society of America*, 1977, *62*(Suppl. 1), S99 (A).

Hutt, S. J., Hutt, C., Lenard, H. G., Bernuth, H. V., & Muntjewerff, W. J. Auditory responsivity in the human neonate. *Nature*, 1966, *218*, 888–890.

Jusczyk, P., Rosner, B., Cutting, J., Foard, C., & Smith, L. Categorical perception of nonspeech sounds in 2-month-old infants. *Perception and Psychophysics*, 1977, *2*, 50–54.

Jusczyk, P., & Thompson, E. Perception of a phonetic contrast in multisyllabic utterances by 2-month-old infants. *Perception and Psychophysics*, 1978, *23*, 105–109.

Kagan, J. The growth of the "face" schema: Theoretical significance and methodological issues. In J. Hellmuth (Ed.), *The exceptional infant* (Vol. 1): *The normal infant*. New York: Brunner/Mazel, 1967.

Kagan, J., Henker, B. A., Hen-Tov, A., & Lewis, M. Infants' differential reactions to familiar and distorted faces. *Child Development*, 1966, *37*, 519–532.

Kaplan, E. The role of intonation in the acquisition of language. Unpublished doctoral dissertation, Cornell University, 1969.

Karmel, B. Z. The effect of age, complexity, and amount of contour on pattern preferences in human infants. *Journal of Experimental Child Psychology*, 1969, *7*, 339–354.

Kaufmann, R., & Kaufmann, F. The face schema in 3- and 4-month-old infants: The role of dynamic properties of the face. *Infant Behavior and Development*, 1980, *3*, 331–339.

Kopp, C. B. A comparison of stimuli effective in soothing distressed infants. Unpublished doctoral dissertation, Claremont University, 1970.

Kuhl, P. Speech perception in early infancy: Perceptual constancy for the vowel categories /a/ and /ɔ/. *Journal of the Acoustical Society of America*, 1977, *61*(Suppl. 1), S39 (A).

Kuhl, P. Models and mechanisms in speech perception. *Brain, Behavior, and Evolution*, 1979, *16*, 374–408.

Kuhl, P. Perceptual constancy for speech sound categories. In G. Yeni-Komshian, J. Kavanagh, & C. Ferguson (Eds.), *Child phonology: Perception and production*. New York: Academic Press, 1980.

Kuhl, P., & Miller, J. Speech perception by the chinchilla: Voiced-voiceless distinction in alveolar plosive consonants. *Science*, 1975, *190*, 69–72.

LaBarbera, V. D., Izard, C. E., Vietze, P., & Parisi, S. A. Four- and six-month-old infants' visual responses to joy, anger, and neutral expressions. *Child Development*, 1976, *47*, 535–538.

Lamb, M., & Sherrod, L. *Infant social cognition*. Hillsdale, NJ: Erlbaum, 1981.

Lewis, M. Infants' responses to facial stimuli during the first year of life. *Developmental Psychology*, 1969, *2*, 75–86.

Lewis, M., & Cherry, L. Social behavior and language acquisition. In M. Lewis & L. A. Rosenblum (Eds.), *Interaction, conversation, and the development of language*. New York: Wiley, 1977.

Lieberman, P. *On the origins of language*. New York: MacMillan, 1975.

Maurer, D., & Barrera, M. E. Infants' perception of natural and distorted arrangements of a schematic face. *Child Development*, 1981, *52*, 196–202.

Maurer, D., & Salapatek, P. Developmental changes in the scanning of faces by young infants. *Child Development*, 1976, *47*, 523–527.

Mehler, J., Bertoncini, J., Barrière, M., & Jassik-Gershenfeld, D. Infant recognition of mother's voice. *Perception*, 1978, *7*, 491–497.

Mendelson, M. J., & Haith, M. M. The relation between audition and vision in the human newborn. *Monographs of the Society for Research in Child Development*, 1976, *41*(4).

Miller, C. L. Developmental changes in male-female voice classification in infancy. *Infant Behavior and Development*, in press.

Miller, C. L., & Morse, P. The "heart" of categorical speech discrimination in young infants. *Journal of Speech and Hearing Research*, 1976, *19*, 578–589.

Miller, C. L., Morse, P. A., & Dorman, M. F. Cardiac indices of infant speech perception: Orienting and burst discrimination. *Quarterly Journal of Experimental Psychology*, 1977, *29*, 533–545.

Miller, C. L., Younger, B., & Morse, P. A. The categorization of male and female voices in infancy. *Infant Behavior and Development*, 1982, *5*, 143–159.

Miller, J. Phonetic determination of infant speech perception. Unpublished doctoral dissertation, University of Minnesota, 1974.

Mills, M., & Melhuish, E. Recognition of mother's voice in early infancy. *Nature*, 1974, *252*, 123–124.

Molfese, D. L. Infant cerebral asymmetry. In S. Segalowicz & F. Gruber (Eds.), *Language development and neurological theory*. New York: Academic Press, 1977.

Morse, P. A. The discrimination of speech and nonspeech stimuli in early infancy. *Journal of Experimental Child Psychology*, 1972, *14*, 477–492.

Morse, P. A., & Cowan, N. Infant auditory and speech perception. In T. Field (Ed.), *Review of research in child development*. New York: Wiley, in press.

Morse, P., & Snowdon, C. An investigation of categorical speech discrimination by rhesus monkeys. *Perception and Psychophysics*, 1975, *17*, 9–16.

Nelson, C. A., & Horowitz, F. D. Infant's perception of visual movement: A review and theoretical analysis (Technical Report No. 94). Lawrence, KS: Research Institute for Early Childhood Education for the Handicapped, University of Kansas, 1980.

Nelson, C. A., Morse, P. A., & Leavitt, L. A. Recognition of facial expressions by 7-month-old infants. *Child Development*, 1979, *50*, 1239–1242.

Newport, E. L. Motherese: The speech of mothers to young children. In N. J. Castellan, D. B. Pisoni, & G. R. Potts (Eds.), *Cognitive theory* (Vol. 2). Hillsdale, NJ: Erlbaum, 1977.

Peterson, G. E., & Barney, H. L. Control methods used in a study of vowels. *Journal of the Acoustical Society of America*, 1952, *24*, 175–184.

Rand, T. C. Vocal tract size normalization in the perception of stop consonants. Paper presented at the meeting of the Acoustical Society of America, Washington, D.C., 1971.

Sameroff, A. J., & Chandler, M. J. Reproductive risk and the continuum of caretaking casualty. In F. D. Horowitz (Ed.), *Review of child development research* (Vol. 4). Chicago: University of Chicago Press, 1975.

Schaffer, H. R. Acquiring the concept of the dialogue. In M. H. Bornstein & W. Kessen (Eds.), *Psychological development from infancy: Image to intention*. Hillsdale, NJ: Erlbaum, 1979.

Seligman, M. E. P. On the generality of the laws of learning. *Psychological Review*, 1970, *77*, 406–418.

Shatz, M., & Gelman, R. The development of communication skills in the speech of young children as a function of listener. *Monographs of the Society for Research in Child Development*, 1973, *38*(No. 5).

Sinnott, J., Beecher, M., Moody, D., & Stebbins, W. Speech sound discrimination by humans and monkeys. *Journal of the Acoustical Society of America*, 1976, *60*, 687–695.

Souther, A. F., & Banks, M. S. The human face: A view from the infant's eye. Paper presented at the meeting of the Society for Research in Child Development, San Francisco, 1979.

Spring, D., & Dale, P. The discrimination of linguistic stress in early infancy. *Journal of Speech and Hearing Research*, 1977, *20*, 224–231.

Sroufe, A. L. Socioemotional development. In J. Osofsky (Ed.), *Handbook, of infant development*. New York: Wiley, 1979.

Streeter, L. Language perception of 2-month-old infants shows effects of both innate mechanisms and experience. *Nature*, 1976, *259*, 39–41.

Sullivan, J. W. and Horowitz, F. D. The effect of intonation on infant attention: The role of the rising intonation contour. *Journal of Child Language*, in press.

Swoboda, P., Kass, J., Morse, P., & Leavitt, L. Memory factors in infant vowel discrimination of normal and at-risk infants. *Child Development*, 1978, *49*, 332–339.

Swoboda, P., Morse, P., & Leavitt, L. Continuous vowel discrimination in normal and at-risk infants. *Child Development*, 1976, *47*, 459–465.

Trehub, S. Infants' sensitivity to vowel and tonal contrasts. *Developmental Psychology*, 1973, *9*, 81–96.

Trehub, S. The discrimination of foreign speech contrasts by infants and adults. *Child Development*, 1976, *47*, 466–472.

Trehub, S., & Rabinovitch, S. Auditory-linguistic sensitivity in early infancy. *Developmental Psychology*, 1972, *6*, 74–77.

Watson, J. B. What the nursery has to say about instincts. In C. Murcheson (Ed.), *Psychologies of 1925*. Worcester, MA: Clark University Press, 1926.

Werker, J. F., Gilbert, J. H. V., Humphrey, K., & Tees, R. C. Developmental aspects of cross-language speech perception. *Child Development*, 1981, *52*, 349–355.

CHAPTER 4

The Role of Temporal Cues in the Development of Language and Communication

Cynthia L. Miller and Joseph M. Byrne

"Rhythms," "reciprocity," "synchrony," "cycles," "turn-taking"—these are only a few of the words that, although relatively recent to our professional jargon, are rapidly approaching the status of buzz words. These terms have been, and continue to be, used in describing various features of infant behavior, of maternal/caretaking behavior, and of caretaker/infant dyadic behavior. Yet, what do these words really mean, or more specifically, what are the implications and the underlying assumptions of the use of these terms in professional as well as everyday nonprofessional parlance? In this chapter, we will explore this question from a variety of perspectives, with the goal of better understanding the infant's experience of time and its relationship of the development of communication skills.

It has been argued that time as a dimension is almost aboriginal in its importance in the young infant's life (Ashton, 1976; Stern & Gibbon, 1979). Yet at the same time, it represents one of the great "uncharted ways" in the study of infant development. Although there are a number of studies that address somewhat indirectly the infant's experience of time, there has been little systematic research directed specifically to this issue; calls for the importance of such research (Stern & Gibbon, 1979) have largely fallen on deaf ears. This is indeed surprising considering the salience of rhythmicity (i.e., temporal predictability) in the infant's behavioral patterns. From the moment of birth, microrhythms in many infant behaviors such as sucking (Wolff, 1968) and crying (Wolff, 1966) can be observed. Even prior to birth, rhythms in more molar features of infant behaviors, e.g., sleep-wake cycles (Roffwarg, Muzio, and Dement, 1966), have been described. Although we have been aware of this rhythmic quality of infant behavior for some 15–20 years now, its significance for the infant's development (except as a descriptor of physiologic processes) has not received extensive speculation until recently. Possibly, one explanation for this "lag" is that, at least in the newborn, these cycles are largely endogenous; in fact, exogenous stimulation may more frequently have a disruptive than a generative effect on neonatal cyclicity (e.g., "jiggling" tends to modify the ongoing temporal patterns of sucking, Kaye, 1977). Thus, we might reasonably ask why it is that the infant's "preprogrammed" rhythms are considered so vital to the infant's adaptation to the outside world.

Part of the answer to this question, we believe, is that these behavioral patterns constitute a "frame" within which the young infant can view the environment, and in that sense, are an important part of the equipment with which the infant approaches the outside world. In addition, however, we should like to propose (as have others, certainly, e.g., Stern and Gibbon, 1979) that timing and the experience of time is an especially critical feature in the development of and competence in communication. In fact, as Kaye (1977) has suggested, these early rhythmic patterns of behavior may indeed constitute the original conversational prototype. Moreover, the perception of temporal features in the environment and the performance of temporally-organized behavior would seem to be vital to skill acquisition in many areas (Ashton, 1976; Lashley, 1951), but most dramatically in the acquisition of communicative competence. As we shall see, both the social and the linguistic components of communicative competence involve precise timing at many levels.

This chapter has two purposes. First, we will examine various ways in which appropriate timing and temporal perception are important to the infant's developing notions of language and communication. Here we will explore the various social and linguistic events that the infant experiences in which temporal features can be seen as critical components. The second purpose is to examine how the infant might be experiencing these events, i.e., infant temporal perception. A variety of diffuse and diverse literatures will be examined that address, both directly and indirectly, three important questions: (a) what are the parameters of time perception in infancy (e.g., memory span), (b) how salient a dimension is time for the infant (e.g., does the infant attend specifically to temporal features as integral components of stimulus events and (c) how can we describe the development of timing processes.

THE TEMPORAL ENVIRONMENT

Clearly, all events in the infant's world unfold in the dimension of time. The first question we need to address ourselves to then is, what is the temporal patterning of these events, and how is it arranged or regulated within the context of the ongoing stimulus event in order to promote the infant's appreciation for timing in communication? In this section, we will explore three sources from which the infant might glean such information: (a) the temporal features of the "typical" mother/caretaker-infant interaction, e.g., turn-taking sequences and mother-infant games, (b) the general temporal features of speech and language, and (c) the specific features of the mother's behavior (both social and linguistic) that seem to highlight the dimension of time.

Temporal Cues in the Social Environment

Perhaps the clearest example of how temporal parameters can direct the structure of ongoing interactions is conversational "turn taking," or speaker switching. Very elegant descriptions of the physical (e.g., facial and vocal) and temporal cues that control speaker–listener interchanges have been provided by a number of studies of adult–adult conversations (Duncan & Niederehe, 1974; Jaffe & Feldstein, 1970). The production and reception of these cues are considered critical to the maintenance of harmony between speaker and listener and to effective communication in general. Certainly, Emily Post would consider interrupting a speaker a very rude behavior indeed!

Thus, one of the primary tasks of the mother and infant during a social exchange is synchronizing or systematizing their turn-taking behaviors. In recent years, with a shift in methodological focus to the *sequential* analysis and description of dyadic behavior (Lamb, Suomi, & Stephenson, 1979) we have seen repeated demonstrations of such synchrony or reciprocity developing in the mother–infant relationship (cf. Schaffer, 1979 for an excellent review of this literature). One of the first studies to alert us to this alternating nature of mother–infant behavior was that of Lewis and Freedle (1973) in which nonrandom orderings of specific behaviors within the mother–infant dyad were dramatically revealed. Since that time, a number of studies have revealed similar results for a variety of different behaviors. For example, Kaye (1977) has conducted exquisite observations of mother–infant feeding interactions in which he has observed precise temporal patternings in each partner's behavior. Sucking, which typically follows a relatively predictable pattern of bursts and pauses (Wolff, 1968), is generally accompanied (during a burst) by a relatively inactive mother, but is then followed (during a pause) by maternal behaviors such as jiggling, vocalizing, and looking (Kaye, 1977). The cessation of jiggling is a signal to the infant that sucking may now resume. This pattern (suck-jiggle-jiggle stop-suck) is presumably controlled by the mother as she adapts her behavior to the spontaneous temporal patterning of the infant's sucking. However, this sequence of behaviors does resemble quite closely a turn-taking interaction, and more likely than not contributes to the infant's learning about these temporal rules of conversation. Indeed, Kaye (1977) has observed that over the first few weeks of life, the "jiggle-stop to suck" latency becomes shorter, suggesting that the infant is adapting herself to the mother's signals. Similar types of alternating sequences have also been observed in mother–infant gaze behavior (Stern, 1974) as well as in vocal exchanges (Bateson, 1975; Lewis & Freedle, 1973). Thus, at least the rudiments of the sequential organization of dyadic behaviors are present even in the newborn infant (Kaye, 1977). The extent to which the infant participates in these interactions out of some "prewired" appreciation for behavioral alternation with a partner (Jaffe, 1978) is still a matter of speculation. However, it is clear that the rhythmic patterns of behavior endogenous to the newborn are adaptive in the sense that, at the very least, the mother can predict and thus adapt to her infant's rhythms (Schaffer, 1979). Whether in fact the infant follows the mother's temporal organization (Condon & Sander, 1974a, 1974b) is quite a different issue and will be considered briefly later.

Yet another form of interaction in which temporal cues appear to play an important role is the mother–infant game. Some well-known games whose success appears contingent upon temporal organization are "peek-a-boo" and the everpopular "gonna getcha." It has been argued that early in infancy, these games are characterized by temporal regularity, and that later they are characterized by the establishment of temporal expectancies and subsequent violations of those expectancies (Stern, 1974, 1977). That the infant can form temporal expectancies and exhibit anticipatory responses has been suggested by Moore, Borton, and Darby (1978) and by Eisenberg (undated). Moreover, the success of manipulating temporal cues in playing games with the infant is seen in naturalistic situations by the joy that the infant exhibits to the resolution of temporal uncertainty (Stern, 1974, 1977).

Temporal Cues in the Linguistic Environment

The other major input component within the infant's immediate environment of course is linguistic. Mothers vocalize frequently to their infants, especially in situations that can be viewed as social-communicative, as opposed to caregiving (Lewis & Freedle, 1973). The pattern of maternal vocalizations, as well as the phonemic structure of the language itself, can also be characterized with respect to temporal parameters.

The temporal properties of the structure of the linguistic system can be described on both molar and molecular levels. The molar level (e.g., turn taking) has been alluded to previously. Essentially, as Jaffe and Feldstein (1970) have noted, the fundamental unit of communication is the dialogue and not the monologue. Thus, inherent to the evolution of communication must also be the evolution of means by which this dialogue can flow smoothly (i.e., cues for signaling speaker switches). Although there are a variety of vocal and facial cues that serve this function (Duncan & Niederehe, 1974; Jaffe & Feldstein, 1970), temporal cues appear to play a role as well. For example, listeners do not typically interject until a pause of sufficient duration has alerted them that the speaker has completed her turn (Jaffe & Feldstein, 1970). Thus, in addition to turn taking in the general kinesic sense as discussed earlier, the infant must also acquire knowledge of the rules of conversational turn-taking in the vocal sense. That is, the infant eventually must learn that a pause in the vocal channel is an especially significant communicative signal. Based upon studies of infant vocal conditioning, Bloom (1979) has suggested that, at a very early age, infants do seem to appreciate the significance of vocal–vocal contingencies and the alternating sequencing of these behaviors.

On a slightly more molecular level are the pauses that signal syntactic or semantic boundaries (Boomer, 1978; Ladefoged & Broadbent, 1960). Ultimately, language comprehension is contingent upon the ability to appreciate the segmentation of these linguistic units. Finally, even at the level of the phoneme and the syllable, temporal cues are critical to both speech production and speech perception. Certainly, the very articulation of speech requires precise and complex sequences of vocal maneuvers (Denes & Pinson, 1963; Lieberman, 1977). In addition, many phonemic contrasts are differentiated only by their temporal features. For example, [be] and [we] differ only in the duration of the initial formant transitions (DeLattre, Liberman, & Cooper, 1955; Liberman, DeLattre, Gerstman, & Cooper, 1956), whereas [ba] and [pa] differ primarily in the latency between vocal closure and the onset of periodic voicing (Abramson & Lisker, 1970). Numerous examples of the importance of durational cues to the perception and production of phonemic contrasts in speech can be cited. Later in this chapter, we shall discuss a few of these within the context of the infant's perception of these temporal features of speech and language.

The discussion thus far has been limited to those characteristics of speech and language, and of conversation in general, that have been observed in the mature adult–adult linguistic system. However, an even more dramatic illustration of the importance of temporal cues (and our awareness of their importance as adult speakers of the language) can be seen in the speech that is addressed specifically to infants. "Motherese" (Newport, 1977), or infant-directed speech, refers to a whole collection of modifications that mothers (and others) use in the speech that they direct to young infants and language-learning children. On the whole, these modifications can be characterized by exaggerations in many of the features that we consider important to effective communication, both linguistic and affective (Garnica, 1977; Remick, 1976; Sachs, Brown, & Salerno, 1976; Stern, Spieker, Barnett, & MacKain, in press). And indeed, it appears as if we do consider temporal cues to be important, since they also are subject to these same modifications or exaggerations. On a very general level, we can describe this speech as *slow*. For example, two specific features of motherese that contribute to this slowed pace are longer and more frequent pauses, as well as elongated phonetic segments, such as vowels (Garnica, 1977; Sachs et al., 1976; Stern et al., in press). Thus, it appears as if the temporal parameters of speech and language are important for communication between adults. Moreover, the observation that we tend to emphasize these cues in our language-teaching behavior toward infants and young children (Garnica, 1977; Sachs et al., 1976; Stern et al., in press) might further attest to their importance in the development of effective communication.

INFANT PERCEPTION OF TEMPORAL INFORMATION

It is clear that the social and language-learning environment is replete with temporal information that the infant must interpret and learn how to use. In this section, we will explore quite briefly various research areas that address, directly and indirectly, the infant's experience of time. These diverse areas of research can be very generally classified as: (a) the infant's ability to "estimate" time; (b) the infant's ability to discriminate temporal cues; (c) the effect of manipulating temporal patterning on the infant's behavior (in naturalistic and seminaturalistic settings); and (d) neonatal interactional synchrony.

Time Estimation

Data relevant to the infant's ability to "estimate" time come primarily from studies of temporal conditioning. In this research the question has been posed: Can the infant estimate the duration of a time interval by exhibiting a conditioned response at the end of that interval? The evidence that we have on this question is somewhat unclear but may be understood better by considering both the nature of the stimulus *and* the nature of the response in determing conditionability (cf. Fitzgerald & Brackbill, 1976; Lancioni, 1980). Essentially, two types of responses have been measured in these studies, autonomic and somatic. In studies of classical autonomic conditioning, conditionability to temporal intervals (generally around 20 seconds) has been demonstrated for both pupillary dilation and constriction reflexes (Brackbill, Lintz, & Fitzgerald, 1968; Fitzgerald, Lintz, Brackbill, & Adams, 1967) as well as for heart-rate responses (Stamps, 1977; Stamps & Porges, 1975). Furthermore, temporal conditioning appears to be superior to auditory conditioning, at least for the pupillary reflexes (Brackbill et al., 1968; Fitzgerald et al., 1967). Stereotype conditioning, or the conditioning to *temporal patterns,* is also possible in young infants (1–3 months), though shows a slower rate of acquisition and less consistency across responses, thus suggesting it as more difficult and more sensitive to individual differences than simple temporal conditioning (Brackbill & Fitzgerald, 1972). With respect to heart-rate conditioning, the data are less consistent but possibly more interesting. Specifically, it has been observed in more than one study that, following repeated presentations of a signal at regular intervals, the omission of that signal elicits a heart-rate *deceleration* in newborn infants (Stamps, 1977; Stamps & Porges, 1975). Thus, the infant's sensitivity to temporal patterns is evidence by the elicitation of this *attentional* response, one that is rarely observed in newborns (Graham & Jackson, 1970).

Studies employing somatic response measures have been somewhat less success-ful in demonstrating temporal conditioning. Reflexes such as eye blinks and sucking can be classically conditioned to auditory and/or tactile stimuli, but apparently not to temporal cues (Brackbill & Fitzgerald, 1972; Brackbill et al., 1968). This appar-ent interaction between stimulus and response modalities has unfortunately not been systematically investigated further. However, it is an intriguing observation and may have implications for neurological processes underlying the experience of time and temporal intervals.

Another indication of the infant's ability to estimate time comes from a recent, and quite extensive, study of Eisenberg (undated). In this study, psychophysiologic (EEG) and behavioral responses of neonates were measured to a series of auditory stimuli, with intertrial intervals (ITI) ranging from 13 to 16 seconds. Examinations of the behavioral data suggested that, after some number of trials, most infants began to exhibit "anticipatory responses" that occurred approximately at the mean of the various ITI durations. Since her study was not designed specifically to examine this issue, however, several methodological considerations make this study less than ideal for testing hypotheses about temporal perception and/or estimation. Thus, at present, interpretation of these data must be made with caution. Nevertheless, the suggestion that neonates can not only estimate time but can also compute the mean of variable temporal intervals is sufficiently intriguing to warrant more direct investigations of this phenomenon.

The issue of the infant's response to variable time intervals has been discussed briefly by Stern and Gibbon (1979) in their speculations about the sorts of timing mechanisms infants employ in organizing environmental input. In an earlier study, Stern, Beebe, Jaffe, and Bennett (1977) described the temporal character of maternal vocal-kinesic input. Very briefly, they organized this input into a hierarchical structure containing "episodes of maintained engagement" (EME), "runs" within those episodes, and "phrases" within each "run." They then computed the durational characteristics of these various units. The results of the study indicated that within any particular EME, the tempo was fairly regular. Each "run," as well as the "phrases" within each "run," imposed moderate variability upon that regular tempo. Gross changes in temporal patterning only occurred between EMEs. Based on these results, Stern and Gibbon (1979) demonstrated that the temporal organization of these units can be described by scalar timing mechanisms (rather than absolute or Poisson timing mechanisms). Therefore, they postulated, it is quite reasonable to suspect that infants use scalar methods as well in the perceptual organization of that input. Although the extent to which infants in fact do use something akin to scalar timing is an empirical question, the observation of Stern et al. (1977) that mothers tend to use a strategy of imposing moderate variability onto inherent regularity would seem to be consistent with Eisenberg's assertion that infants can learn this sort of pattern and exhibit anticipatory responses to it.

Discrimination

The infant's ability to discriminate temporal cues within the speech signal has been demonstrated almost as often as it has been tested. Young infants, for example, can discriminate voicing information, whether cued by voice onset time (Eimas, Siqueland, Jusczyk, & Vigorito, 1971) or by vowel duration (Eilers, 1977), and whether occurring in initial, medial or final position of a syllable (Eilers, 1977; Eimas et al., 1971; Trehub, 1973). Duration of formant transition cues are readily discriminated both for consonants occurring in initial position such as [be-we] (Hillenbrand, Minifie, & Edwards, 1977) as well as for formant transitions occurring *within* a stimulus complex (Miller and Byrne, in press). Miller and Byrne presented to newborn infants computer-synthesized versions of the diphthong [ai], in which the transition between the component vowels was either 1 or 500 msec. As early as 30 hours of age, infants were found to be sensitive to this stimulus feature. Moreover, the heart-rate response of these infants was *greater* to the stimuli with longer interphonemic transitions. This latter result may have implications for the infant's early processing of the "slowed pace" of infant-directed speech (Garnica, 1977; Sachs et al., 1976; Stern et al., in press). In addition, even very brief stop burst cues (e.g., those that differ by as little as 24 msec) are discriminated by young infants (Miller, Morse, & Dorman, 1977), as is the duration of the frication information contrasting fricative consonants (Eilers & Minifie, 1975; Holmberg, Morgan, & Kuhl, 1977). Finally, in adult listeners the presence of a very short period of silence within a syllable is sometimes sufficient to cue a phonetic contrast (e.g., inserting silence between the /s/ and the /l/ of /slit/ will be perceived by adults as /split/). Morse, Eilers, and Gavin (1980) recently demonstrated young infants to be sensitive to this temporal speech cue as well. Thus, at the level of the phoneme and the syllable, infants appear to be quite sensitive to a variety of temporal/durational information. It should be noted as well that, in most cases, the discrimination that is observed in these infants is similar in form to adult listener discrimination of the same stimuli (Eimas et al., 1971; Miller et al., 1977).

In addition to the cues signaling phonetic contrasts, temporal perception is involved in speech perception and production at higher levels as well. For example, every speech act involves precise temporal sequencing of vocal maneuvers (Lieberman, 1977). In addition, the production of words and strings of words obeys various syntactic rules of temporal order. Little is known of the infant's abilities at these higher levels of speech perception. For example, how and when does the infant begin to appreciate the rules of phonological sequencing (i.e., that some phonemes cannot follow others)? Word recognition and the temporal ordering of syllables within a word or words within a phrase have not yet been investigated. There is some evidence that infants can discriminate individual syllabic contrasts within a multisyllable (Goodsitt, Morse, Cowan, & VerHoeve, 1981), but this evidence does not directly address the question of whether infants appreciate that a change in the *sequence* of syllables results in a change of meaning. Finally, of interest in future research will be the investigation of the infant's appreciation of silence when it cues extralinguistic information such as speaker switching (Jaffe & Feldstein, 1970).

The perception and discrimination of temporal order, although not investigated with respect to speech and language, has been examined within the context of the infant's perception of rhythm and rhythmic sequences. For example, employing a sequence of tone bursts, Demany, McKenzie, and Vurpillot (1977) have shown that infants (age not specified) exhibit renewed attention when a familiar "rhythm" (i.e., temporal sequencing of the tones) is changed. Similarly, Marcell (1979) demonstrated auditory rhythm discrimination in infants as young as 1.5 months and visual "rhythm" discrimination (sequences of light flashes) in 3.5-month-olds. Furthermore, by 7 months, infants seem able to respond to "amodal" qualities of temporal order (Allen, Walker, Symonds, & Marcell, 1977). Following habituation to a particular rhythm in one modality, these infants dishabituate to a different temporal sequence regardless of modality and appear to treat similar temporal sequencing as equivalent, even when presented in a different sensory modality (Allen et al., 1977). Finally, evidence is now accumulating that infants seem to appreciate the temporal correlations of a bimodal stimulus (Dodd, 1979; Spelke, 1979). That is, they can match a temporally specified visual stimulus to its auditory counterpart (Spelke, 1979), and they seem to prefer synchronous relationships between speech and lip movements to asynchronous relationships (Dodd, 1979).

Another feature of the infant's perception of temporal cues, and relevant to the infant's more general understanding of stimulus events, is the rate at which events unfold within a stimulus display. Byrne (1982), using a habituation-dishabituation paradigm and monitoring total visual fixation times, presented to 3-month-old infants a geometric 3-dimensional stimulus moving in a 120° arc. This stimulus was presented in a right–left trajectory at either a "slow" (34.8 deg./sec) or a "fast" (103.3 deg./sec) speed. The results showed that irrespective of order of presentation (i.e., slow/fast vs. fast/slow), the infants exposed to a *change* in speed exhibited a significantly greater increase in visual fixation time than infants exposed to no such change. These results were interpreted to suggest that the young infant can perceive the temporal component of a stimulus event, and that a change in this component is sufficient to rerecruit the previously-habituated response of visual attention.

In a second study, Byrne (1982) investigated the influence of speed of movement on object recognition. The procedure was identical to that employed in the first study, except that following habituation, the shape (square vs. cross) rather than the speed of the object was changed. Speed of movement (i.e., fast vs. slow) was varied between subjects, so that half of the infants were presented with the two shapes moving at a fast speed and half at a slow speed ("fast" and "slow" were defined as in the first study). Thus, of interest in this study was the ability of 3-month-old infants to discriminate object shape despite its movement through space, and further, whether the speed at which the object would influence this discrimination. The results revealed that, at both fast and slow rates of movement, infants were able to discriminate object shape (i.e., they exhibited visual fixation dishabituation following the stimulus change). Similar effects have also been observed by Day and Burnham (1981).

The combined results of these studies have several implications for, and raise several additional questions about, the infant's perception of temporal information. First, it is clear that 3-month olds are sensitive to temporal information. Since the difference between the two speeds employed by Byrne was quite large, however, this study does not address the limits of this ability. In future research, it will be of interest to investigate smaller temporal differences and to document the lower bounds of this ability. Attention to temporal information does not seem to preclude attention to other stimulus dimensions, however, since shape discrimination was observed in 3-month olds despite the movement of these shapes through space. Thus, these two studies suggest that both physical and temporal properties of stimuli are salient to infants. The extent to which they are differentially salient awaits further research, especially in light of the suggestion by Stern and Gibbon (1979) that temporal information may be more salient to young infants than are physical stimulus properties.

These two studies, although important, have only begun to scratch the surface of

the questions before us in considering the infant's perception of time and its relevance to understanding and organizing the environment. Several immediate research questions may be posed. First, related to the issue of the differential salience
of temporal vs. physical stimulus properties is that of the infant's ability to extract
the temporal component of stimulus invariance (i.e., to recognize the temporal
similarity among a variety of diverse stimulus events). Stern et al. (1977) have
reported that, in interactions with infants, mothers tend to organize both vocal and
kinesic behaviors in similar temporal patterns. Thus, the extent to which infants can
generalize across these different behaviors and extract the common temporal pattern
may be important to the development of communication. Finally, and perhaps most
interstingly, will be investigations of the relationship between the infant's perception of time and the development of contingency awareness. It has been argued, for
example, that perceiving a contingency between one's own behavior and environmental consequences may be a critical feature in promoting both social and cognitive development (Ainsworth & Bell, 1974; Schaffer, 1979; Watson, 1972, 1979).
Thus, one of our most important questions must be to investigate the temporal parameters of interaction that might facilitate this type of awareness. On
a more general level, it will also be of interest to examine the effects of temporal
patterning on the infant's understanding of action–consequence sequences more
generally.

The Effects of Temporally Specified Events
on Infant Behavior

As indicated earlier, temporally specified events in the infant's social/interactive
world abound. Feeding schedules and sleep-wake cycles serve as macrorhythms to
regulate the infant's daily living. Within a single social interaction (e.g., feeding or
playing), time is not only an organizational force, but also serves to cue specific
events and expectations within the interaction. Stern et al. (1977) have described in
elegant detail one way in which mothers organize the temporal nature of their
infant's interactive experiences. Within the more physiological domain, the infant's
sensitivity to temporal organization is seen in the observation that sleep-wake cycles
and cyclic activity levels change in the first weeks of life, presumably as a function
of the feeding and sleeping schedules imposed (by the caretaker) on the infant's own
endogenous rhythmicities (Marquis, 1941; Parmelee, Wenner, & Schulz, 1964).
Similarly, within a feeding interaction, for example, changes in temporal parameters of burst-pause sucking occur in the first few weeks, again apparently as a
function of the mother's patterns of "jiggle-stop" (Kaye, 1977). Thus, sensitivity
to exogenous cues seems to be reflected in changes in the infant's own inherent
rhythmicities within the first weeks of life.
    Evidence of the infant's response to temporal rhythmicity has also been revealed
in many studies of soothing and state manipulation. In almost every modality,
stimuli that are temporally predictable (i.e., rhythmic) tend to be soothing to the

neonate and young infant, whereas aperiodic stimulation tends to arouse the infant (Brackbill, 1970; Byrne & Horowitz, 1981). Furthermore, with respect to consoling, infants appear to respond (i.e., by changing state) optimally to some frequencies over others (Guthrie, 1976; Pederson & Ter Vrugt, 1973; Ter Vrugt & Pederson, 1973; Van den Daele, 1970, 1971). Manipulation of infant affect can be accomplished by varying or violating temporal expectancies, as in games (Sroufe, 1979; Stern, 1974, 1977; Stern & Gibbon, 1979). In other situations, changes in the tempo of maternal activity appear to have an affect on the infant's response to that activity. Field (1977), for example, found that a slowed pace of maternal imitation of the infant's behavior was more effective in eliciting and maintaining infant responsiveness than was a heightened level of activity. More recently, Arco and McCluskey (1981) have reported somewhat different effects of changing the pace of maternal activity on infant responsiveness. In this study, mothers were requested to either speed up or slow down the pace of their normal play activities with their infants. The results demonstrated first, that infants seemed to prefer (i.e., demonstrate positive affect to) the "natural" rhythms of their mothers' play routines, and second, that faster play was preferred to slower play. This latter result seems to be in contrast with the findings of Field (1977). Unfortunately, however, these data were confounded in two ways: (a) the sequence was presented in a fixed order, and (b) changes in the tempo of play also resulted in concomitant changes in other features of the mother's behavior. Thus, additional research employing this type of quasiexperimental design would be useful to resolve this ambiguity.

Interactional Synchrony? We turn finally to a discussion of possibly the most dramatic report of the effects of temporal patterning on infant behavior presented within the last decade. Research investigating the dynamics of adult–adult conversations has suggested that these interactions tend to be characterized by "interactional synchrony" (Condon & Ogston, 1967), that is, that speakers and listeners seem to "tune in" to each other, by demonstrating similar vocal-kinesic rhythms during these conversations. Listeners, for example, exhibit patterns of motor movement that appear to be time locked to the linguistic boundaries (e.g., phonemic junctures) of the speaker's vocal behavior. More recently, this work has been extended to the behavior of neonates. Employing microanalytic observational techniques, Condon and Sander (1974a, 1974b) have reported that neonates (12 hours to 2 days of age), in interaction with their mothers, exhibit body movements that are precisely time locked to the adults' speech patterns, even at the level of phonemic structure. The observation of this type of vocal-kinesic entrainment in the newborn infant has mind-boggling implications for the development of language and communication, and thus demands closer examination.

The Condon and Sander study has been challenged on a variety of methodological grounds. Rosenfeld (1981) has provided a provocative critique of this work that explores some of these problems. First, we must question the accuracy with which judgments of phonemic boundaries were made. Since these judgments were made without the benefit of electronic acoustic analyses (e.g., spectrograms), it is questionable whether adult listeners could make judgments with confidence regarding the juncture of connected phonemes. Indeed, considering the context dependency of speech and language (Liberman, 1970), it is questionable whether any such judgments could be made at all, even with spectrographic analyses. We know, for example, that the clarity and the duration of a phonemic transition depends not only upon the nature of the phoneme itself (e.g., whether it is a consonant or a vowel), but also on its context (e.g., surrounding phonemes). The nature of linguistic coarticulation is such that clearly defined boundaries between phonemes are rare (Liberman, 1970), and this is especially true for the time units employed by Condon and Sander (i.e., it is unlikely that a phoneme boundary will be evident for one 1/30 sec unit). Finally, Condon and Sander did not report any measures of reliability for these phonemic judgments, further challenging their accuracy.

A second methodological question also concerns the issue of judgment precision. Condon and Sander (1974a, 1974b) employed as their unit of analysis an interval of 1/30 sec. Although they report high interobserver reliability estimates for body movement judgments, the value of these estimates can be questioned on two grounds. First, they do not report that in making kinesic judgments, observers were blind to the vocal channel. As Rosenfeld (1981) points out, linguistic units (e.g., syntactic boundaries) have a powerful influence on our judgments about the co-occurrence of other activities (Ladefoged & Broadbent, 1960). Assuming even a small error of judgment, Rosenfeld reports that the "synchrony" observed completely disappears. In his analysis, which was based upon the actual published data of Condon and Sander (1974b), Rosenfeld shifted the neonatal behavior by one film frame, and discovered that even this small adjustment destroyed the observation of synchrony. Thus, even if adult judges made only microscopic errors of judgment, the results could be significantly biased. This issue becomes even more important when we consider that with similar procedures McDowall (1978) reported an inability to achieve acceptable levels of interobserver reliability at intervals of less than 1/8 second.

In view of these methodological issues and considering the import of such a finding, it is remarkable that there have been virtually no attempts at replication. McDowall (1978) has attempted to replicate this finding with adults, however, and has been largely unsuccessful. In his observations of adult conversations, McDowall analyzed the movement of 18 body parts of 57 combinations of interactants. Of the 57 opportunities for synchrony to occur, only one was significant at an acceptable alpha level. This result contrasts sharply with those of Condon and Ogston (1967), and particularly of Condon and Sander (1974a, 1974b), who reported evidence of synchrony in all 14 of their neonate–adult pairs. The only attempt that we are aware of to replicate the infant findings (Dowd & Tronick, 1982) has also been unsuccessful. Since one of the frequent criticisms of the Condon and Sander (1974a, 1974b) work has been the definition of the phonemic unit (see below for a discussion of this issue), Dowd and Tronick employed spectrographic analyses of the mothers' speech in an attempt to define these units precisely and empirically. Measurement precision was also increased by recording infants' arm movements and computing their spatial coordinates. The spectrographic displays and spatial displacements of the infants' arms were viewed and analyzed simultaneously. These procedures were designed to reduce the judgment error (see below) that may have been present in the Condon and Sander work. Once again, evidence to support the claims of Condon and Sander did not obtain. Interpretation of these data must be made with caution, however, since (a) this work has not yet been published, (b) the methodological improvements (and the use of somewhat older infants) that Dowd and Tronick employed render the study not a true replication, and (c) clear phoneme boundaries simply do not exist in running speech or connected phonemes (Liberman, 1970). Thus, it is not clear that using spectrograms is particularly useful in locating these boundaries. Nevertheless, both of the only attempts (to our knowledge) to replicate Condon's work (Condon & Ogston, 1967; Condon & Sander, 1974a, 1974b) have failed.

Although these methodological problems and reports of failure to replicate might be sufficient to challenge the notion of neonatal interactional synchrony, Rosenfeld (1981) also suggests a number of logical arguments that add to the skepticism about these findings. In order to lend credulity to these findings, a number of questionable assumptions must be made. For example, we must assume that connected phonemes have precise boundaries, the validity of which has been discussed. Second, we must assume that the speech of the mother is truly rhythmic (i.e., temporally predictable). Rosenfeld (1981), in yet another reanalysis of the Condon and Sander published data, found little evidence of rhythmicity (i.e., the recurrence of temporal patterns) in the mother's speech, thus challenging this assumption. Stern (1981) also has suggested that neonatal interactional synchrony probably depends upon the provision of a constant rhythm by the mother. Without the presence of recurrent rhythmic patterns, it is inconceivable how the neonate might organize her movements to match the speech patterns of her mother. Finally, Rosenfeld (1981) cites a number of additional assumptions about the nature of infant behavior (e.g., assumptions about infant reaction time, about the "innate" motivation to respond to phoneme boundaries, etc.) that seriously challenge the notion of neonatal interactional synchrony.

Despite the above critique, however, we are still in the position of having before us a finding that we cannot explain theoretically. Until such time that a true attempt at replication fails in public, we must accept these data, and we can only wonder what they might mean about the development of language and communication. Such innate preprogramming would be spectacular if true, and the sheer wonderment of it should motivate us to explore this issue with more vigorous empirical research.

DEVELOPMENT IN TIMING MECHANISMS

Throughout this chapter we have touched periodically, though somewhat tangentially, on the issue of development. We have suggested, for example, that part of the process of development in the early months consists of learning to adapt, and even possibly to override, one'e own endogenous rhythms to conform to those of the outside world (Ashton, 1976). We have not, however, discussed more general issues of development and will, therefore, attempt such an analysis here. The shift from endogenous to exogenous control over behavior is almost a given in most discussions of behavioral development. In order to address the issue of *how* this occurs, we need a much fuller explication of the processes that underlie both endogenous and exogenous control. Within this framework, two immediate issues are: (a) what are the mechanisms (i.e., clocks) by which infants experience time, and (b) how are these clocks modified or expanded to encompass an ever-increasing set of behaviors and experiences?

The question of clocks has been addressed in part for exogenous timing by Stern and Gibbon (1979) and in part for endogenous timing by Ashton (1976). Ashton proposed that the human newborn comes equipped with a "central pacemaker" which serves both to encode and organize the external world, as well as to regulate one's own behavior. This pacemaker, argues Ashton, beats at approximately 1–1.2 Hz, and its locus appears to be the hippocampus. As evidence for this cycle frequency, he cites two sources of data. First, as noted earlier, the infant's sucking pattern is impressively rhythmic, and within an individual infant, displays quite predictable sequences of bursts and pauses (Wolff, 1968). In addition, as Wolff (1968) has demonstrated, this rhythm operated with a cycle frequency of about 1 Hz. The second line of research employed to support this hypothesis is the now quite extensive literature on neonatal consoling. Once again, not only is periodic stimulation (in any modality) superior to aperiodic stimulation in consoling a distressed infant (Brackbill, 1970; Byrne & Horowitz, 1981), but the most effective periodicity of this stimulation appears to be 1–1.2 Hz (Ambrose, 1969; Guthrie, 1976; Pederson & Ter Vrugt, 1973; Ter Vrugt & Pederson, 1973; Van den Daele, 1970, 1971). Sucking, of course, is also an effective pacifier. Ashton (1976) proposes that this particular frequency of stimulation is soothing to infants because it matches the internal beat of the central nervous system. Perhaps this process is similar to the process of habituation (e.g., if the frequencies of internal and external stimulation match, there is no need for active processing of or attention to the external stimulus, and thus the whole system slows down). In any event, there does appear to be support for the existence of this "central pacemaker" and for the suggestion that its frequency is about 1–1.2 Hz. Somewhat later in development, this frequency apparently increases to around 6 Hz (Ashton, 1976; Lenneberg, 1967), but how or when this change occurs is unknown.

Ashton's (1976) discussion centers primarily on endogenous mechanisms. Although he notes the importance of exogenous timing control as well, he does not suggest how the two might be related (e.g., developmentally). The only attempt that we are aware of to explain how the infant times exogenous stimulation is that of Stern and Gibbon (1979). As noted previously, Stern and Gibbon (1979) propose that the infant uses scalar timing methods in making estimates of, and in generating temporal expectancies from, the environment. The three modes of timing discussed by Stern and Gibbon (1979)—absolute, Poisson, and scalar—are differentiated with respect to the relationship between the mean and the variance of specific temporal intervals. In scalar timing, the variance increases proportionately with increases in the mean. Thus, an interval of $1 \pm .2$ sec is functionally equivalent to an interval of $2 \pm .4$ sec. The assertion that infants use this method of timing is based on the observation that the temporal pattern of the input that the mother provides the infant can be described in these terms, and that the infant appears to respond to this patterning (Stern et al., 1977). Clearly, more direct experimental evidence would be useful here. However, until such evidence is offered, the scheme proposed by Stern and Gibbon (1979) would seem to be our most reasonable estimate.

What, then, is the nature of development within these two models? Stern (1981) has offered the provocative (and frankly, somewhat unappealing) suggestion that there is no development in the *ability* to time. The ability to estimate time per se, according to this argument, is innate; what develops is the infant's ability to apply this knowledge to an increasingly larger set of environmental events. That is to say, the infant begins to appreciate that social interactions and other forms of environmental stimulation can all be described and understood in the dimension of time. With development, then, comes the ability to understand the temporal dimensions of various environmental events (as well as the fact that these temporal parameters might be different from one's own endogenous rhythms).

In the absence of any evidence directly relevant to this proposal, it is difficult to quarrel with Stern's position. However, notable within this model is its apparent assumption of linearity (i.e., that development is simply an additive process of increasing the set of events which can be timed). With respect to the first premise of this argument, the evidence does seem to support the notion that experiencing the world in the temporal dimension is an innate human quality. The striking rhythmicity of neonatal behavior could not suggest otherwise. However, if both Ashton (1976) and Stern and Gibbon (1979) are correct in their analyses of infant timing mechanisms, then we might have reason to question this assumption of linearity (i.e., that the relationship between endogenous and exogenous mechanisms is quantitative rather than qualitative). Specifically, we would suggest that infants may indeed use different clocks at different stages of development. If in fact the world operates in scalar units, this would seem to be inconsistent with the view of the central pacemaker as a "neural counter" (Ashton, 1976). Scalar timing is a process by which the variance around a mean increases proportionately with increases in the mean. It is difficult to imagine how a neural counter which presumably "ticks off" impulses and estimates time by the number of accumulated "ticks," could estimate scalar time accurately within this type of system. Thus, we would propose that the process of development might be one which begins with a neonate who attempts to understand exogenous temporal systems with reference to this internal pacemaker. When this system proves inadequate, revisions are made in the system itself. Perhaps this is the elusive shift from endogenous to exogenous control for which we have been searching. Perhaps as the infant develops an appreciation for the temporal dimensions of the external environment, the exogenous and endogenous become dissociated. In this way, the endogenous rhythms continue to provide some control over the infant's own actions such as sucking and crying, while a growing appreciation for exogenous timing mechanisms allows the infant to coordinate her activities with these external rhythms as well as to generate temporal expectancies regarding this external stimulation. We should recall at this point that the infants studied by Stern et al. (1977) were 3 to 4 months of age, an age at which infants are becoming somewhat freed from endogenous control mechanisms. For example, reflexes are beginning to disappear, suggesting reduced entrainment to the endogenous environment, and the ''fake cry'' is beginning to appear, also suggesting reduced involvement of endogenous rhythmic mechanisms. Thus, the fact that this age range is significant for other aspects of the infant's development as well suggests that a major change in the mechanisms of temporal perception and temporal control is not an implausible hypothesis from which to work.

Clearly, such a speculative account underscores the important need for empirical research in this area. With specific reference to the above proposal, we would suggest that a fruitful way to begin would be to conduct a Stern and Gibbon (1979) type of analysis on mother–infant interactions during the newborn period. Such an analysis would answer the first of our questions: Is the mother's temporal organization of her input the same or different at these two levels of development, and how does the infant respond to this organization? In addition, however, a considerable amount of experimental work (e.g., manipulating temporal organizations) and observational work (e.g., investigating the development of temporal patterning in the infant's behavior and in interactions with others) still remains before we can make more informed speculations about the *process* of development within a temporal world.

FUTURE DIRECTIONS

It is clear that the experience of time and temporal perception play a large role in the infant's experience of temporal events. It is also clear that, on some level, the infant's perceptual apparatus is sensitive to the dimension of time. However, in examining the literature devoted to these two problems, there arise several issues that are not at all clear, and in fact, may even appear paradoxical. In this section, we will discuss some of the issues that are still before us, and suggest ways in which we might begin to explore them.

Who Follows Whom and When?

There is general agreement that during the early stages of the developing mother–infant relationship, the mother adapts her behavior to ''fit in'' with the endogenous rhythms of the newborn (Kaye, 1977; Schaffer, 1979). In contrast, however, the role of the infant (other than providing the rhythms to which to adapt), and more importantly, of *development* in the infant's role, is not terribly clear. For example, Condon and Sander's work, if replicable, suggests quite clearly that the *infant's* movements follow the temporal patterns of the *speaker's* utterances. Further, within the first few weeks of life, the infant's macrorhythms (sleep-wake, activity levels) begin to conform to an exogenously imposed schedule (Marquis, 1941; Parmelee et al., 1964), as apparently do some microrhythms, such as sucking bursts (Kaye, 1977). With respect to turn taking in vocal-kinesic interchanges, most agree that by around 6 months of age infants are quite able to "take their own turns" and are no longer entirely dependent on a partner to "demonstrate" mutual temporal roles (Schaffer, 1979; Trevarthen, 1977). Surely, at some point, the infant comes to appreciate communicative role requirements. However, just these few examples suggest that the problem may not be quite as simple as we would like to believe. More than likely, what we are dealing with is a gradually unfolding, complex series of *different* processes. For example, changes in cyclicity of activity levels as a function of externally imposed feeding schedules is probably quite a different process from that involved in learning to take one's turn at the appropriate time in a conversation. Thus, one of our tasks at this point is to develop a functional analysis of these various processes. This will involve more detailed descriptions in our methodological strategies (e.g., to look more directly at the effects of external stimuli on the infant's ongoing rhythmicities). Simple sequential and/or correlational data may not serve us well for very much longer as we begin to approach process, rather than product, questions. The question of how behavioral control changes from primarily endogenous to primarily exogenous mechanisms is probably the paramount question of development.

What is the Functional Salience of Time as a Dimension for the Infant?

We have seen that the infant is sensitive at a very early age to the temporal properties of stimuli (Byrne, 1982). However, there are virtually no data that speak to the nature or the limits of that sensitivity. Stern and Gibbon (1979) suggest that temporal features of stimuli have an essential nature about them that makes them more salient than other physical properties of the stimuli. For example, the infant must habituate to the temporal dimensions before proceeding to an analysis of the physical structure of a stimulus event (Stern & Gibbon, 1979). In that the most salient feature (for us) of neonatal behavior is its rhythmicity, this suggestion seems quite viable. However, there are two sources of evidence that seem to be inconsistent with this position. First, if temporal features do possess a sort of amodal quality, we should expect to see cross-modal transfer of temporal information from the very beginning, which appears not to be the case (Allen et al., 1977; Marcell, 1979).

More troublesome, however, is an apparent paradox between the results of the Stern and Gibbon (1979) report and those of temporal conditioning studies (Brackbill et al., 1968; Fitzgerald et al., 1967; Stamps, 1977; Stamps & Porges, 1975) with respect to the role of temporal regularity and variability. Specifically, Stern and Gibbon (1979) suggest that, as in other features of infant attention, the most effective way to recruit the infant's attention to time is to impose a moderate amount of variability into the temporal sequencing of events (e.g., vocal behaviors). By presenting stimuli at constant intervals, one habituates the infant to time and allows for the processing of other features of the stimuli. In direct contrast to this, however, the results of temporal conditioning studies suggest that attention to time (i.e., temporal conditioning) is *facilitated* by presenting stimuli at constant intervals. We would presume that imposing variability upon that regularity would interfere with conditioning. The results of Eisenberg (undated) would seem to be relevant here, but at the present time it is not entirely clear how (i.e., she did report "conditioning" effects when stimuli were presented according to a schedule of variability around a mean). In addition, the studies described above that are either completed or in progress may speak more directly to both a) the relative salience of temporal cues with respect to other stimulus properties, and b) the differential effects of variable versus constant temporal patterning. In any event, it is an intriguing paradox, and one that would benefit from further investigation. Given the substantial differences between these two types of research strategies, we may discover that the results are not inconsistent at all.

Skill Acquisition

Another issue that has arisen from this discussion is the relevance of temporal perception and temporal patterning for behavioral acquisition. Two related, yet distinct, skills are important here: (a) the perception of time, as time intervals and duration, and (b) the sequential ordering of events in time. Certainly the latter, and probably both, are critical for the acquisition of temporally specified behaviors (e.g., throwing a ball, reaching and reach–grasp coordination, and even vocalization and the distribution of phonemes into words.

Thirty years ago, Lashley (1951) first emphasized the importance of understanding the serial ordering of behavior and the relevance of timing to that ordering. Essentially, Lashley argued that the performance of a skilled motor act requires that the individual formulate a priori a plan of action for that behavior. This plan includes not only decisions about the sequences of the component behaviors, but also about the temporal patterning of those components (e.g., the duration of each component, pauses beteen each, etc). A similar analysis was offered by Bower (1977) in his description of skilled versus unskilled reach–grasp behavior. During the early stages of this action, according to Bower, reaching and grasping are not well coordinated temporally, that is, the grasp occurs either too early or too late for the infant to be successful. In the final stages, however, the temporal control of grasping (i.e., after the hand has made contact with the object) is achieved and the infant is successful.

According to Lashley (1951), and extended somewhat later by Bruner, Oliver, and Greenfield (1967), the acquisition of skilled motor acts is a process by which an essentially temporal behavioral dimension (i.e., ordering of component behaviors in time) becomes translated into a spatial dimension (i.e., the entire act is conceptualized and planned *beforehand,* and then simply unfolds). This type of process is evident in our daily experiences with learning new behaviors. Driving a car, for example, presents such a situation to the learner. In the initial stages, many a car is stalled because the learner has not mastered the clutch–brake sequence or the precise temporal coordination of releasing the clutch simultaneously with depressing the accelerator. The skilled driver, however, performs these temporal processes habitually, and Lashley (1951) and Bruner et al. (1967) contend, spatially. Another example of this, more relevant to the present discussion, is the production of speech and language, a skilled motor act par excellence. Running speech is a series of coarticulated phonemes (Liberman, 1970). In producing speech, we do not, for example, produce a succession of isolated, self-contained phonemes, but rather our vocal articulators are in a constant state of anticipation or preparing for the next phoneme (Lieberman, 1977). Moreover, for adult speakers of the language, this process is largely unconscious. In considering the acquisition of speech, from Lashley's position, we might speculate that the process of babbling is one whereby the infant is actively learning about this temporal sequencing (e.g., how the articulators must be positioned in order to produce the current phoneme and simultaneously to prepare for the next).

This, then, is one conception of the *product* of skilled motor performance (i.e., the transition from a temporal to a spatial mode). The *process* by which this occurs, however, is an issue that has received very little theoretical and/or empirical attention. Both Lashley (1951) and Ashton (1976) propose that the control over these behaviors is largely endogenous; that is, it is unlikely that the environment provides either temporal or physical cues upon which to base these sequential decisions. Lashley (1951) argues that this plan of action must arise from within, and Ashton (1976) further suggests that the time base for this plan is the "central pacemaker" refered to earlier, which for the infant appears to operate at a frequency of 1 to 1.2 Hz. Unfortunately, however, these arguments are based largely on indirect inferences from the available data; we have no direct empirical evidence either to support or to refute these proposals.

Once again, we must conclude that much remains to be investigated with respect to the processes by which skilled motor acts become skilled (i.e., smooth and rhythmic). Although we know a fair amount about the sequencing of the component behaviors, we know virtually nothing about the temporal control over these components. In summarizing this problem, Ashton (1976) has used the analogy of dancing: "we easily learn where to put our feet, but learning when takes longer. Knowing when is the mark of a good dancer or a mature person" (pp. 625–626).

Methodological Implications

Ultimately, the question we have been posing throughout this chapter is, how infants organize their temporal experiences? How they chunk experiences into temporal units? Unfortunately, as is the case so many times in infancy research, the way we phrase the question has more than a trivial effect on the answer that we receive. At the same time, however, it is difficult to know how to phrase the question without already knowing the answer. To leave the existential and enter the concrete, the issue here is, how do we, as investigators, temporally organize the environment that we are observing. Can we really be confident in the beginnings and ends of our "runs," "episodes," "time-ins," and "time-outs," or whatever other organizational structure we devise? Certainly, those who have attempted to employ such organizational schemes have not been unaware of this problem, and most have employed reasonable criteria for defining these structures. But, until we know more about how the *infant* perceives and distributes temporal patterns, these schemes will remain largely arbitrary.

A similar situation exists in the development of observational codes. For example, how long a delay is necessary before a *behavior* can no longer be considered a *response,* 1 second, 3 seconds, 10 seconds? Recent studies of mother–infant interaction, for example, have frequently adopted ≤ 3 seconds as the appropriate interval for defining a contingency between mother and infant behaviors or for defining the beginning of a new bout of activity (Stern et al., 1977). However, this decision has been based largely upon evidence from the operant conditioning literature (Millar, 1972; Millar & Watson, 1979; Watson, 1967), which has employed only a limited number of responses. Thus, a number of questions arise. First, to what extent is this "contingency" interval appropriate for *all* infant behaviors (e.g., is the time course of contingency awareness necessarily the same for smiles and vocalizations)? Second, might this interval be different for mother and baby? Perhaps the mother will consider as a response any infant behavior that occurs as long as 10 seconds following a maternal behavior, whereas the mother must follow an infant behavior immediately for the *infant* to perceive a contingency. Once again, as noted previously, it is important that we begin to investigate more systematically the temporal dimensions of the infant's contingency awareness. Moreover, if we are to study caretaker–infant interactions from a transactional perspective (Sameroff & Chandler, 1975), it may also be important to examine the *mother's* contingency attributions. It is possible, for example, that using the same temporal criteria when coding mother and infant behaviors may be inappropriate. Another issue concerns the measurement of the duration of various behaviors. This question is especially relevant to studies of mutual gazing (i.e., how long does a "gaze" have to last before it can be called a gaze rather than a glance?). Many other examples can be cited, but the point is that the codes we devise for observing mothers and babies derive from our own assumptions and perceptual limits and may bear little resemblance to the way in which the infant parses these experiences. Stern et al. (1977) have provided a useful starting point for this research by describing the temporal properties of selected maternal behavioral episodes. However, it is critical that we begin to understand more about the infant's perception of these events (through both laboratory and observational means), if only to have more data upon which to base these methodological decisions.

FINAL COMMENTS

In this chapter, we have attempted to outline various ways in which temporal cues enter the world of infant communication. With respect to social interaction and social relationships, it appears as if mothers order their infants' temporal worlds quite carefully, in order to optimize a smooth-flowing interaction. The endogenous rhythms attending the infant from birth are exploited as the mother attempts to adapt her rhythms to those of the infant. At the same time, however, the infant is learning that perhaps the world operates on a somewhat different schedule and that to function effectively she must do some adapting as well. The process by which the primary control of the temporal patterning of behavior changes from endogenous to exogenous mechanisms is not clear; what is clear is that it happens and that the process is probably gradual and complex. On the linguistic level, we have seen that temporal factors are critical to both the perception and the production of speech and language. The infant, even at a very early age (i.e., less than 2 months), appears to be sensitive to many of these cues (Eilers, 1977; Eilers & Minifie, 1975; Eimas et al., 1971; Miller & Byrne, in press; Miller et al., 1977; Morse et al., 1980). Extensive experience with an environment that tends to exaggerate these cues, such as motherese (Garnica, 1977; Sachs et al., 1976; Stern et al., in press), would seem to reinforce their importance to the infant, and also may facilitate the development of more mature perceptual and articulatory skills (Liberman, 1970; Lieberman, 1977).

Certainly, the ideas presented here are not novel. In recent years, the focus on the temporal ordering of behavior has replaced almost entirely the previous focus on the specific content, or components, of behavior (Lamb et al., 1979; Schaffer, 1979). Yet, integrative, convergent research still eludes us. Thus, our purposes in writing this chapter were, (a) to attempt a preliminary integration of the available data, and (b) to outline some of the issues that are still before us as we try to come to grips with this very important feature of the infant's early experience with language and communication. The ''time'' has come and the ''time'' is now!

REFERENCES

Abramson, A. S., & Lisker, L. Discriminability along the voicing continuum: Cross-language tests. In *Proceedings of the Sixth International Congress on Phonetic Sciences, 1967.* Prague: Academic Publishing House of Czechoslovakian Academy of Sciences, 1970.

Ainsworth, M. D. S., & Bell, S. M. Mother–infant interaction and the development of competence. In K. S. Connolly & J. S. Bruner (Eds.), *The growth of competence.* New York: Academic Press, 1974.

Allen, T. W., Walker, K., Symonds, L., & Marcell, M. Intrasensory and intersensory perception of temporal sequences during infancy. *Developmental Psychology*, 1977, *13*, 225–229.

Ambrose, A. (Ed.). *Stimulation in early infancy.* New York: Academic Press, 1969.

Arco, C. M. B., & McCluskey, K. A. ''A change of pace'': An investigation of the salience of maternal temporal style in mother-infant play. *Child Development*, 1981, *52*, 941–949.

Ashton, R. Aspects of timing in child development. *Child Development*, 1976, *47*, 622–626.

Bateson, M. C. Mother-infant exchanges: The epigenesis of conversation interaction. *Annals of New York Academy of Sciences,* 1975, *263,* 101–113.

Bloom, K. Evaluation of infant vocal conditioning. *Journal of Experimental Child Psychology,* 1979, *27,* 60–70.

Boomer, D. S. The phonemic clause: Speech unit in human communication. In A. W. Siegman & S. Feldstein (Eds.), *Nonverbal behavior and communication.* Hillsdale, NJ: Erlbaum, 1978.

Bower, T. G. R. *A primer of infant development.* San Francisco: W. H. Freeman, 1977.

Brackbill, Y. Acoustic variation and arousal level in infants. *Psychophysiology,* 1970, *6,* 517–526.

Brackbill, Y., & Fitzgerald, H. E. Stereotype temporal conditioning in infants. *Psychophysiology,* 1972, *9,* 569–577.

Brackbill, Y., Lintz, L. M., & Fitzgerald, H. E. Differences in the autonomic and somatic conditioning of infants. *Psychosomatic Medicine,* 1968, *30,* 193–201.

Bruner, J. S., Oliver, R. R., & Greenfield, P. M. *Studies in cognitive growth.* New York: Wiley, 1967.

Byrne, J. M. The influence of velocity of movement on object shape discrimination in 3-month-old infants. Unpublished doctoral dissertation, Univ. of Kansas, 1982.

Byrne, J. M., & Horowitz, F. D. Rocking and soothing intervention: The influence of direction and type of movement. *Infant Behavior and Development,* 1981, *4,* 207–218.

Condon, W. S., & Ogston, W. D. A segmentation of behavior. *Journal of Psychiatric Research,* 1967, *5,* 221–235.

Condon, W. S., & Sander, L. W. Neonate movement is synchronized with adult speech: International participation and language acquisition. *Science,* 1974, *183,* 99–101. (a)

Condon, W. S., & Sander, L. W. Synchrony demonstrated between movements of the neonate and adult speech. *Child Development,* 1974, *45,* 456–462. (b)

Day, R. H., & Burnham, D. K. Infants' perception of shape and color in laterally moving patterns. *Infant Behavior and Development,* 1981, *4,* 341–357.

DeLattre, P. C., Liberman, A. M., & Cooper, F. S. Acoustic loci and transitional cues for consonants. *Journal of the Acoustical Society of America,* 1955, *27,* 769–773.

Demany, L., McKenzie, B., & Vurpillot, E. Rhythm perception in early infancy. *Nature,* 1977, *266,* 718–719.

Denes, P. B., & Pinson, E. N. *The speech chain.* Murray Hill, NJ: Bell Telephone Laboratories, 1963.

Dodd, B. Lip reading in infants: Attention to speech presented in- and out-of-synchrony. *Cognitive Psychology,* 1979, *11,* 478–484.

Dowd, J. M., & Tronick, E. Z. The temporal organization of infant links movements. Paper presented at the International Conference on Infant Studies, Austin, TX, 1982.

Duncan, S., & Niederehe, G. On signaling that it's your turn. *Journal of Experimental Social Psychology,* 1974, *10,* 234–247.

Eilers, R. Context-sensitive perception of naturally produced stop and fricative consonants by infants. *Journal of the Acoustical Society of America,* 1977, *61,* 1321–1336.

Eilers, R., & Minifie, F. Fricative discrimination in early infancy. *Journal of Speech and Hearing Research,* 1975, *18,* 158–167.

Eimas, P. D., Siqueland, E. R., Jusczyk, P., & Vigorito, J. Speech perception in infants. *Science,* 1971, *171,* 303–306.

Eisenberg, R. B. Infant perception of speech and nonspeech sounds: Final report, R-01-HD-00732. Report to the National Institute of Mental Health, unpublished, undated.

Field, T. M. The effects of early separation, interaction deficits, and experimental manipulations on infant–mother face-to-face interaction. *Child Development,* 1977, *48,* 763–771.

Fitzgerald, H. E., & Brackbill, Y. Classical conditioning in infancy: Development and constraints. *Psychological Bulletin,* 1976, *83,* 353–376.

Fitzgerald, H. E., Lintz, L. M., Brackbill, Y., & Adams, G. Time perception and conditioning an automatic response in human infants. *Perceptual and Motor Skills,* 1967, *24,* 479–486.

Garnica, O. Some prosodic and paralinguistic features of speech to young children. In C. Snow & C.

Ferguson (Es.), *Talking to children: Language input and acquisition.* London: Cambridge University Press, 1977.

Goodsitt, J., Morse, P., Cowan, N., & VerHoeve, J. Infant speech perception in a multisyllabic world. Paper presented at the meeting of the Society for Research in Child Development, Boston, 1981.

Graham, F. K., & Jackson, J. C. Arousal systems and infant heart-rate responses. In L. P. Lipsitt & H. W. Reese (Eds.), *Advances in child development and behavior* (Vol. 5). New York: Academic Press, 1970.

Guthrie, R. J. The effects of fixed and variable frequency rocking on arousal and sleep state proportions in 2-month-old infants. Unpublished masters thesis, Univ of Western Ontario, 1976.

Hillenbrand, J., Minifie, F. D., & Edwards, T. J. Tempo of formant-frequency change as a cue in infant speech discrimination. Paper presented at the meeting of the Society for Research in Child Development, New Orleans, 1977.

Holmberg, T., Morgan, K., & Kuhl, P. Speech perception in early infancy: Discrimination of fricative consonants. *Journal of the Acoustical Society of America,* 1977, *Suppl. 1,* (a) S99.

Jaffe, J. Parliamentary procedure and the brain. In A. W. Siegman & S. Feldstein (Eds.), *Nonverbal behavior and communication.* Hillsdale, NJ: Erlbaum, 1978.

Jaffe, J., & Feldstein, S. *Rhythms of dialogue.* New York: Academic Press, 1970.

Kaye, K. Toward the origin of dialogue. In H. R. Schaffer (Ed.), *Studies in mother–infant interaction.* London: Academic Press, 1977.

Ladefoged, P., & Broadbent, D. E. Perception of sequence in auditory events. *Quarterly Journal of Experimental Psychology,* 1960, *12,* 162–170.

Lamb, M. E., Suomi, S. J., & Stephenson, G. R. *Social interactional analysis.* Madison, WI: University of Wisconsin Press, 1979.

Lancioni, G. E. Infant operant conditioning and its implications for intervention. *Psychological Bulletin,* 1980, *87,* 513–534.

Lashley, K. S. The problem of serial order in behavior. In L. A. Jeffress (Ed.), *Cerebral mechanisms in behavior: The Hixon symposium.* New York: Wiley, 1951.

Lenneberg, E. H. *Biological foundations of language.* New York: Wiley, 1967.

Lewis, M., & Freedle, R. O. Mother–infant dyad: The cradle of meaning. In P. Pilner, L. Kramer, & T. Alloway (Eds.), *Communication and affect: Language and thought.* New York: Academic Press, 1973.

Liberman, A. M. The grammars of speech and language. *Cognitive Psychology,* 1970, *1,* 301–323.

Liberman, A. M., DeLattre, P. C., Gerstman, L. J., & Cooper, F. S. Tempo of frequency change as a cue for distinguishing classes of speech sounds. *Journal of Experimental Psychology,* 1956, *52,* 127–137.

Lieberman, P. *Speech physiology and acoustic phonetics.* New York: MacMillan, 1977.

McDowall, J. Interactional synchrony: A reappraisal. *Journal of Personality and Social Psychology,* 1978, *36,* 963–975.

Marcell, M. M. Auditory and visual discrimination of rhythmic sequences by 1 1/2 and 3 1/2 month-old infants. *Dissertation Abstracts International,* 1979, *39(11-B),* 5615–5616.

Marquis, D. P. Learning in the neonate: The modification of behavior under three feeding schedules. *Journal of Experimental Psychology,* 1941, *29,* 263–282.

Millar, W. S. A study of operant conditioning under delayed reinforcement in early infancy. *Monographs of the Society for Research in Child Development,* 1972, *37*(2, Whole No. 147).

Millar, W. S., & Watson, J. S. The effect of delayed feedback on infant learning re-examined. *Child Development,* 1979, *50,* 747–751.

Miller, C. L., & Byrne, J. Psychophysiologic and behavioral response to auditory stimuli in the newborn. *Infant Behavior and Development,* in press.

Miller, C. L., Morse, P. A., & Dorman, M. F. Cardiac indices of infant speech perception: Orienting and burst discrimination. *Quarterly Journal of Experimental Psychology,* 1977, *29,* 533–545.

Moore, K. M., Borton, R., & Darby, B. L. Visual tracking in young infants: Evidence of object identity or object permanence? *Journal of Experimental Child Psychology*, 1978, *25*, 183–198.

Morse, P. A., Eilers, R., & Gavin, W. Exploring the perception of the "Sound of Silence" in early infancy. Paper presented at the meeting of the International Conference on Infant Studies, New Haven, CT, 1980.

Newport, E. L. Motherese: The speech of mothers to young children. In N. J. Castellan, D. B. Pisoni, & G. R. Potts (Eds.), *Cognitive Theory* (Vol. 2). Hillsdale, NJ: Erlbaum, 1977.

Parmelee, A. H., Wenner, W. H., & Schulz, H. R. Infant sleep patterns from birth to 16 weeks of age. *Journal of Pediatrics*, 1964, *65*, 576–582.

Pederson, D. R., & Ter Vrugt, D. The influence of amplitude and frequency of vestibular stimulation on the activity of two-month-old infants. *Child Development*, 1973, *44*, 122–128.

Remick, H. Maternal speech to children during language acquisition. In W. von Raffler-Engel & Y. Lebrun (Eds.), *Baby talk and infant speech*. Amsterdam: Swets & Zeitlinger, B. V., 1976.

Roffwarg, H. P., Muzio, J. N., & Dement, W. C. Ontogenetic development of the human sleep dream cycle. *Science*, 1966, *152*, 604–619.

Rosenfeld, H. M. Whither interactional synchrony? In K. Bloom (Ed.), *Prospective issues in infancy research*. Hillsdale, NJ: Erlbaum, 1981.

Sachs, J., Brown, R., & Salerno, R. Adult speech to children. In W. von Raffler-Engel & Y. Lebrun (Eds.), *Baby talk and infant speech*. Amsterdam: Swets & Zeitlinger, B. V., 1976.

Sameroff, A. J., & Chandler, M. J. Reproductive risk and the continuum of caretaking casualty. In F. D. Horowitz (Ed.), *Review of child development research* (Vol. 4). Chicago: University of Chicago Press, 1975.

Schaffer, H. R. Acquiring the concept of the dialogue. In M. H. Bornstein & W. Kessen (Eds.), *Psychological development from infancy: Image to intention*. Hillsdale, NJ: Erlbaum, 1979.

Spelke, E. S. Perceiving bimodally specified events in infancy. *Developmental Psychology*, 1979, *15*, 626–636.

Sroufe, A. L. Socioemotional development. In J. D. Osofsky (Ed.), *Handbook of infant development*. New York: Wiley, 1979.

Stamps, L. E. Temporal conditioning of heart rate responses in newborn infants. *Developmental Psychology*, 1977, *13*, 624–629.

Stamps, L. E., & Porges, S. W. Heart-rate conditioning in newborn infants: Relationships among conditionability and heart-rate variability. *Developmental Psychology*, 1975, *11*, 424–431.

Stern, D. N. Personal communication, December 1981.

Stern, D. N. Mother and infant at play: Dyadic interaction involving facial, vocal, and gaze behavior. In M. Lewis & L. A. Rosenblum (Eds.), *The effect of the infant on its caregiver*. New York: Wiley, 1974.

Stern, D. N. The first relationship: Infant and mother. In J. Bruner, M. Cole, & B. Lloyd (Eds.), *Developing child series*. Cambridge: Harvard University Press, 1977.

Stern, D. N., Beebe, B., Jaffe, J., & Bennett, S. L. The infant's stimulus world during social interactions: A study of caregiver behaviors with particular reference to repetition and timing. In H. R. Schaffer (Ed.), *Studies in mother-infant interaction*. London: Academic Press, 1977.

Stern, D. N., & Gibbon, J. Temporal expectancies of social behavior in mother-infant play. In E. B. Thoman (Ed.), *Origins of the infant's social responsiveness*. Hillsdale, NJ: Erlbaum, 1979.

Stern, D. N., Spieker, S., Barnett, R. K., & MacKain, K. The prosody of maternal speech: Infant age and context related changes. *Journal of Child Language*, in press.

Ter Vrugt, D., & Pederson, D. R. The effects of vertical rocking frequencies on the arousal level in two-month-old infants. *Child Development*, 1973, *44*, 205–209.

Trehub, S. Auditory-linguistic sensitivity in infants. Unpublished doctoral dissertation, McGill Univ., 1973.

Trevarthen, C. Descriptive analyses of infant communicative behavior. In H. R. Schaffer (Ed.), *Studies in mother-infant interaction*. London: Academic Press, 1977.

Van den Daele, L. D. Modifications of infant state by treatment in a rocker box. *Journal of Psychology*, 1970, *44*, 161–165.

Van den Daele, L. D. Infant reactivity to redundant proprioceptive and auditory stimulation: A twin study. *Journal of Psychology*, 1971, *78*, 269–276.

Watson, J. S. Memory and "contingency analyses" in infant learning. *Merrill-Palmer Quarterly*, 1967, *13*, 55–76.

Watson, J. S. Smiling, cooing, and "The Game." *Merrill-Palmer Quarterly*, 1972, *18*, 323–339.

Watson, J. S. Perception of contingency as a determinant of social responsiveness. In E. B. Thomas (Ed.), *Origins of the infant's social responsiveness*. Hillsdale, NJ: Erlbaum, 1979.

Wolff, P. H. The causes, controls, and organization of behavior in the neonate. *Psychological Issues*, 1966, *5*(No. 1, Monograph No. 17).

Wolff, P. H. The serial organization of sucking in the young infant. *Pediatrics*, 1968, *42*, 943–956.

SECTION II

THEORETICAL AND METHODOLOGICAL ISSUES CONCERNING THE MECHANISMS OF COMMUNICATION DEVELOPMENT

Introduction

Carol Harding

The chapters contained in this section are about *meaning,* as all discussions of communication development basically are, to the extent that they examine change in the child's ability to interpret and behave with meaning. However, these chapters are about another level of meaning as well, that is the meaning imposed by those who study communication on the events of early life. There is a concern for what the researcher is interpreting (and perhaps misinterpreting) about the communication of others.

A confounding factor in any psychological study is the researcher's inability to become disentangled from the human condition. Psychological theories may profit from this entanglement; what else can we theorize about from such an intimate perspective? However, scientific methodology is at risk in that objectivity seems impossible. This is particularly the case in communication research. The researcher is part of the communication system being investigated. His/her ability to interpret the meaning of others' behaviors (itself a communicative ability) is the researcher's only means for examining communication. Even when hidden behind video cameras or imbedded in macroamounts of microanalyses, the researcher is making decisions about what behaviors to focus on, how to segment the flow of events, and/or whether or not frequency, type, or other characteristics of the behaviors might be important.

It is the theoretical basis of these decisions as well as their effect on research findings that the chapters in this section are trying to both ascertain and evaluate. Questions are raised about how children change and about how the meaningfulness of their behaviors changes. More important, however, are the researchers' concerns when making decisions as to how to detect and characterize these changes and what methodology best permits examination and, ultimately, explanation of these changes. Specifically, questions are raised about (a) the validity of our hypothetical constructs, for example, social and/or communicative competence (Chap. 11), symbolism in play and language (Chap. 8), and intention (Chaps. 5, 6); and (b) the usefulness of the methodology and level of analyses employed (Chaps. 7, 9, 10, 11). It is clear from these chapters that evaluation and continuing reevaluations of theories and methodologies are necessary.

HYPOTHETICAL CONSTRUCTS

A useful suggestion for communication researchers attempting to disentangle themselves from their study can be found in Hofstadter's (1979) remarkable treatise on Gödel, Escher, and Bach, all of whom were masters at representing entangled situations and clarifying them. Hofstadter (1979) concluded, "How you describe a tangled situation . . . depends how far back you step before describing. If you can step far enough back, you can often see the clue that allows you to untangle things" (p. 692). Whether or not communication researchers have been able to step far enough back is open for review. However, several clues in the form of constructs have been untangled from the mass of data on communication.

The construct "intention" is the focus of two chapters (Chaps. 5, 6). Neither questions intention as a construct, but instead posits it as a given in the interpretation of communication. However, its significance for the researcher is questioned. As do the authors in several of these chapters, Scoville emphasizes the importance of evaluating the criteria used in specifying and understanding the existence of a construct such as intention. Although I disagree with his decision about these particular criteria, his call for their evaluation is critical.

Symbolic conduct is another example of a hypothetical construct often tangled in among our studies of communication. Zukow's chapter takes some researchers to task (Bates, Benigni, Bretherton, Camioni, & Volterra, 1979; Bates, Bretherton, Share, & McNew, in press) for their interpretations and perhaps misinterpretations of symbolic acts in children's behavior.

Greenberg's discussion of social and communicative competence emphasizes the necessity of evaluating what it is we think we are studying. Whether or not the competencies we assume to be related (e.g., social and communicative competence) are in fact related may be most clearly observed in nontypical populations where one competence is absent or delayed. Although it is obvious that Greenberg's work has practical applications for the deaf population, it also has implications for understanding how processes, such as social competence and communication, may function in other populations as well. Greenberg's emphasis on the development of valid operationalizations to be used in addressing different theoretical questions is indicative of a pervasive concern expressed in all these chapters for relating methodology to theory.

In each of these examples, as well as others presented in these chapters, it is not clear whether the researcher is right or wrong in the decisions made about the constructs being studied. More definitive answers to the meaningfulness of the constructs being posited are needed. However, it appears those answers are not available. Continuing the open discussion and reevaluation begun in these chapters should lead to a more coherent and complete theory of communication development.

METHODOLOGY AND EVIDENCE

Much of the discussion in the chapters is about how methodological changes could add to what we already know about communication development. We already know, for example, that children communicate, or at least are interpreted as communicating, even before they begin to talk. We know that mothers (and other caregivers) use certain language forms when talking with young children and that perhaps this speech to children contributes to language acquisition. We know that children use conventionalized behaviors when they play and when they talk. We know that infants can be included in interactions that look social and even conversational. We know that parents have ideas and expectations about their own and their child's behavior. However, it is not clear that we understand the meaning of these observations or that we know how these bits of data fit into our theories.

Two issues about the methodology used to formulate and test theories are raised in these chapters. The first deals with the level of observational interpretation used; the second, with the statistical procedures employed.

Different types of information based on interpretations of empirical data are presented as evidence in support of theories. The problem is how does one know when information presented is adequate evidence? Again, I turn to Hofstadter (1979) for his clever thoughts and words. He used Lewis Carroll's infinite regress paradox as a reference and concluded, ''If you want to show that A is a fact, you need evidence: B. But what makes you sure that B is evidence of A? To show that, you need meta-evidence: C. And for the validity of that meta-evidence, you need meta-meta-evidence—and so on, ad nauseam'' (Hofstadter, 1979, pp. 693–694).

The concern of Hayes, Ninio and Wheeler, and Scoville for the validation of the psychological reality of constructs by those involved (for example, the parent) addresses the requirements for metaevidence. If you want to verify evidence, can you do better than to have the one who has committed the act confess? Probably not. However there is still scientific risk involved. For one thing, there is always the chance for an invalid confession—perhaps the individual misunderstood the question or actually performed the culturally relevant act without giving it explicit thought. In addition, at its best, this evidence, even as that collected by the event recorder, will have been interpreted according to some theory, in this case the individual's theory of why and how s/he behaves or why and how his/her child behaves. When Scoville, for example, focuses on whether or not the parent attributes intentionality to the child rather than taking the risk as a researcher of misinterpreting the child's behavior, he has traded, it appears, his theory of intention for the parent's. The parent's point of view is an interesting topic of study and will add to our knowledge of what parents think they and their child are doing, but this approach is not inherently any more scientifically or theoretically satisfying than any other. All evidence undergoes interpretation based on theory; some on layers of interpretation such as the researcher's interpretation of the subject's interpretation. Although the technique of asking the subject (or the subject's parent) to describe and frame her own behaviors provides evidence and probably very good evidence, we cannot be confident that we have all the information we need.

Bohannon and Hirsh-Pasek (Chap. 9) provide a good example of how reseachers must continually question whether or not they are making the most of the evidence available to them. When it becomes apparent that what the observer and, in some cases, the participant "know" to be true does not match the findings after analyses of the data, then the researcher must question not only his/her insights but also the methodology used. Bohannon and Hirsh-Pasek have come upon a way to analyze data on speech to children that makes the statistical findings more compatible with their theory and other evidence of the function of speech to children.

Sugarman (in press) concluded an excellent discussion on empirical and logical issues in the study of communication by stating: "We need to know how to exploit the wealth of circumstantial evidence that is currently or potentially available to us, as does a good judge, who once in a while reaches a true verdict." I agree, and the methodologies presented in these chapters will help to build this wealth of evidence. However, I am still not certain how we will know when the verdict is or is not true.

These chapters represent the basics of the process of scientific inquiry. They are full of questions, assertions, and criticisms, directed at self as well as others. In addition to providing information about the meaning of early communication development, the process represented in these chapters should serve to further the meaningfulness of scientific endeavor.

REFERENCES

Bates, E., Benigni, R., Bretherton, I., Camioni, R., & Volterra, V. *The emergence of symbols: Communication and cognition in infancy.* New York: Academic Press, 1979.

Bates, E., Bretherton, I., Share, C., & McNew, S. Names, gestures, and objects: The role of context in the emergence of symbols. In K. Nelson (Ed.), *Children's language* (Vol. 4). New York: Gardner Press, in press.

Hofstadter, D. R. *Gödel, Escher, Bach: An eternal golden braid.* New York: Basic Books, 1979.

Sugarman, S. Discussion: Empirical vs. logical issues in the transition from prelinguistic to linguistic communication. In R. Golinkoff (Ed.), *The transition from prelinguistic to linguistic communication: Issues and implications.* Hillsdale, NJ: Erlbaum, in press.

CHAPTER 5

Development of the Intention to Communicate: The Eye of the Beholder*

Richard Scoville

Several years ago, in an undergraduate biology course, I had the fascinating experience of watching a flower grow in reverse. With a rapid, fluttering motion, a crocus folded its petals into a bud, which rapidly grew smaller and smaller as the leaves receded toward the base of the stem, gradually twining themselves around it. Soon there remained only a single shoot, no longer recognizable as a crocus, ineluctably retreating until it dived beneath the sand, which, for good measure, sprang into the spot, leaving behind a smooth featureless surface. The trick, of course, was engineered by the use of time-lapse film run backward. But the effect was meaningfully reminiscent of the progress of research in language development over the past twenty years. It is as if we have been running the film backward, frame by frame, examining the growth of a flower, trying to determine the exact moment at which a flower really becomes a flower. As we have searched for signs of language in ever younger infants, we have been forced to confront many of the assumptions and facile definitions that could be more readily sidestepped in studying the language of older children. What, for instance, is the most rudimentary form of behavior that qualifies as language? How do we discriminate between infant behaviors that are intended as messages and those that are not? How can we correctly interpret the content of such messages?

To the developmentalist, discontinuous change is problematic. It demands expla-

* The author wishes to acknowledge an intellectual debt to Joanna Ryan (1974), whose thoughtful essay provided inspiration for the ideas presented here. I thank Barbara Lawrence and Carol Harding for helpful discussion of these issues.

nation; and the explanation often requires a shift in the level of analysis. For example, children begin producing multiword utterances around their second birthday, and from the point of view of stochastic models of syntax (such as pivot grammar) the appearance of syntactic relations appears as a discontinuous change in behavior. Bloom (1973), by recognizing that the inferable semantic structures of multiword utterances are also inferable in earlier, single-word utterances, was able to show that the transition to syntactic speech is the result of continuous changes operating at the semantic level. An analogous problem currently confronts those who seek to explain the apparently discontinuous appearance of illocutionary utterances and gestures around the age of 10–12 months, the "magic moment" at which the infant initially seems to be trying to send messages to another person. A developmental explanation of this apparently novel capability will be achieved only when it can be shown to be the product of some continuing developmental process. But what aspects of behavior are subsumed in this process? What is the appropriate descriptive vocabulary for the changes that occur during this period? These questions address basic assumptions concerning the theoretical constructs that will guide research in this area, and suggest behaviors that might index those constructs; and so at least tentative answers must be advanced before programmatic research in this area can proceed very far.

The present essay is concerned with one such construct, communicative intention. A growing consensus among students of early language development maintains that descriptive continuity in children's communicative behavior can be traced back to a time around the child's first birthday. Many observers agree that at this point infants begin to be aware that certain of their behaviors, including gesture and vocalization, may be used not to gain direct access to a goal, but to induce another person to behave (Bates, 1979; Braunwald, 1978; Bretherton, McNew & Beeghly-Smith, 1980; Harding & Golinkoff, 1979). In brief, at about this time the infant begins to intend to communicate with others. From this point, but not before, it is possible to describe the child's communicative behavior in terms of an underlying semantic structure, defined as including both an illocutionary and a propositional component.

For example, Bates (1976) describes an early use of imperative signals by one of her subjects, Carlotta:

> C. [age 13 months] is seated in a corridor in front of the kitchen door. She looks toward her mother and calls with an acute sound *ha*. Mother comes over to her, and C. looks toward the kitchen, twisting her shoulders and upper body to do so. Mother carries her into the kitchen, and C. points toward the sink. Mother gives her a glass of water, and C. drinks it eagerly. (p. 55)

Here the illocutionary component of Carlotta's behavior might be characterized as a request, an attempt to enlist her mother's assistance by the use of signals—in this case vocalization and pointing. The propositional component, the content of C's message, involves her knowledge that there is water in the kitchen, that mother can be instrumental in providing a drink, and that C is to be the beneficiary of her mother's action.

Together, the illocutionary and propositional components constitute a semantic structure, which we might gloss as a request for a drink. This structure adequately describes the message as long as we allow that the child's repertoire of signals and her knowledge of the relationship between the objects and persons involved may be quite different from those of an older child or adult. But more important is the fact that, by assigning the child's behavior a semantic structure, we are able to trace its development. A 13-month-old child might ask for a drink by pointing and vocalizing, while at 30 months s/he may simply say, "Need some juice, Mommy." By categorizing both of these events as *requests*, we are able, at least in principle, to describe the intervening developmental changes in his/her utterances as the gradual acquisition of increasingly linguistic means for accomplishing the same kinds of tasks (see Bruner, Roy, & Ratner, in press). In this way, the description of children's early communicative behavior in terms of its underlying semantic structure has formed the basis for a rich and growing literature describing the development of language during the second year (Bloom, 1973; Dore, 1974; Greenfield & Smith, 1976; Rodgon, 1976).

From a logical standpoint, the determination of the communicative intention of a signal is required for its propositional content to be specified (Bennett, 1976). This can be argued from first principles by appeal to Grice's (1957) criteria for linguistic behavior, namely, that the speaker intends that the hearer should do or believe something, and that he also intends that the hearer should understand that this intention is part of the motivation for the speaker's behavior. But we can get at essentially the same notion in a less convoluted way by pointing out that, in order to discover the content of a child's message, we must know that his/her behavior is in fact a signal: that it is meant to influence the hearer in some way. In the above example, we may assume that Carlotta's looking at her mother along with the vocalization alerted her mother to the communicative nature of this particular episode. Given that mother understood C's behavior to be a signal, she then proceeded to discover the content of C's message by carrying her into the kitchen. More specifically, in this single word example, the identification of the illocutionary component of C's behavior as a request guides the choice of semantic elements that might be included in the propositional component, as well as the semantic relations between them. Without some indication of an intention to communicate, there is no reason to propose a semantic structure to account for the child's behavior. Thus, the construct of intentionality is inextricably bound up with the process of semantic description.

In cases where the child performs conventional signals—recognizable words, gestures such as pointing, etc.—communicative intention is more readily inferred. Since the use of conventional signals by adults is generally restricted to intentionally communicative situations, their performance by the child implies that s/he intends to communicate, and the assignment of a semantic structure can proceed based on the form of the signal, any accompanying behavior, and the context in which the signal is produced. (These "rich interpretations" are subject to intense debate concerning their precision and validity, but their status as intentional communication seems uncontroversial. See Bloom, Capatides, and Tackeff, 1981; Golinkoff, 1981; Howe, 1981, and references therein.) Thus, the child who looks at her mother, holds up a stuffed animal and says "Kitty!" is easily assumed to be intending to communicate, since the word itself provides convincing evidence. The importance of communicative intention for the specification of semantic structure is especially apparent when, as sometimes happens, conventional signals are produced in noncommunicative situations (e.g., in solitary play, in the crib, etc.). In these cases the illocutionary component of the utterance is unclear, and hence the elements to be included in the semantic structure cannot confidently be specified. As we extend our analysis to younger children whose behavior less closely resembles the conventional words and gestures of the adult, the specification of communicative intention becomes problematic. And to the extent that the child's intentions are brought into question, the semantic description of his/her behavior is similarly problematic.

Thus, from a developmental perspective, our account eventually reaches a point of discontinuity. If we are unable reliably to assign semantic structure to the behavior of 6-month-old infants, it is not easy to see how prelinguistic, nonillocutionary behavior develops continuously into the semantically structured communication that emerges during the second year. A developmental account of the transition to intentional communication requires a redefinition of the child's behavior, a shift to a new level of analysis. Since we ultimately wish to explain the emergence of communicative intentions, our descriptions of the changes that occur during this period cannot be cast in terms that presuppose those intentions (Dennett, 1971). For example, Greenfield and Smith (1976) designate certain of their subjects' early vocal signals as *volitions,* which they describe as

> a particular kind of Performative. Its basic function is to obtain some desired response from the person addressed. The most common examples of this category are *mama,* used to request something, and *no,* used to reject something. (p. 51)

Volitions appear at around 12 months in Greenfield and Smith's data. They are distinguished by "standardized intonations and gestures," and are "often repeated until the desired response is obtained." Now, phrases such as "desired response," "used to request" and "used to reject" all assume a communicative intention; hence, volitions are defined by the child's having a particular kind of intention. The presence of the intention is indexed by gesture, intonation, and persistence. (Note that these behaviors do not constitute the intention, because the intention can be recognized by a variety of different behaviors in different combinations; behavior merely gives evidence that an intention is present. See also Bates, 1979, p. 35.) As employed by Greenfield and Smith, that is, to provide a vocabulary for the description of later language development, intentional categories such as *volition* are both reasonable and useful. But the present question involves the process by which the infant originally comes to have such intentions. For this work, *volition* is useless. For example, we might longitudinally examine a group of children from 6 to 15 months, looking for volitions. We would note instances of the children's behavior that increasingly exhibit behavioral evidence of volition, and by establishing criteria for the behavioral indices we might be prepared to conclude that volitions, together with their accompanying intentions, appear at, say, 12 months. But although we would have gained a bit more experience with the phenomenon, we would be no closer to explaining its development. Since volition is defined in terms of intentions, and since an intention is something one either has or one does not, we are left wondering how, at precisely 12 months, the child has suddenly picked up this particular bit of mental apparatus.

Furthermore, it is disturbing that the age at which we conclude that the child acquires volitions is partially a function of the behavioral criteria we select. If our criteria are loose, if we are prepared to say that a rising intonation contour is sufficient to denote volition, we will mark their appearance at about 7 months (Tonkova-Yampol'skaya, 1973). But if we require that any volition must exhibit rising intonation contour, a discrete pointing gesture with extended finger, and eye contact, and at least two persistent repetitions, then our proposed age of acquisition will be considerably later. If one assumes communicative intention to be resident in the child and not merely in one's descriptive system, the fit of the behavioral criteria is crucial. But on what grounds are we to loosen or tighten them?

Recent developmental studies of early communication have dealt with the problem of intentionality in several ways. One approach has been to focus on the "conversational" structure of prelinguistic interactions between infants and parents beginning in the first few months of life (Stern, 1977). This tactic tends to eschew intentional interpretations of the infant's behavior in favor of descriptions of the reciprocal contingencies in the behavior of the dyad. However, the behaviors selected for study are typically those that will later figure in intentional communication, including vocalizations (Anderson, Vietze, & Dokecki, 1977; Bateson, 1975; Freedle & Lewis, 1977; Snow, 1977), mutual or object-oriented gaze (Collis & Shaffer, 1975; Scaife & Bruner, 1975; Stern, 1974) and facial expressions (Tronick, Als, & Adamson, 1979). These studies show that during the first year the infant becomes increasingly responsive and autonomous in his/her social behavior. Early on, the reciprocal structure of interaction is imposed by the adult, who responds contingently to the infant's behavior. By the end of the first year, the infant is able to initiate and sustain interaction; in short, his/her social behavior looks increasingly intentional.

Insofar as descriptions of dyadic behavior are restricted to the temporal and contingent structure of behavior, they cannot settle the issue of communicative intention, although they provide information about age-related changes in possible behavioral indices of intentionality. But the question of which behavior patterns are to be taken as indicators of communicative intention remains open.

A second approach to the developmental description of communicative intention is conceptually quite simple. It proposes very loose criteria for the presence of intentionality, and so purports to find full-blown communicative intentions in very young infants. Two passages from Trevarthen (1977) illustrate this strategy:

> The responses of infants to persons . . . show that they may not only express communications to persons when less than two months old, but that they well and quickly locate communicative acts of an attentive partner . . . Very young subjects have consistently exhibited preferences for physical constellations of stimuli that, in the ordinary world, are unambiguous signs of attempting communication. (p. 234)

> Since the psychological situation for the baby's expressive mouth movements is, in general, similar to that between two persons engaged in speaking together, and since the movement of lips and tongue resemble the movements adults make with the mouth while speaking, we feel justified in labelling [the] weakly voiced mouth activity of the infant [at 7 weeks] *prespeech*. (p. 251)

Why not use intentional categories to describe the behavior of neonates? For one thing, it flies in the face of currently accepted ideas about the cognitive capacities of young infants. But more importantly, to most observers, including mothers, the behavior of very young infants simply does not appear to be motivated by a desire to produce a specific effect on the listener. Pratt (1978, reported in Bruner et al., in press) found that mothers' interpretations of their infants' cries were initially cast in physical terms: hunger, pain, etc. At around 26 weeks, mothers' interpretations began to be framed in intentional terms. As the maternal behaviors required to terminate a bout of crying changed from "organic" (feeding, diapering, etc.) to "psychological" (providing an object, distraction), mothers began to interpret the cries intentionally, as *requests* for a change of state. For Pratt's mothers the intentionality of their babies' signals depended not simply on the form of the behavior, but upon the apparently psychological nature of their causes, which in turn were revealed by the children's responses to the mothers' actions. Thus, this second approach ultimately fails to deal with some important changes that occur in communicative behavior before the child's first birthday. To resolve the problem of communicative intention by radically relaxing the criteria for intentionality does damage to parents' common-sense notion of what intentional communication is all about, and like other nativist arguments, treats the problem of development by defining it out of existence.

A third approach to the emergence of communicative intentions reduces the level of analysis from linguistic to cognitive by pointing out that the intention to communicate can be interpreted as the execution of a particular sort of sensorimotor scheme. In one version of this view, the child intends to communicate when s/he is able to use an object to engage another person in interaction or to use another person's actions as a means for obtaining an object (Bates, 1976; Bates, Camaioni, & Volterra, 1975). So defined, communicative intention involves Piagetian Stage 5 tertiary circular reactions (Piaget, 1952); and a number of investigators have presented evidence consistent with the hypothesis that Stage 5 in the development of causality is coincident with the use of such schemes (Harding & Golinkoff, 1979;

Sugarman, 1978; but cf. Corrigan, 1979). In Piagetian terms, it is reasonable to describe the earlier means–end relationships of Stage 4 in intentional terms. The child who opens a box in order to find a hidden toy appears to anticipate the finding of an unseen object and engages in one scheme (opening) with the intention of exercising the other (manipulating the toy) (Piaget, 1952, p. 148). In this view, then, the appearance of communicative intentions marks the extension of earlier intentional behavior to new, more complex social situations.

This and similar formulations of communicative intentions, unlike Trevarthen's, have the virtue of suggesting specific developmental hypotheses related to the emergence of illocutionary behavior (Bates, 1979; McCune-Nicolich, 1981). They are therefore potentially useful in extending our account of communicative development into early infancy.

Although the cognitive approach to the study of communicative intention successfully achieves the change in level of description necessary for developmental analysis, the problem of criterion fit remains: What behaviors can be considered as reliable indices of communicative intention? Unfortunately, this question admits no simple answer.

Observers who agree that communicative intentions appear near the child's first birthday point to a particular set of behavioral indices of communicative intention. Bates's (1979) theoretical system defines two early types of illocutions; *protoimperatives* and *protodeclaratives*. In the protoimperative, the child's behavior shows that s/he desires a goal—namely, to exercise some scheme on an object. This goal object is indicated by reaching or pointing and by gaze; desire is indicated by these deictic acts as well as, perhaps, by "effort" vocalization. In addition, the observer's knowledge of the child's previous activity with this or similar objects may also provide evidence for his/her perception of this object as a goal. As long as the child's behavior is directed only at the goal object, we may credit him/her with the intention to obtain the goal, but not with the intention to communicate a request for the object to the adult. This requires that the child direct his/her gesture and gaze at the adult as well as at the goal, typically in an alternating fashion. Thus, the child's behavior seems to indicate that s/he is aware of the potential instrumental relationship between the adult and the object; this awareness plus the child's desire for the object together imply the existence of a communicative intention. Similar criteria of gesture, gaze, object and vocalization have been listed for directive messages by Bruner et al. (in press), Halliday (1979), and others.

The protodeclarative, according to Bates (1979; Bates et al., 1975), is similar, except that here an object is used as a means to obtain some adult behavior. Behavioral indices include pointing at an object while making eye contact with the adult, or extending an object toward the adult while making eye contact, with or without vocalization. Here the goal is the appreciative behavior of the adult; its goal status is presumably inferred from previous experience with the child's behavior in such circumstances.

In addition to the direction and sequence of gestures and gaze and the acoustic properties of the child's vocalizations, two other criteria for the existence of communicative intentions are commonly noted. One, "ritualization," refers to the increasingly conventional nature of the gestures and vocalizations. In recurring episodes, the gestures become more stereotyped and abbreviated and so more intentional looking (Bates, 1979; Bruner et al., in press). A related criterion is the use of phonologically consistent vocalizations in similar situations, that is, in similar contexts with similar accompanying nonverbal behaviors (Braunwald, 1978; Dore, Franklin, Miller, & Ramer, 1976; Halliday, 1975, 1979; Ricks, 1979).

Finally, the child's tendency to modify his/her signals according to the listener's behavior is a further indication of intentionality (Bates, 1979). If the adult is slow to respond, the child is likely to persist in his/her gestures and vocalizations. When the goal is achieved, the infant gives behavioral indications of satisfaction by manipulating the object, responding to the adult's behavior, or simply ceasing his/her signals.

Bates's definitions of protodeclarative and protoimperative require the presence of an object either as instrument or goal, since the alternation of the child's signals between object and adult provides the strongest clue to communicative intention. But the intention to communicate per se does not logically require that the message involve an object, and other accounts of communicative development during this period include requests for help, invitations to play, greetings, etc. (Bruner et al., in press; Halliday, 1975). For example, an invitation to play a well-established game may be indicated by performing part of the actions involved, such as bouncing up and down on an adult knee to request a game of "horsie" (Bruner et al., in press).

To what extent do the behavioral criteria listed above provide adequate evidence for the infant's intention to communicate? Do they indeed show that s/he is aware of the effect of his/her signals on the listener? A traditional but evasive empiricist reply might be simply that one can never be certain about another's mental states and that, once the subject's action in a situation is thoroughly described in terms of its observable behavioral features, nothing is added to that description by the inclusion of an intentional element. I need not dwell on the inadequacy of this reply beyond reiterating that communicative intention is in principle no more inaccessible than any other abstract scientific construct (Feldman & Toulmin, 1975). Its theoretical value lies in its usefulness for organizing and predicting behavioral data. It is a truism that we only know about someone's beliefs and intentions through his overt behavior. But it does not follow that questions about intentionality are necessarily moot.

A more serious criticism of the above criteria is that they are too loose, that they allow us to classify as intentional behavior patterns that on other grounds we would wish to exclude by definition. A comparative example illustrates the fact that the intentional appearance of behavior can be misleading. Consider the neonatal communication system of the mallard duck (*Anas platyrhynchos*). The newly hatched duckling normally spends all of its time in close proximity to its mother and broodmates. The hen orchestrates the behavior of the young by means of two distinct vocalizations, one of which, the *assembly call,* serves to attract the duckling to the hen. She can often be heard to utter this call as the brood moves about on land or water. Occasionally, perhaps while dabbling about in a particularly interesting bit of muck, a duckling may fail to notice that the rest of the brood has moved on. Sooner or later, the straggler will look up from his dabbling, and there ensues a very intentional-looking sequence of behavior: the duckling becomes agitated and, looking about, begins to utter *distress calls*. These serve to attract the attention of the hen, who orients to the sound and begins to approach the lost duckling while uttering the assembly call. When the duckling hears this he begins to move toward the hen until they meet, whereupon the duckling's vocalizations switch from distress to *contact* calls. The hen then leads the duckling back to the brood.

The duckling's behavior in this situation satisfies most of the usual criteria for communicative intentionality in human infants. There is no eye contact at first, since the hen is absent; but in its place we see the duckling looking about, apparently searching for the hen. The distress calls of the duckling appear to be efforts to direct the hen's attention, to elicit her approach and call. The distress calls are accommodated to the hearer's behavior in that the rate of calling is influenced by the presence of the hen's call (Scoville & Gottlieb, 1980). The behavior persists; the calls are uttered in successive bursts of 10 or more rhythmically grouped notes, and the calls terminate when the hen and duckling are reunited. Even though no object is involved, it is likely that a similar behavior pattern by human infants would unhesitatingly be classified as intentional communication.

But for ducklings, such a description is clearly facetious. Ducklings who have been reared in an incubator, who have never seen or heard an adult female mallard nevertheless have the ability to behave in precisely the manner described above. Newborn ducklings approach the maternal call even if they have never heard it before.[1] Ducklings' distress calls are elicited by, among other factors, a reduction in the number of other ducklings in the vicinity (Gaioni, Hoffman, Klein, & DePaulo, 1977) and need not involve the hen at all. Thus, it can be argued that attributing communicative intentions on the basis of gaze, directed action, stereotypy of the form of the signal, persistence, and accommodation of the signal to the hearer's behavior is still not stringent enough. In order to insure that the child's behavior is truly intentional, it might seem necessary to require further criteria.

For example, one might want to include the availability of alternative communicative strategies. It can be argued that intentionality necessarily involves choice, the decision to act in one way rather than in some other way. Operationally, for protoimperatives we might require that the infant exhibit alternative patterns of behavior for enlisting adult services. We might even require that the infant be capable of prevarication, since as noted by Bennett (1964), lying provides unequivocal evidence of choice, and hence of the intentionality of the signal.

However, as noted above, tightening or loosening the behavioral criteria for communicative intention merely shifts the age at which we attribute intentionality to

---

[1] See Gottlieb (1981). Even though no prior exposure to the maternal call is necessary, this perceptual system does require auditory experience for its normal development. This experience is ordinarily provided by the duckling's own prenatal vocalizations.

the child. Furthermore, adjustments in criterion fit ultimately translate into practical decisions about operational definitions that are to some degree arbitrary. For example, Harding and Golinkoff (1979) introduce communicative intention by citing four criteria for intentional vocalizations: (a) eye contact with the adult; (b) gesturing or looking at a goal object; (c) persistence; and (d) termination of the behavior once the goal is achieved. But given the constraints of their procedure, Harding and Golinkoff (1979) credit the child with communicative intention if s/he simply "vocalizes while making eye contact with the mother" at least twice during the test session (p. 36). A strong case could be made that this operational definition is too loose. But my more general point here is that *any* set of behavioral criteria adopted with the aim of fixing a particular point at which the child "acquires" communicative intentionality introduces an artificial discontinuity into the resulting development description. Thus, the correlation of this apparently sudden acquisition with other sensorimotor structures, and hence its developmental explanation, is potentially an artifact of the operational definition. This is clearly a precarious state of affairs and one that is not confined to discussions of communicative intention. Corrigan (1979) has extensively illustrated the same point with respect to the developmental relationship between object concept and single word langage use, while Feldman and Toulmin (1975) discuss more general implications of the problem of behavioral criteria for Piagetian theory.

In spite of the above difficulties, the phenomenon remains: somewhere around 12 months, something new about the infant's behavior leads observers to credit him/her with the intention to communicate, and thus to assign semantic interpretations to his/her signals. Earlier, I claimed that "if one assumes communicative intention to be resident in the child and not merely in one's descriptive system, the fit of the behavioral criteria is crucial." I wish to conclude this chapter by suggesting that not only is this assumption unnecessary, but in addition, there may be positive theoretical gains to be made by considering communicative intentionality from the point of view of the adults who interact with the infant.

Dennett (1971) has suggested that intentional terms are best considered as attributions, as perceptual categories that allow an observer to summarize past regularities in the behavior of a system and to predict its future behavior. The system under discussion need not be an infant, nor indeed, a human agent at all. The more flexible and complex the system, the more appropriate the attribution. Consider a computer program that accepts two numbers input by the user and produces their sum. A description of this very simple, inflexible behavior need not involve intentional terms at all. But now consider a very complex program, for instance the Statistical Analysis System (Helwig & Council, 1979). Anyone who has had the pleasure of using SAS for a large data analysis will recall error messages such as "STATEMENT IS INVALID OR IS USED OUT OF PROPER ORDER." The ensuing discussion with a statistical consultant is customarily phrased in very intentional terms:

Consultant: SAS is trying to tell you that you have to finish a DO-loop with an END statement before you can PROC.

User: Oh I see, it doesn't just assume that the PROC statement closes that loop.

Now, does SAS have communicative intentions? If we consider SAS as a mechanism whose behavior is completely determined by a series of program statements (roughly analogous to a physiological account of infant or duckling behavior), the answer is no. But to the extent that we are ignorant of that mechanism, and to the extent that the system carries out complex series of actions on its own, intentional terminology represents a useful means of describing and interacting with the program.

This is a provocative analogy. It suggests that communicative intentionality may be more appropriately considered to be a property of adults' perception of infant behavior than of the child him/herself. To be sure, caregivers' attributions of intentionality can be expected to rely on behavioral and contextual cues similar to those described above. But the problem of criterion fit has been avoided. The questions of whether the child "really" intends to communicate and hence whether a semantic description of his/her behavior is appropriate, can be replaced by an empirical examination of the developmental relationship between infant behavior and caregivers' perceptions of that behavior. Following Pratt's (1978) lead (see above), the empirical strategy becomes one of discovering those features of infant behavior that are necessary and sufficient to induce parents to interpret the infant's behavior intentionally, and to map out the effects of such attributions on caregiver behavior. To what extent and in what ways does a parent behave differently toward a child who is viewed as trying to communicate as opposed to one whose behavior is determined by organic factors? Ultimately, we would want to know how these changes in parental behavior affect the child's communicative development. In this way, the transition from preillocutionary to illocutionary communication can be seen not as the discontinuous appearance of a qualitatively new class of behavior, but rather as a gradual process involving both the infant and the caregiver.

In all this, at least one conceptual problem can be anticipated. It is unlikely that caregivers' perceptions of communicative intentions are based on consistent, fixed behavioral criteria. We may expect that parents will describe the behavior of even very young infants in loosely intentional terms. For example, an early smile might evoke the comment, "She's trying to tell me she loves me!" In spite of this, we may hypothesize that parents are sensitive to the communicative developments occurring throughout the first year and will reflect this sensitivity by the increasing specificity of the messages they attribute to the child (e.g., request to play a specific game, asking for a particular object), as well as in their reactions to those messages.

The approach to the study of early communication advocated here in no way proscribes the cognitive analysis of prelinguistic communication. Certainly, the changes in infant communicative behavior that occur during the first and subsequent years are based on increasing cognitive capacities, and a developmental explanation of these changes must make reference to the cognitive substrate. But to establish communicative intentionality as a cognitive construct whose existence explains the emergence of the first languagelike behavior is to build a theoretical edifice on very shifty sands indeed. I see no conclusive way to solve the problem of criterion fit a priori, and suggest that intentionality is better considered to be an interpersonal rather than a cognitive category, especially during the transitional period discussed here.

The present reinterpretation of communicative intention may prove particularly useful as we move from descriptions of age-related changes in children's language to investigations of the developmental mechanisms involved in these changes. Recently several authors have suggested that the transition to illocutionary speech is a bidirectional process in which a caregiver's reactions to the infant's behavior serve to segment the infant's world into conventional units of action and establish social and ultimately linguistic meanings for those actions (Braunwald & Brislin, 1979; Harding, this volume; Newson, 1979; Ratner & Bruner, 1978; Ryan, 1974).

> The child may be making noises that are unrecognizable because they are not part of the standard adult vocabulary, but she may be making them in such a way that adults think she is trying to say something. Whether or not it is true that the child "is trying to say something," and whether or not this is something that is in principle ascertainable, it is an important fact about adults that they do behave toward children in this way— that is, as though the child was trying to say something. In an effort to understand what are regarded as attempts at speech, mothers often repeat or extend the child's utterance, or alter some aspect of the non-linguistic context. (Ryan, 1974, p. 201)

In summary, I have attempted to point out some of the difficulties arising from the construct of communicative intentionality, particularly as these relate to the developmental analysis of early communication. A bidirectional model of development may be well served by considering communicative intention not as a causal factor in the production of infant behavior, but as a category of adult perception of that behavior.

REFERENCES

Anderson, B., Vietze, P., & Dokecki, P. Reciprocity in vocal interactions of mothers and infants. *Child Development*, 1977, *48*, 1676–1681.

Bates, E. *Language and context: The acquisition of pragmatics.* New York: Academic Press, 1976.

Bates, E. *The emergence of symbols.* New York: Academic Press, 1979.

Bates, E., Camaioni, L., & Volterra, V. The acquistion of performatives prior to speech. *Merrill-Palmer Quarterly*, 1975, *21*, 205–226.

Bateson, M. Mother–infant exchanges: The epigenesis of conversational interaction. *Annals of the New York Academy of Science* 1975, *263*, 101–113.

Bennett, J. *Rationality.* London: Routledge & Kegan Paul, 1964.

Bennett, J. *Linguistic behaviour.* Cambridge: Cambridge University Press, 1976.

Bloom, L. *One word at a time.* The Hague: Mouton, 1973.

Bloom, L., Capatides, J., & Tackeff, J. Further remarks on interpretive analysis: In response to Christine Howe. *Journal of Child Language*, 1981, *8*, 403–411.

Braunwald, S. Context, word and meaning: Toward a communicational analysis of lexical acquisition. In A. Lock (Ed.), *Action, gesture and symbol: The emergence of language.* London: Academic Press, 1978.

Braunwald, S., & Brislin, R. On being understood: The listener's contribution to the toddler's ability to communicate. In P. French (Ed.), *The development of meaning*. Japan: Bunka Hyoron Press, 1979.

Bretherton, I., McNew, S., & Beeghly-Smith, M. Early person knowledge as expressed in gestural and verbal communication: When do infants acquire a "theory of mind?" In M. Lamb & L. Sherrod (Eds.), *Infant social cognition*. Hillsdale, NJ: Erlbaum, 1980.

Bruner, J., Roy, C., & Ratner, N. The beginnings of request. In K. Nelson (Ed.), *Children's language* (Vol. 3). New York: Gardner Press, in press.

Collis, G., & Schaffer, H. Synchronization of visual attention in mother-infant pairs. *Journal of Child Psychology and Psychiatry*, 1975, *16*, 315–320.

Corrigan, R. Cognitive correlates of language: Differential criteria yield differential results. *Child Development*, 1979, *50*, 617–631.

Dennett, D. Intentional systems. *Journal of Philosophy*, 1971, *68*, 87–106.

Dore, J. A pragmatic description of early language development. *Journal of Psycholinguistic Research*, 1974, *3*, 343–350.

Dore, J., Franklin, M., Miller, R., & Ramer, A. Transitional phenomena in early language acquisition. *Journal of Child Language*, 1976, *3*, 13–28.

Feldman, C., & Toulmin, S. Logic and the theory of mind. *Nebraska Symposium on Motivation*, 1975, *23*, 409–476.

Freedle, R., & Lewis, M. Prelinguistic conversations. In M. Lewis & L. Rosenblum (Eds.), *Interaction, conversation and the development of language*. New York: Wiley, 1977.

Gaioni, S., Hoffman, H., Klein, S., & DePaulo, P. Distress calling as a function of group size in newly hatched ducklings. *Journal of Experimental Psychology: Animal Behavior Processes*, 1977, *3*, 335–342.

Golinkoff, R. The case for semantic relations: Evidence from the verbal and nonverbal domains. *Journal of Child Language*, 1981, *8*, 413–437.

Gottlieb, G. Roles of early experience in species-specific perceptual development. In R. Aslin, J. Alberts, & M. Petersen (Eds.), *Development of perception* (Vol. 1). New York: Academic Press, 1981.

Greenfield, P., & Smith, J. The structure of communication in early language development. New York: Academic Press, 1976.

Grice, H. Meaning. Philosophical Review, 1957, *66*, 377–388.

Halliday, M. *Learning how to mean*. New York: Elsevier, 1975.

Halliday, M. One child's protolanguage. In M. Bullowa (Ed.), *Before speech*. Cambridge: Cambridge University Press, 1979.

Harding, C., & Golinkoff, R. The origins of intentional vocalizations in prelinguistic infants. *Child Development*, 1979, *50*, 33–40.

Helwig, J., & Council, K. (Eds.). *SAS user's guide*. Raleigh, NC: SAS Institute, 1979.

Howe, C. Interpretive analysis and role semantics: A ten-year mesalliance? *Journal of Child Language*, 1981, *8*, 439–456.

McCune-Nicolich, L. Toward symbolic functioning: Structure of early pretend games and potential parallels with language. *Child Development*, 1981, *52*, 785–797.

Newson, J. The growth of shared understandings between infant and caregiver. In M. Bullowa (Ed.), *Before speech*. Cambridge: Cambridge University Press, 1979.

Piaget, J. *The origins of intelligence in children*. New York: Norton, 1952/1963.

Pratt, C. The socialization of crying. Unpublished doctoral dissertation, University of Oxford, 1978.

Ratner, N. & Bruner, J. Games, social exchange and the acquisition of language. *Journal of Child Language*, 1978, *5*, 391–402.

Ricks, D. Making sense of experience to make sensible sounds. In M. Bullowa (Ed.), *Before speech*. Cambridge: Cambridge University Press, 1979.

Rodgon, M. *Single-word usage, cognitive development and the beginnings of combinatorial speech*. Cambridge: Cambridge University Press, 1976.

Ryan, J. Early language development. In M. Richards (Ed.), *The integration of the child into a social world*. Cambridge: Cambridge University Press, 1974.

Scaife, M., & Bruner, J. The capacity for joint visual attention in the infant. *Nature,* 1975, *253,* 265–266.

Scoville, R., & Gottlieb, G. Development of vocal behavior in Peking ducklings. *Animal Behaviour,* 1980, *28,* 1095–1109.

Snow, C. The development of conversation between mothers and babies. *Journal of Child Language,* 1977, *4,* 1–22.

Stern, D. Mother and infant at play: The dyadic interaction involving facial, vocal and gaze behaviors. In M. Lewis & L. Rosenblum (Eds.), *The effect of the infant on its caregiver.* New York: Wiley, 1974.

Stern, D. *The first relationship.* Cambridge, MA: Harvard University Press, 1977.

Sugarman, S. Some organizational aspects of pre-verbal communication. In I. Markova (Ed.), *The social context of language.* London: Wiley, 1978.

Tonkova-Yampol'skaya, R. Development of speech intonation in infants during the first two years of life. In C. Ferguson & D. Slobin (Eds.), *Studies of child language development.* New York: Holt, Rinehart & Winston, 1973.

Trevarthen, C. Descriptive analyses of infant communicative behavior. In H. Schaffer (Ed.), *Studies in mother-infant interaction.* London: Academic Press, 1977.

Tronick, E., Als, H., & Adamson, L. Structure of early face-to-face communicative interactions. In M. Bullowa (Ed.), *Before speech.* Cambridge: Cambridge University Press, 1979.

CHAPTER 6

Acting with Intention: A Framework for Examining the Development of the Intention to Communicate

Carol Harding

Through the course of history, as humankind has attempted to understand its own behavior, one of the recurring issues has been the question of intention, or in Cazden's (1977) words, "the *why* of human behavior." Although any one of us can discuss intentions as both an explanation of our own behavior and a source for our interpretation of others' behavior, these introspections have not led to a consensus in the inference of intention as a basis of behavior. The philosopher Anscombe (1957) attempted to demonstrate that at least some behavior occurs because of preconceived goals or intentions. She concluded that as long as "the question "Why?" *with answers that give reasons for acting*" exists, the concept of intention also must exist (Anscombe, 1957, my italics). The answers need not be verbal (see her discussion of animals and infants apparently behaving with intention, p. 5) and may not accurately explain the behavior, since these answers are, as Anscombe described, only the expression of intention. The fact that for the actor there can be an answer affirms that the behavior was based on an intention.

In addition to this compelling psychological reality of the actor's own intentions, Anscombe presented as evidence of the existence of intention, interpretations of behaviors which require the inference of intention. One such interpretation is implicit in the act of signaling. In order to interpret one's own behavior or another's as a signal, the assumption must be made that one organism can attempt to intentionally affect another. All signals may not be intentional, but in order to possess a concept of signaling, one concedes the possibility that behaviors can be intentional.

Cherry (1978) described communication as the transmission of "signals or signs—audible, visual, tactual. They may be spoken or written words, or numbers, or pictures, or many other forms of physical expression that are said to be *meaning-*

ful or *significant"* (p. 9, his italics). To be "meaningful or significant" assumes
that one partner involved in communication can intend the signal to mean, and the
other can recognize this intention and interpret the signal as meaningful.

In the following discussion, Cherry's description of communication is used to
represent at least the endpoint of communication development as engaged in by
adult humans. The developmental issue addressed is the process through which this
endpoint is achieved. Although refinements in the use and interpretation of meaningful signals probably continue throughout the lifespan, the focus of this chapter is
on the prelanguage period. Investigations of the development of communication
have indicated changes in the use of behaviors during the first year of life (Bates,
1976; Harding & Golinkoff, 1979; Shotter, 1978). It is proposed that these changes
in the development of communication reflect the gradual development of the ability
to act with intention (Harding, 1982b).

The chapter is divided into three parts. In the first part, an argument is made that
in order to examine developmental change in communication, it is necessary to
make inferences about whether or not the infant is acting with intention. This
argument is presented in contrast to arguments that the inference of intention is
unnecessary (cf. Scoville, this volume, chap. 5) and/or unnecessarily unscientific in
studying communication development (cf. Sugarman, in press).

The second part of the chapter presents findings from a short-term longitudinal
study examining communicative change in prelanguage infants within the proposed
framework of the developing ability to act with intention.

The third section proposes an explanation for how developmental change in the
ability to intend to communicate may occur.

INFERRING INTENTION IN THE COMMUNICATION
OF PRELANGUAGE INFANTS

It is not self-evident that the study of communication development requires the
inference of intention, at least when prelanguage infants are involved (see Scoville,
this volume, chap. 5; Sugarman, in press). Although Cherry's (1978) definition of
communication given above assumes intentional signaling, other definitions of
communication require no such assumption. For example, as Wilson (1975) summarized, "communication has been defined as the process by which behavior of
one individual alters the probability of behavioral acts in other individuals" (p.
194).

For psychologists studying communication, such definitions have provided a
scientific approach based on behavioral observation. Fortunately, since presumably
it is agreed that the event of communicative interaction represents something different than events involving behaviors such as a tap on the patella, operational definitions have not necessarily negated the researcher's interpretations of communicative
meaning or the significance of it during interactions. For example, when observing
interactions involving older children or adults in which a conventional communication code is used (e.g., language), the researcher is able to make judgments about
the meaningfulness of the communication to the partners involved, based on knowl-

edge of the shared code. In addition, the researcher is able to use the partners' descriptions of their intentions and interpretations during the interaction as part of the observational data base in describing the interaction. Perhaps even more importantly the researcher, knowing his/her own ability to engage in communicative intentions and interpretations, begins with the assumption that others, at least those who are using conventional communication codes, also engage in intentional communication (cf. John Locke's presumption in his *Essay Concerning Human Understanding*, 1690, that it "will be easily granted to me that there are ideas in men's minds; everyone is conscious of them in himself, and men's words and actions will satisfy him that they are in others").

In contrast, however, when interactions involving prelanguage infants are observed, none of these three conditions apply. There is no conventional communication code to interpret; the infant is unable to corroborate any inferences of interpretation and/or intention attributed to him or her, and, in contrast to the interactions described above, it is not clear that one can (or does, except perhaps in the case of the caregiver) assume that the infant has the competence to intend to communicate.

It could be argued that these difficulties in observing interactions involving infants make an operational definition based on behavioral probabilities essential for the scientific study of infant–adult interactions. However, the argument presented here is that it is in fact *because* of these difficulties that researchers trying to examine the development of communication must not limit their study to observable effects of behaviors. Instead, inferences of the infant's intentions must purposefully be included. If we can agree that communication can be different from other cause/effect reactions and that older children and adults can intend to signal and can intentionally use a communicative code they interpret as having shared meaning, then what we become interested in developmentally is when and how these intentions develop. By attempting not only to observe changes in the infant's behavior but also to interpret these changes within a framework of an increasing ability to act with intention, it is proposed that the process of becoming a communicator may be most clearly examined. By neglecting to infer change in intention as the infant develops, we may observe how interpretations and reactions to his/her behavior change, but miss the critical variable of what it is about the infant's developing abilities that accounts for that change. In observing adult communicative interactions, the researcher implicitly infers that the intention to communicate can be present. In investigating the development of intentional communication, we limit our study if we do not explicitly search for the basis of that intentional behavior.

A LONGITUDINAL STUDY OF THE DEVELOPMENT
OF THE INTENTION TO COMMUNICATE

The study described below examined when and in what ways developmental change occurs in communication, specifically by observing changes in infants' use of communicative behaviors. The term "communicative behaviors" is employed in this study to describe behaviors that *can* be communicative, for example, vocaliz-

TABLE 1
A Developmental Model of Intention as It Relates to Communication Development[a]

Order of Development of the Components of Intention	Component 1: "Awareness of a goal"	Component 2: Behavioral evidence of a plan designed to achieve a goal	Component 3: Behavioral evidence of alternative plans and intermediary actions leading to a goal
	Component 4: Persistence—occurs across other components		
Cognitive Development	Knowledge of means–end relationships During Stage 3, Piaget (1954) states: "Awareness of purpose results in the dissociation between cause and effect" (p. 263).	Knowledge of objective causality Piaget (1954) states: "During this fourth stage the child ceases to consider his own action as the sole source of causality and attributes to someone else's body an aggregate of particular powers" (p. 296)	Knowledge of other person as autonomous sources of action and intermediary actions as means of achieving goals Piaget (1954) states: Beginning with the fifth state, . . . the child increasingly will notice and utilize the intermediaries between his own movements and the culminating point of his acts" (p. 290). He will begin to use new means in achieving goals.

Communication			
Communicativelike behaviors (i.e., vocalizing, reaching, and looking) may occur as "procedures" (see Piaget, 1954) as infant attempts to achieve a goal, but they appear communicative only because of the mother's reaction to them. means ——→ end	Communicative behaviors appear to be directed toward the object or the mother's hand as if to "set them into motion" (see Piaget, 1954). means ————→ end	Communicative behaviors are directed at mother's eyes and patterns of behaviors (such as looking back and forth between object and mother) and indicate that communication has become a goal in itself and is used as a way of contacting another and enlisting her help. means ←— communication —→ end	
Infant performs procedures, such as kicking, banging on table, and vocalizing.	Infant uses communicative behaviors as way of achieving object directly or as a tool to get what he wants (e.g., moving Mom's hand toward toy).	Communicative behaviors directed at mother's eyes and toy.	Communication occurs between infant and mother.
Mother gives him toy or whatever she thinks he wants.	Mother may give him the toy if that's what he thinks he wants.		Mother gets toy for infant or infant tries alternative behaviors.

aReprinted from Harding (1982B).

ing, looking, or reaching (cf. Argyle, 1972; Cherry, 1978; Duncan, 1972), but that are not necessarily used with the intention to communicate. Predictions about changes in these behaviors were based on a developmental model of intention proposed by Harding (1982b). This model, based on a description of intentional behavior presented by Ryan (1970) and related to Miller, Galanter, and Pribram's (1960) classic work on planned behavior, proposes that intention develops in a sequence of three components: (a) awareness of a goal; (b) development of a plan for achieving the goal; and (c) development of coordinated plans involving alternative plans and intermediary goals. A fourth component, persistence, is assumed to occur throughout the development of the other three, dependent on the level of behaviors available.

Table 1 outlines the predicted changes in communicative behaviors and the components of intention theorized as accounting for each level of behavior. Table 1 also outlines the cognitive abilities (based on Piaget, 1954) predicted to relate to each level of development (Harding, 1981; Harding & Golinkoff, 1979).

In addition to the cognitive relationships outlined in Table 1, it was predicted that others' interpretations (particularly mothers' interpretations) of behaviors as communicative would relate to changes in acting with intention. As Anscombe (1957) argued, it is not only within the act itself that intention exists as a basis for behavior, but also in others' interpretations of the act. It was hypothesized that mothers' interpretations of their infants' use of communicative behaviors, particularly mothers' inferences of intention in the infants' actions, would relate to both the mothers' actions toward the infants and to the infants' developing ability to act with intention. Cross-cultural research (Schieffelin, in press) indicates that mothers' inferences about their infants' behaviors may be culture-specific rather than species-specific. However, the hypothesis of mothers' inferences affecting infants' intentions remains plausible, and cultural differences may support rather than refute this hypothesis. Perhaps the evidence that some mothers, for example the Kaluli mothers observed by Schieffelin, do not infer intention, at least not as Western mothers do, may relate to observable cultural differences in later language use. The positing of such a relationship would, of course, require empirical substantiation. In any event, the findings from the study reported here are not assumed to necessarily represent universal patterns.

Twelve infants and their mothers were observed at monthly intervals in both home and laboratory settings over a period of five months beginning when the infants were approximately 6 months old. This time period was predicted to include critical changes in the ability to act intentionally (Bruner, 1973; Piaget, 1954). In addition to the home and laboratory observations, the mothers kept weekly diaries describing their interpretations of changes in their infants' behaviors (see Harding, 1981).

As displayed in Table 2, the data indicated that there were developmental changes in the intentional use of communicative behaviors, and that the ability to communicate developed according to the predicted sequence and was related to performance on Piagetian cognitive tasks (see Harding, 1981). The discussion

TABLE 2
Performance on Cognitive Tasks and Predicted Communication Level[a]

Observed Level of Communication Development	Lower than Stage 3: No Means–end Sequencing	Stage 3: Means–end Knowledge	Stage 4: Knowledge of Object Causality	Stage 5: Knowledge of Causal Agency	Knowledge of Using New Means
Procedures (Level 1)	A-1[b]	B-1 C-1			
Communicative Behaviors Directed at Toy or Mother's Hand (Level 2)			D-1 E-1 F-1 H-1	G-1[c]	A-2[c] C-2[c] A-3[c] C-3[c]
Intentional Gestures (Level 3)				J-1 I-1 K-1 K-2 K-3	E-2[c] F-2[c] H-2[c] F-3[c] H-3[c]
Intentional Vocalizations (Level 4)				L-1[b] B-2 D-2 E-3 G-2 I-2 I-3	J-2 L-2 B-3 D-3 J-3 L-3

[a] Observed relationships between cognitive and communicative development at three different ages for each infant: Time 1: X = 5.8 months; Time 2: X age = 8.3 months; Time 3: X age = 10 months. Each observation is labeled as to infant identification letter and time of observation (e.g., A-1 refers to infant A observed at Time 1). Predicted relationships fall on the diagonal.
[b] Observed performance above predicted performance.
[c] Observed performance below predicted performance.

below summarizes the relationships found between the development of the intention to communicate and cognitive ability and describes the apparent role of the mother as the interpreter of intention.

It was observed, as predicted, that at about 6 months of age (or during Stage 3 in sensorimotor development), at least some infants were beginning to develop schemes which would reproduce interesting events in the environment (i.e., secondary circular reactions as described in Piaget, 1954). It appeared that at first these infants did nothing more than differentiate between means and ends; they learned that certain events lead to others. Global body movements consisting of undifferentiated behaviors at this point in development were used to cause desired events to last (Piaget, 1954, described these movements as "procedures," see pp. 167–271). These global movements appeared to be unorganized means for making things happen and there was little difference in the infants' behaviors in either social or nonsocial situations. This level of communicative development was identified as representing pre-intentionally communicative behavior. The infants appeared aware of a goal (Component 1 of the proposed model), but did not use behaviors in any coordinated fashion and demonstrated neither an instrumental attempt to achieve the toy nor a signal that it was wanted. It appeared that the infants were aware of something they wanted and initiated a global state of activity that led to the achievement of the goal either by coincidence or, more often, through the mothers' action. At this point, the infants may have been aware of one goal of communication, that is, they may have wanted social contact, but this study provided no evidence (and based on the cognitive abilities during Stage 3 there had been no prediction) that behaviors would be used in an intentional way to initiate social contact or to continue interactions.

Although the mothers acted on most of the infants' behaviors, over time the mothers' interpretations and reactions changed (see Table 3). As their infants began to use instrumental behaviors for achieving goals (Piagetian Stage 4), mothers appeared to adjust their behaviors, perhaps based on their interpretations of the infants' increasing abilities (cf. Kaye, 1977). They began to both interpret and react most often to certain behaviors, particularly the conventional communicative behaviors of reaching, eye contact, and vocalizing, and began encouraging their use as communicative behaviors.

During Stage 4 when the infants directed behaviors at instrumentally achieving a goal (Component 2 of the model), the mothers' behaviors continued to occur as a necessary although unsolicited part of achieving the goal. It appeared, as Newson (1978) pointed out, that "in the course of repeated encounters," the mother's behaviors began to "impart to the infant's actions a sense of coherence and goal-directedness which they would not otherwise have" (p. 39). Only as infants became more organized in interpreting the environment (i.e., as they began to sequence

TABLE 3
Behaviors Interpreted as Communicative by Mothers
(listed according to the infants' age at time of report in mothers' diaries)

6 Months	7 Months	8 Months	9 Months	10 Months
Crying (7)[a]	Listening (6)	Associating consequences with words (usually "no") (8)	Waving (12)	Associating own actions with words (11)
Shrieking (4)	Whining (7)		Responding to specific words with correct action (6)	
Fake cough (3)	"Da da" (7)			Using words (7)
Procedures (usually described as occurring to continue a game) (6)	Imitating noises (7)	Babbling (7)		Using words for communication (4)
	Reaching (7)	Active participation in games (12)	Using words and/or gestures with eye contact (7)	
Eye contact during social contact (4)	Screaming (4)	Expectant waiting (3)	Pointing (2)	
Smiling (8)		Eye contact with vocalizations (5)		
Laughing (4)				
Making noises (7)		Using sounds with consistent meaning (5)		
Looking (3)				

[a] (n) = number of mothers reporting behavior.

events and recognize causal agents, Stage 5 behaviors as assessed through cognitive tasks), did they also come to recognize the mother's role in the achievement of goals and the potential of using her as a means.

However, it is not clear from the data whether infants first recognized the mother as a potential agent and then learned how to communicate with her, or whether they first learned the signal value of their behaviors and then figured out to what or whom these behaviors must be directed. Both sequences were observed. Some infants, as had been predicted, appeared to recognize that certain behaviors, particularly eye contact, vocalizing, and reaching, served to activate the mother and directed these behaviors toward her as intentional communication. Other infants, in contrast, appeared only to recognize that their behaviors operated as means to make things happen, and they directed their behaviors toward the desired object as if signaling to it. For example, some infants were observed vocalizing toward the toy they wanted in much the same way they later vocalized toward their mothers. At least for some infants, it appeared that the means for communicating (i.e., the ability to signal with intention), developed prior to the recognition that signaling only works when an animate being responds to it. It is interesting that, even though it is the mother's behaviors which consistently follow the infant's behavior and make the achievement of the goal happen, some infants (at least initially) did not appear to notice the essential role the mother played and instead only connected their own behaviors with the successful outcome.

Once the infants had begun to coordinate their behaviors as signals to the mother in the achievement of goals, alternative plans for communication were developed (Component 3 of the model). As would be expected, the first behaviors used for signaling developed from earlier instrumental behaviors, such as reaching, and only later were vocalizations used. As shown in Table 2, the intentional use of vocalizations was related to performance on Stage 5 cognitive tasks demonstrating the ability to use new means for achieving goals.

Mothers again played a role in the development of vocalizations as communicative behaviors. Mothers not only responded most often to vocalizations, they also used verbal responses and comments as they interacted communicatively with their infants. The infants' recognition of the effects of their own vocalizations probably developed first through the recognition of connections, mediated and carried out by the mothers, between the infants' vocalizations and goal achievement. With the development of the ability to intentionally use vocalizations as signals, the base appears to be established for the development of language as a conventional communication code (see Harding, in press).

Developmental Mechanisms

This study investigated developmental change in the intention to communicate. The investigation of change requires at least the consideration of how that change might occur. In a review of Lock (1978), Atkinson (1980) emphasized the problem that few discussions of preverbal communication development address developmental mechanisms. Atkinson (1980) questioned specifically the interactive process this study supports:

> How does the mother acting as if the child had an intention manufacture such an intention? . . . the main social factor, as far as the development of communication is concerned, is the adult's interpretation of the child's actions as communicative, resulting in the development of intentional structures, but, again, we are offered no insight as to how this is achieved. (pp. 580–581)

Atkinson concluded that the difficulty of discussing developmental mechanisms, at least for the theorists and researchers represented in Lock's (1978) collection,

> emerges from a general failure of approaches adopting "social relations" as a central theoretical construct to say anything clear about the causal role of such notions. (Atkinson, 1980, p. 580)

The study reported in this chapter differs from those reviewed by Atkinson. The central theoretical construct is cognitive development. The infant's cognitive construction of the world is assumed to be basic to social relations and, as Piaget (1971) posited, the developing cognitive structures are assumed to set the parameters within which the environment is known and acted on at any given time. The infant's ability to act in social interactions (e.g., to communicate) is therefore dependent on his level of cognitive development.

In the present study, cognitive level was found to be related to communication development. In fact, specific cognitive abilities were found to precede the development of the related communicative behaviors. In addressing Atkinson's question ("How does the mother acting as if the child had an intention manufacture such an intention?"), the observation that cognitive abilities preceded communication development indicates that the infant's ability to (a) separate events into means–end sequences, (b) recognize causal sequences, and (c) use himself and others as causal agents, provides the means through which the infant begins to recognize the regularity of the causal sequencing of his own behavior and the mother's behavior.

Within the framework of the proposed model of the development of intention, the infant's use of communicative behaviors changes from unorganized to instrumental to intentional because of both his developing cognitive structures and the mother's interpretation and reaction to what she infers as intentional behaviors. As the infant attempts to achieve goals, the mother's behaviors form a consistent part of the means–end pattern. However, as the infant's behavior becomes more organized, the mother appears to become less omniscient in carrying out her role and more specific in her requirements of the infant. By keeping pace with and apparently in advance of the infant's developing cognitive abilities, the mother provides the environment necessary for development, that is, an environment conducive to change (Harding, 1982a).

In his classic treatise on equilibration, Langer (1969) described the process of change as follows:

The child is an active operator whose actions are the prime generator of his own psychological development. When he is in a relatively equilibrated state, he will not tend to change; he will only change if he feels, consciously or unconsciously, that something is wrong. This means that both affective and organizational disequilibrium are necessary conditions for development. (p. 36)

The developmental question, according to Langer, is: "In what way he [the child] is able to assimilate a given type of perturbation at successive stages of development—to recognize that it is a perturbation and that something is wrong" (p. 36).

It appears that the mother's behaviors may both set up the perturbation and prepare the infant for the recognition of it as being something wrong. Her behaviors initially allow the infant's behaviors to become goal-directed (i.e., as the infant becomes cognitively aware of goals, the mother makes his early attempts at goal achievement successful). As the infant operates with more organization, she continues to participate in the achievement of goals. By inferring intent and reacting to his behavior consistently, she orders the infant's behavior in the world. However, the mother appears to anticipate her infant's cognitive abilities (perhaps by reading early signs of transition) and begins to alter her supporting role by requiring more specific behaviors from her infant before she will act. By altering the environment, she sets up the perturbation required for development. This perturbation occurs for both the means–end sequences the infant has cognitively organized and the affective organization of the social context to which he is adapted (see, for example, MacMurray's 1961 discussion of the adaptiveness of the infant's "complete dependence upon an adult human being," p. 48). It is proposed that this disequilibrium brought about within the communicative context of the mother–infant interaction, provides the necessary conditions for, in Langer's (1969) words, "the energetic or emotional force for change in action to be activated" (p. 36). The infant changes his actions and, through the observed sequence of developmental levels, begins to communicate.

CONCLUSION

There is nothing magical about the mother's inference of intention leading to the development of intention in the infant. Rather, her inference influences her behaviors; she acts consistently and contingently on the infant's behaviors, allowing the infant's developing cognitive abilities to operate on and organize an ordered environment. Then the mother's inferences about the infant's increasing abilities appear to lead her to alter her role, thereby setting up a perturbation in the infant's environment. The infant recognizes the violation of both his cognitive knowledge of the world and the social context he is adapted to and reorganizes his behavior.

Although this description is clearly an over-simplification and must be taken in the speculative spirit in which it is presented, it is an attempt to at least address the question of what might account for the changes in communication observed in this study. It is proposed that the issue of developmental mechanisms provide the impetus and direction of future research.

REFERENCES

Anscombe, G. E. M. *Intention.* Oxford: Basil Blackwell, 1957.

Argyle, M. Non-verbal communication in human social interaction. In R. A. Hinde (Ed.), *Non-verbal communication.* London: Cambridge University Press, 1972.

Atkinson, M. Review of A. Lock (Ed.), Action, gesture and symbol. *Journal of Child Language,* 1980, 7, 579–590.

Bates, E. *Language and context: The acquisition of pragmatics.* New York: Academic Press, 1976.

Bruner, J. S. Competence in infants. In J. S. Bruner (Ed.), *Beyond the information given: Studies in the psychology of knowing.* New York: Norton, 1973.

Cazden, C. B. The question of intent. In M. Lewis & L. A. Rosenblum (Eds.), *Interaction, conversation, and the development of language.* New York: Wiley, 1977.

Cherry, C. *On human communication: A review, a survey, and a criticism.* Cambridge, MA: MIT Press, 1978.

Duncan, S. D., Jr. Some signals and rules for taking speaking turns in conversation. *Journal of Personality and Social Psychology,* 1972, 23, 283–292.

Harding, C. G. A longitudinal study of the development of the intention to communicate. Unpublished doctoral dissertation, Univ. of Delaware, 1981.

Harding, C. G. Mechanisms for developmental change in communication. Paper presented at the Third International Conference on Infant Studies, Austin, Texas, March, 1982. (a)

Harding, C. G. The development of the intention to communicate. *Human Development,* 1982, 25, 140–151. (b)

Harding, C. G. Setting the stage for language acquisition: Communicative and cognitive development in the first year. In R. Golinkoff (Ed.), *The transition from implications.* Hillsdale, NJ: Erlbaum, in press.

Harding, C. G., & Golinkoff, R. M. The origins of intentional vocalizations in prelinguistic infants. *Child Development,* 1979, 50, 33–40.

Kaye, K. Toward the origin of dialogue. In H. R. Schaffer (Ed.), *Studies in mother–infant interaction.* New York: Academic Press, 1977.

Langer, J. Disequilibrium as a source of development. In P. Mussen, J. Langer, & M. Covington (Eds.), *Trends and issues in developmental psychology.* New York: Holt, Rinehart & Winston, 1969.

Lock, A. (Ed.). *Action, gesture and symbol: The emergence of language.* New York: Academic Press, 1978.

Locke, J. *Essay concerning human understanding,* 1690.

MacMurray, J. *Persons in relation.* London: Faber & Faber, 1961.

Miller, G., Galanter, E., & Pribram, K. *Plans and the structure of behavior.* New York: Holt, Rinehart & Winston, 1960.

Newson, J. The growth of shared understandings between infant and caregiver. In M. Bullowa (Ed.), *Before speech: The beginning of interpersonal communication.* London: Cambridge University Press, 1978.

Piaget, J. *The construction of reality of the child.* New York: Ballatine, 1954.

Piaget, J. *Biology and knowledge.* Chicago: University of Chicago Press, 1971.

Ryan, T. A. *Intentional behavior: An approach to human motivation.* New York: Ronald Press, 1970.

Schieffelin, B. Cross-cultural perspectives on the transition: What difference do the differences make? In R. Golinkoff (Ed.), *The transition from prelinguistic communication: Issues and implications.* Hillsdale, NJ: Erlbaum, in press.

Shotter, J. The cultural context of communication studies: Theoretical and methodological issues. In A.

Lock (Ed.), *Action, gesture, and symbol: The emergence of language.* New York: Academic Press, 1978.

Sugarman, S. The development of preverbal communication: Its contribution and limits in promoting the development of language. In R. L. Schiefelbusch & J. Picker (Eds.), *Communicative competence: Acquisition and intervention.* Baltimore: University Park Press, in press.

Wilson, E. O. *Sociobiology: The new synthesis.* Cambridge, MA: The Belknap Press of Harvard University Press, 1975.

CHAPTER 7

Interaction, Engagement, and the Origins and Growth of Communication: Some Constructive Concerns*

Alan Hayes

The eras of an intellectual discipline are delineated by sets of central questions, each of which is yoked to a preferred method of inquiry.
Kagan, Kearsley, & Zelazo (1978, p. 1)

THE EMERGENCE OF INTEREST IN SOCIAL INTERACTION IN INFANCY

The Concept of Interaction and the Development of Communication

A series of questions central to contemporary developmental psychology could be summarized in the following form: "How does the capacity for social interaction develop, and what are the implications of social interaction and socialization processes for human development?" The study of social interaction in infancy has assumed central importance in the study of the origins and growth of communication.

* I am pleased to acknowledge the assistance of several people. First, Jacqueline Goodnow and John Murray, my doctoral advisors, for their encouragement, enthusiasm, and gentle criticism of earlier versions of this chapter. I am similarly grateful to my colleagues at the Fred and Eleanor Schonell Educational Research Centre, University of Queensland, for their critical responses to the ideas presented in the chapter. It is, however, to the faculty members and my fellow participants in the Institute on the Origins and Growth of Communication, University of Delaware, 1979, that I extend a particular note of thanks. The many discussions, debates and discourses made the Institute an academic and personal

The term interaction implies a fundamentally reciprocal action, and *action presupposes occurrence in time*. It is therefore not surprising that the description of the temporal course of social interactions has been of considerable interest. Interest in social interaction actually predates development of the technology for recording its temporal dimensions. At the turn of the century, Georg Simmel stated that the central concern of sociology should be the phenomenon of interaction (Kendon, 1975). The term "interaction" is, in fact, Wolff's translation of the German word *Wechselwirkung*, which in essence means "reciprocal effect" or "reciprocal orientation" (Collins & Collins, 1973). Simmel, for example, discussed such topics as the significance of mutual gaze and other forms of interactive behavior (Kendon, 1975), topics which became central to later investigations of social interaction. Simmel's work had a direct influence on the Chicago school of descriptive sociology and the influential symbolic interactionism movement (Kendon, 1975).

Within the Chicago school, George Herbert Mead (1934) developed two themes of particular relevance to the contemporary discussion of social interaction. The first is essentially a recognition of the importance of the intersubjective nature of social interaction:

> We find no evidence for the prior existence of consciousness as something which brings about behavior on the part of one organism that is of such a sort as to call forth an adjustive response on the part of another organism, without itself being dependent on such behavior. We are rather forced to conclude that *consciousness is an emergent from such behavior;* that so far from being a precondition of the social act, the social act is the precondition of it. (Mead, 1934, p. 18, italics added)

However, Mead continued:

> The mechanism of the social act can be traced without introducing into it the conception of consciousness as a separable element within that act; hence the social act, in its most elementary stages or forms, is possible without, or apart from some form of consciousness. (p. 18)

The latter quote embodies Mead's notion of *Social Behaviorism,* and his focus on the importance of studying the behaviors of interaction. The second, and related theme, concerns the importance of the "conversation of gestures":

> Language is a part of social behavior. There are an indefinite number of signs or symbols which may serve the purpose of what we term "language." We are reading the meaning of the conduct of other people when, perhaps, they are not aware of it.

experience of inestimable value. The Institute excited, inspired, and challenged me in many ways, and marked the inception of many of the ideas expressed in this chapter. The magnanimous support of the Carnegie Foundation and the Society for Research in Child Development is most gratefully acknowledged. With that support, distance for one Australian became a little less tyrannous. The material presented in this chapter formed part of a Ph.D. thesis submitted to Macquarie University in December, 1980, and undertaken with the generous support of the New South Wales Department of Education and the Australian Postgraduate Research Awards Scheme. The manuscript was prepared with the support of the facilities of the University of Queensland and the expertise of Mrs. Sannie Pritchard.

There is something that reveals to us what the purpose is in just the glance of an eye, the attitude of the body which leads to the response. The communication set up in this way between individuals may be very perfect. Conversation in gestures may be carried on which cannot be translated into articulate speech. (Mead, 1934, pp. 13–14)

For Mead, communication involved much more than just language. Kendon provides a contemporary corollary: "language does not NEED speech" (Kendon, 1975, p. 13). In other words there are important, nonverbal, aspects of communication that convey intention and meaning, and perform the functions of language without speech. Communication can accordingly be seen to involve gaze, physical proximity, bodily contact, bodily orientation and movement, gestures, head nods, facial expressions, appearance, nonlinguistic and paralinguistic aspects of speech, as well as speech itself (Argyle, 1972). Further, while nonverbal communication emerged as a field of study in its own right (Argyle, 1972; Duncan, 1969), it was also recognized that nonverbal channels were integrally related to language. In Kendon's (1975) words, "If one looks, for example, at how the voice operates in interaction it quickly becomes obvious that the traditional boundary between language and paralanguage cannot be sustained" (p. 13).

For Mead (1934), language arises out of the process in which "an attitude of one individual . . . calls out a response in the other, which in turn calls out a different approach and a different response, and so on indefinitely" (p. 14). This passage clearly underscores the need to study organization of the *turns* of communicative behavior occurring within an interaction. Such temporal dependencies between the aspects of communication both within an individual and between interacting individuals have assumed central importance in the study of social interaction since Simmel's and Mead's work.

Conversation, Dialogue, and the Regulation of Turns

The metaphor of interaction as conversation or dialogue has exerted a powerful influence since Mead's initial formulation. Jaffe and Feldstein's *Rhythms of Dialogue* (1970) was a landmark in the study of the temporal structure of conversation. This work underscores the fundamental importance of dialogue to language acquisition: "No human has ever learned to speak except in a dialogic context, so to this extent the ability to speak presupposes a prior conversation" (Jaffe & Feldstein, 1970, p. 5). Jaffe and Feldstein concluded that conversations have a formal structure in time with invariant mathematical properties. Their analyses also pointed to the existence of both stable characteristics of speakers and variable characteristics that served as "sensitive indicators" of the interaction. Social contexts appeared to modify the characteristics of the dialogue systematically according to the social content of interaction. Jaffe and Feldstein also observed a tendency for conversationalists to match pause lengths. They concluded that the alternation of speaker and listener roles in the dialogue is a neurophysiologically based linguistic universal resulting from the limits of information processing in the human nervous system.

Finally, they successfully modeled the data as a stochastic Markov chain with strong interdependence *between* the conversationalists and proposed that:

> (a) It is possible, and may be profitable, to entertain the notion of a set of "rules" which underlie what might be termed "interactional skill"; and (b) at least several of such "rules" are the necessary consequences of the finite information processing capacities of the neural apparatus. (p. 6)

Following Jaffe and Feldstein's work, turn-taking mechanisms and the organizational rules of conversation have been extensively studied. For example, Kendon (1967) made the important discovery that gaze regulates the flow of conversation and the exchange of speaker and auditor roles. Duncan (1972, 1973; Duncan & Niederehe, 1974) has also devoted considerable attention to describing "the mechanism by which participants in a dyadic conversation effected the smooth exchange of speaking turns" (1973, p. 30). Content of the dialogue, syntax, interaction, paralanguage, and body motion were found to act as signals governing the yielding of the floor by the speaker (Duncan, 1972). In later work, Duncan and Niederehe (1974) also found that auditors employ particular signals (speaker state signals) to register their desire to take the floor.

Overall, the taking of turns in conversation appears to be a universal characteristic of language use (Miller, 1963, cited by Duncan & Niederehe, 1974). It is not surprising, then, that the structure of dialogue has emerged as a vital dimension of the problem of how behaviors are mutually integrated over time (Schaffer, 1979).

Mother–Infant Interactions as Prelinguistic Conversations

Several authors have referred to the "conversational" structure of the prelinguistic exchanges of mothers and infants and to what appears to be "turn taking" in the verbal and nonverbal aspects of the interaction (Brazelton, Koslowski, & Main, 1974; Freedle & Lewis, 1977; Newson, 1974, 1977; Newson & Newson, 1975; Schaffer, 1974; Snow, 1977; Trevarthen, 1977). The precise ordering of the responses of mother and infant gives many interactions the appearance of "well-practiced games" (Bell, 1971). Not only does the interaction give the appearance of a dialogue, but the mother regards the infant's act as meaningful and intentional communicative gestures (Newson, 1974).

The acquisition of the ability to take turns and engage in preverbal dialogue has, in fact, come to be viewed as essential to language development:

> Timing is crucial in the effect of any feedback—reinforcing, comparative or corrective—upon learning. Thus dialogue ought to be acquired or built into the system first so that the specifics of language, object manipulation, social ritual or whatever can then be learned efficiently. Put this way, we can think of dialogue as a necessary context for language acquisition as well as other kinds of learning, and we would be inclined to pursue any phenomenon in early infancy which bears a resemblance to dialogue. (Kaye, 1977, p. 94)

The pursuit of dialoguelike phenomena has included examination of the burst-pause structure of infant sucking during feeding (Kaye, 1977), the coupling of mother–infant gaze (Jaffe, Stern, & Peery, 1973), and the organization of aggregated measures of dialogic behavior (Bakeman & Brown, 1977).

The synchronization of mother and infant behaviors has been a related topic of interest. Newson and Newson (1975) state that "the infant's action sequences are temporally organized so that they can mesh—with a high degree of precision—with similar patterns of action produced by his human caretaker" (p. 440). An influential, although somewhat controversial, study by Condon and Sander (1974) has proposed "a complex interaction system in which the organization of the neonate's motor behavior is entrained by and synchronized with the organized speech behavior of adults in his environment" (p. 101).

It has become commonplace to talk of both the reciprocity and temporal enmeshing of the behaviors of mother and infant. Nonetheless, the extent to which the infant does play a reciprocal role remains to be determined. Is the infant a naturally skilled conversationalist as Newson and Newson (1975) suggest, or are the enmeshed sequences "pseudo-dialogues" (Schaffer, 1979) or "proto-conversations" (Bateson, 1975)?

Reciprocity: Conflicting Interpretations

One of the major changes in the study of infant development in recent years has been an increasing tendency to attribute to the infant the capacity to participate reciprocally in interactions with the surrounding physical and psychological environment. While this trend has been widely acknowledged, the infant's role in interaction is still subject to equivocal interpretations. For example, Trevarthen (1977) has argued that it is the infant who calls the tune in interaction with the mother:

> The communications which we obtain are rich enough in structure to establish that human infants are endowed with a specialized mechanism for human behavioural exchange and that their expressions may exercise a powerful control influence over those of an adult partner when the infant is no more than eight weeks of age. (p. 238)

Further, Trevarthen states that:

> in the communication behaviour of infants 6–12 weeks of age the pattern of action is normally sustained by the mother following and complementing the infant's acts at particular points . . . This is not to say that the infant is not dependent on social stimulation and making precise demands on the mother's acts. (p. 238)

In contrast, Schaffer (1974) accepts the general proposition that the infant is the initiator of many behavioral sequences but, in common with several other researchers (for example Kaye, 1977; Newson, 1977; Whiten, 1977), ascribes the dialoguelike character of the interaction to the mother's skill in *creating* the impression of conversation: "The mother thus allows herself to be paced by the infant. She fills in the pauses between his response bursts, and to do so successfully she needs, of course, sensitivity and an exquisite sense of timing" (Schaffer, 1977, p. 12). The difference between the two positions is a subtle, but fundamental one. It is encapsulated in Trevarthen's use of the phrase "making precise demands on the mother's acts" and his stated belief in the "mutuality" of the developing interaction. For example, in discussing differences between dyads, Trevarthen (1977) states "we gained a clear impression that each mother–infant dyad was developing a different style of mutual activity" (p. 259). His position is explicitly summarized in the following quote:

> I believe a correct description of this behaviour, to capture its full complexity, must be in terms of mutual intentionality and sharing of mental state. Either partner may initiate a "display" or "act of expression" and both act to sustain a sharing and exchange of initiatives. Both partners express complex purposive impulses in a form that is infectious for the other. (Trevarthen, 1977, p. 241)

Trevarthen is not the only author to suggest that dyadic interaction is mutually regulated and to provoke questions about the degree of mutuality. Tronick, Als, and Brazelton (1977), for example, posit mutuality on the basis of analyzing the running correlations between scaled scores of the involvement of mother and infant in interaction. Such a relationship, however, while fascinating, is not sufficient evidence of a contingent link between the mother and infant processes. Jaffe et al. (1973) present data demonstrating that infant gaze has a first order Markov chain structure identical to the Markovity present in the temporal structure of the utterances in adult conversation, and on the basis of this evidence conclude that a common communicational structure is present. But to what extent are the interactions of prelinguistic infants "conversational," "reciprocal," or "mutual"? Implicit in the use of such terms is a notion of interdependence. Such terms imply, in the strongest sense, a strict contingency between the acts of each partner. In less extreme interpretations, to be reciprocal the behavior of each must at least be conditional upon the behavior of the other (Thomas & Martin, 1976). The latter position is consistent with the definition of communication commonly employed by information theorists:

> Communication has been defined as the process by which behavior of one individual alters the probability of behavioral acts in other individuals. . . . In words, the conditional probability that act X_3 will be performed by individual B given that A performed X_1 is not equal to the probability that B will perform X_2 in the absence of X_1. (Wilson, 1975, p. 194)

The demonstration of sequential connectedness of the behavior of mother and infant is a fundamental theoretical issue. If such mutual connectedness can be demonstrated in very young infants, then much of the current theory in cognitive

development will require fundamental revision to account for this important precocity. If, on the other hand, the temporal patterning is coincidental, that is, reflecting the concurrence of events without bidirectional causal connections, then the
proposition that the infant responds contingently may not be a necessary element in
a theory of the development of human communication.

The results emerging from a number of projects suggest that for behaviors like
gaze and vocalization there is sufficient evidence to reject the hypothesis that the
interactions are completely coincidental (see, for example, Hayes & Elliott,
1979;Hayes, 1980; Penman, Friedman, & Meares, 1978). However, at the same
time there is not enough evidence of sequential dependency to say that they are
"conversational," in any strongly contingent sense. Rather, the dependence of the
mother's vocal activation, for example, indicates that she at least *regards* the
interaction as a dialogue, and acts as if her infant were a reciprocating, conversational partner. As Snow (1977) has concluded, the 3-month-old's mother *imposes*
the rules of conversation upon the interaction, rules of which her infant is yet
unaware.

The Role of Chance in the Structuring
of the Patterns of Dyadic Interaction

The dangers of too quickly interpreting patterns of dyadic results as evidence of
reciprocity, without establishing that individual processes are, in fact, sequentially
dependent are becoming increasingly recognized. Recently, Rutter, Stephenson,
Lazzerini, Ayling, and White (1977) presented data which correlated the eye contact data reported in six studies of adult dyadic interactions, with the eye contact
scores predicted to occur by chance alone. Rutter et al. found that the observed and
predicted results were highly correlated, with the relationship explaining at least
97% of the variability. In a further test of the chance hypothesis, Lazzerini, Stephenson, and Neave (1978) computer-simulated the chance occurrences of mutual
eye contact. They found that the frequency and duration of simulated eye contact
from the random simulations were not significantly different from the frequency and
durational data obtained from the records of "real" interactions.

Hayes has indicated that apparent evidence of reciprocity in the facial gaze and
vocalization components of mother–infant interactions may be, in part, the result of
the coincidental pattern of juxtaposition of two processes with fundamentally different temporal structures (Hayes & Elliott, 1979; Hayes, 1980). This is not to suggest, however, that important regularities in dyadic interaction cannot underlie these
apparent coincidences. For both facial gaze and vocalization the interactions are
asymmetrical, a fact which suggests that the gross adaptation of the mother's
interactive behavior when with her infant, provides the redundancy necessary to
ensure the continuance of the interaction. But even more importantly the interaction
continues in a form which provides the infant with important information about the
structure of visual and vocal communication (Anderson, 1977; Hayes, 1978). Mu-

tual facial gaze and nonoverlapping vocalization have fundamental significance for human communication, and the mother seems determined to structure her interactive behavior in a way which maximizes the opportunities for her infant to acquire these basic communicational rules.

The Necessity of Strict Molecular Dependence Questioned

In the discussion of Trevarthen's (1977) interpretations of the infant's role in interaction, presented earlier in this chapter, it was noted that such a position, if validated, had considerable implications for theories of infant development. Such a position has not yet obtained unequivocal support.

MOTHER–INFANT INTERACTION: A MISNOMER?

Interaction or Engagement?

A growing body of evidence, in fact, leads one to question *the extent to which the actions of mothers and infants are reciprocal.* And if their reciprocity is in question, then the legitimacy of the use of the term interaction is also debatable. Interaction was defined above as implying a fundamentally reciprocal action. But to what extent do the behaviors of mothers and infants meet the necessary condition of this definition?

The term *engagement* perhaps provides a better characterization of the dyadic facial gaze and vocal activity (Hayes, 1980). While reciprocity is a necessary condition for interaction to occur, it is not necessary for engagement. The necessary condition for engagement is that the two sets of acts, entities, or structures are, in some way, connected or joined. Connection can result from the actions of one or the other or both of the engaging parties. It is only in the last circumstance—a junction resulting from the actions of both parties—that the engagement may become an interaction.

Engagement,[1] when used in the sense of connection, has a number of mechanistic connotations that are not necessarily implied in the current use of the term, engagement, to describe social phenomena in infancy. Unlike the engagement of clutches or cog wheels, social engagement does not necessarily imply precise synchronization and continuous connection. Rather, mother–infant engagement in early infancy is a tenuous process, with considerable scope for slippage. In further contrast to mechanical metaphors of engagement, the engaging structures are not fixed in form, but are developmentally dynamic. A more appropriate metaphor for social engagement may be the bringing into phase of two wave forms, by the modification of one

---

[1] The term engagement as it will be defined here, is not to be confused with use of it (Stern, Beebe, Jaffe, & Bennett, 1977) in defining the unit, episode of mutual engagement (EME).

wave, relative to the essentially unpredictable changes in the form of the second wave. However, the processes of synchronization or phase alignment are at a higher level, parts of the more general process of "engaging" an immature human being in a set of social contexts; the infant being, at least in early infancy, an unwitting partner.

This leads to the second issue. It will be argued that in early infancy the phase of engagement provides the foundation for the later development of dyadic interaction and linguistic communication. Specifically, it will be asserted that the early engagements of mother and infant have important structural similarities to later phases of social development. A growing body of research evidence suggests that after approximately 6 months of age, infants begin to demonstrate the capacity to participate in complex reciprocal games (Bruner, 1977; Sander, 1975). Also at about this time the first manifestations of social attachment behavior start to appear (Ainsworth, 1969; Ainsworth, Bell, & Stayton, 1974; Bowlby, 1971). However, it seems that patterns of behavior, similar to later interaction and attachment, are present in the dyadic engagements of the first six months of the infant's postnatal life. These patterns are, it is argued, essentially imposed on the engagement by the mother.

The Structural Features of Social Engagements

The dyadic facial gaze and vocal engagements are characterized by two major features. First, the contributions of mother and infant are not symmetrical; mothers spend more time looking at, and vocalizing to, their infants than their infants spend looking at, and vocalizing to them. Rheingold (1966) commented upon this fact:

> The amount of attention and the number of responses directed to the infant are enormous—out of all proportion to his age, size and accomplishments. Under ordinary circumstances, in any human group containing an infant, the attention directed towards him is usually considerable. (p. 12)

Second, the engagements often have the appearance of dialogues. The pattern of dependence evident in the mother's vocal behavior seems to be directed to minimizing vocal overlap, and thereby maintaining vocal alternation.

Both features raise questions about the transition to later development. Before communication can occur, a problem of coordination must be solved (Keenan, 1974). The problem can be succinctly summarized in these terms "to interact effectively, they (the interactants) need to share not only a linguistic code, but also a code of conduct. That is to say, interlocutors need to establish a loose set of conversational conventions" (Keenan, 1974, p. 165). The concept of conversational conventions parallels the broader "mappings" of interaction, or the cultural patterns of ideas about how persons should "act" in relation to others, described by Collins and Collins (1973, p. 148). The early dyadic engagements provide the infant with the first contact with the set of conversational conventions that will circumscribe later communication in the culture to which s/he belongs.

Similarly, according to Bullowa (1975), the key problem of early communication is one of synchronization:

> Let me state the problem: the neonate lives in his own time domain while his caretakers live in theirs. . . . In order for an infant to survive and to come into communication with caretaking adults, infant and adult must somehow come to synchronize their behaviors so that communication and interaction between them can occur and develop. (p. 95)

At least in the first three months of life this process occurs as a result of the mother adapting her timing to the infant's, while at the same time imposing the rules of conversation upon the engagement (Snow, 1977). So, until the infant develops the capacity to reciprocate, the mother must synchronize her behavior with the spontaneous activity of her infant (Schaffer, 1979). The earliest examples of this synchronization are evident in the feeding engagements of mother and infant. Kaye (1977) concludes that "the smooth alternation of turns comes about, when it does come about, by the mother's accommodating her turns to the temporal organization imposed by the infant" (p. 109).

At the level of the actions of both partners, the direction of influence is made from infant to mother, by virtue of the mother's accommodation to her infant. However, the mother influences her infant's behavior inasmuch as she defines the behavioral situations and settings for the infant. Bidirectionality of effects, therefore, operates at two different levels. As Cairns (1977) suggests, for much of infancy and childhood "the mother (or other caretakers) nonetheless determines what kinds of initiations the child can make, and how often, by arranging the circumstances in which he is placed. The relationship may be a two-way street, but the parents determine which lanes are used, and how the traffic is controlled" (p. 3). Clearly, the mother is influenced by her infant, but the extent to which she directly affects her infant's behavior is limited in early infancy. Mothers may attribute intentions to the infant (Richards, 1974) and see their acts as instrumental in determining their infant's behavior, even though as Kaye (1977) and Hayes (Hayes & Elliott, 1979; Hayes, 1980) have shown, changes in the infant's behavior are statistically independent of the mother's behavior, and as such, the extent to which "proto-conversations" are homologous with later communicative forms must be seriously questioned.

Kaye has suggested that three phases may characterize the engagement situations of infancy and early childhood. In the first phase, the mother attempts to fit her behavior to her infant's "more or less autonomous" behavior. The second phase is marked by the attainment of mutual contingency and is the basis of reciprocal games. In the third phase, there is some form of violation of rule embodied in the game, which serves as a mutual confirmation of the rule embodied in the game. If the rule is disconfirmed, then the process cycles back to the first phase. The extent to which dyads in the first half of the infant's first year go beyond the initial phase is, however, open to question, at least for those aspects of the engagement studied by Hayes. Vocally, the mother's "pseudo-dialogue" (Schaffer, 1977) is often based on strings of monologue in which she takes both parts in order to maintain the engagement. Notwithstanding, the infant is exposed to a vocal stream segmented into conversational units. The exaggerated and simplified form of the mother's utterances may serve to mark the *salient* events in the stream of vocalization. Confronted by the complex, dynamic array of stimulation emitted by a mother, the infant has to develop the ability both to detect the episodic units or events (Sarles, 1975), and segment his or her behavior into "something like the adult pattern of hierarchically nested segmentation" (Bullowa, 1975, p. 96). Mothers may assist in these developmental tasks by slowing the rate of speech, exaggerating the boundaries between utterances, and providing repeated presentations of simiplified linguistic forms (Anderson, 1977; Bateson, 1975; Snow, 1977).

The Content and Meaning of Social Engagements

The "pseudo-dialogues" of the engagement phase eventually provide the infant with aids to identifying the conversational units and relatedly solving the problems of coordination. But conversation is primarily a vehicle for the communication of meaning derived from experience. As with adult conversation the content represents selections from a domain of relevance (Keenan, 1974). Before meanings can be shared, mothers appear to impose a domain of relevance primarily derived from their infant's immediate activity. As Keenan (1974) comments:

> Generally interlocutors expect each other's utterances to relate to some mutually accepted orientation. One of the communication skills which a child must learn is, then, this maxim.

> The notion of relevance implies that the utterance at hand can be assigned a meaning. When we say that an utterances is relevant to some previous talk, we mean that the utterance is referentially or sociologically (as a kind of speech act) tied to the topic or direction of the talk. (p. 175)

Topic-comment structure is a feature of all natural languages (Bruner, 1975). In the engagement phase mothers provide, not only the conversational form, but also the linguistic topic-comment structure of the dialogue. As Bruner (1975) notes, "topic-comment structure reflects an underlying feature of attention" (p. 4). Long before their infants can verbalize topic-comment or subject-predicate structures, mothers attempt to incorporate what they presume to be the baby's objects of attention into the flow of "dialogue."

Viewed in this light, the mother's almost constant attention to her infant serves not only to maximize the probability of mutual facial gaze, but also fulfills a necessary monitoring function. Mothers typically cast fleeting glances to the presumed object of the infant's attention and then resume watching their infant's face

(Hayes, 1980). It was usual for the mother to comment upon the object and weave the comment into the ongoing sequence of the "conversation." But why did the mothers not merely look at the presumed object of attention? Why did they devote the bulk of their time in the engagement to their infant, when the situation was designed in such a way as to provide an alternative object of attention? The answers to these questions are inherent in the characteristics of the infant's behavior during the engagement.

During the neonatal period the baby has, by virtue of his/her immaturity, a very limited set of behaviors with a high degree of "salient regularity, rhythmicity and predictability" (Kaye, 1977, p. 112). With development, rapid enlargement of the infant's behavioral repertoire occurs. During the engagement phase, the increased activity of the infant, coupled with the limited ability to mesh behaviors reciprocally with the mother's actions, leads to a high degree of uncertainty for the mother in the attempt to interlock her behavior with that of her infant. The mother's preponderance of attention to her infant is an obvious way of reducing this uncertainty. The infant's behavior, while spontaneous, is not random. There is "a degree of sequential constraint" in the infant's activity (Collis, 1977), which the mother seeks to detect by carefully monitoring her infant's behavior. As Schaffer (1977) observes, "the mother's task in interacting with her baby is seen to be not one of creating order out of chaos; it is rather a matter of fitting her behavior in with an already existing organization" (p. 5). For the mother's part, "the *when* of her behavior is thus every bit as important as the *how* if she is to achieve a predictable outcome to the encounter" (Schaffer, 1977, p. 13).

The knowledge she gains of her infant's idiosyncratic behavioral repertoire and the regularities of the infant's behavior will later form the basis for the ritualized content of reciprocal games (Bruner, 1975). However, while by dint of her maturity the mother is able to monitor and orchestrate the exchange, such procedures are also necessary because *both* mother and infant are involved in a new social situation and have much to learn about each other (Kaye, 1977; Papousek & Papousek, 1977). The dialogue, therefore, proceeds in the face of considerable uncertainty, because only "one of the two communicating persons is socially sensitive to the effect of what is happening to the other, moment by moment" (Newson, 1974, p. 255). Moreover, the combination of careful monitoring interspersed with periods of co-orientation provides the foundation for the infant eventually to realize the relevance and the meaning of his or her experiences for another. These are essentially the processes of intersubjective awareness, shared meaning and communication. Expressed less prosaically, "only through this delicate ballet of action and reaction between a more experienced and a less experienced human communicator can shared meanings be arrived at" (Newson, 1974, p. 255).

All told, careful monitoring appears to serve several functions. It provides information about *both* the presumed perceptual input to the infant and the infant's behavioral output; it serves to enable coordination of meanings; and last, it gives feedback to the infant that helps determine the infant's emerging definition of self.

A Further Feature of Engagement and its Links to Later Social Attachment

In addition to the monitoring function, the mother's preponderance of attention to her infant has been interpreted as an example of adult "framing" of infant activity (Fogel, 1977). Framing seems to be an important characteristic of the engagements of adults and infants and provides some interesting insights into the significance of the social contexts of infant behaviors. Hayes (1980) has provided a detailed examination of visual framing which allows the concept to be extended. Briefly stated, these results suggest that, with development, infant attention to the mother decreases, and attention to the novel object and the wider environment increases concomitantly.

These results—the mother's stable frame and her infant's increasing exploration—show some interesting parallels to behavior in later infancy and early childhood. Compare, for example, explanations of the dynamics between the infant's growing social bonds and the equally pressing need to explore the wider environment, in terms of the concept of attachment and its evolutionary utility (Ainsworth, 1963, 1969; Ainsworth et al. 1974; Bowlby, 1971; Marvin, 1977). Ainsworth et al. (1974) summarize the argument:

> It is an advantageous arrangement for an infant to be activated to explore without straying too far from an adult who can protect him if he encounters danger, for him to be programmed to maintain a reasonable degree of proximity on his own account without requiring that the adult be always alert to do so, and for him to be activated to seek quickly a close proximity or contact should he become alarmed. (p. 104)

In the engagement phase the infant is relatively immobile. However, the use of vision is a first means of exploring the distal environment while the mother's visual framing ensures social contact when the infant changes attention from environment back to mother (Blehar, Lieberman, & Ainsworth, 1977). Unlike the older child who maintains contact by actively keeping within a "set goal distance" (Ainsworth et al., 1974), "the young infant's attachment behavior is not yet goal directed," and "the mother usually behaves in such a manner that proximity and contact are predictable outcomes of his attachment behavior" (Marvin, 1977, p. 30).

As the maintenance of "pseudo-dialogue" requires sensitive adjustment of the mother's behavior, so also does the maintenance of "pseudo-attachment." It is also possible to argue that, as the experience of pseudo-dialogue relates to later conversational development, the pseudo-attachments of the engagement phase are the precursors of later developments in the relationship of mother and child. Blehar et al. (1977) have recently provided empirical data relevant to the issue. They compared the en face behaviors of 26 mother–infant dyads, observed at home for periods of 4 hours when the infants were 6, 9, 12, and 15 weeks old, with behaviors in the Ainsworth "strange situation" at 12 months. Post hoc analyses showed clear differences in the patterns of en face behavior for dyads with infants classified as securely attached and those classified as anxiously attached. In discussing the differences, Blehar et al. underscore the importance of differences in maternal sensitivity. Specifically, they suggest that mothers of anxiously attached infants were more likely to be silent and impassive in engagements with their infants. In contrast, mothers of securely attached infants showed greater sensitivity in pacing their behavior to the infant's activity and actively encouraging further "interaction." Again, the essentially mother-directed pattern of the engagement phase is related to later developments more directly involving reciprocal infant activity.

Social Contexts, Intersubjectivity, and Infant Development

To date, the discussion has suggested that both communication and social relationships emerge from the activities of the dyad in the engagement phase. Schematically the situation could be represented as in Figure 1. The interlocking of the mother's behavior in the engagement phase produces dyadic phenomena that give rise to two,

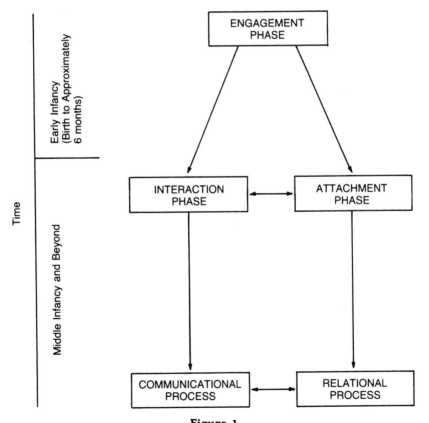

Figure 1.

Schematic Representation of the Emergence of Processes of Communication and Relational Development from the Engagement Phase of Early Infancy.

parallel and interconnected, strands of development—the communicational and the relational. Both strands mutually influence each other. Throughout childhood, adults provide the "scaffolding" (Bruner, 1975) for the processes of development in each strand; progressively reducing the adult-imposed structure as ontogeny proceeds and the child becomes more capable of autonomous regulation of social behavior. Advances in communicational ability lead to changes in the structure of the relationship between child and adult. And the maintenance of the relationship becomes less dependent upon immediate behavioral interaction, moving increasingly toward a state of mutual enmeshing of plans (Maccoby, 1979). With progressive consolidation of the relationship, the child gains increasing scope for active involvement in the exploration of the world (Ainsworth et al., 1974) and the construction of reality (Piaget, 1955).

It is not currently possible to describe in any detail the links between the communicational, relational, and cognitive strands. One specific proposal, however, is that the social context of development serves to overcome the "problem of the match" (Hunt, 1961). The problem of the match is an old one. In Brown's words, "it is a widespread assumption of developmental psychologists of quite divergent theoretical viewpoints that the distance between the child's existing knowledge, and the new information he must acquire, is a critical determinant of how successful training will be" (in press). Vygotsky's concept of the "zone of proximal development" brings into the problem of the match the social context of development (Wertsch, 1979). Summarized, the zone of proximal development is the distance between the problem-solving performance characteristic of the child's current developmental level and the "level of potential development" determined by observing performance under the guidance of an adult or a generally more expert problem solver (Wertsch, 1979). As a result of such aided performances, the child learns about his/her capacities and progressively moves towards autonomous expertise (Brown, in press). In this framework, development explicitly involves capitalizing on the transactions between the external, essentially social, context and the child's increasing capacity actively to explore the environment.

The importance of viewing ontogeny as an active process of interaction between child and environment is not new. Piaget's theory (1953, 1955, 1970) centrally embodies this notion. However, while Piaget admits that "persons are obviously the most easily substantiated of all the child's sensorial images" (1955, p. 46), he underrates the importance of social mediation in determining infant development (Gratch, 1979; Newson & Newson, 1975), an underrating common to many theorists in developmental psychology.

One theorist at whom the same criticism cannot be leveled was George Herbert Mead (1934). Gratch has provided a fascinating comparison of the theories of Piaget and Mead, emphasizing their respective positions on the ontogenetic development of language and thought. For Mead the infant is an active, "unreflective" entity embedded in a social context. At first, the infant's knowledge is context bound, and awareness only linked to the completion of activities. Mind is present when the infant can leave the "flow of conduct" and obtain the "ability" to attend to events as relevant to various possible lines of activity" (Gratch, 1979, p. 441):

> Thus, putting things in perspective was Mead's metaphor for thought, and he viewed such perspective-taking in communicative terms. The infant contacted the world in the context of a social field, and Mead believed that through taking the role of the "other" person or thing or larger setting—the child would come to construct ideas of thing, self and society. (p. 441)

Mead (1934), accordingly, viewed communication as central in the process of developing thought:

> When, in any given social act or situation, one individual indicates by a gesture to another individual what this other individual is to do, the first individual is conscious of the meaning of his own gesture—or the meaning of his gesture appears in his own experience—in so far as he takes the attitude of the second individual toward that gesture, and tends to respond to it implicitly in the same way that the second individual responds to it explicitly. Gestures become significant symbols when they implicitly arouse in an individual making them the same responses which they explicitly arouse, or are supposed to arouse, in other individuals, the individuals to whom they are addressed; and in all conversations of gestures within the social process, whether external (between different individuals) or internal (between a given individual and himself), the individual's consciousness of the content and flow of meaning involved depends on his thus taking the attitude of the other toward his own gesture. (p. 47)

The central point is that "it is the other who gives the gesture meaning by his response to it" (Gratch, 1979, p. 442). The activity of the "other" in the engagement phase marks the beginning of the process of conferring meaning on the infant's acts. The mother thus *confers* the status of gestures upon the infant's acts. In Mead's conceptualization, this is the necessary prerequisite to the infant's later reflective recognition of these acts as communicative gestures per se.

Vygotsky's view of the ontogeny of "higher mental processes" resonates with, and amplifies, the central themes of Mead's account, although it is not clear that Mead influenced Vygotsky's thought. Vygotsky argued that higher mental functions appear first on the "interpsychological" (i.e. social) plane and only later on the "intrapsychological" (i.e. individual) plane. Wertsch (1979) quotes Vygotsky: "The means for influencing oneself originally were means of influencing others or others' means of influencing an individual" (p. 2).

Taken together, the viewpoints of Mead and Vygotsky permit one to speculate that the engagement phase may contribute to later development primarily to the extent to which it provides the child with, first, the repeated experiences of influencing another, and second, with the experience (albeit more limited) of being influenced by another. In addition, the child experiences the basic forms of social interaction that provide the structure for the interpsychological processes outlined by Vygotsky. Schaffer (1977) concludes that:

given an inherent basis of pre-adaptation and the necessary means, the additional
factor required seems to be just the sheer opportunity, repeated day after day for month
after month, of taking part in dialogue-like exchanges. And it is here that the mother's
ability to set up and sustain such exchanges becomes so important. (p. 11)

While the appropriateness of referring to the pseudo-dialogues of the engagement
phase as "exchanges" is questionable, the important point remains. The infant is
enmeshed in the "language-game" (Wertsch, 1979). Through the process of engagement the infant, like his/her older problem-solving peer:

comes to understand the task situation as a result of behaving (under someone else's
guidance) as if she/he understood it . . . the definition of situation which is presupposed in an adult-adult interaction, is created in adult–child interaction while
carrying out the other-regulation language game. (Wertsch, 1979, p. 21)

During the engagement phase, the process of connection involves limited "other-
regulation" of the infant's behavior by the mother, but, by her actions, she appears
to be playing the "language-game" as if her infant's activity actually were part of
an interpsychological process. The infant's attainment of an awareness of the contingency between his/her acts and the mother's behavior is required before the
process can be legitimately labeled interpsychological.

The engagement phase may, therefore, be the forum for the development of
metapsychological processes, such as Flavell's metacommunication (Gratch,
1979). Prior to the development of some degree of communication, intersubjectivity, and shared meanings, some "understanding" of the importance of such
processes interpsychologically must be present. That "understanding" need only
involve the crude differentiation of self from others, means from ends, and the
exogenous regulation of behavior from the endogenous.

A Theoretical Limitation

To all of the previous discussion, a clear cavaet is in order. The description of the
engagement phase presented so far and the discussion of constructs derived from
other conceptualizations (e.g. those of Piaget, Mead, Vygotsky, Newson and
Newson, and Schaffer) do not constitute an explanatory theory of early ontogenetic
development and its social context. At this stage in the history of developmental
psychology, the hypothetical constructs employed are only loosely tied to a "nomo-
logical network" (Cronbach & Meehl, 1955). There are clearly insufficient links
both between the observable phenomena and the constructs—"social context,"
"social determination," "intersubjectivity," "shared meaning," "interpsychological process," "intrapsychological process," and "engagement"—to
enable the exact processes of ontogenetic change to be explained. The conceptualization is unavoidably pretheoretical at this stage of its formulation.

As Markham (1975) has argued in reply to Newson and Newson (1975), the new wave of hypothetical constructs currently represents statements of the author's metaphysics, rather than the parts of a coherent theory. To adapt the classic McLuhanism, "the metaphor is the message." Gratch (1979) has warned:

> It is all too easy to notice a mutual regulation between an infant and a mother and conclude there is communication without simultaneously asking in what way such communication differs from the communication between two adults or children and adults. It is all to easy to note an infantile performance in a particular context that seems most intelligent and not wonder if the specificity of that performance to that context implies a different form of knowing rather than just the ignorance of the other contexts. For example, it is indeed impressive that children come to talk in the 2nd year of life to significant others, but what accounts for the fact that such talk does not become self-guiding until much later? (p. 458)

The currently held models and metaphors of infant development are essentially generating new ways of viewing old data and changing the focus of the search for the agents of ontogeny. The process of ontogeny, however, remains insufficiently specified. *How,* for example, does "the sheer opportunity . . . of taking part in dialogue-like exchanges" (Schaffer, 1977, p. 11) *lead* to conversational competence? And how are the behaviors of the developing mother–infant dyad to be interpreted? In particular, how close is the match between the observer's interpretations of an engagement and the participants' interpretations? The nature of the infant's interpretations—the infant's "psychological reality"—is a "bedeviling problem": one that confronts the psychologist with "the considerable conceptual task of justifying the choice of constructs or explanatory systems as maps of the child's epistemology" (Sameroff & Harris, 1979, p. 358). The mother's "psychological reality" may be somewhat more accessible, but still raises a number of perennial questions about the methods to be used to gain access. For either infant or mother, an interest in the interpretations or meaning of social events—the participants' epistemology—raises major questions of method. Method is the point to be considered in the next section, concentrating especially on the question: "How appropriate are current microanalytic approaches to the study of social acts?"

SOME METHODOLOGICAL ISSUES IN THE STUDY OF COMMUNICATIVE BEHAVIOR IN EARLY INFANCY

A Possible Change in Method

Microanalyses clearly have made it possible to ask and answer a number of questions about mother and infant behavior. Without microanalyses, for example, it would not have been possible to ask if the behaviors of mother and child were truly reciprocal. And we would not have gained such a strong picture of the extent to which the mother "frames" the exchanges and imposes a dialoguelike structure upon them.

What we need, however, is a way of keeping some fine attention on the stream of behavior, and some precise methods of analysis, while at the same time blending into such work some of the concepts from more recent approaches to the study of social behavior. Such blends are rare. One example, however, flows from consideration of how the stream of behavior is divided into acts, events or states.

One of the assumptions underlying the current use of event recorders is that issues of salience and meaning have been avoided by defining the acts, events, or states from the researcher's perspective. Duncan and Fiske (1977), for example, define the act as "the smallest unit of observation used by an investigator but not further subdivided or analyzed in a given study" (p. 309). This is a convenient, but not compelling, definition. As Bullowa (1975) points out, "there is always a problem of when to stop looking at smaller-and-smaller-sized units" (p. 114). But what is an appropriate basis for deciding on the "natural" units of analysis?

Altmann (1965) provides the following guidelines:

> Like other problems in classification, categorizing the units of social behavior involves two major problems: when to split and when to lump. If one's goal is to draw up an exclusive and exhaustive classification of the animal's repertoire of socially significant behavior patterns then these units of behavior are not arbitrarily chosen. On the contrary, they can be empirically determined. One divides up the continuum of action wherever the animals do. If the resulting recombination units are themselves communicative, that is, if they affect the behavior of other members of the social group, then they are social messages. Thus the splitting and lumping that one does is, ideally, a reflection of the splitting and lumping that the animals do. In this sense, then, there are natural units of social behavior. (p. 492)

Altmann's position raises at least two crucial issues for the study of social engagement and interaction in infancy. First, how does one decide where the infant has divided the continuum of action? In other words, what constitutes sufficient evidence of the infant's segmentation of the stream of another's behavior? Perhaps the surface topography of the infant's behavior is not a sufficient basis for imputing effects of the mother on her child. Second, how much, and what features, of the mother's behavior is the infant processing, and how is this information being organized? Currently, these are questions that have not been addressed in studies of mother–infant interaction, except in cursory fashion. Bell (1968) says, in discussing the problem of the appropriate level of complexity in studies of interaction:

> It is necessary to select a level of complexity at which responses will be defined. Most investigators of parent–child interaction have set a minimum level which is appropriate to a social system, the discrete actions of each participant being at least of sufficient complexity to be recognized by the other and perceived as relevant. (p. 66)

However, Bell's definition still begs the question, "How is discrete action to be defined, and what is the basis upon which a third party, the observer, decides on the perceived relevance of that action to another?"

Given the problems of defining acts, events, and states, why then has the discrete behavioral approach persisted as the primary approach to the study of engagement and interaction? The answer, in part, lies in the "safety" of dealing with discrete behavioral categories at a microlevel of analysis. If a mechanistic model is adopted, and the subjective importance of behavior ignored, then precise definition of the act, event or state by the observer is scientifically appropriate and defensible. The problem only becomes significant when an attempt is made to link activity at the microlevel to organizing principles at the macrolevel. The introduction of a cognitive processing, active organism into the picture changes the scene quite fundamentally. Once constructivist conceptualizations are admitted, the definition of acts, events, or states in isolation from the actors is no longer sufficient.

Pribram (1965) provides a further insight into the dimensions of "safety" in microanalysis. He contrasts the characteristics of micro- and macrolevel analyses in the social sciences with analyses at these levels in physics:

> The physicist's macroscopic universe is the more stable predictable one: "It does not hurt the moon to look at it" (Eddington, 1958, p. 227). For the most part it is as he moves to ever more microscopic worlds that uncertainties are asserted. The scientist concerned with social matters finds it just the other way around: it seemingly does little harm to the man to look at him; but seriously look at his family, his friendship, or his political–economic systems and what you had started out to look at changes with the looking. Here indeterminancy comes to plague the macrostructure; it is in the stabilities of microanalysis that the mirage of safety appears. (p. 448)

The very nature of current event recorders and microlevel analyses enhances the illusion of stability.

The act of event recording involves certain assumptions about the way the stream of another's behavior is perceived. Apart from the problem of functional equivalence of the units (Hayes, 1981), the act of event recording also involves untying features from the covarying relationship they have to the other contemporaneous aspects of the behavioral stream. At present, we have insufficient knowledge of how features of mother and infant displays such as looking, touching, vocalizing, and smiling dynamically relate. An attempt has been made to code these features singly and then aggregate the results and look at sequences of combinations such as looking and vocalizing (Gunn, Berry, & Andrews, 1979). But do mothers (and infants) act in this way in vivo? Recent research in event perception suggests that people perceive a flowing, dynamically changing stimulus array—not just a procession of static images shifting location in space and time (Johansson, von Hofsten, & Jansson, 1980). Aspects of the dynamic display are assimilated to organising structures and assigned differential salience. Microanalyses of event recordings of discrete behaviors or crude aggregates of behaviors cannot take sufficient account of the dynamic perceptual processes operating in vivo. In short, the models currently imposed on the data by microanalytic researchers can be criticized on a number of important grounds.

In the haste to adopt and master the current styles of microanalytical models, the central role of the participants' perceptual and cognitive capacities has been over-looked (Parke, 1978). Most microanalytic approaches have, in part, been fueled by a reductionist desire to reduce interactional behavior to its most elementary level, and to understand more complex phenomena by "combining well-understood fun-damental parts" (Magoon, 1977, p. 657). But in this process the meaning of the "parts" to the participants has been ignored.

Problems and Prospects in Studying Constructions

Constructs operate as part of a theory. The theory may be primitive or naive (Baldwin, 1967; Heider, 1958); it merely serves to organize our systems of con-structs. As Kelly (1955) stated:

> A theory need not be highly scientific in order to be useful. All of us order the daily events of our lives by constructions that are somewhat elastic. Under these construc-tions our anticipations of daily events, while not scientifically precise nevertheless surround our lives with an aura of meaning. (p. 18)

The study of the naive theory that a mother, for example, builds of her infant may provide an insight into the meanings she assigns to the infant's behaviors. Further, it may provide a basis for determining the principles by which she perceptually organizes and conceptually interprets that behavior. As scientists we require what Schutz called "constructs of the second degree" (Magoon, 1977), by which he meant constructs about the constructs of the social actors we seek to describe.

This is problematic. It is one thing to attempt to describe behavior as an external observer and another to describe the way people think about their behavior. Essen-tially this is the problem of "etic" versus "emic" description. Blurton-Jones and Woodson (1979) adopt the following stance:

> we are not concerned . . . with the way people think about their behavior (the "emic" approach): we are interested in the way in which it can be observed that they behave (the "etic" approach). . . . (p. 99)

Collins and Collins (1973) frame the problem in anthropological or sociological terms, as that of describing what exists in a culture (emic) and the generalizations and categorization of the observer from outside the culture being observed (etic). Scientific generalization and communication necessitate translation of emic data into etic form. So not only are the mother and infant's "meanings" involved, but also the observer's. Blurton-Jones and Woodson warn against confusing etic and emic approaches. For them, as observers, meaning is "the most observable feature of the preceding, contemporary and subsequent behavior of parent and child, and some observable features of the situation" (p. 99). But does this solve the problem of deciding on the units of behavior to be analyzed? I think not.

Focusing on the processes of event perception in mother–infant interaction may provide valuable clues to the feature of the infant's repertoire that *mothers* construe as salient. Examination of the way persons perceive the stream of another's behavior and organize it cognitively may provide a more efficient basis for understanding the temporal organization of engagements than overlaying essentially ad hoc models on microanalytic data. Again, it should be recognized that the range of models that can be applied to such data is potentially infinite, limited only by the imagination of the researcher, the biases of the data collection techniques, and current conceptions of the phenomena being described.

A more productive direction for research may be in consideration of the match between mothers' subjective organization of infant behavior and the data generated by the researcher's analyses. Such a course seems to offer greater hope of bringing the salient features regulating interaction into sharper focus. Microanalyses, as currently applied, would seem to involve a high probability that the salient features of the interaction will be swamped by the mass of marginally relevant, discrete behavioral events. Succinctly put, such microanalyses seem to offer considerable potential for burying the salient interactional signals in a cacophony of behavioral noise. In contrast, working back from the subjective data to the behavioral analysis may provide richer insights into the process of differential perception of the salient features in the highly diverse display of infant action.

The seminal work of Newtson (1976) provides an interesting set of take-off points for such a research program. Newtson has extensively examined the way in which people unitize the ongoing behavior of others. He regards the break points that individuals report in the stream of another's behavior as high information points. Post hoc analyses of the behaviors surrounding the break points reported by individual mothers may facilitate the identification of the salient features of the infant's behavior to which the mother responds in interaction. As Lieberman (1979) has argued, the marriage of subjective methods and behavioral analyses may ultimately provide a better basis for understanding the organization of behavior. Further, such an approach should facilitate the enunication of the links between molecular and molar levels of organization.

Newtson has also provided data suggesting that the level of unitization of ongoing behavior varies systematically as a function of the predictability of the behavioral events used for unitization. Variations in the unitization of behavior may prove to be useful indicators of developmental change at the level of the relationship. They may also provide inferential evidence of the conceptual frameworks within which mothers view their developing infant.

Newtson's (1976) work provides one example of how a new approach may be possible, combining new concepts and methods, not abandoning close attention to the stream of behavior, but adopting instead a new way of conceptualizing and studying it. With such approaches, developmental psychologists may begin to ask a number of questions concerning social behavior in infancy which have long been overlooked.

REFERENCES

Ainsworth, M. D. The development of infant–mother interaction among the Ganda. In B. M. Foss (Ed.), *Determinants of infant behaviour* (Vol. 2). London: Methuen, 1963.

Ainsworth, M. D. Object relations, dependency and attachment: A theoretical review of the infant–mother relationship. *Child Development*, 1969, *40*, 969–1025.

Ainsworth, M. D., Bell, S. M., & Stayton, D. J. Infant–mother attachment and social development: "Socialization" as a product of reciprocal responsiveness to signals. In M. P. M. Richards (Ed.), *The integration of a child into a social world*. London: Cambridge University Press, 1974.

Altmann, S. A. Sociobiology of rhesus monkeys. II: Stochastics of social communication. *Journal of Theoretical Biology*, 1965, *8*, 490–522.

Anderson, B. J. The emergence of conversational behavior. *Journal of Communication*, 1977, *27*, 85–91.

Argyle, M. *The psychology of interpersonal behaviour* (2nd ed.). Harmondsworth: Penguin, 1972.

Bakeman, R., & Brown, J. V. Behavioral dialogues: An approach to the assessment of mother–infant interaction. *Child Development*, 1977, *48*, 195–203.

Baldwin, A. L. *Theories of child development*. New York: Wiley, 1967.

Bateson, M. C. Mother–infant exchanges: The epigenesis of conversational interaction. *Annals of the New York Academy of Sciences*, 1975, *263*, 101–113.

Bell, R. Q. A reinterpretation of the direction of effects in studies of socialization. *Psychological Review*, 1968, *75*, 81–95.

Bell, R. Q. Stimulus control of parent or caretaker behavior by offspring. *Developmental Psychology*, 1971, *4*, 63–72.

Blehar, M. C., Lieberman, A. F., & Ainsworth, M. D. Early face-to-face interaction and its relation to later infant–mother attachment. *Child Development*, 1977, *48*, 182–94.

Blurton-Jones, N., & Woodson, R. H. Describing behavior: The ethologists' perspective. In M. E. Lamb, S. J. Suomi, & G. R. Stephenson (Eds.), *Social interaction analysis: Methodological issues*. Madison, WI: The University of Wisconsin Press, 1979.

Bowlby, J. *Attachment and loss* (Vol. 1): *Attachment*. Harmondsworth: Penguin, 1971.

Brazelton, T. B., Koslowski, B., & Main, M. The origins of reciprocity: The early mother–infant interaction. In M. Lewis & L. A. Rosenblum (Eds.), *The effect of the infant on its caregiver*. New York: Wiley-Interscience, 1974.

Brown, A. L. Learning and development: The problems of compatibility, access, and induction. *Human Development*, in press.

Bruner, J. The ontogenesis of speech acts. *Journal of Child Language*, 1975, *2*, 1–19.

Bruner, J. Early social interaction and language acquisition. In H. R. Schaffer (Ed.), *Studies in mother–infant interaction*. London: Academic Press, 1977.

Bullowa, M. When infant and adult communicate, how do they synchronize their behaviors? In A. Kendon, R. M. Harris, & M. R. Key (Eds.), *Organization of behavior in face-to-face interaction*. The Hague: Mouton, 1975.

Cairns, R. B. Beyond social attachment: The dynamics of interactional development. In T. Alloway, P. Pliner, & L. Krames (Eds.), *Attachment behavior*. New York: Plenum Press, 1977.

Collins, O., & Collins, J. M. *Interaction and social structure*. The Hague: Mouton, 1973.

Collis, G. M. Visual co-orientation and maternal speech. In H. R. Schaffer (Ed.), *Studies in mother–infant interaction*. London: Academic Press, 1977.

Condon, W. S., & Sander, L. S. Neonate movement is synchronized with adult speech, interactional participation and language acquisition. *Science*, 1974, *183*, 99–101.

Cronbach, L. J., & Meehl, P. E. Construct validity in psychological tests. *Psychological Bulletin*, 1955, *52*, 281–302.

Duncan, S. D., Jr. Nonverbal communication. *Psychological Bulletin*, 1969, *72*, 118–137.

Duncan, S. D., Jr. Some signals and rules for taking speaking turns in conversation. *Journal of Personality and Social Psychology*, 1972, *23*, 283–292.

Duncan, S. D., Jr. Toward a grammar for dyadic communication. *Semiotica*, 1973, *9*, 29–46.

Duncan, S. D., Jr., & Fiske, D. W. *Face to face interaction*. New York: Halsted Press, 1977.

Duncan, S. D., Jr., & Niederehe, G. On signalling that it's your turn to speak. *Journal of Experimental Social Psychology*, 1974, *10*, 234–247.

Fogel, A. Temporal organization in mother–infant face-to-face interaction. In H. R. Schaffer (Ed.), *Studies in mother–infant interaction*. London: Academic Press, 1977.

Freedle, R., & Lewis, M. Prelinguistic conversation. In M. Lewis & L. Rosenblum (Eds.), *Interaction, conversation and the development of language*. New York: Wiley, 1977.

Gratch, G. The development of thought and language in infancy. In J. D. Osofsky (Ed.), *Handbook of infant development*. New York: Wiley, 1979.

Gunn, P., Berry, P., & Andrews, R. Vocalization and looking behaviour of Down's syndrome infants. *British Journal of Psychology*, 1979, *70*, 259–263.

Hayes, A. Mother–infant interactions—coincidental conversations? *Sociolinguistics Newsletter*, 1978, *9*, 37–38.

Hayes, A. *Visual regard and vocalization in mother–infant dyads*. Unpublished doctoral dissertation, Macquarie University, 1980.

Hayes, A. Levels of description and explanation in studies of mother–infant engagement and interaction. In A. R. Nesdale, C. Pratt, R. Grieve, J. Field, D. Illingsworth, & J. Hogben (Eds.), *Advances in child development: Theory and research*. Nedlands: University of Western Australia Press, 1981.

Hayes, A., & Elliott, A. G. L. Gaze and vocalization in mother–infant dyads: Conversation or coincidence? Paper presented at the biennial meeting of the Society for Research in Child Development, San Francisco, March, 1979.

Heider, F. *The psychology of interpersonal relations*. New York: Wiley, 1958.

Hunt, J. McV. *Intelligence and experience*. New York: Ronald Press, 1961.

Jaffe, J., & Feldstein, S. *Rhythms of dialogue*. New York: Academic Press, 1970.

Jaffe, J., Stern, D. N., & Peery, J. C. "Conversational" coupling of gaze behavior in prelinguistic human development. *Journal of Psycholinguistic Research*, 1973, *2*, 321–329.

Johansson, G., von Hofsten, C., & Jansson, G. Event perception. *Annual Review of Psychology*, 1980, *31*, 27–63.

Kagan, J., Kearsley, R. B., & Zelazo, P. R. *Infancy: Its place in human development*. Cambridge, MA: Harvard University Press, 1978.

Kaye, K. Toward the origin of dialogue. In H. R. Schaffer (Ed.), *Studies in mother–infant interaction*. London: Academic Press, 1977.

Keenan, E. Conversational competence in children. *Journal of Child Language*, 1974, *1*, 163–184.

Kelly, G. A. *The psychology of personal constructs* (Vol. 1. *A theory of personality*). New York: Norton, 1955.

Kendon, A. Some functions of gaze-direction in social interaction. *Acta Psychologica*, 1967, *26*, 22–63.

Kendon, A. Introduction. In A. Kendon, R. M. Harris, & M. R. Key (Eds.), *Organization of behavior in face-to-face interaction*. The Hague: Mouton, 1975.

Lazzerini, A. J., Stephenson, G. M., & Neave, H. Eye contact in dyads: A test of the independence hypothesis. *British Journal of Social and Clinical Psychology*, 1978, *17*, 227–229.

Lieberman, D. A. Behaviorism and the mind: A (limited) call for a return to introspection. *American Psychologist*, 1979, *34*(4), 319–333.

Maccoby, E. E. Parent–child interaction. Paper presented at the biennial meeting of the Society for Research in Child Development, San Francisco, March, 1979.

Magoon, A. J. Constructivist approaches in educational research. *Review of Educational Research*, 1977, *47*(4), 651–693.

Markham, K. A. Towards a theory of infant understanding: A response. *Bulletin of the British Psychological Society*, 1975, *28*, 108–110.

Marvin, R. S. An ethological-cognitive model for the attenuation of mother–child attachment behavior. In T. Alloway, P. Pliner, & L. Krames (Eds.), *Attachment behavior*. New York: Plenum Press, 1977.

Mead, G. H. *Mind, self, and society*. Chicago: University of Chicago Press, 1934.

Miller, G. A. Review of J. H. Greenberg (Ed.), Universals of language. *Contemporary Psychology*, 1963, *8*, 417–418.

Newson, J. Towards a theory of infant understandings. *Bulletin of the British Psychological Society*, 1974, *27*, 251–257.

Newson, J. An intersubjective approach to the systematic description of mother–child interaction. In H. R. Schaffer (Ed.), *Studies in mother–infant interaction*. London: Academic Press, 1977.

Newson, J., & Newson, E. Intersubjectivity and the transmission of culture: On the social origins of symbolic functioning. *Bulletin of the British Psychological Society*, 1975, *28*, 437–446.

Newtson, D. Foundations of attribution: The perception of ongoing behavior. In J. Harvey, W. Ickes, & R. Kidd (Eds.), *New directions in attribution research* (Vol. 1). Hillsdale, NJ: Erlbaum, 1976.

Papousek, H., & Papousek, M. Mothering and the cognitive head-start: Psychobiological considerations. In H. R. Schaffer (Ed.), *Studies in mother–infant interaction*. London: Academic Press, 1977.

Parke, R. D. Parent–infant interaction: Progress, paradigms, and problems. In G. P. Sackett (Ed.), *Observing behavior* (Vol. 1): *Theory and applications in mental retardation*. Baltimore: University Park Press, 1978.

Penman, R., Friedman, J., & Meares, R. The temporal structure of vocalization and gaze behaviour in mother–infant dyads. Unpublished manuscript, University of Melbourne, 1978.

Piaget, J. *The origin of intelligence in the child*. London: Routledge & Kegan Paul, 1953.

Piaget, J. *The construction of reality in the child*. London: Routledge & Kegan Paul, 1955.

Piaget, J. Piaget's theory. In P. H. Mussen (Ed.), *Carmichael's manual of child psychology* (Vol. 1; 3rd ed.). New York: Wiley, 1970.

Pribram, K. H. Proposal for a structural pragmatism: Some neuro-psychological considerations of problems in philosophy. In B. Wolman & E. Nagle (Eds.), *Scientific psychology: Principles and approaches*. New York: Basic Books, 1965.

Rheingold, H. L. The development of social behavior in the human infant. In H. W. Stevenson (Eds.), Concept of development. *Monographs of the Society for Research in Child Development*, 1966, *31*(5, Serial No. 107), 1–17.

Richards, M. P. M. First steps in becoming social. In M. P. M. Richards (Ed.), *The integration of a child into a social world*. London: Cambridge University Press, 1974.

Rutter, D. R., Stephenson, G. M., Lazzerini, A. J., Ayling, K., & White, P. A. Eye-contact: A chance product of individual looking? *British Journal of Social and Clinical Psychology*, 1977, *16*, 191–192.

Sameroff, A. J., & Harris, A. E. Dialectical approaches to early thought and language. In M. Bornstein & W. Kessen (Eds.), *Psychological development from infancy: Image to intention*. Hillsdale, NJ: Erlbaum, 1979.

Sander, L. W. Infant and caretaking environment: Investigation and conceptualization of adaptive behavior in a system of increasing complexity. In E. J. Anthony (Ed.), *Explorations in child psychiatry*. New York: Plenum Press, 1975.

Sarles, H. B. A human ethological approach to communication: Ideas in transit around the Cartesian impasse. In A. Kendon, R. M. Harris, & M. R. Key (Eds.), *Organization of behavior in face-to-face interaction*. The Hague: Mouton, 1975.

Schaffer, H. R. Early social behaviour and the study of reciprocity. *Bulletin of the British Psychological Society*, 1974, *27*, 209–216.

Schaffer, H. R. (Ed.). *Studies in mother–infant interaction*. London: Academic Press, 1977.

Schaffer, H. R. Acquiring the concept of dialogue. In M. H. Bornstein & W. Kessen (Eds.), *Psychological development from infancy: Image to intention*. Hillsdale, NJ: Erlbaum, 1979.

Snow, C. E. The development of conversation between mothers and babies. *Journal of Child Language*, 1977, *4*, 1–22.

Stern, D. N., Beebe, B., Jaffe, J., & Bennett, S. L. The infant's stimulus world during social interaction: A study of caregiver behaviours with particular reference to repetition and timing. In H. R. Schaffer (Ed.), *Studies in mother–infant interaction*. London: Academic Press, 1977.

Thomas, E. A. C., & Martin, J. A. Analyses of parent–infant interaction. *Psychological Review*, 1976, *83*, 141–156.

Trevarthen, C. Descriptive analyses of infant communicative behaviour. In H. R. Schaffer (Ed.), *Studies in mother–infant interaction*. London: Academic Press, 1977.

Tronick, E. D., Als, H., & Brazelton, T. B. Mutuality in mother–infant interaction. *Journal of Communication*, 1977, *27*, 74–79.

Wertsch, J. V. From social interaction to higher psychological processes: A clarification and application of Vygotsky's theory. *Human Development*, 1979, *22*, 1–22.

Whiten, A. Assessing the effects of perinatal events on the success of the mother–infant relationship. In H. R. Schaffer (Ed.), *Studies of mother–infant interaction*. London: Academic Press, 1977.

Wilson, E. O. *Sociobiology: The new synthesis*. Cambridge, MA: The Belknap Press of Harvard University Press, 1975.

CHAPTER 8

Criteria for the Emergence of Symbolic Conduct: When Words Refer and Play Is Symbolic*

Patricia Goldring Zukow

The nature of the relationship between the emergence of symbolic conduct in play and in language has recently been the focus of considerable theorizing and empirical investigation (Bates, Benigni, Bretherton, Camaioni, & Volterra, 1979; Fein, 1979; Gardner, in press; Huttenlocher & Higgins, 1978; McCune-Nicolich, 1981; Nicolich, 1975; Shotwell, Wolf, & Gardner, 1982; Veneziano, 1981; Rocissano, 1982; Zukow, 1980, 1981a, 1981b). The major thrust of child language research and theory during the past decade has been an attempt to clarify what a child can comprehend and produce, when, and under what circumstances. Less interest has been directed toward the precursors to language. (See Golinkoff, 1981, for a review of the evidence for semantic relations prior to speech). Recently, Bates and her colleagues have noted that prelinguistic children engage in activities such as delayed imitation, "symbolic" play, and tool use that correlate with comprehension and production measures of language acquisition. Currently, Bates and others are exploring how these so-called spontaneous predilections/propensities of children are related to language acquisition. This issue *is* important. However, the enterprise has been permeated by subtle cultural and theoretical biases which must be addressed.

These biases have led to an overestimation of the child's referential activities in both domains. In this chapter I argue that the symbolic status of activities the-

* Preparation of this manuscript was supported in part by a Spencer Foundation Grant to Patricia M. Greenfield.

oretically and operationally defined as "symbolic" play[1] in current use by most researchers is open to question. In particular, since "symbolic" play invariably entails the manipulation of objects in culturally recognizable activities, these situations will be examined carefully in the discussion that follows. In addition, the questionable nature of activities taken to be referential in play points to a similar problem with respect to the symbolic status of early word use. Clearly, overestimating the child's abilities in language or in play obscures the "true" interrelationship which is posited to exist between conduct emerging in these symbolic domains. In answer to this problem, candidate criteria for assessing the symbolic status of activities in both domains are proposed and discussed. The implication of using these criteria for future research is explored.

CURRENT THEORETICAL APPROACHES TO THE EMERGENCE OF SYMBOLIC CONDUCT

Current approaches to symbolic development (Bates et al., 1979; Bates, Bretherton, Shore, & McNew, in press; Fein, 1979; Fischer, 1980; Gardner, in press; Huttenlocher & Higgins, 1978) are derived from an amalgamation of the theoretical approaches advocated not only by Piaget (1962), but by Vygotsky (1967, 1978) and Werner and Kaplan (1963) as well. Among those approaches Bates and her colleagues have proposed the most articulated theoretical position. Bates and her coworkers (Bates, 1976; Bates et al., 1979; Bates et al., in press) focus on the relationship between language acquisition and cognition during the later stages of the sensorimotor period and the early preoperational period. Their work on cognition follows from a Piagetian framework, although they have extrapolated and innovated from other theorists (Werner and Kaplan's 1963 approach to symbol formation) and from other disciplines (e.g., the philosopher Peirce's system of classifying signs, 1955). The Piagetian assumption that sensorimotor knowledge serves as a basis for further intellectual development has been extended to the level of representation. It does not follow that symbolic conduct should first appear in action (e.g., in play, and subsequently in language). However, the Piagetian perspective (1962, p. 75) may, in fact, implicitly bias most of us, including Bates and her coworkers to expect symbolic conduct to appear first in action.

Bates et al.'s conceptualization treats the interrelationship between the emergence of nonverbal symbols in play and in language. Bates et al. (1979) define *prerequisite,* not in terms of a direct causal model, but in terms of a model of behavior based on shared origins. Such a model suggests some underlying cognitive structure that both language and cognition share in some way. This model does not predict a particular sequence of acquisition as a causal model would. Bates et al.

[1] Symbolic activities in the nonverbal domain have been called symbolic play (Piaget, 1962), nonverbal representation (Veneziano, 1981), nonverbal symbols (Bates et al., 1979), and semiotic conduct (Inhelder, Lezine, Sinclair, & Stambak, 1971).

assert that in a model of homology through shared origins, positive correlations derived from observed linguistic and cognitive behavior reflect the sharing between cognitive and linguistic systems. However, Bates et al. (1979) describe prerequisites to language as follows:

> developmental dependence such that one system requires input from another in order to derive or build its structure . . . Great borrowing going on, in which language is viewed as a parasitic system that builds its structures by raiding software packages of prior or parallel cognitive capacities. (p. 6)

To say the least, these statements appear to be quite contradictory. That is, "shared origins" and "parallel cognitive capacities" suggest no particular sequence of acquisition for particular aspects of language and cognition, while describing the relationship between language and cognition as "parasitic" suggests that behaviors ought to appear first in cognition and then in language. In the next section, we will see that the latter is advocated by Bates et al. for the emergence of symbolic conduct.

Although Bates et al. are careful to state that acquisitions do not necessarily appear in cognition prior to language, they do argue for a smooth transition from sensorimotor comprehension and action to symbolic comprehension and action (including speech). This conceptualization apparently envisions a slight shift from nonverbal to verbal means of comprehension and action, while the views of Piaget, Vygotsky, and Werner and Kaplan, in contrast, characterize the shift as more of a quantum leap. Bates et al.'s perspective may have arisen partially to refute theories that propose that language arises independently of other capacities from a built-in language acquisition device (Chomsky, 1965; McNeill, 1966). From Bates et al.'s point of view, language is a natural outgrowth of prior cognitive abilities. Bates et al., as well as Greenfield (1975, 1978), have argued that language does not spring forth with no roots in cognition. On the contrary, they both propose that action and language arise from underlying cognitive structure. However, the theoretical framework and empirical data that Bates et al. marshall to support their arguments are not convincing. The discussion that follows will analyze and criticize their theoretical stance. (For a critique of Bates et al.'s complex statistical methods, see Rocissano, 1979, and of their operational definitions of symbolic activities, see Zukow, 1980.)

To understand Bates et al.'s (1979) position, their definition of *symbol* and *naming* must be considered in detail. First, they offer this definition of symbol.

> The comprehension or use, inside or outside of communicative situations, of a relationship between a sign and its referent, such that the sign is treated as belonging to and/or substitutable for its referent in a variety of contexts; at the same time the user is aware that the sign is separable from its referent, that is, not the same thing. (p. 43)

Second, Bates et al. (in press) proposed the following definition of naming:

> The use of a symbol to recognize, categorize, identify, or otherwise label a referent as a member of some known class of entities or as an instantiation of a known unique

individual. This naming act may be carried out for the purpose of identifying the referent for an intended listener, or in a private act of recognition for oneself. When used communicatively, a naming act may be the major point of an utterance or it may be a subsidiary act in the service of making further points about that referent. Similarly, in private cognition a naming act may be carried out in isolation, or as a subsidiary act within a higher relational or predicative construction. (p. 1, manuscript)

Bates et al. support their contention that there is a smooth transition from sensorimotor to linguistic knowing by proposing that children first employ *nonverbal symbols* to name when engaged in *indexical acts* and gradually come to name with verbal symbols. An indexical act is defined in this chapter (not by Bates et al.) as an occasion during which an individual is engaged in a culturally recognizable activity. (While Bates et al. and most adults may interpret the child's acts as such, we do not know if the child interprets her/his acts in the same way). In most research, young children are characterized as playing when participating in such activities. Because Bates et al. make the assumption that the child's doing of an indexical act entails identifying, recognizing, or classifying of objects, culturally appropriate manipulation of objects is conceived as naming. The discussion that follows will examine Bates et al.'s assumptions on several levels. First, are indexical signs symbols? Second, does engaging in an indexical act, doing a recognizable cultural act, name?

First, Bates et al. claim that indexical signs are "symbolic" in Peirce's sense (1955), that is, being engaged in an act that indexes an activity or object, to the self or to some other participant, constitutes symbolic activity. The examples cited by Bates et al. are invariably characterized by appropriate object use in a culturally recognizable activity, that is, in cultural acts. For example, being in or displaying a state called "readiness-to-sit" on an object that affords sitting, such as a tree stump, indexes chair or sitting. That is, the state, "readiness-to-sit," identifies, recognizes, and/or categorizes the tree stump as a chair or the act as sitting (Bates et al., 1979, p. 6; Bates et al., in press, p. 3, manuscript). Thus, the use of a "symbol," the doing of a cultural act, such as a display of "readiness-to-sit," is naming. Bates et al. support their claim that indexical signs are "symbols" by arguing that the relationship between an index and the activity in which it participates is arbitrary for the child. Bates et al. have introduced the notion of arbitrariness into the criteria for judging a behavior as symbolic. Peirce's symbol does have an arbitrary relationship with its object. However, Piaget's "symbol" is Peirce's icon. For Piaget the symbol in "symbolic" play, for instance, refers to the relationship between the signifier and the signified based on physical resemblance. Given that indexical signs are "symbols," Bates et al. assert that children use them to name. The following discussion will refute the idea that indexical signs are "symbols" in Peirce's and in Piaget's sense and that these children are naming.

Bates et al. claim that indexical signs are no less "symbolic" than words since they are related in an arbitrary way to the phenomena they index. According to Peirce (1955), whom Bates et al. quote extensively and whose system of signs is explicitly preferred to Piaget's, an *index* is related to the object it stands for by its participation in the same event or phenomena. *Symbols* have been defined by Peirce as signs that are related to their referents by means of a rule or arbitrary convention. Bates et al. argue that, for the child, indices are no less arbitrary than symbols. That is, Bates et al. claim that indices are symbols. For example, knowing that a shoe goes on a foot is a purely arbitrary connection. A shoe does not convey its function of fitting or protecting a foot. The association between shoe and foot obeys the simple learning principle of spatio-temporal contiguity alone. That these behaviors are cultural in the sense that they could probably only have been acquired through social observation is not refuted in the present discussion. Bates et al.'s interpretation *may* be correct for the child's first momentary encounter with shoes. However, Bates et al. do not consider whether the first experience changes what the child knows about the world.

The world becomes more differentiated as the child interacts with it (Gibson, 1969; Gibson, 1979). This theoretical position suggests that the connection between shoe and foot is not arbitrary at all. The child and shoe are not paired in some static moment. The pairing is a dynamic process. Once a shoe has been put on the child's foot, what the child knows about the world has been altered. The interaction between child and shoe opens up possibilities and disclosed limitations for movement. Thus, the opening in the shoe affords putting something in it; the child's foot affords an ankle that turns, a sole that flexes, and toes that can wiggle into just such a foot-shaped opening. The shoe affords a surface that separates hot sand or cold snow from tender feet. The shoe and the foot not longer are related arbitrarily at all, but are part of an available, understandable everyday event for the child. Bates et al.'s interpretation of spatio-temporal contiguity overlooks the dynamic interactive nature of events. That is, how things are related is not arbitrary but emerges as the coparticipants continuously interact with the perceptually available particulars in the situation. From this point of view, indexical signs are not arbitrary and, therefore, are not symbols (nor are they necessarily icons).

Secondly, Bates et al. assert that the use of a "symbol," indexical sign, to recognize, categorize, or identify something as an instance of a member of a class of objects is naming. I have argued above that indexical signs are not arbitrarily related to their objects nor are they icons and, therefore, are not symbolic. Now I will refute Bates et al.'s claim that indexical acts categorize objects or events. First, Gibson's (1979) theory of the direct perception of the affordances of objects accounts for the child's use of objects without attributing categorization or classification to children beginning to talk. Further, according to Ginsburg and Opper (1969), sensorimotor schemes apply to particular objects over time rather than to collections of objects. For instance, recognizing a shoe by wiggling your foot as if to put the shoe on does not imply that shoes belong to a class. That is, recognizing that shoes have affordances or have properties is not naming. Perhaps Bates et al. have been misled because in an activity an individual must direct attention to what is being done and must be aware of the properties of the object in order to act. However, that is not naming. Naming conveys that the individual has noticed that x is an instance of X; it is not merely that someone is actively engaged with an x or is xing. It is more conservative and parsimonious to assume that the child is acting on the basis of what is perceptually present than that the child categorized the object to access its function, or vice versa.

The arguments presented in this section refute on a theoretical level Bates et al.'s contention that "nonverbal symbols," engaging in culturally recognizable acts, constitutes symbolic conduct. Children may indeed engage in culturally recognizable activities before they use language referentially. The question is whether these acts are referential for the child.

THE EFFECT OF CULTURAL AND THEORETICAL BIASES ON THE ASSESSMENT OF SYMBOLIC CONDUCT IN PLAY

Children who are just beginning to talk engage in activities which are often mistakenly interpreted as symbolic or referential. There are at least two sources for these errors: cultural and theoretical. First, these overinterpretations exemplify a well-documented interactive, cultural style common to middle-class caregivers in Western cultures (Kaye, 1976; Snow, 1977; Wertsch, 1978, 1979; Wood, Ross, & Bruner, 1976). These caregivers continually treat children's behavior as if the child performs at higher levels of complexity than the child's actual performance. On the positive side, numerous researchers have speculated or assumed that this interactive style is the major means by which children acquire (cultural) knowledge of the world (Ochs, 1982; Ryan, 1974; Shotter, 1978; Trevarthen, 1979; Wikler, 1976; Zukow, Reilly, & Greenfield, 1982). However, this interactive style may have a less positive side effect. As researchers and middle-class adults, we may have attributed more advanced functioning to children than the evidence actually supports.

Most researchers studying the emergence of symbolic play make the implicit assumption that the children are doing cultural acts. A child's acts may mimic the appropriate use of objects without the child comprehending how those manipulations are linked to a cultural event. Children probably acquire these behaviors by observing caregivers as they unwittingly model or intentionally demonstrate everyday activities. In our culture we attribute adult intentions to very young children (Shotter, 1978; Trevarthen, 1979). When most of us observe a toddler manipulating a cultural object, we interpret the child's acts in terms of the act's significance to an observing adult; thus, children's "intentional" acts are primitive gestures (Clark, 1978). These acts are unintentionally communicative, even though the child is not intending to communicate and the child is engaged in an act different from the adult interpretation. For instance, even though Bates et al. explicitly state that the child probably does not comprehend the cultural event (stirring's relation to food preparation), a fragment of behavior is taken to be part of "an activity typically associated with the object" (Bates et al., 1979, p. 42). This implies that the child has a model of the actions that comprise the event without knowing what that event represents culturally; the child has the form but not the function. At first the child may not, in fact, have a model of the entire sequence nor even of the fragment enacted. That is, moving a spoon about in a bowl may not be stirring or even "deferred imitation" but rather following the affordances revealed by objects. For instance, a spoon handle is graspable as is the side of a bowl. The configuration of the two in hand affords new possibilities for action. The bowl invites penetration by the spoon and the spoon as an extension of a rotatable arm can explore the limits of movement afforded by the rim of the dish. While these acts are directed, they do not necessarily constitute stirring to the child. To attribute, without appropriate criteria, to the child that the act engaged in is stirring rather than directly perceiving affordances is an overrich interpretation.

Second, our theoretical biases may be another source of error. In particular, Piaget's conceptualization of cognitive development may have misled us. If the child is seen as coming to know the world independently and/or play is viewed as a predominance of assimilation over accomodation, then we may overestimate the capacities of children and underestimate the role of the caregiver. On the one hand, each child is seen as, in some sense, reinventing the world. The focus is upon the child's activities with animate and inanimate objects in the world and not upon a two-way, negotiated interaction. Due to Piaget's influence, we have envisioned a miniature Western scientist setting off to sample life. Since the child's spontaneous interactions with the world are the raw material with which the child tests and modifies her or his hypotheses about the world, caregiver input is seen as interfering, or superfluous at best.

Although we no longer believe that cognitive development is a natural unfolding or simply the establishment of associative connections, we do assume that the interactions with the world that are necessary for development occur naturally. At the appropriate time, the elements in the environment that are necessary for further development are assumed to be available to the child. No explanation is made to account for the presence or absence of these elements. The elements are simply there. However, we have overlooked the fact that this is a carefully tailored and very cultural affair. The organized, interactional nature of everyday activities is implicit. We can no longer ignore the caregiver who is preparing and repairing the child's experiences in the world, nor can we ignore what makes these interactions with the world cultural.

On the other hand, some other aspects of Piaget's theory may also have inadvertently blinded him and his adherents to the importance of caregivers. Play has been defined as activities in which there is a predominance of assimilation over accomodation. By definition, then, in play the child is not conforming or accommodating to the world to a very great degree. That is, in play ongoing events are incorporated into and interpreted in terms of the child's own cognitive structures. Therefore, interactions to which the child accommodated in the first place to acquire the structures that produce play have been ignored entirely and/or have been considered irrelevant. In sum, caregiver input, the original source of many experiences, has been ignored due to the definition of play as a predominance of assimilation over accommodation and due to the view that the child comes to know the world independently.

Ignoring the original source of experiences (e.g., caregiver input) that led to the child's representations may have led researchers to overestimate the child's symbolic abilities (cf. Fein, 1981). Children's play activities have been interpreted as if the activities displayed serve the same symbolic function for children as for adults. For example, putting toy food up to a doll's mouth *is* evidence for cultural knowledge of miniature object use but it is unclear if that behavior stands for feeding someone. The child has probably observed caregivers, siblings, or peers treating dolls in that way and may be imitating those activities rather than abstracting this behavior from her/his own eating experiences (Zukow, 1980, 1981a, 1981b). In both cases, the child clearly has a mental representation of the event but what is ambiguous and must be addressed is whether that representation is a "prefiguration," "a sort of representation in material acts and not yet in thought" (Piaget, 1962; Inhelder et al., 1971) or whether it is truly symbolic.

CANDIDATE CRITERIA FOR SYMBOLIC PLAY

What constitutes symbolic play is at issue. By and large, what has been defined as play are the activities in which children display their culturally organized knowledge of the world and its objects (Rocissano, 1982; Veneziano, 1981; Zukow, 1980, 1981a, 1981b). Apparently, objects are first manipulated on a nonspecific sensory level, then in a manner which explores their physical properties, and later in culturally recognizable ways (Rocissano, 1979, 1982; Zukow, 1980, 1981a, 1981b). Because the display of culturally recognizable activities has been overinterpreted as referential without appropriate evidence, this aspect of play will be addressed most carefully in the discussion that follows.

Some notions that the philosopher Ryle (1949) introduced may lead us to a more adequate definition of symbolic play. He defined *knowing-how* as the knowledge that can vary in the degree of skill displayed (e.g., a person can comb hair or sing either well or poorly), and *knowing-that* as knowing the truth of certain principles and applying them in activities. That is, a child may "know how" to manipulate objects such as putting a cup to a doll's mouth with varying degrees of skill without "knowing that" putting a cup to the doll's mouth constitutes giving the doll a drink. At the level of "knowing-how," the child may be following affordances or imitating. When the child "knows-that," the child's acts refer.

"Knowing-that" you are giving the doll a drink may be more than one step away from "knowing-how" to put the cup to the doll's mouth. The evolution of play that Inhelder et al. (1971) describe shows a progression from unskilled displays of culturally recognizable activities to skilled displays. To assess symbolic conduct they stress the child's ability to enact these activities skillfully in new situations. Thus, symbolic conduct does not simply entail skill, "knowing-how." Further, symbolic conduct is not bound to the original observation in all its detail, but is generalized competently to situations that are less and less closely allied to the initial modeled act. The move from awkward to skilled can be characterized as the difference between "knowing-how$_1$" on the basis of directly perceivable affordance and "knowing-how$_2$" on the basis of perceptually absent information. Although the latter may be coherent reenactments of culturally recognizable activities that reinstantiate events observed in past, they do not refer. Again, "knowing-how" to put a cup up to a doll's mouth is not "knowing-that" you are giving the doll a drink. Perhaps, when the child can competently engage in this activity in novel situations we can say that the child "knows-that" (s)he is giving some new doll a drink. Fischer's model (1980) provides a means to examine and confirm this conceptualization experimentally. In his discussion, he suggests the experiences that would provide a basis for moving from sensorimotor skill (knowing-how$_1$) to representation (knowing-how$_2$) to abstraction of a principle or rule (knowing-that).

To differentiate "knowing-how" from "knowing-that," we can consider that feeding a doll can be taken three ways. First, the child's action may emerge from direct perception of the *indexical* characteristics of the events. During indexical play, interacting with the situational particulars (e.g., objects, events, persons) directs the child's actions from moment to moment. A mental image need not be posited to explain the basis for the child's acts. That is, putting a spoon up to a doll's mouth may not be "feeding the doll," but rather directly perceiving the perceptual relationships or affordances objects display (Gibson, 1979). For instance, a spoon handle is graspable as is the side of a doll. The configuration of the two in hand affords new possibilities for action. The mouth invites partial penetration by the edge of the spoon and the spoon, as an extension of a rotatable arm, can explore the limits of movement of its edge afforded by the lips of the doll. While these acts are directed, they do not necessarily depend on mental images nor denote feeding the doll to the child. In order to attribute to the child that the act engaged in is feeding rather than directly perceiving affordances, one must accept unproven assumptions about the symbolic meaning of the action for the child.

Second, the child's action may be only an *instantiation*. Instantiations are reenactments or going through the motions of activities observed in the past on the basis of a mental image. Take an action that is often interpreted as symbolic play, "pretending" to feed imaginary food to a doll (Shotwell et al., 1979; Veneziano, 1981; Wolf & Gardner, 1979). Investigators have assumed that the child treats the doll as if the doll stands for an animate being (Bates et al., 1979; Bates et al., in press). Similarly, other researchers have assumed that the child has imaginary food in mind when placing an empty spoon near the doll's mouth (Fein, 1979). The child may be simply displaying cultural knowledge of conventional miniature object use (Dunn & Wooding, 1977; El'Konin, 1971; Huttenlocher & Higgins, 1978; Rocissano, 1979). That is, caregivers put empty toy spoons up to the mouths of dolls and make smacking noises when playing with their children. At first, children may merely imitate these activities ("knowing-how") after a delay without "knowing-that" eating is being represented to more culturally competent observers. Further, such sequences can be expected to be truncated since they may be based upon incomplete images of events observed in the past. In addition, present actions may be awkward, since they may not be tailored to present objects but to past observations.

Third, *denotations* designate a culturally recognizable act *for the child.* That is, the activity enacted stands for feeding (knowing-that) for the child as well as the observer(s). When the researcher or caregiver has evidence that the child can improvise, interact spontaneously to the dynamic particulars of a new situation, we have some evidence to argue that the child "knows-that$_2$" (s)he is doing a particular act. In order to differentiate between these three interpretations of object use during culturally recognizable activities: index, instantiation, and denotation, the researcher can refer to data that documents the acquisition of the activity and/or to interactional data that displays how the child interprets the activity.

To understand the difference between instantiations and denotations, compare the two following excerpts from naturalistic videotaped interactions (Zukow, 1980, 1981a, 1981b). In this interaction sequence, Alice's mother requested that Alice give the dolly seated next to Alice a drink. Her mother touched her fingers to her thumb as if her hand were a cup and extended the "cup" toward Alice. Alice touched her hand to her mother's, made a fist, and put her hand to the doll's mouth. It might seem reasonable to attribute to Alice the knowledge that she was giving the doll a drink rather than merely reenacting a routine in which she cups her hand and touches it to the doll's face. That is, this might be considered symbolic behavior rather than an instantiation of appropriate miniature object use. However, Alice turned her hand over as she touched her hand to the doll's mouth so that the imaginary water would have spilled out. Further, when her mother requested that Alice return the cup, Alice cried because she thought that her mother wanted the miniature comb and brush that were clutched in her left hand. Alice surely did not understand that the return of an imaginary cup was being requested. Thus, this child can engage in cultural activities with appropriate objects although the child's performance is often fragmentary, less than competent, and not clearly symbolic.

In the following fragment, the child's gestures to her doll make available to us that she was not engaged in some routine based on past observation. Her ability to interact spontaneously to the dynamic particulars of the situation displayed that she "knew-that" she was engaged in a particular act. Her actions referred to a culturally recognizable activity. Jeri and her mother were seated on the bed looking at a picture book. During this interaction Jeri's mother pointed to an elephant in the book and asked, "What's that?" Jeri replied, "ā::" (Elephant). Jeri picked up her doll and said, "be ɔ::" (Baby. Elephant.). Next she looked at the doll and rotated it toward the book while saying, "beɪbi, ɔ::" (Baby, elephant). She lifted the doll away from the book, looked at it full face, and then put the doll at her side. At this point, it was not clear if this was spontaneous action or some routine she had learned from her mother! However, a few moments later her mother exclaimed, "O:::h!" while looking at a new page. Jeri pointed to the page saying, "oω." She turned to the doll and attempted to get its attention by tugging on its dress. Next Jeri brought her hand to a position directly above the doll's eyes and paused. Then while looking at the doll, Jeri moved her hand in a trajectory that was led by pointing her index finger directly at the picture in the book. She repeated a variant of her mother's exclamation, "aω::" to coincide with the point's projected destination in the book. Jeri's exquisite timing in the execution of this communicative point clearly displayed that she "knew-that" she was showing a particular picture in a particular book to a particular doll, that this was symbolic play.

In the first interaction, the child's instantiation of a familiar routine, giving the doll a drink, was partially based on an incomplete demonstration by her mother as well as upon similar events observed in the past. From the interaction it is evident that the child was not responsive to the particulars of the situation. Turning her cupped hand over so that the imaginery water would have spilled out is at cross purposes to giving the doll a drink. In the second fragment, the child's actions denote a culturally recognizable event for her as well as for the observer. She displays this to us by treating the doll as if it could see. When she showed the doll a particular picture in a book she improvised, so that her actions were tailored to the particulars of the situation (e.g., the trajectory of her point appropriately directed the doll's gaze to the picture in the book). From the history of the interaction and the child's ability to improvise as circumstances unfold, we can make more accurate judgments of symbolic conduct in play.

CANDIDATE CRITERIA FOR SYMBOLIC WORD USE

In early language as well as in play, culturally recognizable acts have been taken to be symbolic. Children who are beginning to talk are acquiring the conventional use of words (Veneziano, 1981). However, several theorists (Bates et al., 1979; Greenfield & Smith, 1976; Piaget, 1962) have noted that early word use is not necessarily referential. Some early uses of words, performatives, are described as indexical rather than referential. A pure performative is part of the activity in which it participates and does not refer to something other than itself, for example, saying "Bye-bye" while waving bye-bye (Greenfield & Smith, 1976). This observation has been overlooked in most research. In our research, more often than not, the use of words in culturally recognizable ways is taken to be referential.

Perhaps, as Savage-Rumbaugh (1979) suggests, the symbolic status of word use in children has not been questioned since the vast majority of children become competent speakers. However, the symbolic status of word use among nonhuman primates has been challenged. Because the language performance of nonhuman primates has come under very close scrutiny (see *Behavioral Brain Sciences,* 1978, for a review of this issue), word use by apes is being reevaluated much more stringently than research conducted with children. Savage-Rumbaugh (1979) has suggested the following criteria for symbolic word use production: (a) nonprompted, spontaneous word use, (b) generative word use, and (c) referential rather than associative word use. According to Savage-Rumbaugh (1979), the difference between referential and associative word use can be conceived of as "what the word represents" and "when to use the word." The latter seems to describe performatives in that the word is the event and not a description of it.

Lexical items emitted by children during the early emergence of language have been variously categorized as encoding semantic function (Greenfield & Smith,

1976), as functional or substantive (Bloom, 1973) as members of adult grammatical categories (Snyder, Bates, & Bretherton, 1981): there is no common agreement among researchers. Further, there is no consensus about what might constitute referential word use.

Snyder et al. (1981) have considered the referential status of early word use among children of 13 months in some detail. They note that researchers have considered contextual flexibility, and content and composition, as well as comprehension versus production to determine the onset of reference. Snyder et al.'s findings echo the asymmetry between comprehension and production found by many researchers. Although comprehension leads production, a large proportion of comprehended items are limited to a particular context, "when to use the word," while production items more often appear in several appropriate contexts. Snyder et al. suggest that items enter the child's repertoire in context-bound situations and through experience become generalized. The ability to use a word in many contexts may lead to a developmental shift. Eventually the child may assume that a new word applies to a class of referents that vary from situation to situation. Given this assumption, a significant positive correlation between both vocabulary size and proportion of flexible items in production would be expected. Since the proportion of context-flexible lexical items in production correlated positively and significantly with total vocabulary, Snyder et al. suggest that the ability to use a word appropriately in new settings may be evidence for an insight into reference. Thus, more stringent criteria for symbolic word use and symbolic play stress the spontaneous, competent display of culturally recognizable acts in new settings.

CONCLUSION

The interrelationship between the emergence of symbolic conduct in language and in play is unknown. Correlational and descriptive studies have shown that symbolic conduct in play and in language are yoked (Bates et al., 1979; Shotwell et al., 1979). How one domain might influence the other is an open question. Researchers have suggested that symbolic word use may precede symbolic play (Lieven & McShane, 1978), that the influence is bidirectional (Veneziano, 1981), and that nonverbal symbols appear before verbal ones (Bates et al., 1979). The first step toward clarifying these issues is the use of more stringent criteria for identifying symbolic conduct.

REFERENCES

Bates, E. *Language and context: The acquisition of pragmatics.* New York: Academic Press, 1976.

Bates, E., Benigni, L., Bretherton, I., Camaioni, L., & Volterra, V. *The emergence of symbols: Communication and cognition in infancy.* New York: Academic Press, 1979.

Bates, E., Bretherton, I., Shore, C., & McNew, S. Names, gestures, and objects: The role of context in the emergence of symbols. In K. Nelson (Ed.), *Children's language* (Vol. 4). Hillsdale, N.J.: Erlbaum, in press.

Bloom, L. *One word at a time.* The Hague: Mouton, 1973.

Chomsky, N. *Aspects of the theory of syntax.* Cambridge, MA: MIT Press, 1965.

Clark, R. A. The transition from action to gesture. In A. Lock (Ed.), *Action, gesture, and symbol: The emergence of language.* London: Academic Press, 1978.

Dunn, J., & Wooding, C. Play in the home and its implication for learning. In B. Tizard & D. Harvey (Eds.), *Clinics of developmental medicine: The biology of play, 62.* London: Heinemann Medical Books, 1977.

El'Konin, D. Symbolics and its function in the play of children. In R. E. Herron & B. Sutton-Smith (Eds.), *Child's play.* New York: Wiley, 1971.

Fein, G. G. Echoes from the nursery: Piaget, Vygotsky, and the relationship between language and play. In E. Winner & H. Garner (Eds.), *Fact, fiction, and fantasy in childhood.* San Francisco, CA: Jossey-Bass, 1979.

Fein, G. G. Pretend play in childhood: An integrative review. *Child Development,* 1981, *52,* 1095–1118.

Fischer, K. W. A theory of cognitive development: The control and construction of hierarchies of skills. *Psychological Review,* 1980, *87,* 477–531.

Gardner, H. Developmental psychology after Piaget: An approach in terms of symbolization. *Human Development,* in press.

Gibson, E. J. *Principles of perceptual learning and development.* New York: Appelton-Century-Crofts, 1969.

Gibson, J. J. *The ecological approach to visual perception.* Boston: Houghton Mifflin, 1979.

Ginsburg, H., & Opper, S. *Piaget's theory of development: An introduction.* Englewood Cliffs, NJ: Prentice-Hall, 1969.

Golinkoff, R. M. The case for semantic relations: Evidence from verbal and nonverbal domains. *Journal of Child Language,* 1981, *8,* 413–437.

Greenfield, P. M. The grammar of action in cognitive development. In D. Walter (Ed.), *Human brain function.* Los Angeles: Brain Information Service/Brain Research Institute, University of California, Los Angeles, 1975.

Greenfield, P. M. Structural parallels between language and action in development. In A. Lock (Ed.), *Action, symbol and gesture: The emergence of language.* London: Academic Press, 1978.

Greenfield, P. M., & Smith, J. H. *The structure of communication in early language development.* New York: Academic Press, 1976.

Huttenlocher, J., & Higgins, E. T. Issues in the study of symbolic development. In A. Collins (Ed.), *Minnesota Symposia on Child Psychology, 10.* New York: Crowell, 1978.

Inhelder, B., Lezine, I., Sinclair, H., & Stambak, M. The beginnings of symbolic function. *Archives de Psychologie,* 1971, *41,* 187–243.

Kaye, K. Learning by imitation in infants and young children. Paper presented at the meeting of the Society for Research in Child Development, Minneapolis, 1976.

Lieven, E., & McShane, J. Language is a development social skill. In D. J. Chivers & J. Hervert (Eds.), *Recent advances in primatology.* London: Academic Press, 1978.

McCune-Nicolich, L. Toward symbolic functioning: Structure of early pretend games and potential parallels with language. *Child Development,* 1981, *52,* 785–797.

McNeill, D. The creation of language by children. In J. Lyons & R. Wales (Eds.), *Psycholinguistic papers.* Edinburgh: University of Edinburgh Press, 1966.

Nicolich, L. M. *A longitudinal study of representational play in relation to spontaneous imitation and development of multiword utterances: Final report.* 1975 (ERIC Document PS007 854).

Ochs, E. Talking to children in Western Samoa. *Language in Society,* 1982, *11,* 77–104.

Peirce, C. S. *Philosophical writings of Peirce.* In J. B. Bochler (Ed.), New York: Dover, 1955.

Piaget, J. *Play, dreams, and imitation in childhood.* New York: Norton, 1962.

Rocissano, L. Object play and its relation to language in early childhood. Unpublished doctoral dissertation, Columbia Univ., 1979.

Rocissano, L. The emergence of social behavior: Evidence from early object play. *Social Cognition,* 1982, *1,* 50–69.

Ryan, J. Early language development: Towards a communication analysis. In M. P. M. Richards (Ed.), *The integration of a child into a social world.* Cambridge: Cambridge University Press, 1974.

Ryle, G. *The concept in mind.* New York: Barnes & Noble, 1949.

Savage-Rumbaugh, E. S. Symbolic communication: Its origins and early development in the chimpanzee. In H. Gardner & K. Wolf (Eds.), *Early symbolization.* San Francisco: Jossey-Bass, 1979.

Shotter, J. The cultural context of communication studies: Theoretical and methodological issues. In A. Lock (Ed.), *Action, gestures, and symbol: The emergence of language.* London: Academic Press, 1978.

Shotwell, J. M., Wolf, D., & Gardner, H. Styles of achievement in early symbol use. In B. Sutton-Smith (Ed.), *Play and Learning.* New York: Gardner Press, 1979.

Snow, C. E. The development of conversation between mothers and babies. *Journal of Child Language,* 1977, *4,* 1–11.

Snyder, L. S., Bates, E., & Bretherton, I. Content and context in early lexical development. *Journal of Child Language,* 1981, *8,* 565–582.

Trevarthen, C. Communication and cooperation in early infancy: A description of primary intersubjectivity. In M. Bullowa (Ed.), *Before speech: The beginning of interpersonal communication.* New York: Cambridge University Press, 1979.

Veneziano, E. Early language and nonverbal representation: A reassessment. *Journal of Child Language,* 1981, *8,* 541–564.

Vygotsky, L. S. Play and its role in the mental development of the child. *Soviety Psychology,* 1967, *1,* 6–18.

Vygotsky, L. S. In M. Cole, V. John-Steiner, S. Scribner, & E. Souberman (Eds. and trans.), *Mind in society.* Cambridge, MA: Harvard University Press, 1978.

Werner, H., & Kaplan, B. *Symbol formation: An organismic-developmental approach to language and the expression of thought.* New York: Wiley, 1963.

Wertsch, J. V. Adult–child interaction and the roots of metacognition. *Quarterly Newsletter of the Institute for Comparative Human Cognition,* 1978, *2,* 15–18.

Wertsch, J. V. From social interaction to higher psychological processes: A clarification and application of Vygotsky's theory. *Human Development,* 1979, *22,* 1–22.

Wikler, M. McD. Delusions of competence: A socio-behavioral study of the maintenance of a deviant belief system in a family with a retarded child. Unpublished doctoral dissertation, University of California, Los Angeles, 1976.

Wolf, D., & Gardner, H. Style and sequence in symbolic play. In N. Smith & M. Franklin (Eds.), *Symbolic functioning in young children.* Hillsdale, NJ: Erlbaum, 1979.

Wood, D., Ross, G., & Bruner, J. S. The role of tutoring in problem solving. *Journal of Child Psychology and Psychiatry,* 1976, *17,* 89–100.

Zukow, P. G. A microanalytic study of the role of the caregiver in the relationship between symbolic play and language acquisition during the one-word period. Doctoral dissertation, University of California, Los Angeles, 1980. *Dissertation Abstracts International,* 1981, *42,* 405B. University Microfilms, No. 8113894.

Zukow, P. G. Words on play: A microanalytic study of the role of the caregiver in the emergence of play activities during the one-word period. *The Quarterly Newsletter of the Laboratory of Comparative Human Cognition,* 1981, *3,* 68–71. (a)

Zukow, P. G. The relationship between interaction with the caregiver and the emergence of play during activities the one-word period. Unpublished manuscript, University of California Los, Angeles, 1981. (b)

Zukow, P. G., Reilly, J. S., & Greenfield, P. M. Making the absent present: Facilitating the transition of sensorimotor to linguistic communication. In K. Nelson (Ed.), *Children's language* (Vol. 3). New York: Gardner Press, 1982.

CHAPTER 9

Do Children Say as They're Told?
A New Perspective on Motherese*

John Neil Bohannon III and Kathy Hirsh-Pasek

Few researchers in the area of language development would oppose the claim that children come into the world superbly preequipped to acquire language. The neurological development of the left hemisphere and the structure of the vocal tract and attendant musculature provide considerable support for the contention that language is a modal action pattern in humans (Lennenberg, 1967). At the same time, few would insist that these physiological specializations are sufficient for the normal development of language. Children must have a language environment to supply the raw data to fuel communicative development.

Given these considerations, the question of theoretical import is not, "Does language input affect language development?" No doubt it does. At the most basic level one can observe that children born in America speak English whereas children born in China learn Chinese. The question is, however, "What specific role does the linguistic environment play in fostering this language development?" This chapter will summarize and expand upon current attempts to define the role of input in the child's linguistic development. In particular, we will contrast the strong *innatist* position that argues that input language only triggers the child's innate biases to learn his native tongue with the "motherese" position that puts the impetus of language learning on a maternal language register. This motherese register is said to highlight and perhaps mold certain aspects of language develop-

* The authors would like to thank Larry James, Amye Warren-Leubecker, Rebecca Treiman, Roberta Golinkoff, Kate Garvey, Lynne Feagans, Roger Bakeman, Catherine Snow, and Philip Dale for their editorial assistance in the writing of this chapter.

ment. After outlining these polar positions, we review the current state of the literature on the role of motherese by examining its raison d'etre along with its potential or realized effects on the language learning process. Finally, we suggest that the role of language input in language acquisition is still undetermined. We propose a statistical model that can be used to assess the role of motherese on language acquisition within a number of particular language domains and within the interactional climate in which natural language learning takes place.

POLAR POSITIONS: LANGUAGE GENERALIZATIONS FROM INSIDE OR OUTSIDE?

In Chomsky's (1965) initial formulation of the language learning process, what the child heard determined only the particulars of his native language. Children were thought to be little linguists industriously detecting important grammatical distinctions embedded in a degraded and errorful corpus that was supplied to them by adults. The child's language environment, it was postulated, was too poor to account for his acquisition of rich grammatical relations.

> A consideration of the character of grammar that is acquired, the degenerate quality and narrowly limited extent of [the child's language environment] the striking uniformity of the resulting grammars and their independence of intelligence, motivation and emotional state over a wide range of variation, leave little hope that much of the structure of the language can be learned by an organism initially uninformed as to its general character. (Chomsky, 1965, p. 58)

It was assumed that the task of language learning was too difficult to be left to a naive processor. The length (measured in mean length of utterance or MLU) and complexity of the resulting sentences were too taxing to be useful to a limited information processing machine. Indeed, Bever, Fodor, and Weksel (1965) wrote, "There is little evidence that adults engage in careful limitation of their linguistic output when conversing with children" (p. 470). Yet despite the observed complexity and variability in the input language, children manage to make appropriate linguistic generalizations from the language corpus. Children key into the *ed* marker for verbs like talk-ed and kick-ed, but never mistakenly conclude that the *ed* embedded in the terms *bed* and *red* earmark these words as verbs.

Given the evidence then that children from diverse backgrounds, with varied levels of intelligence, and from diverse linguistic environments all learn language with apparent ease and regularity, researchers turned to an nativistic theory of language acquisition. Proponents of this view argue that children come to the language task equipped with extensive preexisting knowledge of general language structures (noun, verb, etc.). This allows them to deduce the regularities of their specific grammar from mere exposure to the speech of adults.

While all the cognitive machinery suggested by Chomsky's language acquisition device has not been accounted for, a number of findings do illustrate the fact that the child approaches language learning with a fair amount of linguistic bias. Among many examples of a biased processor are Eimas, Siqueland, Vigorito, and Jusczyk's (1971) finding that infants segment the soundstream into discrete phonemes; Kuczaj's (1979) finding that children selectively attend to word endings; Slobin's (1973) contention that learners are predisposed to map conceptual units onto the word unit, and Feldman, Goldin-Meadow, and Gleitman's (1978) finding that the structural parameters evident in the language of deaf isolates is not unlike the emergent structures in natural language acquisition.

Though there is strong evidence to suggest that children come to the task of language acquisition with preexisting knowledge, there is also extensive evidence that these predispositions, void of contact with an input language, would not yield language acquisition. Children who are exposed to spoken language only through the mediums of television or radio have severely retarded language development (Moscowitz, 1978; Sachs & Johnson, 1972). These unfortunate cases highlight the point that mere exposure to the soundstream is insufficient to trigger resultant language. At the very least, children seem to require an input sensitive to their attention such that there is stable correlation between sound and meaning. Thanks to the accumulated evidence of the past 15 years, we now know that the child's predetermined knowledge requires interaction with a mature language user, and that the child's predetermined knowledge may not need to be as extensive as was originally suggested (Chomsky, 1965).

On closer inspection of the language learning environment, investigators discovered that the language input to the child was not so variable and disorganized as had once been supposed. A number of studies now document the finding that adults, almost from the moment of the child's birth (Rheingold & Joseph, 1977), modify their speech in very consistent ways when addressing children. The language addressed to children is composed of short, highly limited sentence types that contain a preponderance of concrete words. These words generally describe important features of the child's immediate environment (for reviews see DePaulo & Bonvillian, 1978; Berko-Gleason & Weintraub, 1978; Snow & Ferguson, 1977). Nor is the child's language environment limited in its exemplars. Moerk (1979) estimated that by the age of four, children have heard over three million simple declaratives and questions addressed to them. This special subset of language behaviors has been called *motherese* because it is typical of mothers' speech to children (Newport, Gleitman & Gleitman, 1977), *baby talk* because it often contains phonological simplifications (Ferguson, 1977) or more broadly, just *speech to children,* since they are the most frequent recipients of this language register. Regardless of the name of the phenomenon, some developmentalists (Moerk, 1975) have come to rely on the speech addressed to children and the characteristics that distinguish this speech from speech to adults, in an effort to rescue language acquisition from the grasp of the strong innatist theories.

In short, the challenge for developmental psycholinguists is to document the nature of motherese, the controlling variables of motherese, and most importantly the effect of motherese on the language-learning process. Some of the efforts generated in the past 15 years of research are reviewed below. These researchers have attempted to shift the impetus of language learning onto the input claiming that language acquisition is molded by rather than triggered by the input language. As we shall see, these efforts have met with some, though as yet limited, success.

CURRENT STATE OF THE LITERATURE: MOTHERESE IN REVIEW

Certain features of motherese have been used to oppose the innatist hypothesis: (a) motherese is a simpler register than speech to adults; (b) the speech addressed to children grows in complexity as the child's linguistic skills emerge; and (c) the more the mothers use motherese, the more quickly their children will acquire language. Although there is some question whether motherese is a simple register from all perspectives (Newport et al., 1977), many researchers argue that motherese is, in general, a simpler register composed of shorter sentences with fewer embedded and dependent clauses, main verbs, and a shorter preverb length (Snow, 1972; and many others) than speech addressed to adults. The rest of this section will concentrate on the last two questions, explanations for the occurrence of motherese, and on the potential effects that it might yield to the language learner.

When and Why Does it Occur?: The Feedback Hypothesis

Motherese has now been observed in a number of diverse contexts ranging from mothers' and fathers' speech to their own and other children (Snow, 1972; Golinkoff & Ames, 1979) to any adults' speech to children (Snow, 1972) to children's speech to other children (Berko-Gleason & Weintraub, 1978; Shatz & Gelman, 1973) to speech to foreigners (Ferguson, 1975; Freed, 1978; Bohannon & Warren-Leubecker, 1982; Berko-Gleason & Weintraub, 1978), retardates (Pratt, Bumstead, & Raines, 1976), dolls (Sachs & Devin, 1976; Bohannon & Warren-Leubecker, in press), pictures of children (Bohannon, Lotz, & Ritzenberg, 1982), and dogs (Hirsh-Pasek & Trieman, in press).

Why certain features of motherese should emerge in these disparate contexts is curious. The simplest explanation is that speakers will "fine tune" the length and complexity of their speech to the perceived or actual comprehension capacities of the listener. This fine-tuning hypothesis is aided by feedback from the listener indicative of the success or failure of the prior communication. Berko-Gleason (1977) stated that adults mark successful communication by nods and statements, such as "yeah," "O.K.," or "sure." She observed further that young children rarely offer such feedback. It may be the lack of these normal adult signals that promotes the characteristics typical of motherese. As such, given an organism that can supply feedback in the communicative interchange but that cannot supply culturally appropriate feedback, we might expect the emergence of motherese.

Bohannon and Marquis (1977) expand on the feedback explanation to suggest that children play an even more active role in controlling the speech that they hear (see Dale, 1976, for a concurring explanation). They found that children tend to signal communicative failure after long complex utterances and success after short, simple sentences. Adults react to these signals in a very stereotypic fashion, simplifying after failures and using longer more complex utterances after successes. Moreover, the probability of the child signaling comprehension to longer, more complex utterances increased over the four month course of the study and the length of subsequent adult utterances increased proportionately. Bohannon & Rondon (1981) supply cross linguistic validation noting the same pattern of interaction in eight monolingual Spanish mothers and their preschool children. The mothers in this study also shortened their utterances following a signal of comprehension difficulty, and the average length of the sentences to which the Spanish children signaled comprehension was positively correlated with the child's age and productive MLU. Even 3-year-old children respond to these signals as adults do when they encounter a speaker who appears younger than they (Bohannon & Warren-Leubecker, in press).

While the feedback explanation is not the only explanation for motherese, it does account for much of the observed data (for evidence counter to the "fine-tuning" hypothesis, see Retherford, Schwartz, & Chapman, 1981). It appears that the child plays an integral role in guiding the course of the communicative interchange. When feedback cues are unavailable, as in the cases of talk to dolls (Sachs & Devin, 1976) and talk to pictures of children (Bohannon, Lotz, & Ritzenberg, 1982), the speaker probably relies on his stereotypic conception of what a child at age X would comprehend. Berko-Gleason and Weintraub (1978) offer some evidence that parents will respond to their perception of what their child knows rather than responding on the basis of the child's actual knowledge (see Ryan, 1978). Such speech adjustments to the perceived comprehension of the linguistically immature listener may also account for the finding that motherese, or doggerel as it was called (Hirsh-Pasek & Trieman, in press), is commonly used to dogs.

In summary, motherese is the linguistic product of those communicative interchanges in which more adept speakers of a language attempt to communicate with less adept language users. Effective communication demands that the one with the superior language skills adapt his speech to the abilities of the listener. The resulting effect is that most speakers will be consistent when addressing the same child. Research data has proceeded beyond the mere observation that maternal language grows in complexity with the child's advancing age and language competence (Snow, 1972; Clarke-Stewart, VanderStoep, & Killian, 1979), to specifying the feedback mechanisms which control this process within the adult–child conversation (Bohannon & Marquis, 1977; Bohannon & Warren-Leubecker, 1982; Bohannon & Warren-Leubecker, in press). Notice that this places an added burden on the immature language learner. The child is the source of the controlling signals that help to tailor the child's linguistic environment. Hence, ineffective or misleading cues could cause variability in the conceptual complexity of the utterances addressed to the child, which may in turn affect his exposure to the linguistic environment necessary for language development.

The Child Influences the Motherese, But Does the Motherese Influence the Child?

As regular, predictable, and invariant as the interactional model of motherese may be when examined at a single age of a particular child (Bohannon & Marquis, 1977), the point of theoretical interest is whether this limited input fosters language acquisition. This issue involves a number of subquestions, not the least of which is "What is meant by assisting language acquisition?"

Some who argue that motherese does effect language development write in terms of affecting the child's conceptual development, vocabulary (Clark-Stewart, 1977; Nelson, 1973) or ability to match a linguistic stimulus to a particular referent (Clarke-Stewart el al., 1979). Others who argue that motherese is basically ineffectual in imparting general language lessons base their arguments on findings in the syntactic domain (Newport et al., 1977). All of these issues properly belong under the rubric of "effects of motherese" though they study very different aspects of the same phenomenon. No one piece of evidence can be taken so globally as to refute claims made in any other domain. Beyond the question of which aspect of language is potentially affected by the linguistic input, there is also the question of the stability of the effect. In other words, one could question whether motherese-related language effects alter the further course of language development. For example, are these effects maintained, exagerrated, or attenuated with the further passage of time?

We will separately report the research that bears on the effect of motherese in language content, function, and structure with particular emphasis on the study of the effects of input on structure or syntax. Only in the domain of syntactic development have the effects of motherese as opposed to more general language input been examined (Furrow, Nelson, & Benedict, 1979; Newport, et al., 1977; DePaulo & Bonvillian, 1978).

In the *content* or *cognitive/semantic* domain, several findings are of interest. Newport et al. (1977) argues that the number of nouns and verbs per utterance in the mother's speech could measure semantic/cognitive learning. Simply put, mothers who talk about more things may have children who also talk about more things. This was found by Furrow et al. (1979) who reported that mothers with larger MLUs have children who use more words. Nelson (1973) and Clarke-Stewart (1977), among others, have observed a positive correlation between the mother's vocabulary and the child's.

Motherese is also thought to encourage the child's understanding of semantic relations by providing the child with a limited range of semantic relationships to map onto the linguistic stimulus (DePaulo & Bonvillian, 1978; Snow, 1972). Within this view, the child's developing ability to comprehend new semantic relationships cue the mother to talk about more abstract and complex aspects of the semantic code.

> Indeed, it is possible that the child's comprehension competence is the "carrier" of the mother's influence from one period to the next. These relations deserve further investigation. (Furrow et al., 1979, p. 439)

The effects of a special input register on the *functional* domain of language had been thoroughly reviewed by Berko-Gleason and Weintraub (1978). Motherese certainly has the effect of attracting the child's attention (Garnica, 1974; Shatz & Gelman, 1973). If children are given a choice of what to listen to, both infants (DeCasper, 1980; Fernald, 1981; Friedlander, 1970), and 5-year-olds (Rileigh, 1973) will prefer the higher and more variable fundamental frequencies characteristic of motherese. The preponderance of yes/no questions and wh questions in the corpus further attract the child while facilitating communicative interaction (Berko-Gleason & Weintraub, 1978). Finally, motherese embodies a number of social *routines* (e.g., "Say 'please' " or "say 'bye-bye' "), many of which explicitly teach the child social aspects of the language, and directives (e.g., "That's it, get the ball, the ball. Reach for the ball. Good girl.") that guide the child's behavior through language. The way in which the mother's language functionally influences the child's learning of things such as turn-taking and dialogue has also been touched upon by Snow (1972) and Greenfield and Smith (1976), among others.

There is no doubt that languge input affects language learning in both the cognitive and functional domains. Yet, because we have neither sufficient data, nor adequate indices of turn-taking skills, referential-semantic mapping strategies, or attention-directing strategies, researchers are unable at present to assess the specific contribution of motherese on these important aspects of language acquisition. If adequate dependent measures were available, one could begin to test the hypothesis that more motherese yields more rapid development in these important areas of language skill than does less motherese. One could identify those aspects of the child's language that emerge because of, or independent of, a tailored and simplified linguistic environment.

In general, the minimum adequate data required to estimate the effects of motherese involve: (a) assessing maternal speech and child speech in conversation at an initial interview (time 1 or T_1), and (b) measurement of the child's language at a subsequent interview (time 2 or T_2). Figure 1 displays the intuitive direction of the motherese effect (arrow *b*) from the mother's speech at T_1 to the child's speech at T_2. Any aspect of maternal speech that is influenced by the child during conversation is represented by arrow *a* above. The feedback model (Bohannon & Marquis, 1977; Berko-Gleason, 1977) argues that cues indicative of the child's ability to comprehend maternal speech controls, in part, the complexity of the mother's speech at that same point in time. Since most the work on the effects of motherese

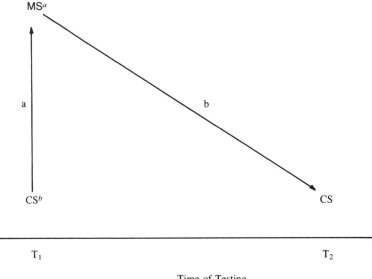

Time of Testing

[a]Maternal speech addressed to child.
[b]Child speech.

Figure 1.
Model of possible causal relations in maternal and child speech.

has been done in the syntactic domain, results from these studies domain can be used to assess the adequacy of this model.

The most comprehensive study on the relationship between motherese and syntax acquisition comes from Newport et al. (1977). These investigators studied 15 mother–child dyads to determine whether individual differences in the mother's speech predicted the child's language growth. The sample ranged in age from 12 to 27 months at T_1 with MLUs ranging from 1 to 3.65. Maternal utterances collected during the first of two interview sessions (MS at T_1 above) were analyzed along a number of syntactic dimensions including well-formedness, sentence length, structural and psychological complexity and sentence type, among others (see Newport et al., 1977, for more thorough discussions of these categories). The children's utterances were collected during two interview sessions (CS at T_1 and T_2 above) and were coded for syntactic complexity (estimated through MLU), mean noun-phrase frequency and length, mean verb-phrase frequency and length, inflection of noun-phrases (plural marking) and auxilliary (modals and tense marking) (see Newport et al., 1977, for further discussion).

As Newport et al. (1977) point out, one must go beyond simple correlations to assess the impact of maternal speech on language growth; simple correlations could reflect "the adjustment of the mothers to their child's age and initial linguistic level . . ." (p. 10). This effect is symbolized by arrow a in Figure 1 above. These authors argued further that, "the amount of the child's improvement over a given time span depends on his age and baseline at the beginning of the interval (this must be so since the language acquisition curves are not linear)" (Newport et al., 1977, p. 10).

To circumvent these potential statistical problems, Newport et al. (1977) employed the following procedures: (a) they obtained a language growth function for each child by computing language differences between T_1 and T_2; and (b) they partialed out any variance in this curve and in the mother's speech (MS at T_1 above) and child's speech at T_2 that was due either to the child's age or his level of language achievement at T_1. The residual variance left in the mother's and child's speech constitutes differences in the linguistic environments alone. By equating subjects for age and base level through partial correlations, they hoped to assess the residual correlations to unveil the effects of motherese on language acquisition.

In summarizing the results of this analysis, Newport et al. (1977) wrote,

> The measures of child language that we take to be indices of universal aspects of language and structure (e.g., number of noun phrases and verb phrases per utterance) are, so far as we can see in this limited study, insensitive to individual differences in maternal speech styles. (p. 27)

In contrast, motherese does contribute to the child's language in what Newport et al. (1977) call language specific, paradigmatic devices (e.g., tense and plural markings that are specific to the language being learned (see Goldin-Meadow, 1981, for a further discussion of differential learning among specific and general properties of language, termed fragile and resilient properties, respectively). By way of example, the mother's use of yes/no questions contributed positively to the child's use of the verbal auxilliary. It appeared that fronting the auxilliary in "*Can* I go here?" feeds the child's listening bias of "attend to the beginning of a sentence" (Shipley, Smith, & Gleitman, 1969). Though a child who is exposed to the auxilliary is more likely to use the auxilliary, it is interesting to note that these children do not use their auxilliaries in the contexts in which they were learned (i.e., the yes/no question). Rather, children appropriately embed the auxilliary within the verb-phrase (e.g., "I *can* go here.") (Gleitman & Wanner, 1981).

A recent study by Cross (1978) has also concluded that no measure of maternal syntactic simplicity "was significantly associated with the higher rate of (language) acquisition" (p. 207). In contrast to the Newport et al. (1977) method described above, Cross (1978) borrowed a paradigm from the field of reading research. She compared eight pairs of children who were matched on measures of language production (MLU and upperbound, mean length of the child's 50 longest utterances) and comprehension (a test of appropriate responding to 100 syntactically different sentences), sex of child, and family size. One child of each pair was 5 to 10 months younger than the other child, thus deriving a group of "accelerated" children and a group of "normal" children. She then compared the speech of the mothers of each child with the assumption that differences in the maternal speech at

T_1 reflect stable differences in the speech directed to the children over time and that these differences might be responsible for the differences between her accelerated and normal children at T_1. Some of her results agreed with Newport's in that the mothers of the accelerated children used fewer unintelligible utterances. On the other hand, Cross found that the mothers of the accelerated children tended to expand and extend their children's utterances much more than the mothers of the normal children, a result not found by the Newport et al. (1977) study.

However, the design of the Cross (1978) study may have little bearing on the issue of general syntactic development. If the Bohannon & Marquis (1977) model is correct in that maternal syntactic complexity is at least partially controlled by the child's ability to understand, then by matching the children on language comprehension there should be no differences between the measures of syntactic complexity from the mothers. As reported above, Newport et al. (1977) realized that same-time measures of maternal language complexity must be some function of the child's language skill at that time. Since Cross (1978) found no differences in maternal syntactic complexity measures (MLU, propositions/utterance, or in the use of 13 different sentence types), the study only adds weight to feedback model of motherese. That is, the mothers' speech was sensitive to the children's matched language capacities and *not* the differences in the children's ages. Therefore, the results of the Newport et al. (1977) study must be relied on to select between hypothetical models of language acquisition that require either: (a) the short, ''simplified'' sentences characteristic of motherese (Klein & Kuppen, 1970), or (b) the extensive syntactic exemplars typical of adult-adult conversation (Wexler & Culicover, 1980). Recently, a study by Furrow et al. (1979) has challenged the Newport data.

The Furrow et al. (1979) critique of the Newport et al. (1977) study is statistical and conceptual in nature. They propose that motherese has qualitatively different effects on the child at different ages and linguistic levels, and that the potential effects of motherese are not equal over time. Motherese in this scenario could have functional impact on the child at age A, (linguistic level A), but primarily a content effect at age C (linguistic level C). This hypothesis echoes a proposal by Berko-Gleason and Weintraub (1978). Under this kind of a model, the potential syntactic influence of motherese on a child's language acquisition could be statistically occluded by equating language level and age when those levels or ages were not actually equal. A child at age 2 years, language sophistication level B, for example, may demonstrate an effect that under Newport's calculations, would show evidence of ''global language learning.'' This effect would be washed out if the 2-year-old's results were equated with the child of 1 year (language level A) whose results demonstrate no susceptibility to the syntactic form of motherese.

Furrow et al. (1979) attempt to control for this confounding by studying a homogeneous sample of seven, one-word speakers who were all 18 months old at the first interview (T_1) and 27 months at the second (T_2). The speech samples from the mothers and the children at T_1 and T_2 were analyzed along a number of syntactic and semantic dimensions. Maternal speech was coded for variables of (a) sentence type (e.g., declaratives, imperatives); (b) structural units (e.g., words, sentence nodes, verbs-main, auxilliary), and also as units; (c) representatives of Brown's grammatical morphemes (e.g., tense, plural); and (d) MLU. Child speech was coded for mean length of utterance, verbs per utterance, noun phrase per utterance, auxilliaries per verb phrase and inflections per noun phrase. Correlations between maternal variables and child language growth were assessed at both T_1 and T_2. The character of the maternal speech over that period did not alter significantly.

There was some agreement in the results reported by Furrow et al. (1979) and the results reported by Newport et al. (1977). Among the concurring results were (a) maternal speech did predict noun-phrase and verb-phrase per utterance, and (b) the use of yes/no questions did predict sentence types. Of five correlations common to both studies (declaratives, yes/no questions, imperatives, interjections, and wh-questions), the direction and general magnitude of correlations were similar in all cases, and in two cases the significance of correlations was agreed upon. (Furrow et al., 1979, p. 433).

In other respects, however, the results of Furrow et al. (1979) are discrepant with findings reported by Newport et al. (1977). First, consistent with their assumptions, Furrow et al. (1979) find that correlations that exist between MS and CS at T_2 are different than correlations noted at T_1 when the child was younger:

> The latter correlations did not replicate those at (T_1). Indeed, in many cases, they were in the opposite direction, the most obvious case being the mother's use of verbs which at (T_1) was a significant negative predictor of child language growth, whereas at (T_2) was positively related to current language level. (Furrow et al., 1979, p. 434)

Furrow et al. (1979) take this to validate the assumption that motherese has an effect, and that this effect changes over the course of the child's development. Yet no measure of the maternal language is available, for example, at time zero or time three to allow us to assess this claim further.

Other discrepant findings between the two studies include Furrow et al.'s (1979) finding that maternal MLU predicts (negatively correlates with) the child's MLU and their finding that the use of syntactically more complex sentences retards the child's language development.

> The greater the number of words, verbs, pronouns, contractions or couplas per utterance used by a mother, the less advancement her child was likely to show over the time period observed. (Furrow et al., 1979, p. 433)

Since utterance length and complexity are hopelessly confounded here, it is impossible to tell whether children respond to the actual length of an utterance due to memory span difficulties or whether characteristics such as number of verbs, etc., lead to the finding. Regardless, the Furrow et al. (1979) study is an indication that at least for holophrastic children, a simplified motherese environment encourages general syntactic development nine months later.

For a number of reasons, both the Newport and Furrow studies should be interpreted with an element of caution. First, the limited sample size of the studies reported above yield correlations that are unstable. In the Furrow et al. (1979) study, the limited number of subjects sometimes resulted in a loss of relevant data points. Some subjects used constructions so infrequently that correlational analysis was impossible. Second, while there was some overlap in the coded variables across the two studies, there were a number of places where the maternal variables, presumed indicative of syntactic complexity, differed. Newport et al. (1977), for example, included maternal variables of psychological and structural complexity that were absent in the Furrow et al. (1979) analysis. It is more difficult to make comparisons between two studies when the syntactic indicators vary. Third, both the Newport and Furrow studies assume that MLU is an indicator of syntactic complexity. Even though a recent study by Fowler, Gelman, and Gleitman (1980) found that MLU was *the* best predictor of language development in normal and retarded children, longer utterances are generally, but not necessarily more complex. That is, length could contribute to psychological complexity (memory limits) without contributing to linguistic complexity. Consistent with this point, one must also be careful to differentiate language acceleration in the child, where input speeds the appearance of specific language productions, from an increase in language use, where aspects of maternal speech increase the probability that previously acquired syntactic structures will appear in more varied contexts.

Even the most cursory review of these important studies leaves the reader pondering the cause of their discrepant findings. At minimum, two hypotheses can be used to explain the divergent results; what we shall call the quantitative and qualitative hypotheses. Under the qualitative hypothesis, maternal language differentially affects different aspects of the child's language development at different times. As noted above, maternal speech may affect functional properties of child language at T_1 with a time lag A (the difference between times of measurement T_1 and T_x) and semantic development at T_2 with lag B. The discrepant results can then be accounted for in the following manner. Furrow et al. (1979) used a homogenous sample and found significant effects of maternal speech on child language. However, their results might not generalize to any other age or linguistic competency group. The quantitative hypothesis asserts that the effects of maternal language are everpresent but their potency is realized differently across different ages. The shape of the relationship (or the slope of the regression lines) changes with the child's advancing age. In this view, it is possible that neither study accurately captured the nature of the effect of maternal speech on their children's language development. Both the quantitative and qualitative hypotheses may be valid.

The issue of the appropriate time lag between times of testing is also unaddressed in the prior studies. Cross (1978), by assessing maternal speech and child speech at the same time, avoids the issue but also avoids the possibility of determining the relationship between maternal language and child language. The Newport et al. (1977) study used a six-month lag between T_1 and T_2 while the Furrow et al. (1979) study used a nine-month lag. It is at least possible that Newport and her colleagues assessed their children (at T_2) before the effects of the maternal speech could be seen in their subject's productive speech. On the other hand, the differences found in the Furrow et al. (1979) study may have disappeared if they had reassessed their sample two months later. It seems to us that many researchers ignore the twin issues of (a) the causal interval between predictor and criterion variables, and (b) the stability of language differences over time (i.e. gains in one period may wash out as the slower children "catch up").

THE NONLINEAR MODEL

The greatest problem for both studies may be inherent in the use of the linear model assumed by the correlation. The linear covariance model presupposes that if there is a relationship between maternal and child speech, the simpler the maternal speech (e.g., the shorter the maternal MLU at T_1), the greater will be the child's language gains between T_1 and T_2, regardless of the child's age or productive MLU at T_1. Taken to its extreme, such a monotonic relationship would mean that children whose productive MLU is 3 morphemes, will show the greatest gains if their mothers only address them in the simplest of sentences (e.g., maternal MLU approximating 1.0). Obviously, the linear model is unlikely. A more likely relationship between maternal speech at T_1 and child speech at T_2 is a nonlinear or nonmonotonic function. The nonlinear model presumes that there is an optimal level of length and complexity in maternal language, where speech that is either too complex or too simple would result in language delay. The more appropriate statistics to estimate nonlinear covariance are hierarchical regression designs that specifically test for a nonlinear component (Cohen & Cohen, 1975). Indeed, a model of this type if assessed with enough dependent measures of different aspects of emerging language at enough successive ages, would test for both the qualitative and quantitative hypotheses. The proposed nonlinear model is detailed below.

For the purpose of simplicity, we have used prior data to make several assumptions. First, we assume that mothers are sensitive to the comprehension abilities of their children (helped in part, by feedback cues from the child). Second, the resultant sentences then provide the primary linguistic data from which the children draw hypotheses concerning competing syntactic rules (Klein & Kuppen, 1970). It is possible that the child's exposure to complex structures used in adult–adult speech also serves a function, but we doubt that it is the primary source. This assumption restricts the experimental designs of studies attempting to test the effects of motherese on child speech to longitudinal designs. Same-time designs (Cross, 1978) may only reflect maternal sensitivity to the child's language level at the time of measurement. Moreover, this assumption implies that measures of child language, especially the child's ability to comprehend, are more appropriate covariates than the child's age, when trying to create groups of children who are homogenous with respect to language development. Third, the basic relationships of the model will be delineated using MLU as the primary data. In the acquisition of the English language, MLU correlates highly with all other measures purporting to assess general syntactic complexity (Newport, 1976; Fowler et al., 1980). However, similar models could be developed for other measures of syntax. Lastly, we will assume a fixed-lag causal interval (difference between T_1 and T_2) for all ages. It is possible that the causal interval between children's linguistic environment and subsequent advancements in the children's language skills changes in some lawful and predictable fashion over the course of normal language development. Yet, for the purpose of clarity, a single, optimum lag will be used for all ages and levels of children.

Under the assumption of the new model, the relationship (arrow *b* in Figure 1) between maternal speech and child language gains is a series of nonlinear functions, a different one for each age and language ability. For all practical purposes, the mother's speech is limited in its ability to become shorter when the child is very young (e.g., is it possible to speak in utterances of *less* than 1.0 morpheme?). Therefore, it is probable that this limitation imposes a skewed distribution on maternal speech, especially when the children are using their first words. Indeed, language users may assume some base level of listener competence when addressing a socially responsive listener (Hirsh-Pasek & Trieman, in press). This base level may provide the only time these curves would contain a significant linear component testable by the standard correlational methods. A test of this notion may lie in the Furrow et al. (1979) study. Even though Furrow et al. (1979) employed the linear model, the very fact that maternal MLU's approximating 1.0 are so rare may have led to their significant finding.

Figure 2 shows the series of hypothetical nonlinear functions relating child MLU gains between T_1 and T_2 and maternal MLU as it should look in a design using children of four different ages (assuming language abilities that are homogenous within ages and that increase across ages from beginning to sophisticated language ability) with a fixed time lag between assessments. Note that optimal peaks increase their distance from each other as the child grows older (the number at the top of Figure 2 refer to the child's age in months), reflecting the positively accelerated function of maternal MLU and child's age cited by Clarke-Stewart et al. (1979). This

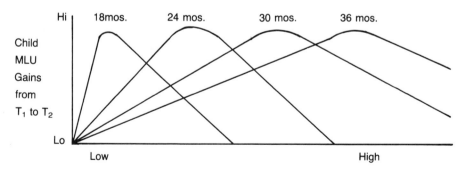

Figure 2.

The nonlinear, interactive model of the effects of maternal speech on language acquisition.

model suggests that simpler is not always better for all children. More sophisticated children probably require more sophisticated language environment (measured by longer maternal MLUs) than younger children to maximize their language development. In fact, it is quite possible that the relationship between maternal speech and child language development is reversed (longer is better) for children as old as 5 or 6 years.

Notice that the shape of the relationships depicted in Figure 2 changes over age. This is a reflection of the interaction between the child's age and linguistic level, and the mother's speech at any point in time (arrow a in Figure 1) with the child's subsequent development. Statistically, this is called a nonadditive model, because it incorporates an interaction term that changes the form of the relationship dependent (in this case) upon the child's initial language level at T_1. Encouragingly, the statistical treatment of nonadditive and nonlinear models is not as difficult as it would appear at first blush (see Cohen & Cohen, 1975, and Stolzenberg, 1980, for a review of these statistical treatments). If the Furrow et al. (1979) design, using developmentally homogenous groups of children (e.g., four groups at ages 18, 24, 30, and 36 months of age, all followed for nine months as depicted in Figure 2) was replicated with adequate numbers of subjects, the statistical analysis would be fairly simple. The details of such an analysis are given in the appendix to this chapter.

CONCLUSION AND DISCUSSION

It is obvious that the input language has a marked effect on the child's language acquisition. How much of an effect the input has, be it in structured language lessons (Moerk, 1975), or in a data base that triggers innate biases (Bates, Bretherton, Beeghly-Smith, & McNew, in press), or exactly what role the input plays in language development is still open to debate. Those who wish to place the impetus of language learning on a highly structured input have concentrated on the study of the limited language register addressed to children, called motherese. They have documented the features of motherese and the environments and variables that elicit this speech. Much of the "simple" nature of motherese seems to be a speaker's response to feedback from their listeners. Mothers simplify their speech because their children fail to comprehend long, complex utterances.

Though we think that the child influences the appearance of motherese, it is still unclear how the motherese affects the child. Studies that investigate the role of language input on functional and semantic properties of the developing child's language fail to assess whether those properties are due to generalized language input or the simplified nature of motherese. Studies that focus on the syntactic influence of motherese yield discrepant results; Newport et al. (1977) noting specific effects and Furrow et al. (1979) reporting more global benefits of motherese.

The Newport et al. study offered no evidence of a global effect of motherese on the general properties of syntactic learning. Recent theoretical arguments from the language learnability literature concur with these results. These investigators (see

Wexler & Culicover, 1980) suggest that exclusive exposure to motherese would not only be ineffective in teaching general syntactic properties (Newport et al., 1977), but would be detrimental to the task of language learning (see Gleitman & Wanner, 1982, for a review). The child who hears only the limited language input of motherese would fail to converge on the appropriate grammar for his language. This child might falsely conclude that he had induced the grammar, hearing no counter examples from the input. In fact, these authors argue, he is not given enough language information to either: correct his hypotheses, to narrow down this hypotheses about the candidate grammars, or to permit him to generate the more complex constructs in the grammar. In short, how could the child, exposed only to motherese, learn to speak the complex language evidenced in his speech by 4 years of age?

These theoretical concerns ally with the Newport et al. (1977) findings and go beyond these findings to suggest that motherese is not an appropriate explanation for the syntactic aspects of language acquisition. On the other hand, a survey of theoretical language acquisition models by Pinker (1979) failed to ascertain any advantage in the Wexler, Culicover, and Hamburger (1975) model over, for example, the Klein and Kuppen (1970) model which requires short, simple exemplars for language acquisition to proceed. Moreover, the Wexler et al. (1975) model entails the simultaneous comparison of all grammatical structures with each presented exemplar, and is possibly a psychologically unrealistic model of language acquisition in children. All children, even the youngest, hear some long (and probably complex) maternal utterances, although rarely. These few utterances may be enough to rescue children from a corpus composed exclusively of short, simple sentences and to allow them to attempt hypotheses about a grammar (e.g., a form of the language-learning device suggested by Wexler & Culicover, 1980). At the same time, most of what the child hears is less complex syntactically. This might be necessary for the child to contrast certain hypotheses about competing grammars (e.g., the model of Klein & Kuppen, 1970). Since none of these theoretical models have yet to be empirically investigated, the claim that motherese is an ineffective language teaching device crucially rests on the Newport et al. (1977) and similar findings.

The present chapter has proposed a different model of maternal–child verbal interaction that may account for the discrepancies between the Newport et al. (1977) and Furrow et al. (1979) studies. Divergent results in the syntactic domain may have been due to psychology's reliance on linear statistical models, even in cases where such models are unwarranted. The Pearson correlation, albeit with an age-partialled modification, relies upon an assumption of linear relationships between the variables. Yet, maternal speech and child language development are both admittedly nonlinear functions of development with age. The most plausible model relating the mother's verbal behavior to the child's emerging linguistic skills is also nonlinear. Given these propositions, it only remains to test the new model utilizing curvilinear relationships assessed by hierarchical, step-wise regression designs that test for the significance of a nonlinear component (see Appendix 1).

Results from these new analyses may support the original Newport et al. (1977) contention or, in contrast, they may support the Furrow et al. (1979) claim. In either event, the hypothesis that motherese assists the process of language acquisition differentially over time, deserves further inspection. New data involving the model proposed in this chapter may help factor out those language domains that are triggered by, or alternatively, molded by the child's linguistic environment.

APPENDIX

The statistical model used by both Newport et al. (1977) and by Furrow et al. (1978) is defined by Equation 1, where y and x are the deviation scores of child speech at T_2 and maternal speech to the child at T_1, respectively. The b_{yx} term is the slope of the regression line of y on x.

Equation 1. $y = b_{yx} x + e$

This assumes that the relationship between y and x is linear in both parameters and variables. A simple test of this assumption involves solving for a nonlinear regression component in the variable x, as in Equation 2. The $b_{yx^2 \cdot x}$ regression weight accounts for the proportion of nonlinear convariance independent of the linear component. The obtained R^2 from Equation 2 can be divided by the R^2 from Equation 1 in an F ratio ($df = n - a - 1$, where a is the number of component terms in the equation) to determine the significance of the additional variance of y accounted for by the nonlinear component. Another method to test the significance of the additional b-weight would be a simple t-test of the new weight (Cohen & Cohen, 1975).

Equation 2. $y = b_{yx} x + b_{yx^2 \cdot x} x^2 + e$

Newport et al. (1977) went further to propose what is called a modifier variable which also influences the relationship between maternal speech (x) and subsequent child language development (y). In her study, the modifier variables were the child's initial age and language level, or simplified here as a single variable for the purposes of demonstration as z in Equation 3. In Equation 3, the b's are unstandard regression weights which determine the relative contribution of x and z on the prediction of y. Again, this equation assumes the regression of y on x and z is linear in both parameters and variables. This model assumes further that the effects are additive. That is, that the variance in y accounted for by x and z is contained in the weighted/additive combination of x and z, where the weights are determined by the ordinary least squares. A comparison of Equation 3 with Equation 1 in another F test will test for the significance of the additive contribution of x and z on y.

Equation 3. $y = b_{yx} x + b_{yz \cdot x} z + e$

In general, higher-order models should be tested to justify the reliance on the simpler models. A regression weight for a xz cross-product may be included to assess the degree to which the relationship between y and x varies as a function of differing levels of z (Cohen & Cohen, 1975). That is, the y, x relation is nonadditive because x interacts with z. The equation for this is displayed in Equation 4 where the $b_{y(xz) \cdot x,z}$ unstandard regression weight term accounts for the interaction between x and z with the main effects of x and z held constant. In fact, Furrow's assumption of a changing relationship between maternal speech and child speech at differing times of measurement would seem to argue for just such a interaction. A further F test between Equations 3 and 4 would test for the nonadditive or interaction effects of z and x, on y.

Equation 4. $y = b_{yx} \, x + b_{yz.x} \, z + b_{y(xz),z} \, xz + e$

In addition, the present chapter argues for a further test based on a nonlinear component relating maternal speech (x) at T_1 with the child's speech (y) at T_2. If a curve with a single inflection point is assumed, this relationship may be tested using Equation 5. The $b_{y(x^2).x,z,xz}$ term is the unstandardized regression weight of the contribution of a nonlinear regression of y on x with the linear effects of x, z, and the interaction of x and z held constant. This equation would be used as the denominator in an F ratio to test actual theoretical relationship between y, x, and z.

Equation 5. $y = b_{yx}x + b_{yz.x}z + b_{y(xz).x,z} \, xz + b_{y(x^2).x,z,xz}x^2 + e$

What was hypothesized in this chapter was a relationship between the mother's speech (x) at T_1 and the child's initial age and language level (z) at T_1, where the facilitative effects of x change as a function of z. As the child grows older the shape of the curvilinear relationship between x and the child's future language development (y) changes substantially (see Fig. 2). This is the definition of an interaction signified by the $b_{y(x^2 z).x,z,xz,x}^2 \, x^2z$ term in Equation 6. The unstandard regression weight holds constant or controls for all the other effects specified in the model. An F ratio comparison of Equations 5 and 6 would be the most accurate test of the hypothesized relationship between maternal language addressed to the child and the child's subsequent language development.

Equation 6. $y = b_{yx} \, x + b_{yz.x} \, z + b_{y(xz).x,z} \, xz + b_{yx^2.x,z,xz} \, x^2 + b_{y(zx^2).x,z,xz,x^2} \, x^2z + e$

(The above equations are hierarchical and must be solved in a step-wise fashion (Cohen & Cohen, 1975). The resultant R^2 terms for each equation may be calculated using several of the standard statistical computer programs currently available, [e.g., the multiple regression section of the Biomedical statistical package (BMDP)]. Since the relative amount of covariance accounted for by each equation is the matter of theoretical import, the exact values of the b weights in each equation can also be tested using t-tests.

REFERENCES

Bates, E., Bretherton, I., Beeghly-Smith, M., & McNew, S. The social basis of language development. In H. Reese & L. Lipsitt (Eds.), *Advances in child development and behavior* (Vol. 16). New York: Academic Press, in press.

Berko-Gleason, J. Some notes on feedback. In C. Snow & C. Ferguson (Eds.), *Talking to children: Language input and acquisition.* Cambridge, MA: Cambridge University Press, 1977.

Berko-Gleason, J., & Weintraub, S. Input language and the acquisition of communicative competence. In K. Nelson (Ed.). *Children's language* (Vol. 1). New York: Gardiner Press, 1978.

Bever, B., Fodor, J., & Weksel, W. On the acquisition of syntax: A critique of "contextual generalization." *Psychological Review*, 1965, 72, 467–482.

Bohannon, J., Lotz, E., & Ritzenberg, D. The effects of experience and feedback on motherese. *The Bulletin of the Psychonomic Society*, 1982, *19*, 201–204.

Bohannon, J., & Marquis, A. Children's control of adult speech. *Child Development*, 1977, *48*, 1002–1008.

Bohannon, J., & Warren-Leubecker, A. The effects of verbal feedback and listener type on the speech of preschool children, *Journal of Experimental Child Psychology*, 1983, in press.

Bohannon, J., & Warren-Leubecker, A. Speech to foreigners: Effects of expectation and feedback. *Journal of Psycholinguistic Research*, 1982, *11*, 207–215.

Bohannon, J., & Rondon, B. The feedback model of motherese in Spanish. Unpublished senior thesis, Univesite del Norte, Columbia, South America, 1981.

Chomsky, N. *Aspects of a theory of syntax*. Cambridge, MA: MIT Press, 1965.

Clarke-Stewart, K. A. *Child care in the family: A review of research and some perspectives on policy*. New York: Academic Press, 1977.

Clarke-Stewart, K. A., VanderStoep, L., & Killian, G. Analysis and replication of mother–child relations at two years of age. *Child Development*, 1979, *50*, 777–793.

Cohen, J. & Cohen, P. *Applied multiple regression/correlation analysis for the behavioral sciences*. New York: Erlbaum, 1975.

Cross, T. Mother's speech and its association with rate of linguistic development in young children. In N. Waterson & C. Snow (Eds.), *The development of communication*. New York: Wiley, 1978.

Dale, P. *Language Development* (2nd ed.). New York: Holt, Rinehart & Winston, 1976.

DeCasper, A. Newborn preference for maternal voice: An indication of early attachment. Paper presented at the meeting of the Southeastern Conference on Human Development, Alexandria, VA, April 1980.

DePaulo, B., & Bonvillian, J. The effect on language development of the special characteristics of speech addressed to children. *Journal of Psycholinguistic Research*, 1978, *7*, 189–211.

Eimas, P., Siqueland, E., Vigorito, J., & Jusczyk, P. Speech perception in infants, *Science*, 1971, *171*, 303–306.

Feldman, G., Goldin-Meadow, S., & Gleitman, L. Beyond Herodotus: The creation of language by linguistically deprived deaf children. In A. Locke (Ed.), *Action, symbol & gesture: The emergence of language*. New York: Academic Press, 1978.

Ferguson, C. Towards a characterization of English foreigner talk. *Anthropological Linguistics*, 1975, *17*, 1–17.

Ferguson, C. Baby talk as a simplified register. In C. Snow & C. Ferguson (Eds.), *Talking to children: Language input and acquisition*. Cambridge, MA: Cambridge University Press, 1977.

Fernald, A. Four month olds prefer to listen to motherese. Paper presented at the meeting of the Society for Research in Child Development, Boston, April 1981.

Fowler, A., Gelman, R., & Gleitman, L. A comparison of normal and retarded language equated on MLU. Paper presented at the Boston University Conference on Language Development, Boston, October 1980.

Freed, B. Foreigner talk: The study of adjustments made by native speakers to nonnative speakers in conversation. Unpublished doctoral dissertation, University of Pennsylvania, 1978.

Friedlander, B. Receptive language development in infancy. *Merrill-Palmer Quarterly*, 1970, *16*, 7–51.

Furrow, D., Nelson, K., & Benedict, H. Mother's speech to children and syntactic development: Some simple relationships. *Journal of Child Language*, 1979, *6*, 423–442.

Garnica, O. Some characteristics of prosodic input to young children. Paper presented at the Social Science Research Council Conference on Language Input and Acquisition, Boston, September, 1974.

Gleitman, L., & Wanner, E. Language learning: State of the art. In E. Wanner & L. Gleitman (Eds.), *Language learning*. Cambridge, MA: Cambridge University Press, 1982.

Goldin-Meadow, S. The resiliance of recursion. In E. Wanner & L. Gleitman (Eds.), *Language learning*. Cambridge, MA: Cambridge University Press, 1981.

Golinkoff, R. & Ames, G. A comparison of father's and mother's speech to their young children. *Child Development*, 1979, *50*, 28–32.

Greenfield, P. & Smith, J. *The structure of communication in early language development.* New York: Academic Press, 1976.

Hirsh-Pasek, K. & Trieman, R. Doggerel: Motherese in a new context. *Journal of Child Language,* in press.

Klein, S. & Kuppen, M. An interactive program for learning transformational grammars. *Computer Studies in the Humanities and Verbal Behavior,* 1970, *3,* 144–162.

Kuczaj, S. Evidence for a language learning strategy: On the relative ease of acquisition of prefixes and suffixes. *Child Development,* 1979, *50,* 1–13.

Lennenberg, E. *Biological foundations of language.* New York: Wiley, 1967.

Moerk, E. Verbal interactions between children and their mothers during the preschool years. *Developmental Psychology,* 1975, *11,* 788–794.

Moerk, E. The mother of Eve: As a first language teacher. Paper presented at the Society for Research in Child Development, San Francisco, March 1979.

Moskowitz, B. Language acquisition. *Scientific American,* 1978, reprints.

Nelson, K. Structure and strategy in learning to talk. *Monographs of the Society for Research in Child Development,* 1973, *38*(Serial No. 149).

Newport, E. Motherese: The speech of mothers to young children. In N. Castellan, D. Pisoni & G. Potts (Eds.), *Cognitive theory* (Vol. 2). Hillsdale, NJ: Erlbaum, 1976.

Newport, E., Gleitman, L., & Gleitman, H. Mother, I'd rather do it myself: Some effects and non-effects of motherese. In C. Snow & C. Ferguson (Eds.), *Talking to children: Language input and acquisition.* Cambridge, MA: Cambridge University Press, 1977.

Pinker, S. Formal models of language learning. *Cognition,* 1979, *7,* 217–283.

Pratt, M., Bumstead, D., & Raines, N. Attendant staff speech to the institutionalized retarded: Language use as a measure of the quality of care. *Journal of Child Psychology and Psychiatry,* 1976, *17,* 133–144.

Retherford, K., Schwartz, B., & Chapman, R. Semantic roles and residual grammatical categories in mother and child speech: Who tunes to whom? *Journal of Child Language,* 1981, *8,* 583–608.

Rheingold, H. & Joseph, J. Speech to newborns by nursery personnel. Paper presented at the meeting of the Society for Research in Child Development, New Orleans, March 1977.

Rileigh, K. Children's selective listening to stories: Familiarity effects involving vocabulary, syntax, and intonation. *Psychological Reports,* 1973, *33,* 255–266.

Ryan, J. Mother's perception of their child's linguistic ability. Paper presented at the Southeastern Conference on Human Development, Atlanta, April, 1978.

Sachs, J., & Devin, J. Young children's use of age appropriate speech styles in social interaction and role-playing. *Journal of Child Language,* 1976, *3,* 81–98.

Sachs, J., & Johnson, M. Language development in a hearing child of deaf parents. Paper presented at the International Symposium on First Language Acquisition, Florence, Italy, 1972.

Shatz, M., & Gelman, R. The development of communication skills: Modifications in the speech of young children as a function of the listener. *Monographs of the Society for Research in Child Development,* 1973, 38(Serial No. 152).

Shipley, E., Smith, C., & Gleitman, L. A study in the acquisition of language: Free responses to commands. *Language,* 1969, *45,* 332–342.

Slobin, D. Cognitive prerequisites for the development of grammar. In C. Ferguson & D. Slobin (Eds.), *Studies of child language development.* New York: Holt, Rinehart & Winston, 1973.

Snow, C. Mother's speech to children learning language. *Child Development,* 1972, *43,* 549–565.

Snow, C., & Ferguson, C. (Eds.). *Talking to children: Language input and acquisition.* Cambridge, MA: Cambridge University Press, 1977.

Stolzenberg, R. The measurement and decomposition of causal effects in nonlinear and nonadditive models. In K. Scheussler (Ed.), *Methodological sociology.* San Francisco: Jossey-Bass, 1980.

Wexler, K., & Culicover, P. *Formal principles of language acquisition.* Cambridge, MA: MIT Press, 1980.

Wexler, K., Culicover, P., & Hamburger, H. Learning theoretic foundations of linguistic universals. *Theoretical Linguistics,* 1975, *2,* 215–253.

CHAPTER 10

Functions of Speech in Mother–Infant Interaction*

Anat Ninio and Polly Wheeler

One of the aspects of language that children have to acquire is how to use speech to perform social acts (Austin, 1962; Grice, 1957; Searle, 1969). Children must learn how to use words, for example, to greet, to request, to regulate an activity with a playmate, or to draw another's attention to something. In trying to understand how children come to learn the social uses of language it is commonsensical to turn to an examination of what models are available for them. When mothers interact with their children the mothers perform such linguistic social acts. An examination of maternal speech to language-learning children, then, will provide basic information about what speech functions are modeled for children and how these functions are carried out by conventional linguistic means. A comparison, along these dimensions, of input language with children's subsequent productions will suggest how the two are related, if at all.

The assumption underlying all theories of language learning is that language acquisition is possible because children can grasp the sense of utterances they hear, independently of understanding the sentences themselves. Language learning, then, is based on the child's matching unknown verbal forms to known meanings (Anderson, 1976; Macnamara, 1972).

Although this idea has the flavor of a real insight into the processes of language acquisition, an attempt to develop it further immediately stumbles against the crucial problem of how to characterize the meanings the child might attribute to the

* The research described in this paper is supported by Grant No. 2467/81 from the United States-Israel Binational Science Foundation to A. Ninio and C. Eckerman.

communications directed at him. Semantically oriented theoreticians like Bloom (1970) and Schlesinger (1971) would claim that young children interpret their experience, and, therefore, the utterances they hear, in terms of broad semantic relations, such as the relation of agents to actions they perform. Language learning at its early stages would, then, consist of acquiring the realization rules by which semantic relations are expressed through linguistic devices such as word order.

This is obviously only one possible way to think of children's organization of their reality in meaningful terms. During the last few years, several investigators have put forward suggestive evidence to the effect that young children primarily organize their experience, and, therefore, interpret the utterances they hear in functional rather than semantic terms. Bates (1976), Bruner (1975), Dore (1975), Halliday (1975), and others put forward the claims that young children are very much adept at interpreting the social meanings of situations they are involved in and are primarily engaged in both interpreting others' intentions in interaction and in expressing their own intentions, whether in prelinguistic or linguistic forms. This approach assigns a prominent role in the child's "reading" of utterances to the pragmatic function of the utterances; furthermore, it sees language acquisition in its primary stages as the learning of verbal forms for the execution of social acts.

According to this school of thought, young children are able to establish mutually interpretable intent with their caregivers because much of their communication is embedded in routinized, repetitive, rule-governed transactions. (Bruner, 1975, 1980; Bruner & Sherwood, 1976; Garvey, 1974; Snow, Dubber, & deBlauw, unpub. ms.). Examples of such "formats," as Bruner calls them, are everyday caretaking routines such as feeding, bathing, diapering; simple games such as peek-a-boo, run-and-chase, build-and-knock-down; and formats for achieving and maintaining joint focus of attention, requesting help, inviting joint action, and the like. Since the range of possible meaning in formats is severely restricted, and since the events are simple and predictable, preverbal infants, it is claimed, are able to establish a shared experience with their adult partners. Within such contexts, communicative intentions can be conventionized and mutually interpreted.

There are indications that early language learning is indeed highly context-specific and that children acquire their earliest verbal forms for the execution of specific sociolinguistic functions. Halliday (1975) has shown that all of his child's first verbal devices were function-specific and unifunctional, and only gradually did the child come to use the same word or phrase for more than one pragmatic function. Bates (1976), Benedict (1979), Bruner (1975), Clark (1974), Snow (in press), and Svachkin (1973) also presented evidence of function specific and context bound acquisition.

It seems that much of this learning is established through simple copying of models presented by adults for the child. The very first verbal forms are probably copied from models experienced as having privileges of occurrence at specified points in formats. They seem to have no semantic content and might be said to be "pure performatives." Such forms are "bye-bye," "hi," "thank you," and utterances embedded in familiar games, as documented by Bruner (1975), Greenfield and Smith (1976), and Nelson (1973). At a more sophisticated level, utterances by adults are used as models for the verbal expression of shared interpersonal meanings. Clark (1974) and Snow (in press) have shown that children sometimes appropriate whole phrases and sentences said by adults in particular situations and use them as unanalyzed wholes to give verbal expression to their intentions. Thus, a child might learn to say "lift you up" as a demand for adults to lift him up, possibly because adults present him with the model "Do you want me to lift you up?" when such an intention is demonstrated by a child nonverbally. Such phrases are obviously learned in, and useful in, specific contexts, for the expression of highly specific intentions. Another form of functionally based learning is, possibly, of simple grammatic formulae used to express a more general pragmatic intention that pertains to several different contexts. Halliday (1975) described such a formula for demanding more of a desired stuff, in the form of "more X." Shatz (1977) has shown recently that mothers' speech exhibits a relatively high degree of form-function correspondence, in that for several functions such as requests and questions for information there exists a major prototypical formula which accounts for the majority of the utterances made with the relevant intent. Thus, the majority of directives had the form, "Can you do X?" Such consistent form-function relations probably enable the child to learn the formula as a relatively flexible device for the expression of similar intentions in differing contexts.

If indeed early language acquisition is largely based on the process of copying adult-provided models for the verbal performance of social acts, the systematic exploration of the process of language learning should include tracing the relationship between adult models and the children's subsequent productions. The success of such an endeavor depends on the correct identification of the social functions of language which are modeled for children in the context of shared social experience. In the rest of this chapter, we are presenting an account of our attempt to identify and classify the shared social uses of language in mother–infant dyads. The work is still in progress, and what we are describing is more how we think about these problems than any final solutions.

In order to obtain a description of the social meanings created in dyadic interaction, we have turned to the mothers and used them as informants on, and interpreters of, videotaped episodes of dyadic activity they had participated in with their infants. In this decision we were motivated by the currently prominent notion in philosophy and social psychology (Bateson, 1955; Cicourel, 1970; Davidson, 1980; Harre, 1979; and especially Erwin Goffman, 1974), that human beings continuously interpret the world and their experience to themselves through the use of schemas of interpretation, which render "what would otherwise be a meaningless aspect of the scene into something which is meaningful" (Goffman, 1974, p. 21). Moreover, we accepted the claim that people are able to give an account of their interpretation of social reality since these interpretative schemas exist within the cognitive field of the person behaving (cf. Wright, 1967). In this we followed one of the established methods of ethnography, the so-called "account analysis" (cf. Carini, 1975; Cicourel, 1970; Garfinkel, 1967; Harre, 1979).

The procedure of an elicitation session is as follows. The experimenter explains the aim of the session to the mother as an attempt to elicit a full description of the taped observation as if to a person who hasn't seen the tape or the actual interaction period. The experimenter asks the mothers to describe the ongoing activity seen on the tapes by the use of questions such as "What is it that's going on here?" (Goffman, 1974, p. 8), "What is happening?" "What are you doing?" The mothers are directed to provide a running commentary on whatever is happening. They are asked to watch the tape for a short while, then stop it and give a description of whatever happened in the section they had been watching. The interviewer lets the mothers pace themselves but he rewinds the tape and asks for further description of sections where some actions were skipped over and not described by the mothers, or if the descriptions were not detailed enough.

The goal of the elicitation procedure is to obtain an utterance-by-utterance description of the social acts performed by the speech of the two participants in the dyadic interaction. These descriptions are to serve as a basic data pool for the construction of a typology of sociolinguistic acts occurring in mother–infant interaction, acts whose meaning is shared by both participants.

Not all social meanings reported by mothers might be equally shared by the children who are their partners in the interactive situation. Adults interpret social situations on many levels, not all of which can be meaningful for a young child. Some meanings are not intended to be shared with the child and thus are a priorily not part of the interpersonally negotiated meaning. Mothers might intend to distract the child from some undesirable activity without his noticing that he was distracted. Mothers might purposefully under-react to a painful or frightening event involving the child in order not to alarm him further. In these cases, mothers actually want to hide their true intentions from their children, and even though they report on them to the experimenter, these are not part of the shared social context.

Mothers might also report intentions which are not shared by their children because they are beyond the children's comprehension. For example, mothers may say that they intended by their acts to shape the child's interests, to make him more intelligent, to keep him facing the camera, or to receive emotionally satisfying responses from him.

When a mother reports as the intention underlying a communication something which is obviously not meant to be shared by her child, she is asked to give an alternative description of the same act. For example, in a situation where a child was playing with the TV set, the mother said, "Why don't you come and play with your ball now?" When she reported on this moment, the mother said she had wanted to distract the child without his being aware of it, since otherwise he would go on playing with the TV set on purpose. She was then asked by the experimenters, "What did you do to achieve this aim?" Such a question usually succeeded in eliciting an answer in terms of overtly communicated intentions. In the present example, the mother said that she had showed another toy to the child and suggested to him that he play with that toy.

Mothers might also describe and explain the ongoing interchange in much too general terms. The experimenter's task is to make sure the mothers come to describe the meaning of every utterance in terms of its relation to what was going on the moment it was uttered. We do not want mothers, for example, to describe ten minutes of interaction as "playing with a puzzle." While this description may be valid for another sort of analysis, it is much too broad a level of description for us, given our interests in language acquisition. "Playing with a puzzle" is not the level of social meaning at which we assume individual utterances are generated or interpreted. It does not seem reasonable to think that children learn verbal forms for a functional unit such as "puzzle play." Rather a meaning of much narrower scope seems reasonable, such as "asking where a piece goes."

The procedure of asking the mothers to describe in detail very short sections of the taped interaction has been found to be most helpful in directing the mothers to an act-by-act level of reporting. If, nevertheless, they provide a too general descriptive statement, it is easy enough to repair this by asking further questions (i.e., about the intended social meaning of individual utterances).

The attempt to classify the social uses of language reported by mothers started off from a theoretical base, since there already existed in the philosophy of language a theory of the social acts that utterances perform. This is the theory of Speech Acts introduced by Austin (1962), developed by Searle (1969), and extended by Holdcroft (1978), Vendler (1972), and others. The theory posits that speech performs social acts such as promising, requesting, cursing, warning, asserting, and so on. Speech acts are identified by their so-called "illocutionary force." Illocutionary force refers to how an utterance is to be taken, given the speaker's intentions and given that the necessary preconditions apply. For example, the utterance, "Please close the door," functions as a request, given that the speaker intends to let the hearer know that that is what the speaker wants, and given that the hearer is capable of carrying out the request.

We have decided to incorporate the idea of a speech act and the types of illocutionary forces listed by speech-act theorists into the formal classificatory system for the description of the social acts performed by the speech of mothers and their young children. We have two reasons for this decision. In the first place, the notion that in speaking, we perform acts of the character described by Speech Act theory is intuitively strongly convincing. In the second place, pilot work has shown that when mothers describe their utterances, they frequently indicate the utterances' illocutionary force. For example, they say that they *asked* the child *to do* so and so, and they *warned* the child *not to do* something, and so forth. Thus, mothers' reports about the function of their utterances is captured at least in part by Speech Act terminology.

Table 1 present the list of speech acts that we have tentatively identified as occurring in mother–infant discourse. The construction of this taxonomy started with the compilation of a comprehensive list of all speech acts we found mentioned in the writings of Speech Act theorists. Then, we deleted all those speech acts which cannot or would not occur in the mother–infant context because they are tied to very different social contexts, such as marrying or pleading a case in court. The remain-

TABLE 1
Speech Acts Occurring in Mother/Infant Interaction

Speech Acts	Examples
Agree (to do)	"All right" "OK. Give it to me and I'll do it."
Agree (with proposition)	"Yes, that's a duck." "That's right."
Answer affirmatively	"Yes."
Answer negatively	"No."
Apologize[a]	"I am sorry." "Sorry, I didn't mean to break it."
Ask for permission	"I am going to read now, O.K.?" "I am going to the kitchen, all right?"
Call	"Sarah!" "Hey!"
Comfort[a]	"Oh, you poor baby!" "Never mind, you'll be all right."
Congratulate[a]	"Mazel Tov!"
Correct hearer's error (in language use)	"That's a *chair*" (and not a duck). "He's *your* father (not *my* father)."
Criticize (for error in motor performance)	"No, it's upside down." "You can't put it in there."
Dare/challenge	"I bet you can't find another wheel." "If you *can* dance, show me."
Declare state of affairs	"We are done playing with the dirty handkerchiefs." "I am a wolf."
Disagree (with proposition)	"No, that's not a duck." "There isn't a ball in that picture."
Disapprove/scold/protest	"What are you doing?" "You naughty little boy."
Elicit completion of word or sentence	"This little piggy went to the . . ." "Umb-rel- . . ."
Elicit imitation	"Say 'doll!'" "Can you say duck? Say 'duck.'"
Exclaim	"Oops." "Wow!"
Give in	"As you wish." "O.K."
Greet upon meeting[a]	"Hi!" "Hello!"
Greet upon parting[a]	"Good night." "Bye-bye!"
Imitate	
Mark transfer of object	"Here."
Perform move in game[a]	"Peek-a-boo!" "Round and round the garden, etc."
Permit (to do)	"All right, *you* do it." (You really insist on it?) OK, tear it up."
Polite response to "Thank you"[a]	"You're welcome"
Polite wish for good appetite[a]	"Bon appetit!"
Polite wish upon sneezing[a]	"Bless you!"
Praise (for motor performance)	"Good!" "That's right!"
Prohibit/forbid	"Don't touch it!" "You are to not crawl under the bed."
Promise	"I'll buy you a watch for your birthday." "I promise we'll go for a walk later."
Question (wh-question)	"What's that?" "Where do you want to sit?"
Refuse (to do)	"No, I can't pick you up right now." "I don't want to do it one more time."

(continued)

Table 1. *(Continued)*

Speech Acts	Examples
Request/propose/suggest	"Let's build a tower." "Give it to me!"
State	"This is blue." "Here is a boat."
State as answer to wh- question	"A giraffe." "Because you lost them."
State intent	"I am going to the kitchen now." "I am going to change your diaper."
Thank[a]	"Thank you."
Threaten to do	"I'll take it away from you." "I'll spank you if you don't stop yelling."
Verbalize–nonfunctional	"Daddy." "This."
Warn of danger	"Be careful, it's hot." "You'll bump your head under the bed."
Yes–no question	"Do you have to go to the bathroom?" "Right?"

[a] This speech act has identical illocutionary force and activity function.

ing categories were tested against the maternal descriptions, and the present short list consists of those speech acts which were actually reported by mothers as occurring in interaction. It should be mentioned that mothers do not consistently use the precise illocutionary verbs identifying given illocutionary forces, but often paraphrase them in various ways. This fact made necessary the disregarding of some finer distinctions between similar speech acts and the construction of wider categories. Thus, "request," "suggest," "propose," and their relatives are grouped into a single category, since it is usually unclear from the parental description how strong was the force with which any particular directive had been uttered. Similarly, "disapprove," "scold," and "protest" are a single category, as are "prohibit" and "forbid." A general category of "state" covers most acts with a declarative intent.

We have also decided to explicitly differentiate between some acts which are not clearly differentiated in Speech Act theory, although their illocutionary force seem not quite the same. We separated praise and criticism for motor performance from positive and negative feedback on labeling, (the latter coded as Agree and Disagree with proposition) since the former have to do with the correctness of actions while the latter with the truthfulness of propositions. We also differentiated between spontaneous statements and answers to questions.

The category of "perform move in game" deserves further comment. There will be eventually several different acts of this type in the category system, each individually defined. An example is the utterance of the phrase "peek-a-boo" in the relevant game. Similar speech acts, occurring in adult discourse, have been recognized by the theorists, such as carried out by the utterance of "check" in chess or "pass" in bridge.

The list presented in Table 1 is still under revision. As more corpora of maternal descriptions are collected, additional speech acts will probably be found to have occurred in mother–infant interaction. According to informal observations, strong candidates for inclusion are "pardon," "declare punishment," and "swear at." The final classificatory system will be the result of the first year's work on this project.

However, it is apparent already that a classificatory system built only on speech act categories would not be sufficient to adequately capture major aspects of the use of speech in mother–infant interaction. In particular, speech act definitions do not always convey how speech fitted into the events of joint activity (e.g., whether a request was used to initiate, to regulate, or to wind up an activity [see also Streeck, 1980]). The indifference of speech act definitions to the specific context in which speech was uttered is a serious shortcoming from our point of view, since we believe, with Bruner (1975), Snow et al. (unpub. ms.), and others, that young children attribute meaning to utterances addressed to them in terms of the (to them) intelligible activity context in which speech is embedded. As we have shown, this view is supported by suggestive evidence on the context-specificity and the narrow functional character of children's early production. Moreover, examination of mothers' reports on the function of their speech clearly reveals that they perceive their own intentions as having to do with the creation of a shared context, either of joint attention or of joint activity. For example, they define an utterance of the type "Do you want to play with Lego?" as an attempt to initiate a new activity with the child, rather than the performance of a speech act such as suggesting or asking a question. Similarly, an utterance of the type "Where's the ball?" is defined as an attempt to direct the child's attention to the ball, rather than as a question or as a request to locate the ball.

The illocutionary force and the activity-related function of an utterance are to some extent independent of each other. The same speech acts might be used for different activity purposes. A request might call for the performance of a novel act from the child, as in "Bring me a book," or it might demand that he stop doing whatever he is currently engaged in (as in "Stop spitting your food out"). Declarations might be used to create roles in fantasy play (as in "I am a witch") or to wind up a game (as in "I am not playing anymore").

Moreover, utterances of different illocutionary force may perform the same function with respect to the ongoing activity. For example, a father in our pilot work used requests, a question, a threat, more requests, and a declaration (in that order) to stop his child from blowing bubbles in his drink, saying, "Stop! Stop! Stop! What are you doing? Father'll take it away. No! Give it to me. Don't do it. That's enough!" (Translated from Hebrew) If we classified these utterances solely by their illocutionary force, we would obscure the fact that they all had the same function in the activity.

These considerations have led us to the conclusion that an adequate classificatory system of speech functions will have to consist of two parts: the first will identify the illocutionary force of an utterance, and the second will identify the utterance's function in the ongoing activity. Table 2 presents a list of activity-related functions of speech abstracted from mothers' descriptions. The list is organized in three

TABLE 2
Activity-related Functions of Speech in Mother/Infant Interaction

Groups	Categories of Speech Functions	Examples
Management of single and joint activity	Regulate hearer's actions	"Put it here." "It's upside down."
	Stop/prevent hearer's action	"Stop it!" "We are not going to play with daddy now."
	Offer to help	"Shall I hold it for you?" "Do you want me to open it?"
	Ask for help	"Come and help me make tea." "Hold it for me."
	Comply to demands for help	"Here is it."
	Make hearer pause in his action	"Just a minute." "Wait a bit, I'll fix it."
	Negotiate new activity	"Do you want to hear a record?" "Call Grandmother on the phone."
	Negotiate renewal of activity	"More swinging?" "Another time?"
	Attempt to end activity	"That's enough." "I am too tired to go on."
	Mark completion of act/activity	"There." "All gone."
	Allocate roles in joint activity	"I will be the clown." "You do it to mommy."
	Allocate turns in turn-taking activity	"Your turn now." "Now Mommy."
	Evaluate hearer's performance	"That's right." "Naughty girl."
	Evaluate speaker's performance	"What a bad mummy you have."
	Perform verbal move in activity[a]	"Peek-a-boo!" "This little piggy went, etc."
	Model hearer's move in activity	"Bye-Bye!" "Hallo, Grandmother, how are you?"
Maintenance of shared attention	Direct hearer's attention to objects and persons	"Look, it's turning." "There's a wheel under the chair."
	Show attentiveness	"What?" "Hm."
	Discuss joint focus of attention	"It fell down." "This doll can talk." "What's that?"
Other	Demand clarification of hearer's intent/request for confirmation	"What do you want?" "You want to walk by yourself?"
	Describe hearer's inner state	"You are happy, aren't you?" "Oh, it hurt you, poor darling."
	Describe speaker's inner state	"Mommy is very tired." "I am still hungry."
	Discuss the nonpresent	"Where is Daddy? At work?" "Remember we went on a train trip?"
	Withdraw from interaction	"I am going to read the newspaper." "Mommy is going to have a nap now."
	Temporary leave-taking	"You wait here, I'll bring you a glass of water." "I am going to the kitchen for a minute."
	Greet upon meeting[a]	"Hi!" "Hello!"
	Greet upon parting[a]	"Good night!" "Bye-bye!"
	Apologize[a]	"I am sorry." "Sorry, I didn't mean to break it."
	Commiserate[a]	"Oh you poor baby!" "Never mind, you'll be all right."
	Congratulate[a]	"Mazal Tov!"
	Thank[a]	"Thank you."
	Polite response to "Thank you"[a]	"You're welcome."
	Polite wish for good appetite[a]	"Bon appetit!"
	Polite wish upon sneezing[a]	"Bless you!"
	Verbalize—nonfunctional[a]	"Daddy." "This."

[a] This category has identical illocutionary force and activity function.

groups dealing, respectively, with the management of joint and single action, the maintenance of shared attention, and a category of "others." As mentioned earlier, the illocutionary force of an utterance and its activity-related function are to some extent independent. Both are needed for the full description of the social uses of most utterances. Thus, an utterance of the type, "I don't want to play anymore," might be cross-classified as a declaration uttered in order to end a joint activity. Similarly, an utterance of the type, "The round piece goes over there," might be classified as a statement uttered in order to regulate the hearer's future actions.

However, not all types of speech acts require further specification in order to convey how the utterances of that act fits into the structure of dyadic activity. Some speech acts are defined in such a way that completely specifies their function in the activity. For instance, the definition of "commiserate" includes reference to the listener's distress; the definition of "thank" includes reference to the hearer's having performed a service to the speaker; the definition of "greet upon meeting" includes reference to the fact of its marking the onset of a new episode of interaction between the speaker and the listener. These speech acts are marked in Tables 1 and 2.

So far we have presented the thinking behind the construction of typology of social functions carried out by speech in mother–infant interaction. The final category system and its coding rules will be the result of analyzing all utterances in 24 tapes of 10-, 18-, and 26-month-old infants and their mothers. After completing the category system, it will be utilized in a longitudinal study of language acquisition. The model of language learning underlying this work is that children are learning to carry out by verbal means the functions captured by this category scheme. For example, they learn how to propose a new activity to a playmate, how to announce their intent to leave the scene temporarily, how to demand a turn, how to draw someone's attention to an object of interest, or how to warn someone of danger. Further, we assume that early productions are in some sense copied from the forms by which parents express these functions.

In the tapes we have collected so far, we have observed three different ways in which parental speech might provide a model for the expression of social functions. First, there are overt attempts to model in appropriate circumstances, such as saying "Say 'Thank you' " when someone has just given the child something. Second, many of the parents' utterances might be directly taken over by the children as appropriate forms for the same functions for which the parents used them. Thus, "No" might be learned as a form of refusal, "Good morning" as a form of greeting, "Let's play with a doll now" as a form of initiation of a new activity. Sometimes, however, it might be sufficient for learning to take place if the parents' utterance gives an indirect expression to what the child wants to say. In particular, utterances whose function is to ask for clarification of the child's intent seem to provide an opportunity for learning of this kind. In such utterances, which occurred frequently in our sample, parents try to guess what the child wished to communicate through his gestures or cries. In one example, a child reached for a bottle and the mothers asked, "Do you want to take your medicine now?" In another example, a child stopped in the middle of being walked and the mother asked, "By yourself?''—meaning, do you want to walk by yourself? From these utterances the child might learn how to ask for his medicine or how to demand to be walking by himself, rather than how to ask someone else what they wanted. Clark's (1974) evidence on the copying of incompletely analyzed units supports this possibility. For example, a child she quotes said, "Sit my knee" when she wanted to sit on an adult's knee, probably copied from an utterance in which the parent offered to seat the child on his knee. On further thought, it is almost impossible for the child to hear a direct model for many intentions that he might want to express. It is not reasonable that a mother would ever ask a child to seat the mother on his knee or to carry her. However, there are many opportunities for the child to hear the same meanings expressed indirectly, as in questions about his wishes.

Our goal is to find relationships between the ways parents perform social acts in words and the ways their children come to perform the same acts. We shall look for regularities in the parental utterances carrying out particular functions in order to find constant, prototypical or formulalike structures, if these exist. A comparison with children's subsequent forms will, we hope, provide some insights into the nature of early language acquisition.

REFERENCES

Anderson, J. R. *Language, memory, and thought.* Hillsdale, NJ: Erlbaum, 1976.
Austin, J. L. *How to do things with words.* J. O. Urmson (Ed.). Oxford: The Clarendon Press, 1962.
Bates, E. Pragmatics and sociolinguistics in child language. In D. Morehead & A. Morehead (Eds.), *Directions in normal and deficient child language.* Baltimore: University Park Press, 1976.
Bateson, G. A theory of play and phantasy. *Psychiatric Research Reports,* 1955, *2.*
Benedict, H. Early lexical development: Comprehension and production. *Journal of Child Language,* 1979, *6,* 183–200.
Bloom, L. *Language development: Form and function in emerging grammars.* Cambridge, MA: MIT Press, 1970.
Bruner, J. S. The ontogenesis of speech acts. *Journal of Child Language,* 1975, *2,* 1–19.
Bruner, J. S. *The social context of language acquisition.* The Witkin Memorial Lecture, Princeton, NJ, May 8–9, 1980.
Bruner, J. S., & Sherwood, V. Early rule structure: The case of peekaboo. In J. S. Bruner, A. Jolly, & K. Sylva (Eds.), *Play: Its role in evolution and development.* London: Penguin Books, 1976.
Carini, P. F. *Observation and description: An alternative methodology for the investigation of human phenomena.* (North Dakota Study Group on Evaluation Monograph). Grand Forks: University of North Dakota Press, 1975.
Cicourel, A. V. The acquisition of social structure. In H. Garfinkel & H. Sacks (Eds.), *Contributions to ethnomethodology.* Bloomington, IN: Indiana University Press, 1970.
Clark, R. Performing without competence. *Journal of Child Language,* 1974, *1,* 1–10.
Davidson, D. *Essays on actions and events.* Oxford: Clarendon Press, 1980.
Dore, J. Holophrases, speech acts and language universals. *Journal of Child Language,* 1975, *2,* 21–40.
Garfinkel, H. *Studies in ethnomethodology.* Englewood Cliffs, NJ: Prentice-Hall, 1967.
Garvey, C. Interaction structures in social play. Paper presented at the New Orleans Symposium on Current Research in Children's Play, 1974.
Goffman, E. *Frame analysis.* Cambridge, MA: Harvard University Press, 1974.

Greenfield, P. M., & Smith, J. H. *The structure of communication in early language development.* New York: Academic Press, 1976.

Grice, P. Meaning. *Philosophical Review,* 1957, *66,* 377–388.

Halliday, M. A. K. *Learning to mean—explorations in the development of language.* London: Edward Arnold, 1975.

Harre, R. *Social being.* Oxford: Basil Blackwell, 1979.

Holdcroft, D. *Words and deeds.* Oxford: Clarendon Press, 1978.

Macnamara, J. Cognitive basis for language learning in infants. *Psychological Review,* 1972, *79,* 1–13.

Nelson, K. Structure and strategy in learning to talk. *Monographs of the Society for Research in Child Development,* 1973, *38*(1–2, No. 149).

Schatz, M. How to do things by asking: Form-function relations in mothers' questions to children. Paper presented at the biennial meeting of the Society for Research in Child Development, New Orleans, March 1977.

Schlesinger, I. M. Production of utterances and language acquisition. In D. I. Slobin (Ed.), *The ontogenesis of grammar.* New York: Academic Press, 1971.

Searle, J. R. *Speech acts.* Cambridge: Cambridge University Press, 1969.

Snow, C. E. Saying it again: The role of expanded and deferred imitation in language acquisition. In K. E. Nelson (Ed.), *Children's language* (Vol. 5). New York: Wiley, in press.

Snow, C. E., Dubber, C., & deBlauw, A. Routines in mother–infant interaction. Unpublished manuscript.

Streeck, J. Speech acts in interaction: A critique of Searle. *Discourse Processes,* 1980, *3,* 133–154.

Svachkin, N. The development of phonemic speech perception in early childhood. In C. Ferguson & D. Slobin (Eds.), *Studies in child language development.* New York: Holt, Rinehart & Winston, 1973.

Vendler, Z. *Res Cogitans.* Ithaca, NY: Cornell University Press, 1972.

Wright, H. F. *Recording and analyzing child behavior.* New York: Harper & Row, 1967.

CHAPTER 11

Pragmatics and Social Interaction: The Unrealized Nexus*

Mark T. Greenberg

. . . reality is not a function of the event as events but of the relationship of that event to past, and future events. We seem here to have a paradox: that the reality of an event, which is not real in itself, arises from other events which, likewise, in themselves are not real. But this only affirms what we must affirm: that direction is all. And only as we realize this do we live, for our own identity is dependent upon this principle.

Robert Penn Warren (1946, p. 384)

During the past decade there has been a series of shifts in emphasis in both the fields of child language and early social development. What is surprising is that neither theorists nor researchers in these historically separate disciplines have fully recognized their shared interests in the child's developing communicative competence. Using the context of caregiver–child interaction, I will explore the interrelationships among measures of "communicative competence" and social behavior at the levels of the utterance and the episode, or conversation. The purpose of this multilevel analysis is to examine in what manner different approaches to the measurement of competence inform us about the developing use of language in social settings. Central to this approach is the issue of context and its recent "discovery" in the fields of early social development and developmental psycholinguistics.

In response to Chomsky's (1957) theory of generative transformational grammar, the study of child language focused on the description and validation of syntactic changes during the early years of life. However, this view of the child communica-

* I wish to express my sincere gratitude to Heather Carmichael-Olsen, Philip Dale, and Catherine Garvey for their helpful guidance and stimulating criticisms of earlier drafts.

tor as a tiny grammarian with a built-in system for abstracting and generating linguistic rules was found inadequate. This notion of a language acquisition device (LAD) with a separate ontogeny from the child's remaining cognitive structures was strongly disputed by Piaget and his colleagues (Sinclair-de-Zwart, 1969). Piagetian theory both challenged the simplicity of the raging nature–nurture controversy with its emergent constructivist position and conceptualized the child's early language as a representation of semantic relations, previously realized at the sensorimotor level of development as action in the world. The recent study of prelinguistic communication has shown even earlier parallels between the roots of communication and sensorimotor development as seen in the works of Bates (1976), Corrigan (1978), Harding and Golinkoff (1979).

Thus, a major shift occurred. Research moved from a focus on syntax to the study of how children express meaning and its relation to cognitive growth. This was paralleled by a shift from structure to process. The question of how children with limited word spans expressed different meanings led to detailed examination of the nonlinguistic context (Bloom, 1970; Scollon, 1979). With the advent of developmental sociolinguistics, the notion of linguistic competence was supplanted by that of communicative competence (Hymes, 1972). Communicative competence entailed not only linguistic competence, the translation of grammar to meaning, but also an awareness of social rules for the use of language. Thus, attention was focused on the important nonverbal and paralinguistic features of communication, as well as on the ability to initiate, repair, and terminate conversation.

The importance of "context" and the study of language as both the result of and the creation of context led to the burgeoning field of pragmatics grounded in the theories of Austin (1962), Grice (1975), and Searle (1969). The evidence that different syntactic structures can manifest the same intention and that various intentions can be manifested by the same syntactic structure led to interest in how children as speakers and listeners come to express and understand both the propositional meaning of the utterance and the communicative intentions of the speaker. The work of Dore (1974) and Halliday (1975) during the prelinguistic and one-word stage and that of Dore, Gearhart, and Newman (1978) during the preschool years, demonstrated both the difficulty and value of examining communication at the level of speech acts or function. Streeck (1980) has cogently critiqued Searle's theory of speech acts as theoretically inadequate for capturing the multiple levels of function apparent in the reality of ongoing discourse.

The emerging field of developmental sociolinguistics views language use not as an end in itself, but as a part of the process of communication which serves to promote social interaction. That is, the process by which infants learn how to use language is the foundation of developing social competence (Bruner, 1975a, 1975b; Kaye, 1977). Recently, there has been growing recognition of the importance of examining the young child's ability to use language in the larger contexts of conversation and ongoing social interaction (Brown, 1980; Camaioni, 1979; Corsaro, 1979; Dore et al., 1978; Mishler, 1979). Garvey (1977) has eloquently illustrated the changing role of language in the context of role and pretend play.

During the past two decades, several analagous shifts have occurred in the study of social development. In keeping with the predominant position of behaviorism in developmental psychology in the 1950s, there was a strong emphasis on descriptive accounts of individual social behaviors that were operationally defined and replicable (Cairns, 1979). Social learning theorists, using a structuralist approach, assigned individual behaviors (or groups of behaviors) to classes of action on a motivational basis (manifestations of latent constructs such as dependency, aggression, etc.). Operant theorists (Bijou and Baer 1961) and later human ethologists (Blurton-Jones, 1972; Smith & Connolly, 1972) attempted to count and describe behaviors without respect to the actor's motivation. The use of "empiricist" methodologies was further supported by the temporary demise of personality theory and trait psychology (Mischel, 1968). The zeitgeist of reductionist theories led to the premature rejection of classificatory schemes and rating scales as useful tools for measurement of social attributes across the life span (Epstein, 1980).

Yet, this radical "empiricism" was gained only with the sacrifice of meaning. The crux of the problem can be simply stated: All instances of a certain behavior do not convey similar meaning or significance. For instance, a smile or cry can represent quite different meanings and be intended to serve different functions, depending upon the environmental and behavioral context. The crucial nature of behavioral context has been most strongly advanced by modern attachment theorists (Ainsworth, Blehar, Waters, & Wall, 1978; Sroufe & Waters, 1977). Drawing on Bowlby's theory (1969, 1973), Ainsworth and her colleagues have hypothesized a series of behavior systems and maintain that a certain behavior (i.e., smiling) might serve different behavior systems (i.e. attachment or sociability) depending upon the context. Greenberg and Marvin (1982) have applied a three-step inductive model in a study of preschooler's reactions to unfamiliar adults that assigns behaviors to particular systems using a contextually based rule structure and examines the patterning of such systems. Similarly, Sroufe and Waters's (1976) model of early emotional development posits that nonspecific arousal may manifest itself in radically different emotions (smiling vs. crying), depending upon the child's schemata of the environmental and behavioral context.

Hinde (1976), in a seminal paper on the study of social interaction, emphasizes that to describe a behavior it is necessary to note not only its citation form but also its quality:

> To describe an interaction, it is necessary first to describe what A did to B (and B to A). They may for instance be talking or fighting or kissing. In addition we must specify how they are doing it—are they talking in an animated or dispassionate fashion? What are they talking about? Are they fighting savagely? Kissing passionately, tenderly, or dutifully? . . . . We may refer to such properties of interactions as qualities, without of course any implication that they cannot be subjected to quantitative treatment. In human interactions such qualities can be as or more important than what the interactants actually did together. (p. 3)

The recognition of the qualitative dimension of social behavior has led to the reintroduction of ratings and classificatory schemes. Ainsworth's classificatory scheme (Ainsworth et al., 1978) for assessing the quality of infant–caregiver attachment is an illustration of the use of a highly reliable and replicable system that focuses both on what the infant does (behavior and patterning) and how the infant does it (quality). Cairns and Green (1979) in a review of methodological techniques have also argued for the validity of behaviorally based ratings for certain questions.

Thus, the study of early social development has progressed from the description of behavioral displays to the examination of the timing and "appropriateness" of such behaviors or behavior systems. Similar to the change in developmental psycholinguistics from the study of linguistic structure to the context-based notion of communicative competence, social development research has shifted from an isolated description of behavior to the study of "social competence" (Greenspan, 1981; Sroufe, 1979; Wine & Smye, 1981). In both fields, context-free approaches to the phenomena of interest have been replaced by the all encompassing constructs of competence. Interestingly, these broad constructs derive their generality from the very fact of their focus on the contextual features/determinants of action and communication. While both the study of child language and social development have evolved toward understanding meaning in context, there has been little confluence in content or hypotheses. Research in child language has mostly ignored nonlinguistic dimensions of social interaction, such as affect or degree of behavioral mesh or complexity. Conversely, research in social development, especially ethology, has relegated language to the status of an entity that should be counted as "verbal behavior" but not interpreted.

As a consequence of the conceptual importance of the notions of "behavioral context" and appropriateness or competence, new methodological approaches may be required. Research in social development has relied on either segmenting social interaction into molecular units of discrete behaviors and their patterning (Sackett, 1979) or molar ratings of the quality/affect of entire sequences of interaction. Linguistic analyses have focused at the level of the discrete unit of the sentence or speech act. A major question arises as to how one might segment ongoing interaction/conversation at a less molecular level that would convey more psychological reality/validity for the participants, without having to summarize only at the holistic level of ratings. Theorists in social psychology (Harre & Secord, 1972), human communication (Pearce & Conklin, 1979), human ethology (Strayer, 1980), sociolinguistics (Corsaro, 1979), linguistics (Garfinkel, 1967) and social development (Brown, 1980; Greenburg, 1980a; Mueller & Brenner, 1977) have recently discussed the similar notions of episode, topic, interaction, and conversation as a viable level for anlaysis.

Newtson, Engquist, and Bois (1977) have demonstrated that naive subjects who are given specific instructions can reliably chunk interaction into perceptually recognized units. The notion that acts are understood not action-by-action but instead in more molar or wholistic units is a basic tenet of Gestalt psychology (Kohler, 1947). This basic quality of human nature endows us with the ability to be consciously (or subconsciously) aware of the nature and path of daily social events and allows us to both project their outcomes and recognize their end states. Pearce and Conklin (1979) have generated a hierarchical model of social meaning for adult communication in which "episodes" are seen as the structural unit by which utterances are "given" both their propositional force and intention. Following the utilitarianly vague definition of Harre and Secord (1972), they define episodes as "sequences of messages which have a starting and stopping point and an internal structure" (Pearce and Conklin, 1979 p. 78). Harre and Secord have envoked the structure of formal episodes (rituals, ceremonies, and games) as models by which the less obvious structure and process of commonly occurring social episodes (enigmatic interactions) can be understood.

The broad purpose of this chapter is to examine the interrelationships of multiple measures of communication and social interaction in the context of mother–child interaction. The measures range from discrete linguistic and social acts of individuals to molar ratings of dyadic interaction. My intention is both to demonstrate the utility of a coding system that examines dyadic interaction at the level of the episode and to examine the relationship between this dyadic approach and other levels or types of analyses. During 8 1/2 minutes of interaction, the following types of measurement were utilized; a message-by-message speech act analysis (e.g., functional communication); an episodic analysis at the level of the dyad (e.g., interaction analysis); ratings of dyadic gratification and communicative competence; and a frequency analysis of discrete affective behaviors.

The protocols utilized to explore these issues involve free play interactions of hearing mothers and their profoundly deaf children. The major reason for using a sample of deaf children was that because their communicative development is largely a function of the age and type of intervention they receive, it can be examined somewhat independently of general intelligence and other maturational processes (Greenberg & Marvin, 1979). Second, as a result of the serious disruption in parent–child communication that results from early childhood deafness (in hearing families), it was believed that atypical patterns of conversation would ensue during both the prelinguistic and early linguistic stages. Since most of this data set has been previously published (Greenberg, 1980a), there will be little elaboration of the sample characteristics, and only selected results will be discussed. The focus of the present report is to detail methods and results of different levels of analysis. (See Greenberg 1980a, 1980b, for additional information and discussion of the results in the context of the socialization and communication of deaf children).

METHOD

Sample

The sample consisted of 28 preschoolers (ages 3 to 5 1/2 years old) and their hearing mothers that were comprised of two groups; half of the sample were educated to use oral communication; the other half, simultaneous communicators, were taught to communicate synchronously in sign language and speech using English syntax. The oral and simultaneous groups were matched on all relevant demographic characteristics and were select samples that were not necessarily representative of their populations.

Systems of Analysis

Summary ratings. Ratings of the communicative competence of each dyad were made from the videotapes using a scale of the Index of Communicative Competence (Schlesinger & Meadow, 1972). The 7-point scale assesses the degree to which both mother and child display mutual or reciprocal understanding of each other's requests, observation, demands, and questions. Communication may occur by speech, vocalization, gesture, sign language, or facial expression. A second 7-point scale was used to assess the degree of mutual or reciprocal gratification that both mother and child derived from the interaction.

Functional communication coding system. This system based on the theory of speech acts, analyzed on a message-by-message basis all communications of both mother and child. Table 1 presents definitions, examples, and information on coder agreement for the 11 mutually exclusive and exhaustive categories encompassing pragmatic and semantic abilities that are represented in communication from the one-word stage in normal hearing children (Bates, 1976; Brown, 1973; Dore, 1974).

The system attempts to sample the major functions of communication; seeking information, gaining another's attention, requesting others to act, teaching another, repeating another, discussing objects, and discussing the self and other's thoughts and actions, as well as assessing the affective dimension of communication (e.g., approval and disapproval). Communications were coded in a manner which took into account both the surface grammatical form and other contextual cues to determine the illocutionary force of the message (cf. Dore et al., 1978).

In addition to this mutually exclusive and exhaustive system, reference to absent objects/persons/events was coded whenever a message with such content occurred. Each child communication was also classified as spontaneous or elicited. Spontaneous communications were defined as those that either begin sequences or interaction and/or were not direct responses to other's previous communications.

Individual social behavior. The frequency of smiles, laughs, and touches were scored for both mother and child, while angry/aggressive behavior, gaze aversion, and the percentage of compliance (to maternal behavior requests and calls for attention) were scored for the child only.

Interaction analysis. The interaction analysis is a system that scores behavior at the level of the dyad itself rather than at the level of each participant. In other words, it is concerned with the structure of interactions of the dyad, not with each individual's separate behaviors. That is, episodes are defined by continued referential or semantic presupposition or contiguity between mother and child (Brown,

TABLE 1
Definitions of Communication Coding System[a]

Category (and Reliability)	Definitions and Examples
1. Questions (R = .88)	Requests for information or confirmation of another's action: "How old are you?" "Is it alright?"
2. Behavior requests (R = .86)	Commands, demands, or requests that call for action: "Would you get me that toy?"
3. Reference to present objects (R = .93)	Declaring the attributes of objects: "This truck is yellow," or nonverbal behavior, such as showing an object.
4. Discuss self-action (R = .90)	Declaring one's own actions, thoughts, or feelings: "I'm building a generator."
5. Discuss other's action (R = .86)	Declaring the actions, thoughts, or feelings of the other: "You're building a house."
6. Approve other's actions (R = .83)	Declaring approval, agreement, an encouragement of the other or the other's actions: "That's nice."
7. Disapprove other's actions (R = .92)	Declaring disapproval, disagreement, or criticism of the other or the other's actions: "I don't like when you scream."
8. Get other's attention (R = .91)	Communications that specifically serve to call or get the attention of another: "Look here, Aaron."
9. Repeat (R = .90)	Copying the other's communication.
10. Declare information (R = .78)	Short declarative statements that are direct responses to questions and don't reference objects: "Yes," "No."
11. Teach (R = .80) (Mother-only)	Mother's communications that specifically function to demonstrate or teach: "See, it goes like this," or nonverbally demonstrating an action.
12. Unclassifiable messages (R = .82)	Verbalizations, vocalizations, gestures, or signs whose function could not be discerned due to message ambiguity, camera angle, or quality of videotape.
13. Reference to absent objects, persons, or events. (R = .98)	Any communication that concerns, objects, persons, or events not present in the room: "I want to swim tomorrow."

[a] Categories 1 through 12 are mutually exclusive and exhaustive.

1980). This definition attempts to operationlize Bruner's notion of joint attention and activity (Bruner, 1975b).

An episode[1] (topic) is defined as occurring when one member of the dyad directs an interactive behavior toward the second member, and the second member responds to that message with another interactive behavior and/or action directly

[1] In order to begin developing semantic agreement among researchers, I have changed the term "bout" (Greenberg, 1980a) to "episode." This alteration is because others (Bruner, 1975a; Garvey, 1980) have used the term "bout" for large units such as gamelike activities. While the unit I have

related to the other. An interactive behavior is one that is directed to the other and may consist of a spoken word, vocalization, sign, gesture, body movement, body contact, or noise. Looking, by itself, is not scored as an interactive behavior. For example, if a mother communicated to her child, "Get the book," and the child either got the book or communicated about it, the mother's message would be defined as the beginning of an episode. If the child did not respond to the mother's message or only looked at the mother, an episode would not have occurred.

An episode ends when 5 seconds have elapsed during which no interactive behaviors have occurred, unless noninteractive activity during the interim is directly related to the topic of the episode. For example, suppose the mother communicated with the child about a toy across the room. The child walked toward the toy, which took more than 5 seconds, but then picked up the toy and communicated to the mother about it. Despite the passage of more than 5 seconds without interactive behavior, the episode is scored as continuing since the interim activity was directly related to the episode topic.

Each time the topic of conversation (e.g., a toy) or interaction/play changed (e.g., a different game begins), a new episode is begun. If two or more episodes occur with less than 5 seconds elapsed between them, they are concatenated into a higher level of analysis, termed an *interaction sequence*. An *episode* measures the amount of time the dyad can interact on a single topic of focus and is conceived of as a distinct social unit, although it may be in some manner related to the preceding or following episode. An *interaction* sequence may contain one or many episodes and constitutes a measure of how long the dyad maintains interaction without a significant break (e.g., a string of social episodes). Each episode was categorized along four dimensions.

1. *Complexity.* A simple episode was one in which there were fewer than two reciprocal chains of behavior between mother and child. A complex episode

---

defined as bout or episode is expandable (by definition) to long sequences, it requires only an A→B exchange. Thus, my definition of episode is similar to that of Messer's (1980) criteria of talk regarding a single toy, in that the episode is of unspecified length and requires joint attention and semantic related-ness. Unlike Messer, however, my criteria for episode permits the topic to be defined not only as a single toy, but also as the use of a number of toys, actions, fantasy, or conversation, as long as there is semantic coherence. When more than one toy is utilized in the same topic, it often follows an explicit verbal or gestural plan that communicates a larger goal or intention, (e.g., "Lets put the people in the airplane!").

It appears that this definition is quite similar to that of Kaye and Charney (1980) in their examination of continuity of topic. Comparing my definition with that of Brown (1980), there are two significant differences. First, Brown defines the initiation and termination of episodes solely from the child's communication and does not require a response from the other. Second, Brown's episodes are defined by pragmatic or psychological presupposition rather than by semantic presupposition, and therefore his episode continues across topics as long as the child appropriately follows or responds to the other speaker(s) (quite similar to my "interaction sequence"). Finally, while Garvey (1980) specifies a 3-part sequence (A→B→A→B) as the minimal criteria for an episode, I only require a 2-part exchange (A→B→A). This differences probably is due to the fact that Garvey is studying peer–peer interaction where interactors often show very fleeting joint attention, while in my protocols of mother–child interaction, the mother acts predictably to secure uptake and continue joint attention through various conversational devices (see Kaye & Charney, 1980).

was one in which two or more reciprocal chains of behavior occurred (e.g., at least A→B, B→A, A→B, B→A).
2. *Topic.* An episode was coded as object-related play or conversation, if its topic was a material object which was present. An episode was coded as nonobject if its topic was an abstract concept, a person (present or absent), or an absent object.
3. *Initiation.* Each episode was coded as mother- or child-initiated, depending upon which person provided the initial behavior that resulted in an episode.
4. *Elaboration.* This dimension reflects elaboration of the other's communication that predictably functions to continue and expand the episode. For example, if the child showed and labeled the toy, and mother responded by communicating a new attribute or discussed an action for the child concerning the toy, the mother was scored as elaborator. However, if mother restated or otherwise only acknowledged what the child had said (e.g., "that's right"), she was not scored as elaborator. An episode may be elaborated by mother, child, both, or neither. Usually, simple episodes were elaborated by neither or only one participant. An episode elaborated by both participants signifies reciprocity or mutality in the expansion or direction of the episode.

RESULTS

Summary ratings. In comparison to the oral dyads, the simultaneous dyads showed a nonsignificant trend ($p = .07$) toward higher ratings of communicative competence. Parental estimates of their child's communicative age (using a revised subscale of the Alpern-Boll Developmental Profile, 1972) also indicated no significant group difference. On both measures, however, there was great within-group variance.

Functional utterance analysis. The strongest substantiation for the conclusion of no group differences in communicative ability was that there were no differences in the percentage use of any of the 11 types of functional communication for either the children or their mothers (see Greenberg, 1980a, for the specific data presentation).

Owing to the fact that no oral vs. simultaneous differences were found on either the utterance analysis or the summary rating of communicative competence, and such competence was a core construct of interest, the sample was dichotomized into high vs. low competence dyads (irrespective of communication method). This was accomplished by splitting the sample at the median on the rating of communicative competence. The heterogeneity of competence levels within the oral and simultaneous groups was evidenced in that each group was split equally, yielding four subgroups each containing 7 dyads; high and low competence subgroups of simultaneous and oral groups. Subsequently, analyses examined differences between both method of communication (simultaneous vs. oral) and level of competence (high vs. low).

The median split on communicative competence was validated in that high-competence children showed a number of significant differences in their distribution of speech acts compared to low-competence communicators; significantly higher use of questions, discussion of self-action, declaring information, and discussion of absent objects/events/persons. Additionally, they received higher scores on the Alpern-Boll Communication Subscale. Thus, it appeared that the rating of communicative competence, functional/speech act analysis, and parental estimates of communication age were in part measuring the same construct (e.g., communicative competence).

Individual social behaviors and interaction analysis. In contrast, the results of both the measures of discrete affective behaviors and the interaction analysis indicated that these indices more often differentiated method groups than level ability groups. On the discrete measures, simultaneous children showed significantly higher compliance to maternal requests and less frequent gaze aversion than did the oral children. Though not significant, simultaneous children had higher mean differences on smile and laugh and lower on aggression. Table 2 presents results on the interaction analysis. As might be expected given the preceding finding, simultaneous children had quite different patterns of interaction. Simultaneous dyads spent significantly more time interacting, longer episode durations, longer

TABLE 2
Interaction Measures by Communication

Measure	Method		Level	
	Simultaneous	Oral	High	Low
Frequency of episodes	12.1	14.4	14.5	12.0
Frequency of interaction	8.0	11.1[b]	9.7	9.4
Mean episode duration	36.7[b]	18.1	27.3	24.2
Mean interaction duration	48.7[b]	25.2	43.3	30.7
Total interaction time	361.0[b]	267.0	370.4[c]	257.7
Mean duration complex episodes	41.6[a]	27.6	36.0	33.3
Mean duration complex interaction	56.3[a]	32.4	50.0	38.8
Complex episodes (%)	69.0[b]	50.5	67.8	51.7
Simple episodes (%)	31.0[b]	49.5	32.2	48.3
Child initiated (%)	49.2	44.6	51.3	42.5
Mother initiated (%)	50.8	55.4	48.7	57.5
Mother elaborated (%)	24.3	32.8	17.2	38.8[c]
No elaborator (%)	17.1	27.5	19.7	25.8
Both elaborate (%)	58.6[a]	39.7	63.2[b]	34.5
Object focus (%)	88.4	91.5	82.9	95.9
Nonobject focus (%)	11.6	8.5	17.1[a]	4.1

[a] $p < .05$.
[b] $p < .01$.
[c] $p < .001$.

interaction durations, had a larger percentage of complex and fewer simple episodes, and more episodes that were jointly or mutually elaborated. Additionally, simultaneous children showed a significantly higher percentage of communications that were spontaneous (37%) than did oral children (20%).

In comparison, few differences were found as a result of level of communicative competence; for example, no differences were found for compliance, positive affect, spontaneity of communication, or mean length of episodes or interactions. High-competence communicators did show less aggression, longer total time in interaction, more episodes that discussed absent topics, and more mutually elaborated and fewer mother-only elaborated episodes. However, these findings are partially confounded by the fact that the most complex and mature interactions were shown by the subgroup of high-competence simultaneous children, while the least complex were the low-competence oral children (see Greenberg, 1980, for detailed analysis of the subgroups).

DISCUSSION

Simply stated, with a very heterogeneous sample, knowledge that a group of children had similar or dissimilar communicative ability did not significantly enhance prediction of the nature of their ongoing social interaction. Summarizing these complex findings, dyads and children who showed higher communicative ability on a number of static dimensions of communication competence demonstrated few differences on measures of either the complexity or length of their interactions or measures of affect, compliance, or spontaneity. Conversely, simultaneous and oral mothers and their children showed no differences on static indicies of communicative competence. However, compared to oral dyads, simultaneous dyads showed more complex, sociable, and contingently responsive social interaction.

These findings do not point to greater validity for analysis at the level of either the speech act or interaction/episode. Instead, the results demonstrate that the levels assess different domains of social communication, and that researchers should be cognizant of what measures will assess dimensions of a particular latent construct. In the present study there appear to be two largely uncorrelated sets of measures that assess two different constructs. On the other hand, the analysis of speech acts and the rating of mutual understanding (communicative competence) assess the domain of communicative competence (i.e., the ability to comprehend and use language in social contexts). On the other hand, the episode/interaction analysis and the discrete social behaviors assess "interactional competence" an aspect of the broad construct of social competence (i.e., the ability to appropriately engage in sustained and coordinated social exchanges). This basic aspect of social competence may be assessed at many different levels/stages and is relevant throughout the lifespan (Anderson & Messick, 1974; Argyle, 1969; Stern, 1974).

Interestingly, the three different approaches to measuring interactional competence (i.e., ratings of dyadic enjoyment, discrete social behaviors, and the interaction analysis) all converged to show at least moderately significant correlations. It is, of course, not surprising that smiling should be associated with longer, more complex social episodes or that gaze aversion, noncompliance, and low rates of child initiation and elaboration should also co-occur. Similarly, significant relationships were found between the two measures of communicative competence: ratings and analysis of speech acts. When two measures do not correlate (or show different patterns of results), it is possible that (a) they are reliable measures of separate constructs (the present conclusion); (b) they are both unreliable measures of the same construct; or (c) they are unreliable measures of different constructs. I believe that there is sufficient evidence for the first conclusion, because the measures have shown adequate reliability and most importantly the convergent validity of multiple measures of the constructs lends support to their reality. Unfortunately, the ratio of sample size to measures prevented the use of factor analysis to either document the separation of the two constructs or to examine the possibility of domains within each construct. As Ragosa (1979) has suggested, the use of multiple measures to assess a construct leads to increased construct stability and validity and is basic to the use of linear structural equations, a valuable tool in longitudinal analyses.

Due to the radical differences in the processes of educating deaf children by oral vs. simultaneous (total communication) methods (Meadow, 1980; Greenberg, 1980b), the constructs of communicative and interactional/social competence appear unrelated. The total communication approach is (ideally) characterized by acceptance of the child's communicative acts in any modality and a priority on the encouragement of ''natural'' self-expression and the use of language as a vehicle for social interaction. On the other hand, the oral method discourages communicative expression by means other than the child's oral skills, which are shaped through the endless repetition of sounds and words that are often devoid of social meaning or context. It is not surprising that even successful oral children (from an utterance viewpoint) show high rates of noncompliance, low rates of spontaneous communication, and relatively short episodes. In fact, subgroup analyses indicated that low competence simultaneous communicators showed interaction that tended to be more spontaneous and reciprocal than the high competence oral dyads (Greenberg, 1980a).

While the orthogonal appearance of the two constructs may be partly due to this unusual sample, it highlights a number of important differences between domains that also share obvious similarities. First, while communication is basic to coordinated social exchange, it is a necessary but not sufficient condition for interactional/social competence (Anderson & Messick, 1974; Ziegler & Trickett, 1978). Second, at least in naturalistic contexts, the interactional competence of any individual is largely a function of the other participant(s). That is, the individual is responding to what the other provides (or expects the other will provide given the dyad's history) and therefore is constrained by the other. By utilizing episodic analysis and discrete behaviors that reflect the other's action (compliance, spontaneity), this study has adopted both the perspective of the dyad involved in social episodes and that of the individual's (mother or child's) contribution to these episodes. While communicative ability also implies a speaker–listener context, the type of message-by-message speech act analysis performed is, by definition, not dyadic (Streeck, 1980).

Third, and most important, the role of affect and motivation are central to interactional competence. Dyadic social performance is influenced by (a) each participant's general desire and social interest (i.e., a stable trait of social motivation); (b) the effect of the specific environmental context on each participant's desire and ability to interact therein (Vandell & Mueller, 1980); and (c) the feelings/desire to interact with a specific other that are the result of the history of their past interactions. The communicative functions that a child expresses are also influenced by the motivation and affect of both the child and other participant(s). However, it is the connection of communicative and social acts on continued and coherent topics as opposed to their abrupt or awkward termination that more specifically manifests affect.

The present data illustrate that how well one can communicate (communicative ability) is not necessarily related to how one uses communication in social contexts. That is, the categorization of language into units based on intention or function (speech acts) may assess ability to use basic forms, but they are not an adequate measure of interactional or conversational competence. Knowledge of how often, or even if, a communicative form is displayed provides basic understanding of the developmental appearance of such forms. However, the analysis of speech acts is realtively context free and therefore provides information only about the social use of language at the level of the utterance (Brown, 1980; Streeck, 1980). The fundamental question is, how can analysis of speech acts can be embedded in the larger framework of emergent social interaction (e.g., how can pragmatics be analyzed at the level of dyadic interaction?). As Pearce and Conklin (1979) state, the analysis of speech acts would be greatly improved by embedding such acts within the ongoing episode. Corsaro (1979) has developed such a system which examines each utterance in terms of its contribution to establishing or maintaining a conversational topic/focus. This system, while not primarily addressing the affective aspects of interaction, demonstrates the viability of such an approach.

We believe that the present operationalization of episode analysis has been quite useful, and while the analysis did not assess affect per se, it was strongly related to such measures. In spite of the necessity to use videotape and often view sequences numerous times to ensure valid and reliable divisions of the interaction into episodes, it is the only available method other than ratings to examine the organization of ongoing behavior. While episode analysis is more time consuming than live coding of discrete behaviors, its product is a small number of variables that are amenable to statistical analysis. We have found that it provides a useful clinical summary of the structure of the dyad's interaction, and in that sense appears to reflect a phenomenologically useful perspective of the psychological reality of the dyad. We believe that such an approach begins to capture Hinde's notion of operationalizing the quality of social interaction. Such an approach is akin to that of family interaction research which examines the flow of topics and their control and interruption as a measure of family pathology (Waxler & Mishler, 1970).

The methodological approach of episode analysis is a quite general notion in which the level or unit and subunit of interest may be chosen by individual investigators. Recent examples include the analysis of early mother–infant games (Gustafson, Green, & West, 1979), the developing structure of early peer interaction (Mueller & Brenner, 1977), the structure of role play (Garvey, 1977, 1980), the features of control and pathology in caregiver–child relationships (Westerman & Havstad, 1980), the structure and sequence of social exchanges in preschoolers (Strayer, 1980), and topic maintenance in early parent-child interaction (Kaye & Charney, 1980; Messer, 1980). In a novel approach, Brown (1980) has developed a measure of the number of exchanges in which each participant maintains topic relevance (MLE, or mean length of episode). Using an analyses at the episode level, one might choose to examine different features of each episode: who initiates and how, who elaborates and how, the degree of mesh or reciprocity, characterization of the different types of interactions, ratings of dimensions such as the affective nature of each episode, the metacommunication used in informing each other of the plan of action, issues surrounding the termination of interaction and, of course, its length and complexity. I believe that the development of reliable and valid operationalizations of such features to answer different questions will lead to considerable advance in our ability to understand both the development of, and individual differences in, communicative and social competence.

REFERENCES

Ainsworth, M., Blehar, M., Waters, E., & Wall, S. *Patterns of attachment.* Hillsdale, NJ: Erlbaum 1978.
Alpern, C. D., & Boll, T. J. *The developmental profile.* Indianapolis, IN: Psychological Development Publications, 1972.
Anderson, S., & Messick, S. Social competency in young children. *Developmental Psychology, 1974, 10,* 282–293.
Argyle, M. *Social interaction.* Chicago: Aldine, 1969.
Austin, J. *How to do things with words.* Oxford: Oxford University Press, 1962.
Bates, E. *Language and context: The acquisition of pragmatics.* New York: Academic Press, 1976.
Bijou, S. W., & Baer, D. M. *Child development* (Vol. 1): *A systematic and empirical theory.* New York: Appleton-Century-Crofts, 1961.
Bloom, L. *Language development: Form and function in emerging grammars.* Cambridge, MA: MIT Press, 1970.
Blurton Jones, N. (Ed.). *Ethological studies of child behavior.* Cambridge: Cambridge University Press, 1972.
Bowlby, J. *Attachment and loss* (Vol. 1). *Attachment.* New York: Basic Books, 1969.
Bowlby, J. *Attachment and loss* (Vol. 2). *Separation.* New York: Basic Books, 1973.
Brown, R. A. *A first language: The early stages.* Cambridge: Harvard University Press, 1973.
Brown, R. The maintenance of conversation. In D. R. Olson (Ed.), *The social foundations of language and thought.* New York: Norton, 1980.
Bruner, J. From communication to language—a psychological perspective. *Cognition,* 1975, *3,* 255–287. (a)
Bruner, J. The ontogenesis of speech acts. *Journal of Child Language,* 1975, *1,* 1–19. (b)
Cairns, R. B. *Social development.* San Francisco: Freeman, 1979.
Cairns, R. B., & Green, J. A. How to assess personality and social patterns: Observations or ratings? In R. B. Cairns (Ed.), *The analysis of social interactions.* Hillsdale, NJ: Erlbaum, 1979.

Camaioni, L. Child-adult and child–child conversations: An interactional approach. In E. Ochs & B. Schieffelin (Eds.), *Developmental pragmatics.* New York: Academic Press, 1979.

Chomsky, N. *Syntactic structures.* The Hague: Mouton, 1957.

Corrigan, R. Language development as related to stage & object permanence development. *Journal of Child Language,* 1978, *5,* 173–189.

Corsaro, W. A. Sociolinguistic patterns in adult–child interaction. In E. Ochs & B. Schieffelin (Eds.), *Developmental pragmatics.* New York: Academic Press, 1979.

Dore, J. A pragmatic description of early language development. *Journal of Child Language,* 1974, *2,* 343–350.

Dore, J., Gearhart, M., & Newman, D. The structure of nursery school conversation. In K. Nelson (Ed.). *Children's language (Vol. 1). New York: Gardner Press, 1978.*

Epstein, S. The stability of behavior: II. Implications for psychological research. *American Psychologist,* 1980, *35,* 790–806.

Garfinkel, H. *Studies in ethnomethodology.* Englewood Cliffs, NJ: Prentice Hall, 1967.

Garvey, C. *Play.* Cambridge, MA: Harvard University Press, 1977.

Garvey, C. The emergence of conversational episodes with friends. Presented at the Conference on Developmental Pragmatics, SUNY/Buffalo, October 1980.

Greenberg, M. T. Social interaction between deaf preschoolers and their mothers: The effects of communication method and communication competence. *Developmental Psychology,* 1980, *16,* 465–474. (a)

Greenberg, M. T. Hearing families with deaf children: Stress and functioning as related to communication method. *American Annals of the Deaf,* 1980, *125,* 1063–1071. (b)

Greenberg, M. T., & Marvin, R. S. Attachment patterns in profoundly deaf preschool children. *Merrill-Palmer Quarterly,* 1979, *25,* 265–279.

Greenberg, M. T., & Marvin, R. S. Reactions of preschool children to an adult stranger: A behavioral systems approach. *Child Development* 1982, *53,* 481–490.

Greenspan, S. Defining childhood social competence. In B. Keogh (Ed.), *Advances in special education* (Vol. 3). Greenwich, CT: JAI Press, 1981.

Grice, H. P. Logic and conversation. In P. Cole & J. L. Morgan (Eds.), *Syntax and semantics* (Vol. 3): *Speech acts.* New York: Academic Press, 1975.

Gustafson, G. E., Green, J. A., & West, M. J. The infant's changing role in mother-infant games: The growth of social skills. *Infant Behavior and Development,* 1979, *2,* 301–308.

Halliday, M. *Learning how to mean.* London: Edward Arnold, 1975.

Harding, C. G., & Golinkoff, R. M. The origins of intentional vocalizations in prelinguistic infants. *Child Development,* 1979, *50,* 33–40.

Harre, R., & Secord, P. *The explanation of social behavior.* Oxford: Basil Blackwell, 1972.

Hinde, R. On describing relationships. *Journal of Child Psychology and Psychiatry,* 1976, *17,* 1–19.

Hymes, D. *Towards communicative competence.* Philadelphia: University of Pennsylvania Press, 1972.

Kaye, K. Toward the origin of dialogue. In H. R. Schaffer (Ed.), *Studies in mother-infant interaction.* London: Academic Press, 1977.

Kaye, K., & Charney, R. How mothers maintain dialogue with two-year-olds. In D. R. Olson (Ed.), *The social foundations of language and thought.* New York: Norton, 1980.

Kolher, W. *Gestalt psychology.* New York: New American Library, 1947.

Meadow, K. P. *Deafness and child development.* Berkeley, CA: University of California Press, 1980.

Messer, D. J. The episodic structure of maternal speech to young children. *Journal of Child Language,* 1980, *7,* 29–40.

Mischel, W. *Personality and assessment.* New York: Wiley, 1968.

Mishler, E. G. Meaning in context: Is there any other kind? *Harvard Educational Review,* 1979, *49,* 1–19.

Mueller, E., & Brenner, J. The origins of social skills and interaction among playgroup toddlers. *Child Development,* 1977, *48,* 854–861.

Newtson, D., Engquist, G., & Bois, J. The objective basis of behavior units. *Journal of Personality and Social Psychology,* 1977, *35,* 847–862.

Pearce, B. W., & Conklin, F. A model of hierarchical meanings in coherent conversation and a study of indirect responses. *Communication Monographs,* 1979, *46,* 75–87.

Ragosa, D. Causal models in longitudinal research: Rationale, formulation, and interpretation. In J. Nesselroade & P. Baltes (Eds.), *Longitudinal research in the study of behavior and development.* New York: Academic Press, 1979.

Sackett, G. P. The lag sequential analysis of contigency and cyclicity in behavioral interaction research. In J. Osofsky (Ed.), *Handbook of infant development.* New York: Wiley, 1979.

Schlesinger, H. S., & Meadow, K. P. *Sound and sign: Childhood deafness and mental health.* Berkeley, CA: University of California Press, 1972.

Scollon, R. A real early stage: An unzippered condensation of a dissertation on child language. In E. Ochs & B. S. Schieffelin (Eds.), *Developmental pragmatics.* New York: Academic Press, 1979.

Searle, J. *Speech acts.* Cambridge: Cambridge University Press, 1969.

Sinclair-de-Zwart, H. Developmental psycholinguistics. In D. Elkind & J. H. Flavell (Eds.), *Studies in cognitive development: Essays in honor of Jean Piaget.* New York: Oxford University Press, 1969.

Smith, P. K., & Connolly, K. Patterns of play and social interaction in preschool children. In N. Blurton Jone (Ed.), *Ethological studies of child behavior.* Cambridge: Cambridge University Press, 1972.

Sroufe, L. A. The coherence of individual development: Early care, attachment, and subsequent developmental issues. *American Psychologist,* 1979, *34,* 834–841.

Sroufe, L. A. Socioemotional development. In J. D. Osofsky (Ed.), *Handbook of infant development.* New York: Wiley, 1979.

Sroufe, L., & Waters, E. The ontogenesis of smiling and laughter: A perspective on the organization of development in infancy. *Psychological Review,* 1976, *83,* 173–189.

Sroufe, L. A., & Waters, E. Attachment as an organizational construct. *Child Development,* 1977, *48,* 1184–1199.

Stern, D. N. Mother and infant at play: The dyadic interaction involving facial, vocal, and gaze behaviors. In M. Lewis & L. A. Rosenblum (Eds.), *The effect of the infant on its caregiver.* New York: Wiley, 1974.

Strayer, F. F. Child ethology and the study of preschool relations. In H. C. Foot, A. J. Chapman, & J. R. Smith (Eds.), *Friendship and social relations in children.* New York: Wiley, 1980.

Streeck, J. Speech acts in interaction: A critique of Searle. *Discourse Processes,* 1980, *3,* 133–154.

Vandell, D. L., Mueller, E. C. Peer play and friendship during the first two years. In H. C. Foot, A. J. Chapman, & J. R. Smith (Eds.), *Friendship and social relations in children.* New York: Wiley, 1980.

Warren, R. P. *All the king's men.* New York: Harcourt, 1946.

Waxler, N. E., & Mishler, E. C. Sequential patterning in family interaction: A methodological note. *Family Process,* 1970, *9,* 211–220.

Westerman, M. A., & Havstad, L. F. A pattern-oriented model of caretaker-child interaction, psychopathology, and control. In K. Nelson (Ed.), *Children's language* (Vol. 3). New York: Gardner Press, 1980.

Wine, J. D., & Smye, M. D. (Eds.). *Social competence.* New York: Guilford Press, 1981.

Ziegler, E., & Trickett, P. K. IQ, social competence, and evaluation of early childhood intervention programs. *American Psychologist,* 1978, *33,* 789–798.

CHAPTER 12

The Relation Between Concept Formation and Semantic Roles: Some Evidence From the Blind*

Anne Dunlea

Visual information has been implicated as an explanation for many facets of the process of language acquisition as it normally progresses. It is thought to be important in fostering early parent–infant interaction, facilitating the emergence of gestural referencing strategies, providing the child with a stimulus for hypothesizing about what language encodes, and supplying the parents with clues about what a young child's early verbalizations mean. And vision seems to be crucial in the infant's conceptualization of the environment on which early language development may depend.

These aspects of communicative development were reflected in the major themes of the Institute and, not surprisingly, vision was repeatedly inferred as an underlying mechanism in language acquisition. A few examples are illustrative: the presentations of Brazelton, Stern, and Tronick each stressed the importance of eye-gaze behavior in early dyadic interaction; Bates discussed a continuity from preverbal to verbal performative structures in which visually based gestures play a crucial role; Golinkoff presented research in which the infant's visual perception of role reversals provides evidence of an underlying concept of agent and recipient. Moreover,

* I am deeply indebted to the children and their families, who so generously shared their early years. Much of the data reported here was collected in collaboration with Elaine Andersen and Linda Kekelis, and I thank them for many comments and suggestions throughout the study. I would also like to thank Patricia Greenfield and Bernard Comrie for several helpful discussions. This research was funded by a grant for the improvement of dissertation research from the National Science Foundation (#BNS-7920350), by a grant from the Spencer Foundation (E. Andersen, P.I.), and by a Morkovan Fellowship for predoctoral research from the University of Southern California.

visual information was used to operationalize various theoretical constructs, notably inferring communicative intent. This was thought to minimally involve the infant's producing goal-directed behavior in conjunction with looking at, or gesturing toward, its caregiver (cf. Harding, 1982, for further development of this construct). But despite its importance, there has been little effort to explicitly evaluate the role of visual information in the emergence of communicative competence. For example, research has not yet examined how development progresses when visual information is not available. The motivation for the investigation discussed below is precisely this; it is drawn from a project designed to evaluate the extent to which visual information can account for the process of language acquisition by documenting and comparing early communicative development in children with varying degrees of vision.

Six children, two blind, two with a small amount of residual vision (well within the range of legal blindness), and two fully sighted were participants in an 18-month longitudinal study from the onset of "words" through the two-word period. Data are drawn from parental diaries, individualized experiments, and audio and video records of monthly home visits which were comprised largely of spontaneous interactions between the subject and caregivers, siblings, or the researchers. Various developmental scales were administered periodically. The focus of the study was to document early semantic development, broadly defined to include lexical development, evolution of referential strategies, the emergence of propositional structures and developments in the use of illucutionary force (cf. Dunlea, 1982). The investigation is a companion to, and an integral part of, a comprehensive ongoing project at the University of Southern California documenting the emergence of communicative competence in blind children through the multiword period (cf. Andersen, in prep.; Andersen, Dunlea, & Kekelis, in prep.; Anderson, Dunlea, & Kelelis, 1982, 1979; Kekelis, 1981).

This chapter focuses on one aspect of semantic development, the early production of multiterm utterances. The first section presents a very brief summary of some of the principle ways in which vision plays a crucial role in the emergence of word meaning. This is presented in order to lay a foundation for the second section, which provides a more detailed discussion of how access to visual information affects the way in which words are first combined. In particular, the analysis contributes to a more general theoretical issue, since it provides evidence that semantic roles do appear to reflect the child's underlying conceptualization of events and relations which obtain between entities in the world.

FIRST WORDS

In ascribing meaning to words, children appear to abstract certain salient attributes from early referents and use these as a basis for extending the domain of application for words (Bowerman, 1976, 1978; Clark 1973; Nelson, 1973a, 1979; Rescorla, 1980). This process is essential in helping the child move from using a word as a "name" for a specific referent, to using words as symbolic vehicles to denote a heterogenous class of referents. It is the cognitive process of categorization that permits the inclusion of entities and events that are distinguishable from one another. Thus, the underlying mechanism in lexical development is inferred to be categorization schema, which enable the child to assimilate new and recognizably different referents to a set, yet at the same time permitting these referents to retain their own identity. The overwhelming evidence is that perceptual attributes, particularly the visual recognition of shape, size, and movement are crucial in the child's classification of referents and also appear to underlie adult categorization and the structure of many lexical fields (Andersen, 1978; Clark, 1977; Lehrer, 1974; Rosch, 1973, 1975, 1977). Since there seems to be a human propensity to exploit perceptual features in constructing sets of objects and defining lexical classes that operates from infancy, blind infants may be expected to extend the domain of application for early words as the result of the same categorization process, though the extraction of criterial features should reflect the relative salience of nonvisual information. For example, haptic sensation of surface contour and audible or olfactory sensation may be criterial (see also Fraiberg, 1977; Urwin, 1978).

An analysis based on diary records and individualized experiments documenting the range of use of the children's first 100 words suggests that this is not the case (cf. Dunlea, 1982, for detailed description of methodology).

Despite similarities in the content of vocabularies with respect to the distribution of lexemes among 10 mutually exclusive categories (e.g., terms for actions, objects, social functions), there are important qualitative differences that clearly distinguish the blind and sighted children. For example, there were no idiosyncratic forms in the blind children's lexicons, and there was a zero mortality rate for early words. Most important, the blind children's applications were considerably more restricted than sighted children's and suggest that words function as specific names for a protracted period of time. Approximately half of their lexemes remained firmly tied to the original context throughout the diary study and many of the forms that were not context-bound referred to specific people or food. These are marginal instances of generalization, since identifying different tokens of, for example, a type of oatmeal cookie is very different from constructing a class of "cookie" comprised of different varieties of cookies. The extensions that did occur were typically applied to only one or two referents and only 8% to 13% of each of their first 100 words were overextended. In contrast, sighted children as reported in the literature (see especially Rescorla, 1980) and in this study overextend over one third of their early lexemes, and almost all terms are extracted from their original context and are applied to a wide variety of referents. To the extent that the blind children did generalize words, perceptual information (largely tactile) seems to be especially important. Individualized experiments were used in an effort to elicit generalizations from the blind children by presenting them with new exemplars for terms that were not extended in the diary record. Similar probes were used to determine whether a word that was nonextended in production was generalized in comprehension. In line with the diary evidence, the children responded only when presented with familiar tokens, suggesting that words are not functioning as symbols for classes of referents.

At the same time that the blind children failed to objectify the word-referent relationship, they did not appear to engage in spontaneous classifying strategies and it was impossible to elicit classifications in experimental probes even after training and task simplification. Classification was observed in the sighted subjects and has been reported elsewhere in both spontaneous behavior and experimental investigations (Anglin, 1977; Nelson, 1973b; Rescorla, 1981; Ricciuti, 1965).

Thus, behavioral and linguistic evidence from the blind children appear to corroborate each other to suggest that the sensorimotor schemata for sorting elements of the environment by abstracting various criterial features is not functioning at the same level for blind children as it is for sighted children at the onset of language. The blind children have difficulty in precisely those areas of lexical development where visual information can provide input about the world and can be a stimulus for forming hypotheses about the nature and meaning of words as symbolic vehicles.

The effect of limited classifying behavior on early lexical development is further complicated by an apparent lack of decentration. In sighted children, decentration is seen in language when children move from referring to their own actions and to the objects on which they are themselves acting, (e.g., saying "down" as climbing off chair, or "cookie" while eating) to referring to the actions of others and to the objects on which others act (e.g., "down" as observes parent climbing down a ladder) (cf. Bates, Benigni, Bretherton, Camaioni, & Volterra, 1979; Greenfield & Smith, 1976; Lock, 1980). This process was not observed in the blind children, with the result that during the single-word period, language is used exclusively to identify objects as they are encountered or actions as they are performed, except in making requests (cf. Dunlea, 1982). This lack of decentration is paralleled by an absence of symbolic play. Even such autosymbolic schemes as pretending to eat, sleep, or wash were not observed (cf. Nicholich, 1975). Bates et al. (1979) have suggested that these developments are highly correlated with the emergence of symbolic language, though no causal relation is implied. Although Zukow (1980) has convincingly argued that many of the activities that are considered instances of "symbolic play" in sighted children actually reflect the child's ability to use culturally prescribed patterns, it is interesting that this behavior and the developments with which it is correlated are not observed in very young blind children.

To summarize, the analysis of early lexical development indicates that blind children acquire lexical forms for a long period of time before they fully recognize the nature of words. And, during the single-word period, they never use words with the expressive power achieved by sighted children at this stage. Yet from this shaky foundation, the blind children go on to combine words. But the analysis presented below reveals that they cannot capitalize on the range of combinatorial meanings that are discovered and encoded by sighted children.

EARLY WORD COMBINATIONS

During the past decade, a number of researchers have used a modified case grammar approach to analyze the semantic roles that are expressed in children's early
multiword utterances (Arlman-Rupp, van Niekerk de Haan, & van de Sandt-Koenderman, 1976; Bloom, 1973; Bowerman, 1973; Braine, 1976; Brown, 1973;
Leonard, 1976; Miller, 1979; Retherford, Schwartz, & Chapman, 1981; Schlesinger, 1971; Kernan, 1969). The analyses suggest that there is an impressive consistency among children acquiring a variety of different languages to begin expressing combinatorial meaning principally through a limited number of semantic
relations (e.g., agent + action, demonstrative + entity) and through forms which
encode negation, recurrance, and attribution, though there is some variation with
respect to the order of emergence and relative frequency of these within a given
corpus. The explanation for this consistency may involve both the child's increasing
use of the roles that are encoded in maternal input (Retherford et al., 1981; Snow,
1977) and the hypotheses that the basic relations constitute a universal core that is
actualized by the child's cognitive schemata for organizing and representing real
world physical and social relationships (Brown, 1973; Golinkoff, 1981; Miller,
1979).

However, the investigation of relational meanings is not without its problems
since semantic roles are not overtly observable but must be inferred on the basis of
"interpretive analysis." This method has been criticized for overestimating the
child's cognitive capacities and for assuming that the child's conception of events is
the same as the adults (Howe, 1976, 1981; Rogdon, 1977). In particular, Howe
(1976) has arugued that children are incapable of conceptualizing the distinction
between agents, possessors, recipients, and so on, during the sensorimotor period.
It appears that if semantic role analysis is to be preserved in child language research
it must be demonstrated that the proposed roles reflect the child's parallel or prior
cognitive schematicization of the relations which obtain between entities and events
in the world. While this would not *prove* the validity of the semantic categories
themselves for young children since symbolic and conceptual knowledge are not
directly equatable (cf. Piaget, 1962), it would represent a valid description of real-
world knowledge. Such a description may in turn provide a basis for the child's
making linguistic inductions about the semantic system.

Some of the evidence that infants possess the nonlinguistic conceptual constructs
implied by the assignment of semantic relations is provided by Golinkoff (Golinkoff, 1981; Golinkoff & Kerr, 1978; Golinkoff & Harding, 1978). Using a habituation paradigm, Golinkoff and her colleagues have demonstrated that children during
the sensorimotor period can recognize action role reversals that reflect changes in
agent and recipient roles occurring in carefully constructed films. The crucial point
is that these action role categories appear to have psychological validity in infants'
perception of events. Other investigations suggest that the concepts of possession
(Golinkoff & Markessini, 1980) and recurrence and negation (cf. Gratch, 1975)
also emerge during the sensorimotor period.

This research raises an issue of considerable relevance in investigating the role of visual information in the relationship between conceptual and linguistic development. If the way in which young children perceive and categorize the world is parallel to the semantic relations they encode, what happens when the child has limited access to visual information? If the claim is valid that semantic relations reflect the child's prior schematicization of events perceived in the world, it should follow that the children who have somewhat different concepts as the result of visual impairment will express qualitatively different relationships in their early utterances. Such an analysis can help evaluate the extent to which a child's own conceptualizations are the source of early utterances and the extent to which hypothesized ontogenetic universals (the core relations) require conceptual knowledge for actualization.

The research presented below is a preliminary attempt to explore this issue by evaluating the relations expressed in the first multiword utterances of 5 children with varying degrees of vision.

METHOD

The analysis is based on a corpus of transcripts of media-recorded interactions that spontaneously occured during monthly home visits between the subjects and their caregivers and/or the researchers. Approximately 45 minutes of such interactions were transcribed for each session according to the procedures established by Ochs (1979).

All sessions from the first occurence of multiword utterances were analyzed. Because children begin to combine words at different ages and because they advance in their ability to use combinatorial patterns at different rates, it is not possible to present the same number of sessions for each child. However, by grouping together the relations expressed within a specified mean length of utterance (MLU) range for each child, we can establish a cohesive picture across the various subjects (e.g., prior to MLU 1.50 and above 1.50).

Mean Length of Utterance was computed for each of the children's samples using the conventions established by Brown (1973, p. 57) except that self-repetitions, imitations, and formulaic (unanalyzed) speech were excluded.

All of the children's spontaneous intelligible utterances of two or more words which had specifiable illocutionary force[1] were analyzed and coded for the presence of eight core semantic roles, and the expression of a predicate, supplemented by

---

[1] A prior analysis assigned each of the children's utterances to one of 13 mutually exclusive illocutionary categories (e.g., Identification/Description, Request for Object, Draw Attention) or to a category of "no" or "indeterminate" force based on explicitly defined contextual criteria and the analysis of type of utterance (e.g., imitation, spontaneous utterance, self-repetition). Interobserver reliability on this analysis was 87.7% using Cohen's Kappa, (which takes into account the effect of chance agreement (Bakeman, 1979; Sachet, 1979). (The illocutionary analysis revealed an implicational hierarchy in the emergence of illocutionary acts which can be explained by facts of language and cognitive complexity, cf Dunlea, 1982.)

eight additional categories which are frequently observed in early language. The rationale for excluding utterances of no clear illocutionary force is that the interpretation of communicative utterances in the context in which they are uttered constitute maximally interpretable data. We can only speculate about "meaning" when a child is playing with language or reconstructing portions of past events to himself, and so on. "Build-up" or "replacement" sequences (cf. Bowerman, 1973; Braine, 1970; Weir, 1962) were analyzed once in their fullest form.

The five subjects who participated in this portion of the study represent a range of visual function from total blindness (subject A) to full vision (subject E). Table 1 indicates the level of visual function, sex, age range, MLU range, and number of sessions and utterances analyzed for each child.

TABLE 1
Visual Function, Sex, Age Range, Number of Analyzed Sessions, Number of Analyzed Utterances and MLU Range for Each Subject

Subject	Sex	Amount of Vision	Age Range	Number of Sessions Analyzed	Number of Utterances Analyzed[a]	MLU Range
A	Male	None	1;5;8–2;1;13	8	348	1.03–2.50[b]
B	Female	Light perception	1;9;11–2;4;13	9	231	1.11–2.01
C	Female	Shadow or more, part of one eye	2;1;23–2;4;5	3	34	1.04–1.29
D	Female	Form, periphery of one eye	1;4;8–1;8;18	5	305	1.42–1.60[c]
E	Male	Full vision	1;8;10–2;0;9	5	122	1.05–1.86

[a] Only a few multiterm utterances appear during first sessions analyzed.
[b] MLU range varied during final sessions; no pattern of consistent increase was evident.
[c] Subject more advanced when first located; information about earliest word combinations not available.

The classification system and examples of each of the categories are presented below. Case roles used in the analysis of semantic relations include:

Agent (Agt):   The animate instigator of the action identified by the verb.
                Daddy laugh. (as F laughs)
                This was extended to inanimate objects which seemed to function as animate beings in representational play (e.g., "Dolly drink"). (Relevant only for children with vision.)

Object (O):   A person or thing whose role is characterized by the interpretation of the verb itself, but which typically directly receives the force of the action.
                Me throw *the ball*. (as child throws ball)

Locative (L):   Indicates the location or spatial orientation of the state or action specified by the verb.
                Baby *here*.
                Baby *in chair*.

Instrument (I):	The inanimate object or force causally involved in the action or state described by the verb.
	Mommy cut *knife*. (As M slices food with knife)
Experiencer (E):	The being affected by the action or psychological state specified by the verb.
	He wants bottle. (child describing why cousin is crying)
	I hear it. (child hears a cuckoo clock sound)
Possessor (Poss):	The person or thing belonging to or habitually associated with another person or thing.
	Dolly hair. (Touching doll's hair)
	The possessed item was indicated as *Possession* (Possn)
Recipient (Dative R):	The person or object who receives or was intended to receive some object through the action specified by the verb.
	Give *me* cookies. (child requesting cookies)
Benefactive (B):	The person or object which benefits from the action specified by the verb.
	Do it for *me*. (child requesting assistance in activating toy)
Comitative (Com):	The animate being who participates with the agent in carrying out the activity specified by the verb.
	I go *daddy*. (child announcing she will accompany her father to work)

Whenever a predicate was explicitly encoded, it was classified as "Action/State." Thus:

Action/State (A/S):	The activity or condition specified by the verb.
	I *combing*. (child combing his hair)
	I *like* candy. (child describing psychological state of self)
	Predicate adjectives were included in this category
	I *silly*. (child commenting on self)

In addition, eight other categories were used in classifying the children's utterances:

Conjunctive (Conj):	The specification of two or more co-occurring beings of objects.
	Daddy doggie. (on seeing F and dog enter room together)
Demonstrative (Dem):	The specification of some particular referent through the use of a demonstrative pronoun or adjective.
	That big. (child specifying a toy)
Negation (N):	Any term used to express refusal, rejection, denial, disappearance, discontinuation, or nonexistence with respect to some object, person, activity, or state.
Entity (Ent):	The identification of some object or being as an instance of a class without action on that object or being.
	It's a *lion*.
	That *froggie*.

Recurrence (Rec):   The specification of, or request for reappearance, or further instance of beings, objects or activities.
More candy. (As M gives child another piece of candy)
Tickle *again*. (child requesting to be tickled again).
Some researchers have differentiated the categories "recurrence"
(more) from "repetition" (again) (Bloom, 1973). The two are
combined here since they both express the predicative function of
additional instance.

Attribute (Attr):   The expression of some quality pertaining to an object or person.
Big truck. (child playing with large toy truck)
Vanilla candy. (child eating vanilla flavored sweet)

Want Statement
(WS):   Because of its prevalence among the blind children, instances of
"(I)-want X" were tallied separately.
Initially, these were simply instances of identifying a desired object
or activity (e.g., "(I) want cookie"), but in time they became more
explicitly complex statements of the form "I-want + Act + Obj"
(e.g., "I want play record"). Such instances were coded as WS +
Action + Object (WS + A + O).

Question (Q):   This was used for formulaic WH-questions requesting the "name"
of an entity.
What this. (Picking up an unfamiliar toy)
Who that. (Seeing a new person in room

Further Considerations Involving the Coding System

Self vs. other. The convention was adopted to use a subscript s (self) to
indicate agency, action, experience, and so on which specifically involved the
child; and to use a subscript o (other) to indicate similar information related to
another.

Uncoded morphemes. The decision was made not to code instances of deter-
miners, quantifiers, or prepositions, since there were no instances in which the
children used these productively in the present data. Similarly, combinations of
verb + particle were counted as a single unit, (e.g., "fall down," "stand up") as
were verb phrase chunks (e.g., "take bath," "make bed").

Stereotypic speech. The semantic relations expressed in stereotypic speech
(use of formulaic language) were not analyzed, but the total number of instances in
which such speech functioned communicatively in each session is indicated[2]

Uninterpretable utterances. Utterances which contained unintelligible
segments were not analyzed, but the total numbers of such speech are tallied.

---

[2] "Stereotypic speech" refers to the use of unanalyzed language patterns which are characteristically
used by othrs, akin to delayed echolalia. This is frequently reported among young blind children (cf. Fay,
1973). However, stereotypic speech was often used communicatively by the blind children in this study
(e.g., "Did you have a nice nap?" on waking; "Wanna blow dry your hair, Teddy (= child)" as a
request to have hair dried), see Dunlea (1982), and Andersen, Dunlea, & Kekelis (1982).

Other excluded utterances. Politeness and greeting formulas ("Thank you," "Hi, Annie") were not included in the analysis, nor were any instances of nursery routines and other ritualized games.

Results

There are two factors which have implications for comparison between subjects. First, child C is just entering the two-word stage and the analysis of her data should be regarded as "suggestive." Second, there is an unusually high proportion of unintelligible utterances in the data from child D. It was often this subject's longest utterances which contained unintelligible segments and classification of her interpretable speech may somewhat underrepresent the frequency with which she encodes three semantic roles in a single utterance. On the other hand, the subject appears to be a "Gestalt" language learner (cf. Peters, 1977) and it is not clear that the lengthy utterances represent fully analyzed constructions.[3]

The eight core relations, plus the four frequently occurring three-term constructions, account for 68% of the sighted child's intelligible utterances, well within the range of 60%–70% generally reported for these categories (Brown, 1973; Retherford et al., 1981). The pattern is similar for the two children with residual visual function. In child D's data they represent 64% of the analyzable corpus and in C's, 72%. In contrast, these constitute less than 35% of the corpora for the children with no useful vision (34% for B and 31% for A). This is in part explained by the effect of stereotypic speech. If stereotypic utterances are excluded from the analysis, the basic relations account for 50% of each of their utterances, still lower than the norm largely because these children produced a greater number of "want statements."

It could be argued that "want statements" should be analyzed as instances of Action/State (of self) + Object. If this procedure is adopted, the blind children's utterances do fall within or exceed the normal range for use of the basic relations, providing the effect of stereotypic speech is removed. The core relations and common three-term constructions would then account for 80.7% of subject A's intelligible utterances, and 68% of B's. Because "want x" statements are well-attested expressions which represent highly reinforced formulas (especially in the blind children's repertoires), they reveal very little about the child's propensity or ability to encode the internal state of an experiencer. Such utterances are therefore retained as a separate category in the analysis.

The semantic relations encoded by each of the children expressed as percentages of total multiword utterance types satisfying the specified criteria are presented in Table 2. In order to distinguish the very earliest strategies for each subject, multi-term expressions encoded before a child had an MLU of 1.50 are separated from those occuring in sessions when the child's MLU exceeded 1.50.

A cursory glance suggests only a few differences associated with the degree of available visual information. The superficial similarity of the presence or absence of particular relations misleadingly implies that the blind and sighted children talk

---

[3] The Gestalt strategies used by this child were first observed by Andersen (undated).

TABLE 2
Semantic Relations Expressed as Percentages of Total Multiword Utterances for Each Child Assessed in Sessions Prior to MLU 1.50 and as MLU Approach 2.0

Child	MLU 1.01–1.49 Vision					MLU 1.50–2.00[g] Vision				
	A	B	C	D	E	A	B	C	D	E
No. of Utterances	43	32	34	85	22	306	199	Ø	220	100
Agt + A/S[h]			5.8[b]	8.2[a]	9.0				2.7[a]	4
(self)	(4.6)	(6.2)		(5.9)		(10.4)	(1.5)		(2.7)	
A/S + O[h]			5.8[a]		4.5	1.0[a]	.5[a]		8.6[a]	19.0
(self)	(9.3)	(6.2)	(14.5)	(5.9)	(13.6)	(7.5)	(6.5)		(5.9)	(3)
Agt + O[h]	0.0	3.1[b]	0.0	5.9[e]	0.0	0.0	0.0		0.0	1.0
(self)				(2.3)						
A/S + L[h]	0.0	0.0	0.0	0.0	4.5	0.0	0.0		0.0	1.0
Ent + L[h]	0.0	6.2[b]	23.5[f]	0.0	4.5	2.0[c]	1.5[b]		.4	20.0
Poss + Possn[h]			2.9		4.5	.3	1.0			3.0
(self)	(4.6)			(5.9)					(5.4)	
Ent + Attr[h]	0.0	12.5[d]	0.0	0.0	4.5	.6[d]	4.5[d]		0.0	5.0
Dem + Ent[h]	4.6	0.0	0.0	2.3	13.6	1.0	.5		2.3	6.0
Agt + A/S + O[i]	0.0	0.0	0.0		0.0	.3	.5[b]		.9	
(self)				(4.7)		(7.5)	(3.0)		(5.4)	(5)
Agt + A/S + L[i]	0.0	0.0	0.0	0.0	0.0	0.0	.5			6.0
(self)							(2.0)		(.4)	
Agt + O + L[i]	0.0	0.0	0.0	0.0	0.0	0.0	0.0		0.0	0.0
A/S + O + L[i]	0.0	0.0	0.0	0.0	0.0	0.0	0.0		0.0	0.0
Neg + A/S	0.0	0.0	0.0	8.2[a]	18.2	0.0	0.0		2.7[a]	6.0
Neg + Ent	44.2	3.1[a]	0.0	0.0	0.0	.6	1.5[a]		0.0	2.0
Rec + Ent or A/S	0.0	12.5	0.0	0.0	0.0	2.3[a]	2.5[a]		1.4[a]	1.0
(self)							(1.5)			
Q	0.0	0.0	5.8	14.1	18.2	2.0	0.0		5.9	1.0
WS	9.3	9.4	0.0	1.2	0.0	12.4	9.5		5.0	1.0
WS + A/S + O or L	0.0	0.0	0.0	0.0	0.0	4.6	9.0		.4	2.0
St. Speech	16.3	25.0	2.9	5.9	0.0	42.2	24.6		.9	0.0
Conj.	0.0	0.0	11.8	0.0	0.0	0.0	1.0		0.0	4.0
Unintell.	7.0	6.2	26.5	29.4	4.5	4.3	27.1		47.3	9.0
Other	0.0	9.4	0.0	0.0	0.0	1.0	1.0		1.3	1.0

[a] All instances are requests.
[b] All instances refer to past events.
[c] All intances are questions.
[d] All instances are familiar patterns.
[e] All but one instance are requests.
[f] All instances are habitual locations.
[g] May not total 100 due to rounding off.
[h] Hypothesized Core Relation.
[i] Common 3-term construction.

about the same kinds of events in the same way. In fact, very significant qualitative distinctions are revealed by a finer grained analysis of the nature of the children's expressions. A particularly robust difference is captured in the contrast between utterances relating to the self and those referring to others. Other systematic distinctions emerging from this examination are indicated in the footnoted information in Table 2. This information will be synthesized below in order to specify more precisely the variation in the expression of semantic relations which characterizes the blind and sighted children. Thus, an important procedural point is that the initial application of ''categories'' may not reveal the most interesting qualitative distinctions among groups of children, even though such categories may be a useful starting point for analysis. Rather, the data must be permitted to suggest further hypotheses and levels of analysis which can amplify or explain the results. Moreover, in the discussion section I will suggest that it is the differences revealed in the finer grained analysis which provide the strongest evidence for positing a relationship between concept formation and semantic roles.

Core two-term relations. The first observation is that the sighted child is the only one who uses all eight of the core relations. ''Entity + Attribute'' is not seen in data from the subjects with residual vision, and while instances of this occur in the speech of the two blind children, they tend to be common associations such as ''nice bath'' and ''little horse'' (one subject has a ''little'' horse and a ''big'' horse). My impression from studying all of the children's language data is that the visually impaired subjects have generally not abstracted attributional features from the items with which they were initially associated. One exception to this is the cutaneously sensed feature, ''cold,'' which occurs in single-word expressions for all of the blind children. Attributes are not especially frequent in the sighted child's two-word utterances, but analysis of his single-word utterances indicate that he is generalizing this kind of information and has started to abstract the critical features which define attributional terms. ''Action/State + Location'' is not observed in the data from the three children with no form vision and occurs infrequently in the sample from D, who has minimal peripheral vision for form. In an apparent paradox, the visually imparied children do encode the location of entities. But notice that almost all uses are to ask a question about the location of something (e.g., ''where ball'') or to comment on past or habitual events. Such instances involve the children's expressing relations which have been previously encoded by others and which refer to events that do not vary from day to day. For example, blind children encode familiar locative information such as ''froggie bath'' (in reference to a bath toy) or ''daddy work'' but they do not produce innovative constructions to express aspects of less common ongoing events. In contrast, the sighted child encodes new information about locations (e.g., ''bubble chiar'' on observing a bubble float onto a chair). Thus, *novel information concerning the location of objects or actions and concerning qualities of objects is not observed in data from the three most visually imparied children* and occurs infrequently in the language of the subject who has only limited vision.

The various combinations of Agent, Action, and Object occur in data from all of the children (except C, for whom data is very limited), but there are significant differences as to how these roles are used. (For all of the children, Agt + A/S and A/S + O are relatively frequent, but Agt + O is very rare.) Whenever the totally blind children express Agt + A/S relations, they are encoding ongoing information about themselves. For example, they frequently encode information such as "I running," "I eat," or "I sit-down," as they perform the relevant action. In such instances the verbalization accompanies the behavior. It is strikingly similar to their use of language during the single word period in which "stand-up" or "jump" or "walk," and so on, co-occur with the specified activities. It is possible that the blind children regard such expressions as an intrinsic component of the event itself rather than as a symbol that is distinct from the elements it encodes (cf. Dunlea, 1982). Again, the blind children's encoding only their own activities points to an absence of decentration in both single and multiterm utterances. This is in striking contrast to the sighted child who only encodes the agentive role in two-term utterances when someone else is the agent! As a rule, D, who has some form vision, encodes her own agency in statements, but the agency of others in requests (e.g., "you wind," to request that M start a music box). The other child with residual vision, C, only uses this role in talking about shared past events (e.g., "Daddy fall," referring to event on preceding day). Only a quarter of the sighted subject's A/S + O constructions involved activities of which he was the instigator. In contrast, all four visually impaired children used this relationship to encode information about themselves, except when they made requests. In summary, *ongoing information about the independent agency of others, or about the events caused by the independent agency of others, is virtually unattested in any of the visually impaired children's early multiterm utterances.*[4]

Not surprisingly, the visually impaired children typically encode only those possessive relationships in which they are the possessor. A striking exception is when A said "your baby," on touching a doll his mother was holding.

Finally, "Dem + Ent" constructions are used by all children, generally with the illocutionary force of identifying the specified entity. There were predictable differences in the use of the demonstrative itself since the blind children used it only to refer to objects they were touching ("this dolly," while holding a doll) or for audible objects ("that (a) motorcycle," on hearing a motorcycle pass the house).[5]

Common three-term relations. Three-term relations are just evolving in the children's productive language and there are no instances in the data from C. None of the samples encode Agent or Action/State with both Object and Location. The other commonly reported constructions pattern quite similarly to the two-term

[4] This finding corroborates Urwin's (1978) analysis of early combinatorial speech for one blind child in which independent agency of others was not encoded. Information about other semantic roles was not fine grained enough to permit comparison with the present data.

[5] It would be fascinating to investigate how (whether) the blind children interpret the distal/proximal distinction of *this* and *that*, but there is insufficient data to even speculate about the issue here.

utterances, with the blind children's expressions generally encoding self-agency except in requests and occasionally in re-encoding past events. Notice though that the sighted child's Agt, A/S, O constructions also tend to be self-agentive, which supports the position that there is a general developmental progression in which children move from talking about the "self" to "others" as they acquire various structures.

Negation and recurrence. Recurrence appears relatively infrequently, but follows a now predictable pattern: The blind children use recurrence only in making requests, whereas the sighted child used recurrence to comment on or describe an ongoing event. Negations of both Action/States and Entities are more frequent than recurrence for all children. Again, the sighted child uses negation in assertions while two of the blind subjects (B and D) use it only to request the cessation of some event or to reject an offer. But, a very surprising difference is that all of the totally blind subject's (A) negations are assertions. He uses negation principally to express tactile awareness of disappearance or "all goneness" as in "no banana" (on feeling his tray-table where pieces of banana had been after he had eaten them all) and "no circle" (after dropping a lid that he called a "circle"). The word "no" also appears in this subject's stereotypic speech when he reproduces such admonitions as "no stove/hot" on approaching the oven. There is no clear explanation for why this subject produces negation constructions in many of the ways suggested for sighted children (cf. Bloom, 1973) while the other visually impaired children do not, but it is very evident that he explored and extracted much of the meaning associated with "no" during the single-word period and his understanding of the term is more fully developed than any other term among his first 100 lexemes (cf. Dunlea, 1982).

Want statements. These are very rare in the sighted child's corpora, but are well attested in the data from the blind children. Of particular interest is the fact that B begins to refer to both objects and locations in want statements, even though these roles are rare in her other constructions. Examples of such utterances are "want ride the box" (box = special toy), "wanna go outside the car" and "want stand up at the box" (this time, "box" refers to a toy chest on which B wanted to stand so that she could touch some pictures on the wall above it).

Other. Isolated instances of other codable relations were occasionally observed, but there are no particular trends to point out. The semantic roles which are infrequent in other studies of child language are virtually unattested in the present data. Instruments, Benefactives, Experiencers, and Comitatives do not appear at all; Indirect Object Datives are limited to the construction "give me X." A few conjunctives are used.

The two children with no useful vision each produced a few combinations which were difficult to analyze. For example, subject B (2;2;2) produced the following very long request, for which it is impossible to classify the terms with confidence, in an effort to get her mother to push her along in a large empty box from the family room to the kitchen (B is in the box at the time): "you go riding mommy kitchen car'' (''you'' = B). The status of *car* is particularly problematic. When A was 25 months old he began to use question structures apparently to identify objects. For example, ''Is that spoon?'' (on picking up a spoon), ''Is it the glass?'' (on picking up an unfamiliar glass; determiner is incorrect). It is unclear whether these are further instances of stereotypic speech, an interactive strategy (someone always replied), or a genuine request for information.

To summarize then, the results indicate that the visually impaired children produce many of the same basic relations that have been identified in other studies of early combinatorial language for children acquiring a variety of different languages; however, only the sighted child produced all eight of the core relations first proposed by Brown (1973). The proportion of fundamental roles expressed by not only the verbal sighted child but also the two children with residual vision was within the normal range reported in previous studies (60% to 70% of all their interpretable multiterm utterances), but the two children with no useful vision produced far fewer of these constructions and instead used a large amount of stereotypic speech and ''want statements.''

Fine-grained examination of the information encoded in the semantic categories reveals several important differences that involve access to visual information. First, novel information about the location of events and objects and about the attributes (qualities) of entities is virtually unattested in the language of the four children with visual impairments. Second, although many of the core relations are expressed by the blind children, almost all of these constructions encode events in which the child is the principle agent or possessor. Third, when the visually impaired children *did* encode the roles of other people, it involved requesting things of them or discussing shared past events.

DISCUSSION

Two very different forces can help explain the findings summarized above. On the one hand, the constructions produced by the blind children reflect the deficit of information which they have with respect to the world around them. This deficit not only restricts what the children are motivated to talk about, but also retards certain crucial developmental processes, in particular, classification schemata. On the other hand, the expression of various relations in discussing past events and the use of increasingly complex requests and questions imply that certain adaptive strategies are in operation. Each of these points is considered in turn.

What the blind children express in their emerging propositional structures is limited to those elements of an event for which the child has *direct* experiential information. Consider the event encoded by the adult sentence: *George rolls the ball to Mary*. A sighted child at the two-word stage commenting on this is likely to encode ''ball,'' ''ball roll,'' or even ''George roll ball'' (assuming that perception of an object undergoing a change of state is the likely element to be encoded; cf. Greenfield & Zukow, 1978). Now consider this from the blind child's perspective.

If Mary is blind, she has immediate knowledge of her own existence. She can discover, after the ball has made contact with her, that the object in question is a ball. Note that she must explore her environment *after the event* has been completed in order to identify the ball. If a sighted child encodes ball in this situation, she seems to be encoding an object in change, whereas a blind child is identifying an object just encountered. "Roll (to)" is virtually meaningless. Mary may come to recognize a contingency relationship between hearing a ball roll and the ball's bumping her, but this is unreliable since the ball can miss its mark or be directed to someone other than herself (in a three-way game of catch, for example). Clearly, Mary could never experience an object's rolling action or understand its trajectory. Mary can be *told* by George or someone else that George caused the ball to contact her, or she can infer it, but she cannot "know" it on her own. Moreover, her understanding of George's role is limited to her understanding of what she herself can do and then projecting this to George, because she can not witness George's action (such projection does not occur in this stage of development, cf. Piaget, 1952, and others).

My own observations of blind children suggest that even if the child is able to produce two- and three-word utterances, in the situation described above, the child is likely to encode only "ball." This is because such children have experiential access only to the ball. (It is also possible that they would encode possession, as in "my ball.")

The blind child's concept of the event is different from the sighted child's concept of it, and this is necessarily reflected in what the blind child expresses linguistically. The agent and action relationships that the young blind child productively encodes are those for which she or he has first-hand experience. As a result, most agents expressed are self-agents, and most actions are actions the child can experience more or less in their entirety. The same lack of basic information may also explain why blind children fail to encode locative and qualifying information. But the blind children do have access to a fair amount of first-hand information that is unexploited. It is very surprising that novel information about the location of events and objects, about the qualities of entities, and even about the activities of others is not generated by available nonvisual information. The qualities of sound, texture, taste, and odor do provide information about objects and people in the environment, but it is not encoded. Moreover, it is almost never used as a basis for talking about the activities of others, even though the familiar sounds of a sibling's squeaking swing or a pet dog barking, the sound and smell of a parent cooking, or even, as we have seen, the sounds of burping, laughing, and coughing do provide the child with information about ongoing activities of others.

The difference in perspective resulting from the absence of visual information can account for why blind children do not encode certain aspects of events, but this is further complicated by the children's relative slowness in extracting the criterial features of entities and events that do not depend on vision and by the delayed classification processes thought to underlie extensions. The same failure to extract and classify information during the single-word period presumably prevents the blind child from extracting and encoding information *about* entities in early combinatorial speech. Thus, the fact that blind children do not discuss the qualities of objects in the early multiword period parallels the limited process of extension observed in their corpora during the single-word period. Both developments are rooted in the ability to recognize and extract salient attributes from encounters with entities and events.

This suggests that vision operates as an important stimulus for the processes that *underlie* language acquisition and that information gleaned from other sensory modalities is not a sufficient substitute for visual input in the early stages of development. While the blind have access to a variety of sensory inputs, the principal basis of information is haptic sensation. Taste and smell are of limited use, and auditory information is not nearly as informative as touch. Relatively few objects actually emit sounds, and the audible information that is present reveals little about the function and structure of the entity producing it. In general, auditory and olfactory information are exploited as clues to the presence of something that is already known on the basis of haptic experience. Thus, the deficit observed in the blind children may result, at least in part, from the differences between touch and vision. Vision is unique as the form of sensory input that allows the easy summation of simultaneous spatial information independent of time, and it enables us to establish and maintain a coherent impression of the environment and of entities and events in it without struggling with memory and information retrieval.

Quite simply, the blind must often remember what the sighted can effortlessly reconstruct with a single look. For example, the sighted can instantaneously apprehend the structure and position of objects in a room, whereas the blind must sequentially explore each item through the haptic modality and must then draw together the discrete information in order to synthesize an accurate representation. Moreover, visual perception goes on throughout the waking state, whether or not one fully attends to it, whereas the act of touch is a search for information that implies a conscious effort to obtain sensory stimulation. Thus, the task required of blind children in extracting information about the qualities of objects and in constructing classes of objects and actions is often different and more difficult than the comparable task faced by sighted children, since it may depend on a conscious search and since the memory burden is greater. This task difference leads to a developmental deficit during the sensorimotor period, though no conclusions can be drawn from this study about the blind children's ultimate development.

Yet, the fact that the blind children encode an increasing number of roles in their requests in order to more precisely indicate what activity, object, or information they want is actually an adaptive strategy which increases their access to the environment. Similarly, talking about shared past events with their caregivers allows these children to maximize the probability that they and their addressees have a common focus of attention, just as the use of visual cues aids sighted children in talking about the "here and now." Moreover, it is also possible that some of these events were previously encoded by the caregiver.

The interaction between the conceptual deficit and the adaptive strategies points to a uniform ontogenetic progression in the acquisition of language. Most of the core relations that have been proposed as "universals" are expressed by the blind children within the confines of the information that is available to them suggesting that these are an intrinsic or natural development in early combinatorial speech, but that they cannot be actualized in the absence of a supporting conceptual framework.

Golinkoff and her colleagues have demonstrated that children in the sensorimotor period use at least some of the conceptual schemata implied by the assignment of semantic relations in their perception of events and relations that obtain between entities in the world. The present investigation takes a complementary approach with a very special population and proposes that the kinds of events and relations for which blind children have a paucity of cohesive information are precisely those events and relations which fail to be encoded in their early langauge. Both of these approaches suggest that early multiterm utterances do reflect the child's underlying cognitive schemata and they point to a parallel between conceptual and linguistic development. The present investigation also demonstrates the crucial role of vision in the emergence of meaning, for it functions as stimulus in activating linguistic development. The children's early productive word combinations are mediated by their own conceptual space and appear to reflect information that is accessible and meaningful to them.

REFERENCES

Andersen, E. S. Lexical universals of body part terminology. In J. Greenberg (Ed.), *Universals of human language* (Vol. 3). Stanford, CA: Stanford University Press, 1978.

Andersen, E. S. Personal communication, undated.

Andersen, E. S. Conversational skills: Effects of visual impairment in appropriateness. (In preparation).

Andersen, E. S., Dunlea, A., & Kekelis, L. Blind children's language: Resolving some differences. Paper presented at the Stanford Child Language Research Forum, 1982.

Andersen, E. S., Dunlea, A., & Kekelis, L. The role of visual stimuli in the acquisition of communicative competence: Reconciling some difference. (In preparation).

Andersen, E. S., Dunlea, A., & Kekelis, L. The emergence of communicative competence in blind children. Unpublished research proposal, Spencer Foundation, 1979.

Anglin, J. *Word, object and concept development*. New York: Norton, 1977.

Arlman-Rupp, A. J. L., van Niekerk de Haan, D., & van de Sandt-Koenderman, M. Brown's early stages: Some evidence from Dutch. *Journal of Child Language,* 1976, *3*, 267–274.

Bakeman, R. Lectures presented at the Institute on the Origins and Growth of Communication, sponsored by the Society for Research in Child Development, Newark, Delaware, June–July 1979.

Bates, E., Benigni, L., Bretherton, I., Camaioni, L., & Volterra, V. *The emergence of symbols.* New York: Academic Press, 1979.

Bloom, L. *One word at the time: The use of single word utterance before syntax.* The Hauge: Mouton, 1973.

Bowerman, M. *Early syntactic development: A cross-linguistic study with special reference to finish.* Cambridge: Cambridge University Press, 1973.

Bowerman, M. Semantic factors in the acquisition of rules and word use and sentence construction. In D. Morehead & A. Morehead (Eds.), *Normal and deficient child language*. Baltimore: University Park Press, 1976.

Bowerman, M. The acquisition of word meaning: An investigation of some current conflicts. In N. Waterson & C. Snow (Eds.), *Development of communication: Social and pragmatic factors in language acquisition.* New York: Wiley, 1978.

Braine, M. D. S. The acquisition of language in infant and child. In C. E. Reed (Ed.), *The learning of language.* New York: Appleton-Century-Crofts, 1970.

Braine, M. D. S. Children's first word combinations. *Monographs of the Society for Research in Child Development,* 1976, *41*(Serial No. 164).

Brown, R. *A first language: The early stages.* Cambridge, MA: Harvard University Press, 1973.

Clark, E. V. What's in a word? On the child's acquisition of semantics in his first language. In T. E. Moore (Ed.), *Cognitive development and the acquisition of language.* New York: Academic Press, 1973.

Clark, E. V. Universal categories: On the semantics of classifiers and children's early word meanings. In A. Juilland (Ed.), *Linguistic studies offered to Joseph Greenberg: On the occasion of his sixtieth birthday.* Saratoga, CA: Anma Libri, 1977.

Dunlea, A. The role of visual information in the emergence of meaning: A comparison of blind and sighted infants. Unpublished doctoral dissertation, University of Southern California, 1982.

Fay, W. H. On the echolalia of blind and of the austistic child. *Journal of Speech and Hearing Disorders,* 1973, *38,* 478–488.

Fraiberg, S. *Insights from the blind.* New York: Basic Books, 1977.

Golinkoff, R. M. The case for semantic relations: Evidence from the verbal and nonverbal domains. *Journal of Child Language,* 1981, *8,* 413–438.

Golinkoff, R. M., & Harding, C. G. Infant's perception of filmed events portraying case role concepts. Paper presented at the International Conference on Infant Studies, Rhode Island, 1978.

Golinkoff, R. M., & Kerr, L. J. Infants' perceptions of semantically defined action role changes in filmed events. *Merrill-Palmer Quarterly,* 1978, *24,* 53–61.

Golinkoff, R. M., & Markessini, J. 'Mommy sock': The child's understanding of possession as expressed in two-noun phrases. *Journal of Child Language,* 1980, *7,* 119–136.

Gratch, G. Recent studies based on Piaget's view of object concept development. In L. B. Cohen & P. Salapatek (Eds.), *Infant development* (Vol. 2). New York: Academic Press, 1975.

Greenfield, P. M., & Smith, J. H. *The structure of communication in early development.* New York: Academic Press, 1976.

Greenfield, P. M., & Zukow, P. G. Why do children say what they say when they say it? An experimental approach to the psychogenesis of presupposition. In K. Nelson (Ed.), *Children's language* (Vol. 1). New York: Gardner Press, 1978.

Harding, C. G. Development of the intention to communicate. *Human Development,* 1982, *25,* 140–151.

Howe, C. J. The meaning of two-word utterances in the speech of young children. *Journal of Child Language,* 1976, *3,* 29–48.

Howe, C. J. Interpretive analysis and role semantics: A ten-year mesalliance? *Journal of Child Language,* 1981, *8,* 439–456.

Kekelis, L. S. Mother's input to blind children. Unpublished master's thesis, University of Southern California, 1981.

Kernan, K. The acquisition of language by Samoan children. Unpublished doctoral dissertation, University of California, Berkeley, 1969.

Lehrer, A. *Semantic fields and lexical structure.* Amsterdam: North-Holland Publishing, 1974.

Leonard, L. B. *Meaning in child language.* New York: Grune & Stratton, 1976.

Lock. A. *The guided reinvention of language.* London: Academic Press, 1980.

Miller, M. *The logic of language development in early childhood.* New York: Springer-Verlag, 1979.

Nelson, K. Structure and strategy in learning to talk. *Monographs of the Society for Research in Child Development,* 1973, *38*(Serial No. 149). (a)

Nelson, K. Some evidence for the cognitive primacy of categorization and its functional basis. *Merrill-Palmer Quarterly,* 1973, *19,* 21–39. (b)

Nelson, K. Features, contrasts and the FCH: Some comments on Barret's Lexical Development Hypothesis. *Journal of Child Language,* 1979, *6,* 139–146.

Nicolich, L. A. A longitudinal study of representational play in relation to spontaneous imitation and development of multi-word utterances: Final Report. *ERIC Document #PS007 854,* 1975.

Ochs, E. Transcription as theory. In E. Ochs & B. Schieffelin (Eds.), *Developmental Pragmatics.* New York: Academic Press, 1979.

Peters, A. M. Language learning strategies: Does the whole equal the sum of the parts? *Language,* 1977, *53,* 560–573.

Piaget, J. *The language and thought of the child.* London: Routledge & Kegan Paul, 1952.

Piaget, J. *Play, dream and imitation in childhood.* New York: Routledge & Kegan Paul, 1962.

Rescorla, L. Overextension in early language development. *Journal of Child Language,* 1980, *7,* 321–335.

Rescorla, L. Category development in early language. *Journal of Child Language,* 1981, *8,* 225–238.

Retherford, K. A., Schwartz, B. C., & Chapman, R. S. Semantic roles, and residual grammatical categories in mother and child speech: Who tunes into whom? *Journal of Child Language,* 1981, *8,* 583–608.

Ricciuti, H. Object grouping and selective ordering in infants 12 to 24 months old. *Merrill-Palmer Quarterly,* 1965, *11,* 129–148.

Rogdon, M. M. Situation and meaning in one- and two-word utterances: Observations on Howe's "The meanings of two-word utterances in the speech of young children." *Journal of Child Language,* 1977, *4,* 111–114.

Rosch, E. On the internal structure of perceptual and semantic categories. In T. E. Moore (Ed.), *Cognitive development and the acquisition of language.* New York: Academic Press, 1973.

Rosch, E. Cognitive representation of semantic categories. *Journal of Experimental Psychology: General.* 1975, *104,* 192–233.

Rosch, E. Human categorization. In N. Warren (Ed.), *Advances in cross-cultural psychology* (Vol. 1). New York: Academic Press, 1977.

Sachet, G. *Observing behavior, Part II.* Baltimore: University Park Press, 1979.

Schlesinger, I. M. The production of utterances and language acquisition. In D. Slobin (Ed.), *The ontogenesis of grammar.* New York: Academic Press, 1971.

Snow, C. E. Mother's speech research: From input to interaction. In C. E. Snow & C. A. Ferguson (Eds.), *Talking to children: Language input and acquisition.* Cambridge: Cambridge University Press, 1977.

Urwin, C. The development of communication between blind infants and their parents: Some ways into language. Unpublished doctoral dissertation, Cambridge University, 1978.

Weir, R. H. *Language in the crib.* The Hague: Mouton, 1962.

Zukow, P. A microanalysis study of the role of the caregiver in the relationship between symbolic play and language acquisition during the one-word period. Unpublished doctoral dissertation, University of California, Los Angeles, 1980.

SECTION III

USING AND THINKING ABOUT LANGUAGE

Introduction

John Neil Bohannon III and Catherine Garvey

The participants of the Institute were products of diverse theoretical positions and disciplines. Experimental and cognitive psychologists met with sociolinguists and anthropologists. The common problem uniting these varied representatives was their interest in how children learned to communicate and how composite communicative skills interact to evolve mature communicative behavior during childhood. This section reflects the diversity of the issues in research on developing communication in children. A common methodological focus, both in the proceedings of the Institute and in the chapters in this section, is a commitment to describing more completely the communicative act itself and the complexity of the skills required for efficient communication.

Traditionally, developmental psycholinguists have observed children speaking to others or performing some verbal task and have examined the linguistic structure of the children's utterances in isolation from both the children's ability to comprehend the meaning and functions of their own messages and the children's language environment (Brown, 1973). Yet, a rapidly emerging grammatical skill is only one of many processes used by children in situations where *something* must be communicated. For example, an anomaly was noted in older preschool and elementary-grade children. Although the children knew *how* to talk quite well (i.e., used good grammar), they had considerable difficulty in adequately describing specific aspects of events to others (Flavell, Botkin, Fry, Wright, & Jarvis, 1968). Moreover, these children were rarely able to adequately monitor certain dimensions of the quality of their own understanding of utterances addressed to them (Bohannon, 1976; Sonnenschein, Chap. 13).

Every chapter in this last section examines some form of an elemental communication situation. These various methods have asked children to tell a listener about (a) an array of abstract stimuli in the Sonnenschien chapter; (b) a school instruction in the Lloyd, Baker, and Dunn chapter; (c) familiar real-life situations like grocery shopping in the Pace and Feagans chapter, and (d) child games in the Evans and Carr chapter. Given this methodological focus of attempting to analyze the demands and dimensions of the communicative situation, the complexity of the processes involved in how the children *use* language and understand *language use* in these situations is obvious.

If 3- or 4-year-old children were aware of the immensity of the task that lies ahead in their growth toward mature communicative performance, they would surely be discouraged. Fortunately, children are unaware of the cognitive demands, the increasing variety of linguistic alternatives, and the expansion of social and task-oriented activities that they will meet over the next several years. Such situations will require more and more sophisticated communicative behavior. Children's ability to use language to conduct their everyday life—to interact with adults, to learn about the world, to construct play episodes with friends—is impressive. It serves their purposes. Children's effectiveness in familiar communicative situations is real, but it masks (to casual observation) the limitations in their understanding of certain aspects of the communicative process. It also masks the fact that they have not yet begun to reflect on language or on the communicative process. Clearly, young children have not acquired the skill or the conventional means for talking about linguistic objects or their relation to communicative situations.

This section will deal with two general classes of communicative accomplishments. The first class of achievements concerns the increasingly precise or appropriate fit of messages to the speech situation. There are two important aspects of this capability. The first aspect is the identification of the informational requirements of a task. Such identification entails the analysis of a display of objects or of facts, and the specification of the appropriate elements of the display for the *purpose at hand*. The other aspect concerns the analysis of the listener's informational requirements, given the task objects and the features of the display, and in most cases, the prior communications, or text.

The second class of accomplishments is comprised of metalinguistic and metacommunicative knowledge—the understanding, respectively, of the role and function of linguistic objects and the understanding of the purpose and effect of communicative acts. This class of accomplishments concerns children's knowledge of how they do what they do with words. It is a higher order of knowledge that emerges only after children have accumulated considerable experience with the immediate use of words and acts. The display of such knowledge necessarily involves command of conventional means for operating on linguistic or communicative events. To make judgments of messages and acts, children must not only suspend their normal instrumental activity with language, but must also reflect on linguistic objects, assessing their goodness to fit to the speech situation. In most investigations of such abilities, children are required to express their assessment using language to do so.

The Evans and Carr chapter (Chap. 16) is a convenient structure to understand these varied cognitive processes involved in children's communications. They argue that young children suffer from several forms of limitations. Not only are they immature linguistically, but also they must learn the various social conventions and cues from their listeners that control when and what they talk about. If a limited processing capacity is assumed for all humans (and especially children), then there is less of this capacity available to devote any one of the various processes necessary for mature communicative behavior. Thus, children stuggling with the mastery of new linguistic forms may appear socially inept when producing these forms, or unable to reflect back on the adequacy of their productions. Conversely, children who are attending to the social learning aspects of communication may produce more nongrammatical utterances. As both the social and linguistic aspects of communication become overlearned and more automatic in later childhood, then the excess processing capacity may be used for an additional order or level of communicative analysis (see Lloyd, Baker, & Dunn, Chap. 15). Identifying and reflecting on the process of communication, once this ability is achieved, may be expected to feed back into more appropriate and precise communicative performance that could be observed in more diverse situations.

One reason why children may appear to be less than astute as both speakers and listeners is that their primary communicative partners (adults) usually assume the responsibility of maintaining effective communication. Children are rarely asked to evaluate, or even to correct or adjust, the messages of others. When they are so requested, we might expect them to be unable to assess the communicative adequacy of messages, especially messages that are not immediately linked to ongoing activity in which the children are engaged (Sonnenschein, Chap. 13). Moreover, when children are asked to assess communicative adequacy, they probably are drawn to the most salient characteristics of the adult utterances they hear. Sonnenschein found that utterance length was the basis for most young children's judgments.

Yet, what might children do if they are provided an extremely supportive framework within which they can either communicate or make reflections about their own communicative performance. If the Evans and Carr argument is correct, then we might see much more sophisticated behavior from younger children when the proper cognitive supports are available. The Pace and Feagans chapter (Chap. 14) examined the effects of scripts or well-known behavioral routines (like gorcery shopping) on children's memory for stories. They found that children remembered much more and were more able to detect discrepant information when the story was in a familiar script. The Lloyd et al. study found that although children had trouble teaching (communicating with) other children, when allowed to view a videotape of their own communicative failures, some of their young subjects were able to adequately assign responsibility for the communication breakdown to themselves. In addition, some of the more advanced children were able to make suggestions as to how they could have repaired their poor performance. In no cases, however, did the children make other than vague and global suggestions based on personal characteristics of their listeners. Moreover, none of the children appeared to criticize the fit of specific aspects of their messages to the information structure of the task. The Carr and Evans chapter argues that when the children are not concentrating on producing an utterance or remembering the flow of conversation after-the-fact, more cognitive capacity may be devoted to higher metacognitive processes like metacommunicative awareness or reflection on the adequacy of one's own statements.

Thus far the book has offered the reader concentrations on the earliest elements of affective communication in infancy, focusing on the transition from purely social signaling to linguistic expression. This was a major problem area addressed in the 1979 meeting, and it was obviously pursued in some depth. Moreover, the social psychological aspects of learning to use a linguistic signaling system were not forgotten as the role of the caretaker–child relationship is examined in detail, not only in infancy but well into early childhood. The last section also contains contributions written with a keen eye directed to the social context within which the child's communicative act occurs. The Evans and Carr chapter points out quite well that a child's simple description is influenced not only by the child's current linguistic expertise, but also by such things as to whom the utterance is directed, the limited memory and cognitive processing capacity of the child, and the referential context which the child is attempting to describe. Such attention to the *total* context of a child's utterance has yielded a varied and rich source of data to aid explanations of communicative development.

REFERENCES

Bohannon, J. N. Normal and scrambled grammar in discrimination, imitation, and comprehension. *Child Development*, 1976, *41*, 669–681.

Brown, R. *A first language: The early stages.* Cambridge, MA: Harvard University Press, 1973.

Flavell, J. H., Botkin, P. T., Fry, C. L., Wright, J. C., & Jarvis, P. E. *The development of role-taking as communicative skills in children.* New York: Wiley, 1968.

CHAPTER 13

Referential Communication: Why do Preschoolers Confuse Quantity with Quality?*

Susan Sonnenschein

Imagine a situation in which there are two red cups, one big and one small, on a table. A speaker must describe one of the cups so that a listener can pick it out. An adult speaker would probably say, "It's the big one." A 5-year-old speaker, on the other hand, would quite likely say, "It's the red one"—a correct description but an uninformative communication. In attempting to explain why young children are poor communicators, early research utilized global theories, such as egocentrism (Piaget, 1926). However, such theories were incompatible with much of the more recent data (see Asher, 1979, for an extensive review). Consequently, researchers now are taking a more molecular approach to the study of communication skills (Glucksberg, Krauss, & Higgins, 1975; Whitehurst & Sonnenschein, 1981).

Much of the research discussed in this chapter will be in the area of referential communication, which is defined as a communication about an object, location, etc., that would enable a listener to select a referent from nonreferential alternatives. Although referential communication is only one aspect of communication skills, it has received much research attention, not only because of its pervasiveness but also because it is probably a component of various forms of verbal communication (Asher, 1979; Glucksberg et al., 1975). One might argue, however, that the laboratory paradigm used by researchers investigating referential communication skills is highly artificial and does not necessarily allow a true measure of a child's communicative competence. That is true. On the other hand, the advantage of the paradigm is that one can examine and explore in more detail specific processes first

* I am indebted to the children, teachers, and staff of the Baltimore County School district.

noticed in naturalistic situations while controlling for speaker's intention, task effects, etc. Thus, one can more rigorously measure the linguistic skills of interest (Asher, 1979; this shall be discussed in more detail in the final section of this chapter).

Three topics that researchers of referential communication skills have investigated are: the specific types of communications children use, the role that social experience plays, and what young children understand the requirements of adequate communication to be. Obviously, these are three important areas. To understand why children are poor communicators, we need to know how they are communicating and how this differs from what adults do. In order to understand how children become better communicators, we need to assess both their cognitive understanding of communication skills, as well as how they respond to environmental contingencies.

These topics have generally been studied as independent areas. However, their interaction may also be important for theories of communication development. What a preschooler may be learning about communication skills by observing the people around him may be affected by what aspects of the interaction he attends to. This, in turn, may be influenced by the child's understanding of the requirements for a successful communication. And how a child communicates will be, at least in part, a result of what he has learned through his observations.

This chapter combines these three topics by considering *why* children are using certain types of messages, thus enabling us to determine what they may be learning about communication skills from their environment. Research on communication development and social learning provides a framework for considering the issue in more detail.

COMMUNICATION STYLE

In the typical referential communication task (Whitehurst, 1976), a speaker can give either a contrastive, a redundant, or an incomplete communication. Contrastive messages are the minimum necessary for a speaker to distinguish verbally a referent from nonreferents. Redundant messages contain more than the minimum necessary. Incomplete messages are uninformative. For example, imagine a task in which a big, red, striped triangle (the referent) was paired with a small, red, striped triangle. A contrastive message would be "the big one"; a redundant message would be "the big, red, striped one"; and an incomplete message would be "the red one." For the most part, preschoolers' communications are uninformative (Whitehurst, 1976). Both the incidence of informative messages, in general, and redundant messages, in particular, increase with age (Whitehurst, 1976).

The issue for theories of communication development is to understand why children produce certain types of messages. Many theorists have argued that a contrastive style is the most advanced (Olson, 1970). Yet children, as they mature, tend to become redundant—not contrastive—speakers. If we could understand the relationship for the preschooler between message length and message quality, this would help us to determine why the developmental progression over the early school years is toward a redundant rather than a more contrastive style.

What Children Learn From Their Environment

A second focus of communication research has been the role of social experience on development. For example, what are children learning from people in their environment? Modeling, as one social learning variable, has been shown to have major enhancing effects on young children's communications (Whitehurst, 1976). That children may learn to become adequate communicators by observing good models in their environment is not surprising. What is of interest, however, are the specific processes involved. Whitehurst found that preschool communicators improved after witnessing an adult model through an increase in *redundant* messages, even though the model had produced *contrastive* messages (Whitehurst, 1976; Whitehurst & Merkur, 1977).

Whitehurst, Sonnenschein, and Ianfolla (1981) explored the cause of this effect. Kindergartners were exposed to one of six modeling conditions: one-word contrastive, one-word incomplete (ambiguous), two-word contrastive, two-word redundant, two-word incomplete, or mixed contrastive (half one-word and half two-word contrastive messages). In general, the results indicated that children imitated the length rather than the quality of the message that they heard. Children who heard *any* of the three types of two-word messages subsequently gave redundant messages. The authors concluded that preschoolers do not appear to discriminate between ambiguous and informative messages. They appear to be sensitive only to message length, readily imitating a model who uses more adjectives than they do. Children become more informative as a result of listening to a wordy model, but this is simply a byproduct of saying more, not a guiding motive for the child.

THE UNDERSTANDING OF THE REQUIREMENTS
OF ADEQUATE COMMUNICATION

Researchers exploring different aspects of language development (e.g., semantics, communication, syntax) have all displayed interest in young children's metalinguistic awareness (Clark, 1978; Hirsh-Pasek, Gleitman & Gleitman, 1978; Slobin, 1978). The implicit notion guiding such interest is that a child's thoughts about linguistic issues should correlate with production and comprehension. Although many researchers are investigating metalinguistic awareness, too few have explicitly drawn connections between these two aspects of linguistics (cf. Robinson, 1981). Gaining knowledge of young children's metalinguistic awareness is of interest in its own right. However, ultimately we also want to know how, if at all, it affects the child's use of language.

Within communication research some of the questions of interest to researchers exploring metacommunication have been: What is the young child's understanding of the requirements of communication; does he or she think that the message in a communication is important, or perhaps, is it only the outcome that is relevant? Robinson and Robinson (1976, 1977a, 1977b, 1981) have done extensive research assessing what young children think are the requirements for successful communication. They had children observe a speaker–listener dyad play a referential communication game. The quality of the messages (informative, ambiguous) were orthogonally varied with the selection that the listener made (chose referent, nonreferent). After each interaction, the child was asked whether the speaker had communicated adequately. If the listener had selected a nonreferent, the child was asked "whose fault" it was.

Their results showed that young children (around 5 years old) generally blamed the listener for communication failures and asserted that the speaker had done an adequate job, even when the speaker's message had been ambiguous. Older children, on the other hand, blamed the speaker for ambiguous, hence inadequate, messages. The Robinsons concluded that these results were due to a change in the child's notion of what makes an adequate communication. According to the Robinsons, preschoolers judge a communication to be adequate as long as it correctly describes the referent. Thus, an ambiguous message that referred to more than one stimulus would be judged as adequate by the preschooler, if the message correctly described the referent. Only at a later stage of development must a message refer only to the referent in order to be considered adequate.

THE IMPORTANCE OF THE LENGTH OF A COMMUNICATION

In order to improve our understanding of the causes of preschoolers' communication patterns, we need to determine more fully their metacommunicative knowledge. Given that *how much* is said appears to determine the focus of children's attention (Whitehurst et al., 1981), we should consider whether length is one of the factors the preschoolers use to judge the adequacy of a communication. Would a preschooler think that any long message, even an ambiguous one, is an adequate communication?

This chapter consists of three experiments. The first replicates the original Whitehurst et al. research in order to correct a confound in that study (to be discussed in the next section). The second focuses on whether preschoolers confuse length with quality and judge any long communication to be adequate. The third directly assesses the relative salience of message length and message quality for both younger and older children. Are children more likely to attend to the length of a message or to its quality? Although Whitehurst et al. implied that message length may be more salient than message quality for preschoolers, they never directly tested this hypothesis. In the final section of this chapter, the data from the three experiments are discussed in terms of general principles of the development of communication.

WHAT YOUNG COMMUNICATORS LEARN
FROM OTHER SPEAKERS

The major purpose of this study was to replicate the Whitehurst et al. (1981) study showing that preschoolers imitate how much an adult model said rather than the quality of what was said. There was a confound in that study, however: given the construction of the speaker task, it would have been more difficult to produce a two-word incomplete message than a two-word informative one. Therefore, their effect may have been due to task difficulty rather than a discrimination failure on the child's part. Perhaps children exposed to the two-word incomplete model were aware that the messages were ambiguous, but simply had more difficulty producing two-word incomplete messages than two-word informative ones. This study corrects that confound by structuring the speaker task so that it is equally easy to produce either an informative or an uninformative message.

A second purpose of this study was to assess children's performance across different-aged models. In the Whitehurst et al. study, the models were all adults. Other research has shown that children react differently to ambiguous messages given by an adult or by a peer (Sonnenschein & Whitehurst, 1980). Young children are more likely to correctly evaluate the peer's performance. In other words, young children tend to incorrectly evaluate an adult's ambiguous message as being informative. Consequently, in the second experiment, subjects would be asked to evaluate a peer's, rather than an adult's, performance. Prior to doing that, however, we need to ensure that the children would imitate a peer in the same manner as an adult.

In brief, children in this study were assigned to one of three modeling conditions (*two-word contrastive, adult; two-word incomplete, adult; or two-word incomplete, child*) in which they served as listeners in a referential communication task to one of the three types of models. After completing this task, the children performed the speaker's task. (An additional control group did not receive the listener's task.)

The task stimuli were similar to those used in other studies by Whitehurst and his colleagues (Sonnenschein & Whitehurst, 1980; Whitehurst et al., 1981). Both the listener's and the speaker's task consisted of different pictures of geometric forms, three per trial, pasted on 8 × 11 inch paper and inserted in a looseleaf notebook. The stimuli were constructed by combining binary values of the following four dimensions: form (triangle, square), pattern (spotted, striped), size (big, small), color (red, green). A star, hidden by an overlying flap, indicated the location of the referent.

The listener's task consisted of fifteen trials. The dimensions were randomly combined with the restriction that each referent could be described by both a two-word contrastive message (minimum necessary to be informative) and a two-word incomplete message (ambiguous in that it described both the referent and one other stimulus). The speaker task consisted of 30 trials. Each referent could be described by either three two-word contrastive or three two-word incomplete messages. For example, on a typical trial, the referent, a big, red, striped triangle, might be grouped with both a big, green, spotted square and a small, red, striped triangle (the nonreferents).

Seventy-five kindergartners participated in this experiment. There were 15 children in each of the three modeling conditions and 30 children in the *no model* control group. The children were tested individually in an isolated room within the school. They began with a pretest of their ability to discriminate the values of the stimulus attributes (e.g., color, pattern, etc.), followed by the listener's task in which each child served as a listener to either an adult or a peer model. Task roles were then reversed and the child became the speaker. A control group received just the pretest and the speaker's task. No child made any errors on the pretest.

After the pretest, the children were told that they would be playing a game involving pictures similar to the ones they had just seen. They would hear a tape-recording of messages produced by a teacher or a student peer from another school. They were to point to the picture in the looseleaf notebook that they thought the speaker was "talking about." If they chose correctly, they would find a star pasted above the picture upon lifting the opaque flap and consequently would win a marble. The children were shown a snapshot of the teacher or peer speaker and then heard a tape-recording of the messages.

Children in the *two-word contrastive, adult* modeling group heard an adult speaker give two-word contrastive messages (e.g., "the big red one" in the previous example). None of the children in this condition made any errors on the listener's task.

Children in the *two-word incomplete* condition heard the speaker (either an adult or a child) give two-word ambiguous messages which described two of the three stimuli (e.g., for the previous example, such a message would be "the red, striped one"). Half the children in the condition heard an adult model (*two-word incomplete, adult*), the other children heard a peer model (*two-word incomplete, child*). Children in the former group made correct choices on the listener's task 56% of the time (approximately chance-level performance), whereas children in the latter group made correct choices 55% of the time.

Upon completion of the listener's task, the children were told that *they* would now become speakers and would have to "tell about the pictures" so that the experimenter would be able to select the referent. Children were instructed about how to hold the flap so that the experimenter could not see the star above the referent. They were also informed that they would win a marble whenever the experimenter made a correct selection, since that would mean they had done a good job of "telling about it." In fact, to obtain baseline levels of performance undistorted by corrective feedback, the experimenter always chose the referent regardless of the quality of the child's message.

In order to determine whether the type of messages that the children gave was a function of the type of model they heard, separate one-factor ANOVAs, with the modeling condition as the between-subjects factor, were conducted for contrastive, redundant, and incomplete messages. Both the incomplete and contrastive

ANOVAs revealed significant effects ($F(3,52) = 3.36, 4.34, p < .05, 01$, respectively). Children in the *no model* control group gave significantly more incomplete responses and fewer contrastive messages than children in the other three modeling conditions ($t(52) = 3.15, 3.15, p < .05$).

Recall that one purpose of this study was to determine whether the Whitehurst et al. effect (whereby preschoolers produced two-word informative messages after exposure to two-word uninformative models) could have been an artifact of their task. As discussed previously, their task was structured so that it would have been harder to produce a two-word uninformative message than a two-word informative one. Although this study controlled for task difficulty, there were no differences in responding for any type of message as a function of modeling condition ($p > .10$, see Table 1 for mean number of responses).

The children's responses were also classified in terms of the number of dimensions that they used to describe the referent (1, 2, 3, or 4). For example, saying "the red triangle" would yield a score of two. Table 1 depicts the mean of 1-, 2-, 3-, and 4-dimension responses as a function of condition. One-factor ANOVA's, with modeling as the between-subjects variable, revealed no significant effects for either 3- or 4-dimension messages. There were significant effects, however, for both the 1- and 2-dimension messages ($F (3,52) = 4.62, 4.24, p < .001, .025$, respectively). There were significantly more 1-dimension messages in the *no model* control group than in the other three modeling groups ($t(52) = 2.51, p < .05$). There were significantly fewer 2-dimension messages, however, in the *no model* control than in the other three modeling groups ($t(52) = 3.08, p < .01$). There was no difference in responding among the three modeling groups.

TABLE 1
Mean Number of Children's Responses in Experiment I as a Function of Conditions

	Type of Message[a]			
	Contrastive	Redundant	Total Informative	Incomplete
No model	3.07	3.07	6.14	23.86
Ambiguous child	8.14	5.79	13.93	16.07
Ambiguous adult	10.50	3.29	13.79	16.21
Contrastive adult	6.79	8.29	15.07	14.93
	Number of Dimensions Used[a]			
	1	2	3	4
No model	19.36	6.71	3.86	.07
Ambiguous child	7.00	17.14	5.00	.86
Ambiguous adult	4.71	20.79	4.43	.07
Contrastive adult	6.86	13.29	7.79	2.07

[a] Total number of trials was 30.

In general, these results confirm those from Whitehurst et al.'s (1981) study and suggest that preschoolers are more influenced in terms of their own future communications by how much a model says than by the quality of the model's communication.

IS ANY LONG MESSAGE A GOOD MESSAGE?

Why should children be so influenced by how much is said? One possibility is that preschoolers confuse quantity with quality and believe any long message is, by definition, a good one. Research has shown that preschoolers use different criteria than adults for judging the adequacy of a communication. In addition to the research already discussed in which preschoolers judge any correct description of a referent to be an adequate communication (Robinson & Robinson, 1977a), an additional study by Robinson and Robinson (1977b) reveals another interesting criterion. Young children use how a listener responds to a message as a basis for judging the adequacy of that message. Six- and seven-year-olds heard speakers give both ambiguous and informative messages. Regardless of the acutal quality of the message, the children judged the speaker to have done a good job if the listener made a correct selection and a bad job if the listener made an incorrect selection.

In order to test the hypothesis that preschoolers use length in addition to outcome as a criterion for communicative adequacy, children in the following study were asked to evaluate the adequacy of various messages which differed on length, informativeness, and eventual listener outcome. The task was similar to that used in the first experiment; however, in this study, all the pictures were of triangles. Therefore, the only dimensions varying were color, pattern, and size. There were 30 trials. Two task booklets were constructed, one for one-word and one for two-word messages. Although the referents in the two tasks were the same, the non-referent differed to allow for appropriate one- or two-word descriptions.

The procedure was adapted from Robinson and Robinson (1977a). Each child, a kindergartner who had no previous experience with this research, was tested individually in an isolated room within the school. The child was told that he or she would be playing a communication game in which the object was to select the referent described by the speaker. The speaker's messages were presented on a tape-recorder and the children were shown a snapshot of the speaker, a female peer (supposedly from another school where she had played the game with the experimenter several days before).

Half the children heard one-word messages and half heard two-word messages. Regardless of the length of the message, half the messages each child heard were contrastive and half were incomplete (ambiguous, referring to two of the stimuli).

If the subject selected the referent, as indicated by the star above it, the child was told, "You chose the one with the star above it. It went right that time. Did (the speaker) tell you properly which one to pick? (If not: What should she have said?)."

If the child chose a nonreferent, he or she was told, "You chose the one without the star. It went wrong that time. Whose fault was it? Did (the speaker) tell you properly which one to pick? (If not: What should she have said?)."

To determine how children's assessments of message quality were affected by factors such as message length and outcome, children were categorized as stating that the speaker had done an inadequate job if they answered "No" on 70% or more of the trials to the question, "Did (the speaker) tell you properly which one to pick?" The data were then analyzed via a series of X^2 tests to assess whether judgments of speaker inadequacy varied as a function of the quality of the message, the outcome (the accuracy of the listener's choice), or the length of the message.

Table 2 indicates the number of judgments for each of the conditions. More children rated the speaker as having done a bad job when the message was ambiguous rather than informative, $X^2(1) = 23.64, p < .001$. Although this was true in all conditions, when the listener made a correct choice, the majority of children stated that the speaker had performed adequately.

Children were also more likely, in general, to state that the speaker had done a poor job if the listener made an incorrect rather than a correct selection $(X^2)1) = 27.28, p < .001$).

Of primary interest to this study was how the children would evaluate the long messages. An overall X^2 and individual tests for each condition revealed no effect for the length of the message ($X^2 < 1$ in all cases). As can be seen by inspection of Table 2, the children did not take the length of the message into account in their evaluations.

This study supports Robinson and Robinson's (1977b) conclusions that the most important factor in how a young child rates the adequacy of a message is how the listener responds. If the listener makes an incorrect selection, then the speaker is judged to have performed poorly. Although the actual quality of the message does play a role, it is not as important as the outcome.

Although length does not seem to be a factor in how young children *evaluate* communication performance, children, as speakers, *imitate* the length rather than the quality of the model's communications. This finding is somewhat strange, if one assumes that speaking and evaluation ability should both be part of the same communication skill, and how well one performs at one should be indicative of how

TABLE 2
The Number of Children in Experiment II who at Least 70% of the Time Stated That the Speaker had *not* Communicated Adequately[a]

	Good/Correct	Good/Incorrect	Bad/Correct	Bad/Incorrect
1 word	1	4	3	14
2 word	0	3	3	15

[a] There was a total of 19 children in each group. The length of the message was a *between subjects* factor, whereas the quality of the message and the outcomes were *within subjects* factors.

well one will perform at the other. However, an alternate explanation, more in keeping with the data, is that the various aspects of communication (e.g., speaking, listening, evaluation, etc.) may actually be different skills for a young child, as opposed to different facets of the same task (Whitehurst & Sonnenschein, 1981).

Regardless of the possible accuracy of this explanation, however, we still need to determine why a young child's speaking style is more influenced by the length of a message than by its quality. This issue is addressed in the next experiment.

IS MESSAGE LENGTH MORE SALIENT THAN MESSAGE QUALITY?

Whitehurst et al. (1981) suggested that preschoolers imitate the length of a communication rather than its quality because they are more likely to attend to length. However, there has been no direct test of this hypothesis. Thus, the purpose of this study was to test the relative salience of length and informativeness and to determine whether this changes with development. Would younger children find the length of an utterance more salient than its quality? How would older children react?

One way to compare the two dimensions is to have children observe a communication (the standard) and then judge which of two people subsequently communicate in a way more similar to the standard. The two people would vary on whether their messages resemble the quality of the standard communication or the length of the standard communication. The children could also be asked to verbalize the reasons for their choices.

If there is any connection between the dimension one attends to and how one communicates, then there should be developmental changes in saliency. Older children and adults give more informative messages than do younger children. Thus, we might expect older children to attend more to the quality of the communication than to how much was said. Furthermore, the children's answers to "Why did you choose that person?" should give us insight into *specifically* what children attend to when they observe others communicating.

Forty-eight kindergartners, none of whom had participated previously in this research, and 48 fourth graders were assigned to one of four modeling groups. The task in this experiment consisted of 22 trials from the task used in the previous experiment. Each child first served as a listener to a female adult speaker for ten trials. Depending on which of the four modeling groups the child was in, he or she heard the adult speaker give one of the following four message types: one-word contrastive, one-word incomplete (ambiguous), two-word contrastive, or two-word incomplete (ambiguous).

Each child was then told that he or she was going to play a game with four dolls each of whom would try and describe the triangles in the same way as the experimenter. The object was to judge which doll most closely imitated the experimenter.

For the remaining 12 trials the experimenter and the dolls alternated taking turns. On six of the trials, the experimenter continued describing the referent in the same manner as she had been previously. On the alternating six trials, two of the four dolls (which two differed each time) each described the same referent. Each of the four dolls "spoke" in a manner representing one of the modeling conditions (e.g., one-word contrastive, one-word incomplete, two-word contrastive or two-word incomplete). The dolls were paired in all possible combinations, resulting in six doll trials for the child to judge.

Before beginning the task, the child was given several practice trials to confirm that the child understood the instructions. All the children appeared to understand the task requirements. In the actual task, on each doll trial, the child was asked both to choose one of the doll's messages as being more similar to the experimenter's and to explain the reason for his or her choice.

Initial inspection of the data suggested that many of the kindergartners' responses did not focus on either the length of the model's utterance or the quality of the utterance. For example, given a one-word contrastive model, a one-word incomplete doll and a two-word incomplete doll, the kindergartner might choose the latter as being more similar the standard despite differing from it on both length and quality. A three factor ANOVA with grade of the child, length of utterance, and quality of utterance as the between-subjects factors revealed a main effect for grade, $F(1,88) = 26.33$, $p < .001$. In choosing a doll similar to the standard, fourth graders were more likely to base their choice on either the length or the quality of the doll's message ($\overline{X} = .86$) than were the kindergartners ($\overline{X} = .68$).

A second analysis tested whether the majority of the kindergartners' and fourth-graders' judgments of similarity were based on message length or message quality. Children were scored as judging on the basis of length, if the majority of the dolls they chose gave messages the same length as the model's. If the majority of the dolls they chose gave messages that were of the same quality as the model's, the children were scored as judging on the basis of quality. In cases where there was no majority of either length of quality choices, that particular child's data was not included in this analysis. The data indicated that kindergartners judged similarity more on the basis of the length of the utterance ($N = 24$) than on its quality ($N = 15$). This pattern was reversed for the fourth graders (Length N = 14, Quality $N = 27$; $\chi^2(1) = 6.00$, $p < .02$).

Because of the orthogonal pairing of the dimensions, a key trial involved a comparison of a message that was the same length but a different quality than the model's and a message that was the same quality but a different length than the model's. For example, in the one-word contrastive model condition, the two comparison dolls might give a one-word incomplete and a two-word contrastive message.

Children's answers on this trial were analyzed in the same manner as was previously described for the overall pattern of responding ($\chi^2(1) = 11.88$, $p < .001$). As before, kindergartners responded more on the basis of length (N = 32) than quality ($N = 13$). Fourth graders again responded more on the basis of quality ($N = 31$) than length ($N = 17$).

On each comparison trial, the children were asked the reason for their choice. The majority of the fourth-graders' responses (96%) mentioned either the quality of the utterance or its length. For example, "You did a good job, and so did this doll." Or, "You used two words; the doll I chose also did." For kindergartners, however, a different pattern emerged. Much of the time they simply said "I don't know" (60%). However, when they did respond, their answers were not based on either the quality of the communication or its length. Instead, they would state, "You said green, spotted (two-word informative), and this doll also said green (one-word ambiguous)." In other words, they were judging similarity on a much more molecular level than were the older children. This has strong implications for how communication develops and shall be discussed in the next section.

A caveat to these results is necessary, however. One might argue that the reasons that the kindergartners gave may not have been the real basis for their choices. Perhaps children of that age are not good at verbalizing their bases for decisions, and, instead, say the first thing that comes to mind. Although that may, in part, be true, we still must explain the strange choices that the kindergartners often made (e.g., choosing a two-word incomplete doll instead of a one-word incomplete doll when the model was one-word contrastive). Given their strange choices, the most parsimonious explanation is that they were accurately relating the basis for their choices.

What the results from this study suggest is that, for preschoolers, the length of a communication is a more salient characteristic than its quality. With development, however, this changes and the quality of a communication becomes more important than its length. These data offer some support for Whitehurst et al.'s (1981) suggestion that preschoolers may become redundant speakers in the early school years as a byproduct of attending to message length. In other words, what appears to be an increase in informative communications may, instead, be merely an indirect benefit of increasing the length of the communications. Of equal interest are what the data suggest that preschoolers seem to be learning by observing others communicate. Although sometimes the preschoolers focus on general principles, such as how much is said, other times they seem to attend to only the actual words used and, thus, do not abstract general principles that they could apply in other instances.

THE IMPORTANCE OF THESE FINDINGS
TO COMMUNICATION DEVELOPMENT

The intent of these studies was to determine why preschoolers are more likely to imitate how much a speaker has said than the quality of the speaker's utterances. Is it that young children confuse length with quality, thereby assuming any long communication is good? Or do they find message length a more salient dimension than message quality? The data presented in this chapter support the latter reason.

Young children did not judge two-word utterances as better than one-word utterances. There was no difference in judgment due to the length of an utterance. On the other hand, the preschoolers found the length of a communication more salient than its quality in the discrimination task in the third experiment. The effect was the opposite for older children, who found the quality of a communication more salient than its length.

Several interesting implications stem from the data.

Metacommunicative Knowledge: What Is It And Why Does It Occur?

As previously discussed, the issue of metalinguistic awareness is of interest to researchers in many areas of language development. However, due to both space limitations and to concern that different aspects of language may be discrete areas for young children (Bohannon, 1976; Sonnenschein & Whitehurst, 1983), meta-communication shall be the focal topic of this discussion.

Research conducted in the laboratory has indicated that young children have two metacommunicative deficits. They often fail to detect communicative ambiguity or, when they do detect it, they fail to respond appropriately (Flavell, Speer, Green, & August, 1982). They also fail to monitor actively their own comprehension, in part, because they may be applying the wrong standards for judgment (Markman, 1977, 1979). The research from the studies presented in this chapter may shed some light on this issue. Young children may be failing to respond appropriately to ambiguous communications because they may not be attending to the quality of the communication. Thus, what appears to be an inability to detect ambiguity or non-comprehension may, in fact, be inattention to that aspect of the communication. Instead, young children's attention may be focused elsewhere.

It is not clear, however, whether we should discuss metacommunication as a unidimensional or a multidimensional trait. Researchers in several areas of language development have suggested that we must distinguish different levels of metal-inguistic awareness (Clark, 1978; Hirsh-Pasek et al., 1978; Levelt, Sinclair, & Jarvella, 1978). The results of this research are consonant with that suggestion. Although 5-year-olds did not primarily attend to the quality of communications, their judgments about communicative adequacy were based on the informativeness of communications.

What is lacking from this analysis, however, is an explanation of why older children eventually attend to the quality of communications, and whether this change causes children to become better communicators. To phrase the issue in broader terms, what is the relationship between metacommunication and commu-nication? Certain researchers (Flavell, 1976) suggest that metacommunication skills influence communicative skills. Others (Hirsh-Pasek et al., 1978) note that meta-linguistic judgments lag behind speech production and comprehension. And others (Ammon, 1981) argue that there is not necessarily any connection between the two. The nature of the putative relationship between metacommunication and communication becomes more complex if we also consider that there may be different levels of metacommunicative awareness. Right now our knowledge of this relationship is limited. All we know is that with development both metacommunication and communication skills improve. Future research must address: What is the relationship between metacommunication and communication skills, and is this true for all aspects of these skills?

What Do Young Communicators Learn
From Others In Their Environment?

Most researchers would agree that there is a developmental improvement in children's communication skills (Asher, 1979). Having discarded Piagetian notions of egocentrism as an explanatory device, however, we must consider what is causing a child's communication skills to improve. Two ways that children may develop more effective communication skills are by observing competent communicators and by receiving feedback for their own communicative efforts.

Both Whitehurst and Vasta (1975) and Rosenthal and Zimmerman (1978) suggest that observational learning involves some form of selective imitation. That is, only certain aspects of a model's behavior will be imitated. In fact, Rosenthal and Zimmerman (1978) state that observational learning involves "the abstraction of rules and meaningful implications from a model's performance" (p. 85).

The questions for communication development are: What is the young child abstracting from observing others, and why is the child abstracting certain things but not others? From the results of this research, I would like to propose three tentative stages corresponding to different levels of abstraction. The very young child may attend mainly to specifics (e.g., the specific words spoken) and not necessarily abstract more general concepts. For example, in the third experiment, kindergartners frequently explained their choices by stating, "You said green and so did this doll," thus ignoring the more basic concepts of message length or quality. At the next stage, the child may attend to, and therefore probably imitate, the length of a model's communications. In the final stage, although the child is aware of how much is said, the main focus is the quality of the communication (Whitehurst & Merkur, 1977). What causes this developmental progression is not yet known. However, the research presented in this chapter indicates that what a young communicator is noticing in his or her environment (and, thus, probably imitating) changes as the child develops.

The issue of what aspects of a communication are attended becomes a concern if (as seems to be the case) the child attends to irrelevant aspects of a communication, draws incorrect inferences, and uses these as a basis for future performance. If the child were receiving feedback from others as to the "error of his or her ways," the situation would quickly be alleviated. (It would also explain what causes the developmental change in the focus of children's attention!) In fact, when adults give explicit feedback on the adequacy of a communication, children's performance on laboratory tasks quickly improves, as does their metacommunicative judgments (Robinson, 1981). However, recent research by Robinson (1981) shows that in naturally occurring situations in the home and school, adults rarely give children explicit feedback. Thus, the factors that cause developmental changes in young communicator's attention need to be addressed by future research, if we are to understand why communication skills develop.

The Ecological Validity Of The Findings

There are many differences between the discourse that takes place in naturalistic settings and the abbreviated version of referential speech acts addressed in this research. As discussed before, the main reason for conducting research in the laboratory is it allows the investigator to study one aspect of communication skill and control all other relevant task factors. The concern, or course, is whether laboratory findings can be generalized to "real life." Asher (1979) describes evidence indicating that children appear to manifest greater communicative competence in naturalistic rather than laboratory settings. However, the difference may not be due to different referential abilities being sampled but rather to other contextual communicative processes and to nonverbal factors (Ackerman, 1981; Asher, 1979).

Referential communication research has typically focused on the child's communications about a perceptual context. In the laboratory one can control the similarity between stimuli to obtain measures of communicative competence. In "real life," however, stimuli are often so different (e.g., a doll and a book) that mentioning any aspect of one stimulus will differentiate it from the other. Thus, we may get a misleading picture of the child's communicative skills. Furthermore, much of the naturally occurring communications of young children are nonverbal gestures (Asher, 1979).

Differences between naturalistic and laboratory performance may also be due to nonreferential communicative processes. In natural discourse not only is the referential speech act relevant but so is the deictic adequacy of the communication and the previous shared history of meaning between the speaker and the listener (Ackerman, 1981). In other words, a listener may correctly interpret a communication even if the referential aspect of it is inadequate.

Having shown how children in the laboratory will attend to specific aspects of a referential communication, future research should assess how this pattern will be manifested in naturalistic situations where other communicative processes may compensate for attention to irrelevant aspects of the referential speech act. For example, will contextual elements, such as the shared history of meaning, compensate for the young child's referential inadequacies, such as have been discussed in this chapter?

REFERENCES

Ackerman, B. P. The understanding of young children and adults of the deictic adequacy of communication. *Journal of Experimental Child Psychology*, 1981, *31*, 256–270.

Ammon, P. Communication skills and communicative competence: A neo-Piagetian process-structural view. In W. P. Dickson (Ed.), *Children's oral communication skills*. New York: Academic Press, 1981.

Asher, S. Referential communication. In G. J. Whitehurst & B. J. Zimmerman (Eds.), *The functions of language and cognition*. New York: Academic Press, 1979.

Bohannon, J. N. Normal and scrambled grammar in discrimination, imitation, and comprehension. *Child Development*, 1976, *47*, 669–681.

Clark, E. V. Awareness of language: Some evidence from what children say and do. In A. Sinclair, R. J. Jarvella, & W. J. M. Levelt (Eds.), *The child's conception of language*. Berlin: Springer, 1978.

Flavell, J. H. The development of metacommunication. Paper presented at the Twenty-first International Congress of Psychology, Paris, July 1976.

Flavell, J. H., Speer, J. R., Green, F. L., & August, D. L. The development of comprehension monitoring and knowledge about communication. *Monographs of the Society for Research in Child Development*, 1982.

Glucksberg, S., Krauss, R. M., & Higgins, E. T. The development of referential communication skills. In F. D. Horowitz (Ed.), *Review of child development* (Vol. 4). Chicago: University of Chicago Press, 1975.

Hirsh-Pasek, K., Gleitman, L. R., & Gleitman, H. What did the brain say to the mind? A study of the detection and report of ambiguity by young children. In A. Sinclair, R. J. Jarvella, & W. J. M. Levelt (Eds.), *The child's conception of language*. Berlin: Springer, 1978.

Levelt, W. J. M., Sinclair, A., & Jarvella, R. J. Causes and functions of linguistic awareness in language acquisition: Some introductory remarks. In A. Sinclair, R. J. Jarvella, & W. J. M. Levelt (Eds.), *The child's conception of language*. Berlin: Springer, 1978.

Markman, E. Realizing that you don't understand: A preliminary investigation. *Child Development*, 1977, *48*, 986–992.

Markman, E. Realizing that you don't understand: Elementary school children's awareness of inconsistencies. *Child Development*, 1979, *50*, 643–655.

Olson, D. Language and thought: Aspects of a cognitive theory of semantics. *Psychological Review*, 1979, *77*, 257–273.

Piaget, J. *The language and thought of the child*. New York: Harcourt, 1926.

Robinson, E. The child's understanding of inadequate messages and communication failure: A problem of ignorance or egocentrism? In W. P. Dickson (Ed.), *Children's oral communication skills*. New York: Academic Press, 1981.

Robinson, E. J., & Robinson, W. P. The young child's understanding of communication. *Developmental Psychology*, 1976, *12*, 328–333.

Robinson, E. J., & Robinson, W. P. Development in the understanding of causes of success and failure in verbal communication. *Cognition*, 1977, *5*, 363–378. (a)

Robinson, E. J., & Robinson, W. P. Children's explanations of communication failure and the inadequacy of the misunderstood message. *Developmental Psychology*, 1977, *13*, 156–161. (b)

Rosenthal, T. L., & Zimmerman, B. J. *Social learning and cognition*. New York: Academic Press, 1978.

Slobin, D. I. A case study of early language awareness. In A. Sinclair, R. J. Jarvella, & W. J. M. Levelt (Eds.), *The child's conception of language*. Berlin: Springer, 1978.

Sonnenschein, S., & Whitehurst, G. J. The development of communication: When a bad model makes a good teacher. *Journal of Experimental Child Psychology*, 1980, *29*, 371–390.

Sonnenschein, S., & Whithurst, G. J. Training referential communication skills: The limits of success. *Journal of Experimental Child Psychology*, 1983, in press.

Whitehurst, G. J. The development of communication: Changes with age and modeling. *Child Development*, 1976, *47*, 473–482.

Whitehurst, G. J., & Merkur, A. The development of communication: Modeling and contrast failure. *Child Development*, 1977, *48*, 993–1001.

Whitehurst, G. J., & Sonnenschein, S. The development of informative messages in referential communication: Knowing when vs. knowing how. In W. P. Dickson (Ed.), *Children's oral communication skills*. New York: Academic Press, 1981.

Whitehurst, G. J., Sonnenschein, S., & Ianfolla, B. J. Learning to communicate from models: Children confuse length with information. *Child Development*, 1981, *52*, 507–513.

Whitehurst, G. J., & Vasta, R. Is language acquired through imitation? *Journal of Psycholinguistic Research*, 1975, *4*, 37–59.

CHAPTER 14

Knowledge and Language: Children's Ability to Use and Communicate What They Know about Everyday Experiences

Ann Jaffe Pace and Lynne Feagans

INTRODUCTION

Increasingly, it is acknowledged that even a child's earliest utterances are mapped onto knowledge which that child already possesses. This knowledge is both conceptual and procedural (Bruner, 1978; Macnamara, 1972), in that children acquire information about many things in the world as well as knowledge about what to do with what they know. If this is true of the first stages of language acquisition, it should be no less true of older children's use of more complex language forms. As children acquire more knowledge and more integrated knowledge about events in their world, they should be able to use this knowledge both to comprehend complex forms of language, such as narratives about these events, and to communicate effectively their understanding of what they already know. In addition, evidence is accumulating that such competencies may be crucial for success in school (Feagans, 1982).

Recent years have witnessed a growing effort both to characterize in theoretically useful ways the kind of complex knowledge people acquire through everyday experiences and to investigate the development of such knowledge in children. A number of related constructs, such as "schema" (Rumelhart & Ortony, 1977), "script" (Schank & Abelson, 1975, 1977), and "frame" (Minsky, 1975) have been proposed to represent the integrated knowledge structures that apparently develop through repeated encounters with similar events and situations. Schema is probably the more inclusive construct and, most broadly, refers to the representation of a generic concept in memory (Rumelhart & Ortony, 1977). This concept may be of an object, an event, an action, a sequence of actions, or an abstract idea. A script, according to Schank and Abelson (1975, 1977), is a stereotypical action sequence for a common, everyday event. Scripts are acquired for many situations, such as eating in a restaurant, going to bed, shopping in a grocery store, etc.

Katherine Nelson (1977, 1980, 1981), in particular, has been studying the development of such scriptlike knowledge in preschool and early school-aged children. She has found (1980) that even children as young as 3 appear to have acquired ordered, generalized knowledge about familiar events. Moreover, they appear to treat routinized, repeated events as generalizable after only one or a few personal experiences with them, and this understanding is marked linguistically, (e.g., through use of the general present tense form "you eat"). That is, children seem to recognize early that sequences of events which are repeated regularly have a coherent structure of their own with identifiable and interrelated parts. Further, although older children (from 5 to 8 years) will relate more elaborate scripts and use more complex language to report them than will younger children, the basic structure of scripts for commonplace situations has been acquired by age 3 or 4 (Nelson, 1980). "In general terms," writes Nelson (1981), "we can state that the child builds up an event representation from the experience of an event that is structured in specific ways" (p. 105).

These findings are impressive. They suggest that children acquire early rather complex knowledge of events in which they participate repeatedly. While some of these events may be specific to certain households or regions, other activities are common throughout our culture. Thus, children from different backgrounds will have some highly similar experiences and likely will have comparable knowledge of them.

Such shared knowledge becomes the basis for many of the ways in which young children use and explore knowledge. For example, the mutual possession of similar scripts for everyday events, in addition to general knowledge of conversational structure, enables preschoolers to engage in genuinely communicative dialogue (Nelson & Gruendel, 1979). While a sustained dialogue concerning an immediate shared context can occur, shared scripts permit children to discuss or reenact routinized events, such as getting ready for bed, that are part of their general background of knowledge. Likewise, some of the first stories told by children (Applebee, 1978; Stein & Trabasso, in press) are scriptlike, in that they are sequences of episodes relating to some familiar experience.

By the time children get to school, then, their use of language in different contexts should reflect their knowledge of many typical events. In fact, script knowledge is a prerequisite for the successful accomplishment of a number of school tasks. For example, the very first selections in a preprimer from a widely used basal reading series (Houghton Mifflin Reading Series, 1976) require, at least, that students have some version of a TV repair script, an amusement park script, a walking-the-dog script, and a library script. To fully comprehend these stories, children have to supplement the information provided via text and pictures in these readers with their own knowledge of the events depicted. (Interestingly, the teacher's guide to this reader does not suggest assessing students' knowledge of these events prior to their reading of the stories.)

Several cognitive demands are placed on children in such a situation. For one, they have to recognize the event described in the story as an instance of a known script. They also have to fill in, from their own scripts, script elements or "slots" that are not explicitly mentioned in the story but are assumed instead. If children have well-learned and organized scripts for these situations, this should be a rather effortless task. In addition, children have to be able to recognize when a story violates the expectations generated by a script. Scripts permit predictions through generalizations from repeated experiences. However, one narrative device is the introduction of surprise through the violation of usual expectations. Thus, children have to be able to distinguish between the information in their own scripts and that in the story.

In addition, adequate comprehension and especially production of stories require that children have some knowledge of narrative structure. As several authors have argued (Applebee, 1978; Labov & Fanshel, 1977; Stein & Trabasso, in press), narratives in general, whether script-related or not, contain a particular structural framework. For script-related narratives, this framework organizes the substance of the script. For instance, scripts are introduced in a particular way in order to set up what follows. Sequences of activities are told in a prescribed order to preserve the temporal contiguity of the events in the real world, and endings are fixed to allow the listener to know that the speaker has finished. Thus, children telling stories must not only have the script knowledge appropriate to the topic of the narrative, but they must also know how to organize this information so that it can be communicated effectively.

In this chapter, the ability of children to understand and produce narratives about stereotypical experiences is explored through two sets of investigations. The first examines elementary school children's comprehension of narratives about differentially familiar events. The second, a longitudinal study, focuses on the ability of preschool children from different socioeconomic backgrounds both to comprehend and to relate narratives about everyday experiences, such as supermarket shopping. Several issues are addressed through these studies. One concerns how young (4- and 5-year-old) children use their existing knowledge to comprehend narratives. Another concerns the relationship, among children of different ages, between their degree of familiarity with the topic of a narrative and their comprehension of it. Additionally, children's sensitivity to story information inconsistent with their own knowledge is considered. Finally, reasons for differences between children's apparent knowledge of ordinary situations and their ability to relate this knowledge coherently and effectively are explored. Differences in the performance of young children from different socioeconomic backgrounds are examined in order to identify potential sources of school failure.

CHILDREN'S COMPREHENSION
OF SCRIPT-RELATED NARRATIVES

If, by the time children enter kindergarten, they have acquired integrated knowledge of frequently occurring events, this knowledge should affect text comprehension in several ways. First, if a passage essentially relates a script for a common, everyday activity that even 5-year olds may have overlearned, comprehension of such passages should be very good for all elementary-grade students, regardless of age. They should recognize the text as another instance of a well-known event; thus, no developmental differences in comprehension may occur. Second, developmental differences should appear with passages that concern events that would be better known to older children. Further, students of any age should be able to use their existing knowledge of well-known events to supply information not provided explicitly in the texts. Expectations which are consistently associated with certain situations should not have to be stated specifically in a passage. For example, a narrative about supermarket shopping which mentions a grocery cart or basket need not contain an explanation for its use. This information should be part of a person's script for this event and would be considered redundant information by most authors. Therefore, children should be able to comprehend equally well texts which do and do not include such assumed knowledge, if they use their own scripts to supplement explicitly stated information.

In the first of a series of investigations of children's knowledge and comprehension, the first two assumptions were tested (Pace, 1978); results consistent with them were produced. Supermarket shopping and making a peanut butter and jelly sandwich were chosen to represent situations that were predicted to be well known, even to kindergartners. Other events, such as playing a game of checkers or planting a garden, were presumed to be better known by older children, while activities such as making lye soap or making a lithograph were thought to be beyond the experience of most—if not all—elementary school children. "Script-lists" were compiled for the more common events. These lists consisted of the most frequently mentioned—or most apparently necessary—steps in a script. Kindergartners and students in the second, fourth, and sixth grades were asked to tell what they knew about these events; nonspecific probes were used to try to make sure that children were revealing all that they knew. To assess children's knowledge of the more unusual activities, they were simply asked whether they were familiar with these situations. As measured by the script-lists, knowledge of the very common events was nearly perfect across all grades; only three script items in all were omitted. Consistent with expectations, greater variability and greater differences among grades were obtained on the checkers and garden scripts, while no student in any grade revealed specific knowledge of the more uncommon events.

Short narrative passages about these different situations were prepared so that the information in them corresponded to that in the script-lists. Further, for the more common events, two kinds of texts were used "Explicit" passages contained all the script information that would be needed to answer a subsequent set of comprehension questions. In "implicit" passages, information was deleted which groups of college students had judged to be implied by the texts of these passages. Only explicit narratives about the more unusual situations were used. Children in each of the four grades listened twice to one story of each type and then answered questions about them.

Comprehension of the passages about the very ordinary events was very good at all grade levels. Kindergartners performed about as well as sixth graders. A total of only 11 errors were made by the 80 participants, and perfect scores were obtained in many instances. In addition, comparable results were obtained for the explicit and implicit texts. Apparently, all the children knew these events so well that they could supply what the text omitted. While these results do not address children's comprehension of text-specific information that may not be part of a child's existing script, they do show that even 5- and 6-year olds can recognize the apparent topic of a narrative and use their own knowledge of the events described to go beyond the information provided. Thus, young children do seem to have scriptlike or ordered, generalized knowledge of commonplace situations and can utilize it in text comprehension.

By contrast, kindergartners had poorer comprehension that the older children of stories about events less familiar to them, such as playing checkers, and this was true of both the explicit and the implicit passages. An analysis of covariance using script knowledge as the covariate revealed that second graders' scores were significantly higher than those of the kindergarten students. Sixth graders made no errors on the explicit forms of these stories and only two on the implicit forms, while fourth graders made six errors on the implicit passages. However, nonparametric tests produced no significant differences between comprehension of explicit and implicit stories for either the fourth or sixth grades. It is interesting, in this case, that hearing all the information did not seem to benefit the younger children. What they did not know well, they could not comprehend well.

Not surprisingly, the passages about the more uncommon events were the most difficult to comprehend, even though all the required information was provided and even though students could request to hear portions of the narratives again. An analysis of variance performed on the comprehension scores for these stories at all four grade levels produced a significant main effect for grade. A subsequent Newman-Keuls procedure revealed that sixth graders performed much better on these passages than did any other group of students, while kindergartners did more poorly. The reasons for this differential performance are probably several. The results, however, may be related less to the younger children's lack of conceptual knowledge about these passages than their lack of what could be called procedural or strategic knowledge or to their inability to regulate their own degree of comprehension. In other words, they may not have known what to do to comprehend a text concerning something about which they knew little. Among the skills children in kindergarten or second grade may not have developed sufficiently is the ability to monitor and improve their own degree of comprehension (Baker & Brown, 1980;

Pace, 1978), an ability often considered to be an aspect of metacognition (Brown, 1980). Although some behavioral evidence of self-regulatory or planful activity has been described in 2- and 3-year-old children (DeLoache & Brown, 1979), whether or not children will demonstrate the ability to monitor and control their understanding of stories probably depends on the interrelations among task demands, subject matter, and cognitive ability.

Although this study showed that even kindergarten children could use their existing knowledge of everyday situations to comprehend passages which essentially incorporated scripts for these events, most texts obviously do not correspond so exactly to such scripts. More typically, background knowledge has to be invoked repeatedly as part of an ongoing comprehension process. Further, texts may contain information which is inconsistent with the expectations generated by past experience. In such cases, predictions based on existing world knowledge would not be confirmed, and comprehension problems might result. If the utilization of scripts for very well-known events were relatively automatic, in the sense of occurring without conscious awareness, young children in particular may not even detect information which violates their usual expectations. Thus, in some situations, the ready availability of organized knowledge may hinder rather than help comprehension.

To test this possibility, some of the information in the passages about supermarket shopping and the peanut butter and jelly sandwich was changed (Pace, 1979). For example, the script-inconsistent version of the supermarket story had a mother buying a color TV set in the market instead of a bag of cookies. Elementary school children were presented with the normal form of one passage and a changed version of the other. Twelve students each in kindergarten and the second, fourth, and sixth grades listened to the stories, while 12 other children in the second, fourth, and sixth grades read the same passages. One comprehension question for each story pertained to the information that was changed in the script-inconsistent forms. The results were striking. When children listened to the passages, two-thirds of the kindergartners and three-fourths of the second graders failed to detect the altered information. On the other hand, all the fourth graders did so and all but two of the 12 sixth graders. A chi-square procedure used to compare the proportion of children in each of the four grades who were aware of the inconsistent script information was significant. However, when second graders read the passages they performed differently. Two-thirds of this group, as well as the same proportion of the older readers, detected the inconsistent information.

These results are provocative for two reasons. One is the apparent difference between the reading and listening conditions for the second graders. The other is the discrepancy in performance between the younger and older children who listened to the passages. The reading–listening comparison provides some support for the suggestion made by Olson and Hildyard (1977) that information which cannot be obtained from existing knowledge might be understood better if it were presented in writing rather than orally. If this is so, then reading may be one means of getting children to attend to text-specific information. Other possibilities include increasing the salience of the inconsistent information or forewarning children to expect to hear something unusual.

Both procedures were tried in a subsequent study (Pace, 1980), and both seemed to be effective. One simple change was to alert children to the possibility that they might hear something strange or unusual in the story and to caution them to listen carefully so that they could later say what it was. Another change was to increase the strangeness of the inconsistent information so that it was clearly anomalous. For example, the mother in the supermarket passage purchased an elephant, while the child in the sandwich narrative put shoe polish, rather than peanut butter, on a piece of bread. Children in kindergarten and second grade heard either a supermarket or a sandwich story under one of three experimental conditions: an original inconsistent story, but with the prompt, as described; a new, stranger inconsistent story without the prompt; or a new story with the prompt.

Over 60% of the kindergartners and second graders who heard these passages detected the inconsistent information. A comparable percentage of children in both grades noticed the inconsistent information in all altered versions of the narratives when they were alerted to attend carefully to them, and all but one student (a kindergartner) detected the anomaly in the "no prompt" condition for the new stories. These results are considerably better than those obtained in the previous study, in which 75% of the kindergarten and second-grade listeners did not report inconsistencies.

Although the inducements used in this study were effective, the results obtained suggest that special efforts may be needed to get younger children to attend to text-specific information when such information conflicts with their own knowledge. Olson (1976) has proposed that successful comprehension of texts may require recognizing that text is autonomous in the sense that meaning resides in the text itself rather than evolving from the interactive communicative context of oral discourse. This recognition may not come readily to younger children who judge a passage to concern an event which is familiar to them. In such cases, they seem to rely more on their own knowledge or scripts than on the text. To understand that a text is a thing apart from immediate experience and is something that may need to be acted upon in a deliberate way may involve the kind of cognitive "distancing" described by Sigel (Sigel & Saunders, 1979) and therefore be a more sophisticated skill developmentally than the utilization of existing knowledge.

Taken together, these studies indicate that younger children can and do use their own knowledge to comprehend narratives, but that utilization of scripts or complex patterns of generalized knowledge may be a mixed blessing. The possible interfering role of existing knowledge in children's comprehension should be explored further, and attempts should be made to identify when, how, and under what circumstances children begin to treat text as autonomous. Indeed, one of the requirements of schooling may be to learn that text information cannot necessarily be derived from personal experience.

Success in school also seems to require that children communicate what they know effectively and in a way which is consistent with teachers' expectations. To meet this demand, children need to have access to their own experiential knowledge. Although the research reported above demonstrates that even young children can make use of their script knowledge in comprehending narrative passages, questions still remain about the organization of this knowledge in memory, as well as its accessibility to the child without verbal probing by an adult.

In addition, it is not known how children interpret tasks which probe for script or narrative information. Although inability to monitor and regulate one's own performance may hinder a child's comprehension, as already discussed, problems may also arise because all children may not interpret task demands in the same way. Thus, children may be able to monitor their own performance and still be unable to meet teachers' expectations because they misunderstand specific task demands. The ability to understand explicit and implicit task demands is another aspect of metacognition discussed by Brown (1980).

INDIVIDUAL DIFFERENCES IN COMPREHENSION AND PRODUCTION OF NARRATIVES

Questions about children's organization of knowledge, its accessibility to them, and possible contextual influences on interpretation of tasks will be discussed below. These questions are important for understanding individual differences among groups of children in school. Demonstration of differential organization of knowledge by groups of children has obvious implications for how this information might be retrieved and used in learning. It is also important (a) to investigate how children access and use their knowledge base spontaneously, since probing is not always practiced or desired in the classroom situation, and (b) to gain an appreciation of how children understand particular contextual or task demands.

Most of the research on children's ability to recall narratives has not been focused on exploring individual differences nor on its relation to script knowledge. Much research, however, has been aimed at examining whether children conform in their storytelling to adult schemas of stories as well as whether children exhibit the same reactions to violations of schema parts as do adults. For instance, Stein and Glenn (1975, 1979) have formulated a story schema which organizes in a hierarchical and sequential fashion the obligatory and optional elements of a story. These include such elements as major settings, initiating events, consequences, and internal responses. They have conducted a series of experiments with children from first through fifth grade in order to determine whether there appears to be a developmental sequence in the acquisition of a story schema, as well as whether the kinds of connections between episodes in a story (causal or noncausal) affect recall. They found that children most often recalled major settings, consequences, and initiating events, whereas attempts, reactions, minor settings, and internal responses were less often recalled. These findings indicate that even the youngest children were able to recall the central aspects of the stories, although less important and implied information such as internal responses were omitted. In addition, Stein and Glenn found that even the youngest children were better able to remember a sequence of episodes in a story when these episodes were causally, rather than arbitrarily, related. In a later study, Glenn (1980) systematically varied stories, so that some stories contained episodes which were causally related and others were arbitrarily linked. The causally linked stories were better recalled by both first and third graders than the arbitrarily related ones. The stories which had arbitrarily linked episodes produced both omission of episodes and inversion of episodes by the children with much greater frequency than the stories in which the episodes were logically related. This is consistent with the data presented above concerning children's use of scripts, in that conventional information in a script is better recalled than anomolous or arbitrarily inserted information.

Individual differences in the acquisition of story schemas have not been carefully investigated so far. The most interesting and relevant study of social class differences in story retelling was done by John, Horner, and Berney (1970). Although this study was done well before the emergence of the recent literature on story schemas, the results are surprisingly relevant for a focus on individual differences. The researchers found that both lower- and middle-class black first graders produced the basic story elements in the retelling of the book, *Curious George* (Rey, 1941). Social class differences were found, though, in the kind of elements included in the retelling. Middle-class children more often reported phrases which were not in the pictorial representation of the story but had to be inferred from listening to the story. The groups did not differ in the proportion of phrases used which were derived from the pictures displayed during the reading of the book. In addition, the lower-class black children, in comparison to the middle-class black children, included more nontext-based items in their retellings, including redundancies, fillers, irrelevant elaborations, and pictorial details. There was some evidence in a further study that such nontext-based items were less frequent at the end of the school year in groups of lower-class children.

More recently, the narrative and dialogue skills of poverty and middle-class children have been studied at the Frank Porter Graham Child Development Center. The children studied come from a longitudinal intervention project that examines children at high risk for sociocultural retardation (The Carolina Abecedarian Project). The children in this project are being followed from birth through 8 years of age. At school entry, each high-risk child is matched on sex with a low-risk child (middle-class) from his or her public school classroom.

Experiments were designed which examined both narrative and communicative skills which appeared to be important for school (Feagans & Farran, 1981). These experiments were administered in the fall of the kindergarten year. One of these experiments involved reading three kinds of simple stories about a grocery store to the children. These stories contained episodes which were (a) causally or script-related, (b) arbitrarily related, or (c) related by temporal-causal connectives, such as *before* or *after*.

The experiment contained two tasks. First, the child was read a story and asked to act it out with the props provided. If he or she failed to act out the story correctly, it was read again until the child achieved a perfect performance. Thus, trials to criterion was the comprehension measure. Second, the child was asked to paraphrase the same story in his or her own words. No prompts were given to help the child recall the relevant information.

The results from these experiments indicated that the high-risk children were similar to the low-risk children in their ability to act out the stories (trials to criterion), while the groups differed significantly in their ability to retell the information to others (Feagans & Farran, 1981). The high-risk group produced fewer pieces of relevant story information, made more errors in sequencing, and also added much irrelevant information. This pattern is similar to the results reported by John et al. (1970).

In addition, for both groups of children, stories about script-based knowledge were the easiest to comprehend and retell verbally, while the stories containing arbitrarily related events were the most difficult. Thus, these children appeared to use their script knowledge to help in recall in a similar manner to that reported by Pace (1978). Further, the results are parallel to the Pace data even when, as in this study, the children demonstrated perfect comprehension of all the details of the material prior to the retelling.

In a more detailed examination of the errors made on the stories, it appeared that low- and high-risk children were forgetting the same kinds of events in the stories, but there was evidence that high-risk children did not introduce the characters in the stories nor did they give setting or concluding information as often as did the low-risk children (Feagans & Farran, 1980). This was especially true of the stories containing arbitrarily linked events.

These results tend to indicate that although both low- and high-risk children demonstrated perfect comprehension of the stories, the high-risk children lost much of the information in recalling the stories without prompts. These results might be explained in several ways. The most obvious explanation is that these high-risk children had problems in monitoring their own performance; they knew the story but they did not have appropriate strategies to retrieve and produce the story correctly, especially when there were no probes or prompts to aid them in recall. Another possibility is that the poorer retellings of these high-risk children were rooted in a less highly developed story schema. They may have been able to act out the story but had a less-developed hierarchical framework to help them organize recall. On the other hand, it could be argued that these differences were due to the situational demands made on these children, so that the high-risk children were constrained in their recall because of the implicit demands of the task.

In a test of this latter explanation, high-risk children were administered a task in which demands varied. After a warm-up task which included modeling stories for the children, they were presented with three objects and asked to tell a story about them. The objects in one set were ones which could be related by the appropriate script (e.g., a boy, a birthday cake, and candles), while another set was composed of unrelated objects (e.g., a girl, a pole, and a Coke bottle). These two sets of objects were given to the children under two conditions. In a constrained condition, the children were asked to tell a story by introducing the objects in the specific order of their placement on the table. Therefore, in the example given above, the boy was to be mentioned first, then the birthday cake, and then the candles. In an unconstrained condition, the children could mention the objects in any order they desired when telling the story. The results indicated that although the children were certainly affected in their ability to tell a coherent story by the set of objects used, there was no effect for the presence of constraints on the order of mention of the objects. These prekindergarten children were indeed able to tell stories which contained some theme and setting information as well as sequences of events leading to some conclusion, when the objects were script related. With nonscript-related sets of objects, most children were not able to tell a story, but merely mentioned the objects on the table and described some aspect about them.

The results of this study indicate that the children were not affected in their performance by the constraints placed on the task. This tends to minimize the likelihood of the explanation that task demands may alter high-risk children's performance in comparison to low-risk children on a task where there were few constraints. In addition, this task revealed some interesting information about the ability of high-risk children to use either script knowledge or a story schema. It appears that the children indeed were helped by their script knowledge in producing good stories about objects related to events like a birthday party. It was somewhat surprising, though, that these children's performance with the unrelated objects was so impaired. In this condition, the children had to rely on their knowledge of story structure to make up a coherent story. They could not depend on conventional knowledge to define the relationships among the objects. It appeared that the high-risk children were not able to use, or did not have, a schema which was adaptable for this purpose. Questions still remain, though, about the exact nature of the relationship between the structure in memory of script knowledge versus story schema knowledge. In addition, a similar study using a low-risk group as well as children of different ages should be conducted in order to determine whether or not children at low risk exhibit similar differential ability between the two conditions and to assess the developmental progression in children's ability to tell stories under the two conditions. The interesting relationship between script knowledge and story schema knowledge, the former knowledge of the complex structure of events in the real world and the latter knowledge of the typical structure of stories, needs much greater study.

Although results thus far point to differences between poverty and low-risk children on measures of knowledge about stories, information is needed about how these differences may affect school functioning. As a beginning step in examining this relationship, measures of comprehension and retelling of stories in the grocery store task (Feagans & Farran, 1981) were correlated with school achievement within each group. It was found that within the high-risk group, there were substantial correlations of .4 to .7 between the discourse measures and kindergarten achievement scores. The correlations for the low-risk group were much lower. Thus, at least for the high-risk group, the abilities utilized in comprehending and retelling such stories may be among those factors by which these children's functioning in school is assessed.

CONCLUSION

The results obtained from these studies indicate that school children's understanding and production of narratives may vary as a function of story topic, grade or age, and cultural or economic background. Further, the abilities involved in these tasks seem to be related in a practical sense to school adaptation, especially for high-risk children. By the time young children of various backgrounds arrive at school, they apparently have acquired organized, sequential knowledge of events they have experienced in their own lives. They can utilize this knowledge to comprehend narratives about these events, and even children identified as at risk academically can produce acceptable stories dealing with such script-based or experiential knowledge.

However, young children and those from less privileged socioeconomic backgrounds, have difficulty with certain tasks that are related to school. For example, high-risk children have problems in organizing story information coherently in a recall task and in telling relevant parts in the correct sequence, even when the information is relatively familiar to them. In addition, they have difficulty organizing into coherent stories information which is not directly related to their own out-of-school experiences. Even young children from an average school population cannot readily detect text information which is inconsistent with their own expectations for events. Thus, although children can use their existing knowledge to accomplish many tasks, school may place demands on them which many children are not ready or prepared to meet. In order to be able to prevent patterns of school failure and to gain a greater understanding of the kinds of skills that need to be taught, more attention must be directed toward identifying the demands imposed by various school tasks and the capacity of children of different ages and different backgrounds to meet these demands.

REFERENCES

Applebee, A. N. *The child's concept of story*. Chicago: The University of Chicago Press, 1978.

Baker, L., & Brown, A. L. *Metacognitive skills and reading* (Technical Report No. 188). Champaign, IL: Center for the Study of Reading, University of Illinois, 1980.

Brown, A. L. Metacognitive development and reading. In R. J. Spiro, B. Bruce, & W. F. Brewer (Eds.), *Theoretical issues in reading comprehension*. Hillsdale, NJ: Erlbaum, 1980.

Bruner, J. S. The role of dialogue in language acquisition. In A. Sinclair, R. J. Jarvella, & W. J. Levelt (Eds.), *The child's conception of language*. New York: Springer-Verlag, 1978.

DeLoache, J. S., & Brown, A. L. Looking for Big Bird: Studies of memory in very young children. *Quarterly Newsletter of the Laboratory of Comparative Human Cognition*, 1979, *1*, 53–57.

Feagans, L. The development and importance of narratives for school adaptation. In L. Feagans & D. C. Farran (Eds.), *The language of children reared in poverty*. New York: Academic Press, 1982.

Feagans, L., & Farran, D. C. Story comprehension and recall as a function of story structure. Paper presented at the Sixth Biennial Southeastern Conference on Human Development, Alexandria, VA, 1980.

Feagans, L., & Farran, D. C. How demonstrated comprehension can get muddled in production. *Developmental Psychology*, 1981, *17*, 718–127.

Glenn, C. G. Relationship between story content and structure. *Journal of Educational Psychology*, 1980, *72*, 550–560.

John, V. P., Horner, V. M., & Berney, T. D. Story retelling: A study of sequential speech in young children. In H. Levin & J. P. Williams (Eds.), *Basic studies on reading*. New York: Basic Books, 1970.

Houghton Mifflin Reading Series (W. K. Durr, Sr. author). Boston: Houghton Mifflin, 1976.

Labov, W., & Fanshel, D. *Therapeutic discourse: Psychotherapy as conversation*. New York: Academic Press, 1977.

Macnamara, J. Cognitive basis of language learning in infants. *Psychological Review*, 1972, *79*, 1–13.

Minsky, M. A framework for representing knowledge. In P. H. Winston (Ed.), *The psychology of computer vision*. New York: McGraw-Hill, 1975.

Nelson, K. Characteristics of children's scripts for familiar events. Paper presented at the American Psychological Association Meetings, Montreal, September 1980.

Nelson, K. Cognitive development and the acquisition of concepts. In R. C. Anderson, R. J. Spiro, & W. E. Montague (Eds.), *Schooling and the acquisition of knowledge*. Hillsdale, NJ: Erlbaum, 1977.

Nelson, K. Social cognition in a script framework. In J. H. Flavell & L. Ross (Eds.), *Social cognitive development: Frontiers and possible futures*. New York: Cambridge University Press, 1981.

Nelson, K., & Gruendel, J. M. At morning it's lunchtime: A scriptal view of children's dialogues. *Discourse Processes*, 1979, *2*, 73–94.

Olson, D. R. Culture, technology, and intellect. In L. B. Resnick (Ed.), *The nature of intelligence*. Hillsdale, NJ: Erlbaum, 1976.

Olson, D. R., & Hildyard, A. *Literacy and its specialization of language: Some aspects of the comprehension and thought processes of literate and non-literate children and adults*. Toronto: Ontario Institute for the Study of Education, 1977.

Pace, A. J. The influence of world knowledge and metacomprehension ability on children's comprehension of short narrative passages. Unpublished doctoral dissertation, University of Delaware, 1978.

Pace, A. J. The effect of inconsistent script information on children's comprehension of stories about familiar situations. Paper presented at the annual meeting of the American Educational Research Association, San Francisco, 1979.

Pace, A. J. Further explorations of young children's sensitivity to world knowledge-story information discrepancies. Paper presented at the Sixth Biennial Southeastern Conference on Human Development, Alexandria, VA, 1980.

Rey, H. A. *Curious George*. Boston: Houghton Mifflin, 1941.

Rumelhart, D. E., & Ortony, A. The representation of knowledge in memory. In R. C. Anderson, R. J. Spiro, & W. E. Montague (Eds.), *Schooling and the acquisition of knowledge*. Hillsdale, NJ: Erlbaum, 1977.

Schank, R. C., & Abelson, R. P. Scripts, plans, and knowledge. *Advance papers of the Fourth International Joint Conference on Artificial Intelligence*. Tbilisi, Georgia, USSR: 1975.

Schank, R. C., & Abelson, R. P. *Scripts, plans, goals, and understanding*. Hillsdale, NJ: Erlbaum, 1977.

Sigel, I. E., & Saunders, R. An inquiry into inquiry: Question-asking as an instructional model. In L. Katz (Ed.), *Current topics in early childhood education* (Vol. 2). Norwood, NJ: Ablex, 1979.

Stein, N. L., & Glenn, C. G. *An analysis of story comprehension in elementary school children: A test of a schema*. Washington University (ERIC Document Reproduction Service N. ED 121-747), 1975.

Stein, N. L., & Glenn, C. G. An analysis of story comprehension in elementary school children. In R. Freedle (Ed.), *New directions in discourse processing*. Norwood, NJ: Ablex, 1979.

Stein, N. L., & Trabasso, T. What's in a story? In R. Glaser (Ed.), *Advances in the psychology of instruction* (Vol. 2). Hillsdale, NJ: Erlbaum, in press.

CHAPTER 15

Children's Awareness of Communication*

Peter Lloyd, Elaine Baker, and Judy Dunn

This chapter will focus on the significance of knowing about the communication process for the act of communication itself. Such behavior has been termed *meta-communication* by Flavell (1981), and it concerns the child's growing understanding of the nature of the communication process and of how this understanding affects the business of exchanging information and ideas. The area is, as yet, broad, and somewhat ill-defined. Among the topics investigated have been metalinguistic abilities connected with language acquisition (Clark, 1978; Karmiloff-Smith 1981), comprehension monitoring (reviewed in Markman, 1981), and awareness of speaker and listener skills as employed in referential communication tasks (Flavell, Speer, Green, & August, 1981; Patterson & Kister, 1981; Robinson, 1981), while Hakes (1980) has attempted to uncover a link between metalinguistic abilities and the onset of the concrete operational stage of cognitive development. (For a longer list of behaviors involving metacognition see Flavell, 1981.)

Yet, despite the recent growth in this area, metacommunication remains an elusive concept. The theoretical analyses which have appeared thus far (Flavell, 1981; Shatz, 1978) have been insufficiently powerful or simply not available long enough to have an impact on the empirical work being carried out. While these models await empirical validation, we are left with a variety of studies that are

* We gratefully acknowledge the help of Rebekah Boddy, who carried out the pilot study of the "people-building" game and Tom Wood, who has kindly allowed us to quote from his unpublished Ph.D. thesis. We are also appreciative of the editorial assistance provided by Neil Bohannon and Catherine Garvey. If ambiguities remain, they are our responsibility alone.

difficult to evaluate, largely because of any common underlying theory. In such a climate we are reluctant to define metacommunication more precisely than we have in the opening sentences of this paper. We deliberately blur, for instance, the distinction between metacommunication and metacognition, since cognition as a whole (memory, attention, thinking, etc.) is inextricably involved in any communication exercise. Such a course is permissable, particularly when considering the role of social agents in communication awareness and the impact of instructions on the grasp of cognitive skills, both of which topics are discussed in this chapter. We do not totally duck the problem of definition, however, and our concluding section in reviewing the contribution that our approach makes also poses some of the questions that a theory of metacognition must address. Some readers may therefore wish, at this point, to turn to this section before proceeding further.

Finally, by way of introduction, we must stress that the data we are reporting are preliminary results from work in progress. In terms of sample size, some of the experiments are little more than pilot studies and, accordingly, we have refrained from giving quantitative treatment to avoid the spurious respectability with which figures can sometimes endow research. At the same time, the analysis has been detailed and careful and has allowed us to make an assessment of the worth of the techniques developed.

The chapter begins with a brief discussion of the early stages of metalinguistic abilities by drawing on recent English observational studies by Dunn in Cambridge and Wood in Manchester. We then present preliminary results from work in progress on communication skills in 6- to 8-year-olds. In this research a method developed by Lubin (1979) has been adapted to assess the effect of watching video-recording of oneself engaged in communication tasks, in order to reveal what Flavell (1979) calls metacognitive knowledge and experiences. The article concludes with a short section on the conceptual issues that abound in this area by raising questions that need to be addressed in future research.

At first sight it seems surprising that there should be metalinguistic abilities present in the early stages of language acquisition (Clark, 1978; Slobin, 1978), since metacognition has tended to be seen as a high-level activity involved in organizing and monitoring complex cognitive effort (Shatz, 1978). There is, for example, abundant evidence (Flavell et al., 1981; Markman, 1977, 1979; Robinson & Robinson, 1976) to show that children as old as 7 years are having difficulty judging the adequacy of fairly simple messages or instructions, as well as constructing unambiguous messages in their own right (see below for some examples). One solution to this problem (Hakes, 1980) is to point to the spontaneity that seems to characterize early metalinguistic abilities in contrast with the deliberate nature of the activity in older children when they are eventually able to focus on the process itself, *on request*. This ability is only possible once the child is able "to engage in controlled cognitive processing operations" (Hakes, 1980). Such a distinction seems reasonable when one starts to look at actual examples of 2-year-olds' communication skills. Wood (1981) has made observations of mother–child pairs in the home and finds examples of spontaneously exercised metalinguistic skills.

In the following episode taken from Wood (1981), CJ, aged 2:4, refuses to observe the polite practice of excusing oneself in the event of belching.

Child (2:4)	Mother
(Belches)	What d'y' say?
No	What d'y' say
No	tut
	Where's y' manners gone?
	What should y' say?
I'm not sayin "scuse me"	
	(Laughs)
	alright

Wood argues for a number of high-level cognitive prerequisites for the management of CJ's contribution to the episode, including the ability to recognize and reflect upon social/conversational acts; the ability to produce such acts in terms of selecting alternative options; and the ability to express the conceptual products of his reflections in ways which elaborate the intersubjective understandings of the interactants.

Wood's analysis requires corroboration, whatever the arguments about the nature of the inferred cognitive prerequisites, but the phenomenon is convincing enough. The child has criteria for what it is to "say" the polite form appropriately, since, paradoxically, he actually says the words he is declaring he will deliberately withhold.

> When he does produce the actual words it seems clear that he is separating the production of the words and the actual 'doing' of the approved procedure, in that for his words to count as the proper procedure he has to say them in a way which he has no intention of doing. There seems to be no doubt for the child that he has not fulfilled the correct procedure, despite the fact that he has said the words. (Wood, 1981, p. 310).

Furthermore, the child is able to engage in such feats, according to Wood, because of the unique quality of the caregiver–child communication situation; one in which caregiver and child negotiate meaning calling on a host of shared presuppositions. The implication is that for the very young child it is only in such a highly supportive context that metacommunication can take place. It may well be that this remains the single most important reason why communication failure or breakdown is so rare in the home and yet so common even for older children in the laboratory or classroom.

That children under 3 years of age *do* in fact repair their own messages in the face of their mothers' incomprehension, point out ambiguities and illogicalities in their mothers' speech, and comment on what was *said,* in relation to their own actions, is evident in the transcripts of the conversations between mothers and children in the longitudinal study of siblings carried out by Dunn and Kendrick (1982). An example of this follows:

Child: Wasp was in my bedroom. Wasp.

Mother: It was a queen bee.

Child: Queen bee. Come in the door it did. I think it did. I think it go now.

Mother: That's not a queen bee.

Child: Queen bee it is. You *said* queen bee.

Mother: That's not a queen bee. It's a fly. There *was* a bee asleep on the curtain.

The sort of fine-grained analysis of videotaped interactions carried out by Wood shows that while communication failure of the sort common in referential communication tasks is so rare, communication *difficulties* do exist. It is the resources that the child *and* the mother jointly bring to the enterprise that permit resolution. Such a resolution is frequently impossible in laboratory-based studies of communication skills and may often not be possible in the classroom, where the child is having to cope with a decontextualized task situation. It is possible that opportunities for exercising a variety of ''meta'' skills in the supportive situation are precisely what allows the child slowly to dismantle the scaffolding represented by the home environment, leading to the type of reflective and disembedded thinking (Donaldson, 1978) that is needed in complex cognitive efforts.

While Wood, like others (Newson, 1977; Travarthen & Hubley, 1978), has drawn attention to the importance of intersubjectivity in this operation, his analytical focus has tended to be on the child in terms of the cognitive skills that appear to be involved. Others (Robinson, 1980; Beveridge & Dunn, 1980; Wertsch & Schneider, undated) have begun to examine the role of parents and, in Dunn's case, siblings as well. Dunn's observations of children in the home indicate that mothers vary in the extent to which they make explicit the ambiguities in what their children say and in the attention they give to metacommunication. In the study of 20 working-class and lower middle-class 2-1/2-year-olds, Beveridge and Dunn (1980) report that the mothers who encouraged their children to reflect on language differed in a number of important respects in their language and conversational style from the mothers who rarely drew their children's attention to communication problems in this way. They more frequently used language for ''complex cognitive purposes'' (Tough, 1976) to direct the child's attention to his own cognitive processes such as memory, language, and logical inference. Such mothers were also more likely to engage in imaginative play, to discuss and explore motives, intentions, wants, or feelings of the child or of other people, and they were more likely to give a rationalization or justification in their attempts to control the child. In many respects, then, these mothers could be described as particularly child-centered or egalitarian in their attitudes to their children (see Dunn & Kendrick, 1982).

It is not possible to say, at this point, that children reared in this type of linguistic environment develop advanced or superior metacognitive skills. There is some evidence, however, from another Cambridge study (Light, 1979) that children who, at 14 months, had mothers whose speech was classified as being high on ''acceptance'' (Nelson, 1973) scored highly in referential communication tasks when tested at 5 1/2 years. Robinson (1980) has also reported that mothers who deal explicitly with communication failure in the home—"I don't know what you mean"—had children who at 6 years, correctly identified ambiguous messages in experimental contexts.

The work to be described now is part of an ongoing research program investigating metacognitive and communicative skills. The techniques used have included monitoring eye movements while children respond to messages varying in adequacy and using a talking doll as a communication partner. The idea of the latter technique is to engage the child in a tutoring role which encourages the sort of metacognitive activity that is involved in judging another's communication in order to improve their performance. (Results from these methods can be found in Lloyd and Beveridge, 1981.)

The method to be reported in this paper arose from adapting the technique described by Lubin (1979), who asked children to watch videotapes of themselves in a play group in order to study the dynamics of the social relations involved. This technique was applied to a procedure used by Markman (1977, 1979) and Flavell et al. (1981) for the investigation of comprehension monitoring. They asked children to carry out a task, such as building with bricks (Flavell et al., 1981) or performing a magic trick (Markman, 1977) according to instructions provided. The instructions, however, were inadequate in certain ways, being ambiguous, complex, or incomplete. It is how children deal with this inadequacy—as revealed by their performance in the tasks and their reaction to questions about their performance and the instructions—that makes up the data from which inferences about metacognition are drawn. The advantage of this method is that it brings into the open the metacognitive processes that the child must utilize in order to proceed to some resolution of the problem. A limitation of these studies is that they focus exclusively on the comprehension or listening skills as aspects of metacognition. The technique we describe enables, in addition, equal attention to be paid to the speaking or instructing roles.

THE VIDEOMONITORING TECHNIQUE

A two-stage procedure is used in which children first perform a task wich is videotaped, and then watch an edited version of that videotape. An integral part of Stage II is a semistructured interview used to probe their understanding of the experience. To some degree this is an extension of Markman's (1977, 1979) procedure with the additional advantages of a tangible and constantly replayable record. The subjects relive the cognitive task by observing themselves in action and seeing the effects of their behavior on others. They have the opportunity to evaluate their own performance as an instructor or tutor with a peer or as a speaker or listener in a referential communication game. They can also be asked to assess the performance of the other child in the dyad or of performances in interactions in which they had not taken part. By careful editing of the videotape of the original interaction, it is possible to obtain the child's reaction to critical moments during the task. From data of this sort one can infer the extent of the children's understanding of their own cognitive capacities.

The use of a videomonitoring or feedback technique is not new in behavioral research, since it had had a role for some time in the investigation and training of social skills. Forbes and Lubin (1979) have extended the procedure for use with children in studying social relations in play groups. The significance of our procedure is that it is brought specifically to bear on cognitive skills, and by relieving the child of the demands of the task itself (it has already been done; it has only to be watched), the metacognitive process can flourish. In the terms used by Flavell et al. (1981), the subject can be relatively much freer to treat messages, instructions, and task strategies as "cognitive objects for scrutiny and evaluation."

In the studies conducted so far we have used videomonitoring in situations (a) where two children are communicating in a referential communication game; (b) where a pair of children are left entirely alone and one, a previously-taught child, teaches a competitive board game to a naive peer; and (c) where a child attempts to teach simple number skills to one slightly younger. In the peer-tutoring task, particularly, we are watching how children deal with another's ignorance. In so doing, of · course, the tutors frequently reveal their own shortcomings. It is a paradigm that has been successfully employed in educational contexts (Sternberg & Cazden, 1979) and in Piagetian tasks such as conversation (Miller & Brownwell, 1975) and seriation (Lloyd, 1982).

The procedure followed with this method will now be described (taking the referential communication task as our example), and then a sample of the sort of preliminary results obtained will be given.

Stage I

A pilot study has been carried out with six children (3 boys, 3 girls, mean age, 7.1 years) from a primary school in a working class area of Manchester. The children operated in six different pairings. Each pair was instructed in a "people building" game in which one child constructed a person by choosing from sets of heads, middles, and legs. The components varied on a variety of attributes, such as hair style, and head gear, in the case of the heads. Speakers were told to select and describe one component at a time to listeners who were free to ask questions at any time, in order to build the same person as the speaker. The "people" were assembled on velcro-strips attached to a board placed between the participants. The board prevented any visual contact during the game. Each child acted the part of speaker and listener for three trials in each of the six pairings. The study was conducted in a room of the Child Study Unit in the Psychology Department at Manchester University. Sessions were videotaped using two remotely controlled cameras (which allowed split-screen representation of speaker and listener, when required) and lasted about 20 minutes.

Videotape Editing

The videotapes were viewed and transcripts made. Fourteen trials were selected for showing to the children, that is, 2 trials for each pairing plus 2 others. The selection was made according to the following criteria: message informativeness, message modification, listener feedback, and trial outcome. Other factors included clarity and general interest of the session. The extracts were edited onto tapes for use with a portable videotape recorder.

Stage II

The second phase of the study took place one week later in a quiet room in the children's school. Before the children were shown the edited version of the sessions in which they had taken part, they were asked some general questions to establish that they remembered significant features of the game. The videotape was then played and the child was questioned about the performance at the conclusion of each trial. The procedure was flexible and the questioning nondirective. Sometimes the tape was stopped during a trial to get the child's reaction to a particularly pertinent piece of behavior. In practice the children often commented spontaneously and this sometimes led to a portion of a tape being rerun. The second stage lasted about 40 minutes and was audiotape-recorded.

SOME RESULTS

There are two findings we wish to report, one concerning awareness of failure and the other relating to the role of the listener. Questions asked about the communicators' abilities revealed a paradox. Even when a comparison between encoder's and decoder's choices at the end of a trial revealed a mismatch, all of the children typically failed to observe the limitations in the speaker's performance, responding "Yes" to the question "Did X (the speaker) do a good job?" This replicates the finding of Flavell et al. and Markman and is consistent with the tendency for younger children to blame the listener for any mismatch in speaker's and listener's choices, first reported by Robinson and Robinson (1976).

Every one of the children in this study regarded the listener's role in a speaker–listener dyad as more important than the speaker's role. The nature of the listener's role as seen by the children is revealing:

> "Just to listen, read carefully."
> "If I don't ask questions I won't know it."
> "The one for remembering."

It seems from comments like these, and their apportioning of blame for failure, that the listener is regarded as the one who has to do the hard work. There are surely implications here for the performance of children as speakers if they are coming to the task with certain expectations concerning the listener's role. It may be, for instance, that they regard it as sufficient to begin a description and leave listeners to complete it by asking appropriate questions. This kind of response from the listener is very much what most children receive (and presumably come to expect) from their mothers, who frequently play a distinctively supportive role in conversations with their children. It is possible too that the tendency to blame the listener reflects what children expect from their experience with teachers: They expect to be given appropriate rather than inadequate information.

At the same time, however, there were numerous instances of the same children recognizing errors in their own and their partner's performance. Spontaneous comments, such as "Because I didn't tell her enough about it" and "Oh, I did it wrong 'cos I wasn't listening," pointed up the children's recognition of their limitations as speaker or listener. Similarly, statements such as "But she should have asked about it" and "She forgot to say something," related to the performance of others in their communicative roles.

Such paradoxical within-subjects findings of poor performance in the initial task, yet recognition of and accounting for the error in the subsequent videomonitoring session, may be understood with reference to Flavell et al.'s notion that children have difficulty in validating their own inferences. By this they mean that there is an initial feeling of uncertainty about the status of a message, revealed by a hesitation, for example, but it is not sustained and erroneous task completion follows. Furthermore, it may also be that during videomonitoring the opportunity to examine one's own performance in a cognitive task reveals to the child what is actually required. There is possibly a comparison here with the claim made by Vygotsky (1978) that what children can do with help might be more representative of their abilities. (And it should be noted that in the home situation many mothers provide exactly this kind of help—at least in the domain of metacommunication—by drawing their child's attention to ambiguities in the message or to their own problems in following the child's thought.) Assuming that the videomonitoring exercise is something other than training in the task, the implication is that the children should replicate the task after the debriefing session. Their performance might be compared with a control group who repeat without the videomonitoring experience. In any event, there are signs from the pilot study data that the tendency to base psychological theory on the single experiment is unwise. Furthermore, it may take a period of familiarity with the task procedure before the child (or adult, indeed) is able to appreciate what is required and then provide a representative sample of behavior. If psychological experiments are to be regarded as examinations then the standard one study approach is appropriate but that is not what we usually intend. We are typically attempting to measure the child's level of cognitive development, language comprehension, or whatever, based on the premise that our subjects realize what is required of them. At the risk of laboring the point, we are saying that our findings indicate that the child may need to try out the task first to determine what is required. Accordingly, a second administration should be given to assess this possibility. Note we are not talking simply about a practice effect but rather about a procedure that will ensure reliable and representative samples of performance from children. It may well be that improvements categorized as practice effects are sometimes brought about by a reconceptualization of the task requirements. This would be another reason for being skeptical about the single study approach.

A STUDY OF TASK NEGOTIATION

The importance of the construction placed upon the task by participants was the object of a referential communication study carried out by the second author which sought to allow the opportunity for pairs of children to disambiguate, or negotiate between themselves, the nature and requirements of the communication task. Underlying the hypothesis that this opportunity would result in superior performance on a posttest compared with a control group is a view of successful communication requiring negotiation and collaboration between interactants. Such a view is shared by Higgins, Fondacaro, and McCann (1981) that communication "is a simultaneous, interdependent process of social interaction in which the participants intersubjectively and collaboratively determine the purpose and social reality, or 'meaning', of the interchange" (1981, p. 294).

Twenty-four children of both sexes, aged 5.7 to 7.1, were tested in their school in two groups of same-sex pairs equally distributed for age and sex. The communication task required building a two-component teddy bear by mounting on a block separate cards picturing a top and a bottom half from a pool of 8 possible cards for each section. (The permutations resulted from orthogonally crossing 2-value variations of 3 critical features for both halves.) The cards used for any complete 2-component trial were returned to the pool to give a complete set for the subsequent trial. During testing, referent choices were predetermined by E in order to control their frequency and order. Four complete trials were obtained from each dyad during testing with each member describing one component per trial. Verbal interaction between pairs was unconstrained but a screen across the center of the table prevented visual contact.

The experimental treatment was to allow half of the dyads a 4-minute period of free practice, left entirely alone, after the standard instructions. This period was audiotaped using a concealed radio microphone transmitting to a receiver and recorder in an adjacent room. Thus, in addition to using this treatment as an independent variable, it was possible to analyse the transcripts to gain some information about how the task was initially construed and about the process of negotiating a shared meaning.

On immediate posttests, the experimental group were successful in matching teddy bears in 37 out of 48 trials. The corresponding figure for the control group was 2/48. Matchings by chance have been excluded from these results.

The encoders of the control group generally conveyed only 1 out of 3 necessary, critical attributes on any trial. Furthermore, they mentioned more than twice as many noncritical features in their descriptions as the treatment group. Decoders generally did not ask questions or otherwise overtly indicate uncertainty when a message did not refer uniquely to one item out of the array. Indeed, only one dyad asked any questions at all, and this was the pair who achieved the only 2 matching outcomes in the control group data.

It is necessary to note whether any improvement occurs over trials in order to rule out the possibility that the superior performance of the experimental group was due to a straightforward practice effect which is, to some extent, contained within the experimental treatment. It may be argued that this is a more parsimonious explanation of the dramatic difference between the groups. No improvement over trials was observed in the control group, despite close attention to checking of outcomes guided by E after every complete 2-component trial and despite repeated invitations to decoders to ask questions if uncertain to which item the encoder was referring. In contrast with the control group, every member of the experimental group achieved at least one adequate encoding of a target picture card which included reference to the three critical features. When decoding, moreover, every child elicited some new information or requested a repetition by asking a question on at least one trial, demonstrating engagement in purposeful interaction. Performance levels were maintained in a 2-week delayed posttest using different materials.

An analysis of the free-practice transcripts supports the view that the experience contributed to the experimental group's appreciation of what the task involved, for example, to achieve a match not by hoping for success through chance or guesswork but as a consequence of cooperating with one's partner. The opportunity was provided, it appears, for pairs who were later expected to cooperate to begin by negotiating a shared understanding of their task. A replication and elaboration of the study is currently being undertaken to examine more closely the process and effects of negotiation in free practice. (Baker and Lloyd, 1982).

PEER TUTORING TASK

A second area in which we have used the videomonitoring technique has required an older child to instruct a younger child in simple number skills Six tasks taken from Schaeffer, Eggleston, and Scott (1974) were first administered individually by the second author to the older children. They, in turn, were asked to instruct a younger child, with whom they were familiar, in the tasks to "try to get them to do it right." The pairs were left alone to do the task and the interactions were videotaped. Examples of the tasks are *drumtapping,* in which the child has to bang the table with a mallet a required number of times, and *recognition of small numbers,* which asks the child to look at small collections of objects and say how many there are without counting.

Edited videotapes were shown to the older children and to a child who had not taken part in Stage I. Much of the data is only meaningful in the full context which demands quoting at length from protocols. For the purpose of this chapter the foci will be on metacognitive awareness revealed during videomonitoring and self-reports as evidence of how the task was construed. Some of the examples which are less dependent on context have been selected to indicate the type of metacognitve awareness revealed, such as awareness of individual differences in teaching or learning ability; the roles of interactants in a teaching situation; or specific factors which contribute to or affect the tutorial interaction. The examples will be taken from the records of Robert and Deirdre (7 years), both concerning the same extracts of Robert's interactions with his tutee. Robert had generally proved an inadequate instructor: he provided insufficient information initially and then failed to react to tutee failure by modifying his teaching procedure. Deirdre did not take part in Stage I and the tasks and the children were unfamiliar to her.

In viewing the tape, Robert recognized a general difference between himself and the younger child.

E: Do you think it's hard to do?

R: It's easy for *me*

This indicates a clear appreciation of the differential abilities of himself and the other child; what Flavell (1979) places squarely in the category of metacognitive knowledge. Deirdre was able to be more specific about the nature of the perceived difference in task difficulty for the older and the younger child:

Because he was younger than the white boy and he came from another country and he didn't really know.

Although the attribution of difficulties due to culture for a West Indian boy indigenous to England was (probably) mistaken, what is significant is that she is making inferences about the capacities of a child she recognized to be younger. She concludes that he is less knowledgeable.

Evidence from a study of siblings shows, moreover, that children have a firm grasp of some of the differences between their own capacities—cognitive and linguistic—and those of a baby (Dunn & Kendrick, 1982). The first-born children, observed at home, commented frequently on the differences between themselves and their younger siblings, discussing both the limitations of the babies' capabilities, and the changing nature of these capacities. For example:

Laura W. (to baby sibling aged 14 months):
You don't remember Judy. I do.

Sue H. (to another child who has told baby sibling to find his bike):
He can't find his. And he doesn't know where it is.

Robert's conception of the tutor's role is one of a tester rather than a teacher. In the drum-tapping task he describes his function as follows:

R: Miss, I should tell him, just say . . . I think what four is. Then if he gets it right, say "correct."

E: And if he gets it wrong, what then?

R: Just say "wrong, try again."

This interpretation is supported by his comments about another child he watched in the teaching role:

> She never said "correct," she said "er er."

Deirdre, who is the same age as Robert, attributes egocentric limitations to the tutor when asked to say why he did not give more assistance to the tutee.

> Because . . . he (tutor) thought he (tutee) was old enough to know how to do it.
> He thought, er . . . as if he was like *him*.

Further probing and viewing, however, reveal that Robert was not unaware of his failings. He is asked:

E: Was it his fault that he got them wrong or was it your fault?
R: Err . . . my fault.
E: Your fault, why?
R: Cos er . . . I never said anything else to him. You know, to help him.

But the status of "help" for Robert remains uncertain. It may represent the simple "knowledge of results" procedure which he employed in the tasks.

It is Deirdre who is able to suggest strategies by which the tutor might better instruct the pupil. In the following extract she is referring to the performance of a female tutor in the drum-tapping task.

> if she really wanted to help she could go "No, you copy me." One (bangs once) and give the hammer to her and she'd do one-one, and then two-two, three-three, four-four (she mimes two people banging alternately by switching hands).

This is an impressive example of metacognition for it shows that Deirdre is able to monitor the performance, diagnose the problem, and offer a successful alternative strategy that takes account of the tutee's need for a step-by-step approach.

CONCLUSIONS

Despite the appearance of a number of theoretical and research papers in the area of metacognition in the past few years some fundamental conceptual issues await resolution. Nor is it evident that there is a clear way forward empirically, though there is agreement among a number of workers that communication skills represent a profitable line of inquiry (Flavell et al, in press; Greenfield & Dent, 1980; Lefebre-Pinard, 1981; Patterson & Kister, 1981; Shatz, 1978).

In the space remaining we can do little more than raise these questions, recognizing that the search for answers will engage the attention of workers for some years to come.

What is the nature of metacognition? If it is defined as awareness of one's cognitive processes then a conscious process is implied and about this there is fairly general agreement (see Lefebre-Pinard, 1981, for a review). On the other hand, Flavell, who might be considered the father of metacognition, clearly states that the phenomenon need not be at a conscious level. This difficulty may be resolved if we differentiate the monitoring of cognitive activities from reflections about them. Monitoring can obviously be a conscious process, as, for example, in assessing the suitability of a message as you construct it. But there may also be below-threshold monitoring in cases where you suddenly get a feeling of uncertainty about something you said, did, or heard, leading you to recheck the event. Distinguishing conscious from unconscious monitoring is difficult, but measures of attentional strategies in relation to language, such as eye movement recordings (Lloyd & Beveridge, 1981), is one way into this problem and videomonitoring, we suggest, is another.

What is the relationship between metacognition and reflective thinking? Reflective thinking is a major aspect of metacognition but it is not the whole of it. It seems to imply the luxury of time to turn over the products of cognition in one's mind and much metacommunication of the monitoring kind is not of this nature. In developmental terms, reflective thinking is a relatively late accomplishment depending on the acquisiton of what Donaldson (1978) calls disembedded thinking. Piaget goes so far as to call it a new form of cognition, implying complete reconstruction and progressive reconceptualization of the cognitive activity to which it is applied (Piaget, 1977).

What are the antecedents of metacognition? Two questions are involved here: What is the course of metacognitive development, and what are the significant influences on its growth? We have provided only one or two fragments of the overall picture as far as development is concerned, and there is some debate as to whether early examples of metalinguistic abilities are the genuine article or merely precursors (see Hakes, 1980). As for influences, we have pointed to the value of observational studies in demonstrating the role of parents and also of siblings. Teachers are another agent who have been little researched in this respect. A comparison of helping strategies (parent, teacher, peer, etc.) in a theoretical framework that sees control passing from the other to the self is clearly relevant (see Wertsch & Schneider, undated).

How is metacognition to be studied? A major concern of this chapter has been to address this question but, as we indicated at the beginning of this section, there is no unique paradigm offering itself. We can best approach an answer by summarizing the conclusions we have drawn from the use of our method of investigation, which arose very directly out of the 1979 SRCD Institute.

Preliminary results indicate that videomonitoring is a promising technique for uncovering the extent to which children are aware of their own and other's cognitive abilities. This may happen in two ways. For the researcher it may uncover information about the child's metacognitive abilities not hitherto revealed. For the child it may direct attention to limitations in performance that had formerly gone unrecognized by, for instance, assisting cognitive monitoring. The area of communication and instruction skills would seem to offer an appropriate area of investigation since understanding others and making oneself understood are essential prerequisites for cognitive growth. A controlled study is currently underway in which one child teaches a board game to a naive peer. The videomonitoring procedure has also been used in a Piagetian class inclusion task with a 2-year time lag, having children of about 8 years of age engage in a videomonitoring exercise using an edited videotaped recording of their performance when tested 2 years earlier.

Our efforts are currently directed to refining the technique particularly in terms of the criteria for selecting extracts for feedback, assuming it is not desirable to show the whole session. Selection will, of course, be partly determined by the hypotheses under investigation but it should also be possible to establish some general principles. Data interpretation also presents problems. While the responses to some questions can be scored, the most informative analysis is (at least currently) qualitative. A comparison between Stage I performance and Stage II observations is obviously valuable. Controlled studies will be carried out to test for the impact of the videomonitoring experience. Does it, for instance, give rise to a change in performance that is significantly different from a test-retest procedure?

Finally, it is worth making brief mention of an important potential application of the technique. If awareness of errors and inconsistencies as well as of successful procedures is heightened by watching a playback together with a structured interview, then it could have a valuable role to play in the classroom. Individual sessions for each child must be considered impractical, except perhaps for special diagnostic purposes. Preliminary results suggest, however, that it may not be necessary to tailor the procedure so precisely. A child who was able to watch someone else nevertheless revealed a number of illuminating observations on the skills of others. Studies which focus on tasks which closely model classroom experiences could have a useful contribution to make.

REFERENCES

Baker, E. and Lloyd, P. Referential communication tasks and the negotiation of meaning. Paper given at the British Psychological Society Annual Conference, University of York, April 1982.

Beveridge, M. & Dunn, J. Communication and the development of reflective thinking. Paper presented at British Psychological Society Developmental Section Annual Conference, Edinburgh, 1980.

Clark, E. V. Awareness of language: Some evidence from what children say and do. In A. Sinclair, R. J. Jarvella, & W. J. M. Levelt (Eds.), *The child's conception of language*. Berlin: Springer-Verlag, 1978.

Donaldson, M. *Children's minds*. Glasgow: Fontana, 1978.

Dunn, J., & Kendrick, C. *Siblings: Love, envy and understanding*. Cambridge, MA: Harvard University Press, 1982.

Flavell, J. H. Metacognition and cognitive monitoring: A new area of cognitive-developmental inquiry. *American Psychologist*, 1979, *34*(10).

Flavell, J. H. Cognitive monitoring. In W. P. Dickson (Ed.), *Children's oral communication skills*. New York: Academic Press, 1981.

Flavell, J. H., Speer, J. R., Green, F. L., & August, D. L. The development of comprehension monitoring and knowledge about communication. *Monographs of the Society for Research in Child Development*, 1981, *46*, (5, Serial No. 192).

Forbes, D. & Lubin, D. Reasoning and behavior in children's friendly interactions. Paper presented at the meeting of the American Psychological Association, New York, September 1979.

Greenfield, P. M., & Dent, C. A developmental study of the communication of meaning: The role of uncertainty and information. In K. E. Nelson (Ed.), *Children's language* (Vol. 2). New York: Gardner Press, 1980.

Hakes, D. T. *The development of metalinguistic abilities in children*. Berlin: Springer-Verlag, 1980.

Higgins, E. T., Fondacaro, R., & McCann, C. D. Rules and roles: The communication game and speaker-listener processes. In W. P. Dickson (Ed.), *Children's oral communication skills*. New York: Academic Press, 1981.

Karmiloff-Smith, A. The grammatical marking of thematic structure in the development of language production. In W. Deutsch (Ed.), *The child's construction of language*. London: Academic Press, 1981.

Lefebre-Pinard, M. Understanding and auto-control of cognitive functions: Implications for the relationship between cognition and behavior. Paper presented at Sixth Biennial Meeting of the International Society for the Study of Behavioural Development, Toronto, August 1981.

Light, P. *The development of social sensitivity*. London: Cambridge University Press, 1979.

Lloyd, P. Talking to some purpose. In M. Beveridge (Ed.), *Thinking through language*. London: Edward Arnold, 1981.

Lloyd, P., & Beveridge, M. *Information and meaning in child communication*. New York: Academic Press, 1981.

Lubin, D. Presentation to the Society for Research in Child Development Institute on the Origins and Growth of Communication, University of Delaware, July 1979.

Markman, E. M. Realizing that you don't understand: A preliminary investigation. *Child Development*, 1977, *48*, 986–992.

Markman, E. M. Realizing that you don't understand: Elementary school children's awareness of inconsistencies. *Child Development*, 1979, *50*, 643–655.

Markman, E. M. Comprehension monitoring. In W. P. Dickson (Ed.), *Children's oral communication skills*. New York: Academic Press, 1981.

Miller, S. A., & Brownell, C. A. Peers, persuasion and Piaget: Dyadic interaction between conservers and non-conservers. *Child Development*, 1975, *46*, 992–997.

Nelson, K. Structure and strategy in learning to talk. *Monograph of the Society of Research in Child Development*, 1973, *38*(Serial No. 149).

Newson, J. An intersubjective approach to the systematic description of mother–infant interaction. In H. R. Schaffer (Ed.), *Studies in mother–infant interaction*. London: Academic Press, 1977.

Patterson, C. J., & Kister, M. C. The development of listener skills for referential communication. In W. P. Dickson (Ed.), *Children's oral communication skills*. New York: Academic Press, 1981.

Piaget, J. *The grasp of consciousness: Action and concept in the young child*. London: Routledge & Kegan Paul, 1977.

Robinson, E. J. Mother–child interaction and the child's understanding about communication. *International Journal of Psycholinguistics*, 1980, *7-1/2*(17/18), 85–101.

Robinson, E. The child's understanding of inadequate messages and communication failure: A problem of ignorance or egocentrism? In W. P. Dickson (Ed.), *Children's oral communication skills*. New York: Academic Press, 1981.

Robinson, E. J., & Robinson, W. P. The young child's understanding of communication. *Developmental Psychology*, 1976, *12*, 328–333.

Schaeffer, B., Eggleston, B., & Scott, J. Number development in young children. *Cognitive Psychology*, 1974, *6*, 357–379.

Shatz, M. The relationship between cognitive processes and the development of communication skills. In B. Keasey (Ed.), *Nebraska Symposium on Motivation,* 1977. Lincoln, NE: University of Nebraska Press, 1978.

Slobin, D. I. A case study of early language awareness. In A. Sinclair, R. J. Jarvella, & W. J. M. Levelt (Eds.), *The child's conception of language.* Berlin: Springer-Verlag, 1978.

Sternberg, C. & Cazden, C. Children as teachers—of peers and ourselves. *Theory into Practice,* 1979.

Tough, J. *The development of meaning.* London: Allen & Unwin, 1976.

Trevarthen, C., & Hubley, P. Secondary intersubjectivity: Confidence, confiding, and acts of meaning in the first year. In A. Lock (Ed.), *Action, gesture and symbol: The emergence of language.* London: Academic Press, 1978.

Vygotsky, L. S. *Mind in society: The development of higher psychological functions.* Cambridge, MA: Harvard University Press, 1978.

Wertsch, J. V. & Schneider, P. J. Variation of adults' directives to children in a problem solving situation. Northwestern University, no. date. (Mimeograph)

Wood, T. The maintenance and repair of communication between young children and their mothers. Unpublished doctoral dissertation, University of Manchester, England, 1981.

CHAPTER 16

The Ontogeny of Description

Mary Ann Evans and Thomas H. Carr

Three lines of developmental research focus on spoken descriptions as a major topic. The most widely recognized of these is the study of referential communication, which has been carried out largely in the context of Piaget's concept of egocentrism (Asher, 1978; Dickson, 1980; Evans, 1981; Evans & Rubin, 1979; Evans & Rubin, 1983; Glucksberg, Krauss, & Higgins, 1975). This research concentrates on the content of descriptions that are produced by speakers at various developmental levels. A complementary body of literature takes up the influence of verbal descriptions on listeners' memories for scenes or events that have been described (Bacharach, Carr, & Mehner, 1976; Carr, Bacharach, & Mehner, 1977; Olson, 1970; Pezdek, 1980; Wilgosh, 1975). The third line of research is perhaps less obviously relevant. Because infants and toddlers use language mainly to communicate about concrete, temporally proximal situations, many studies of language acquisition and its antecedents can be viewed as studies of verbal description. These studies speak to the content of the earliest descriptions and their emergence from gestural communication systems (Bates, 1976; Carter, 1978a, 1978b, 1979; Greenfield & Zukow, 1978).

In this chapter we draw together some findings from these three lines of research and attempt to integrate them. Our goal is to trace the ontogeny of the description of physical environments and, to an extent, social events with respect to what is described, what kinds of information a description contains, how the description's content is distributed between verbal–symbolic and gestural–enactive modalities, and what effects the description has on the perceptual and cognitive activities of listeners who hear it. We believe that this approach can shed some useful light on the development of communicative abilities in general, the nature of "egocentric" and "nonegocentric" communication in particular, and the large role that description might play in the socially mediated learning of the child.

WHAT IS A DESCRIPTION?

We regard a description as a relatively complex speech act by which the speaker asserts his perspective about a state of affairs in order to create in his listener a shared attention to, and potentially shared understanding of, that state of affairs. As the topics described may be present or absent, real or imaginary, past, present or future, it includes a variety of forms of communication, such as simple assertions, narratives, reports, explanations, predictions, and commentaries. Although these forms are diverse, they all equally qualify as descriptions when they occur in a context in which the speaker asserts a proposition about what he believes to be the case and calls the listener's (or reader's) attention to particular aspects of a state of affairs which have been selected for comment from a range of possible aspects. Three examples follow. The simple statement, "That's a beautiful bird!" uttered as a change of topic while walking in the woods and accompanied by a gesture of pointing, expresses the speaker's appreciation of the bird but also calls the listener's attention to particular aspects of the situation (i.e., the bird and the bird's beauty) that the speaker sees as noteworthy. A set of instructions in which the speaker describes how to do something, make something, or put something together asserts how the speaker believes one should go about the activity, but also successively calls attention to each of the components selected for comment, with the potential result that the listener will go about the activity in a similar fashion. The opening passages of Dickens's *A Tale of Two Cities* convey factual and evaluative information about the state of French and British society which the author believes to be the case, but also call attention to these aspects and inherently request the reader to adopt the same perceptions of the period as those presented by the author. Hence, when "describing," one asserts a proposition about a state of affairs which one believes (or pretends) to be the case, and does so with the belief that the listener can come to share the same perspective as opposed to other perspectives as a result of that speech act.

On this basis, we attribute four potential psychological functions to description. First, a description calls attention to some particular aspect of a situation via the selectivity of its propositional content. Second, the propositional content asserted by a description reveals what the speaker believes to be the case and as such acts as a window (albeit sometimes faulty) to his understanding and evaluation of a situation. Third, a description influences the listener's perceptions, beliefs, or understanding of a situation. As an example, substituting "horrible" for "beautiful" in the bird description would likely induce profound changes in the listener's cognitive and emotional expectations about what would be encountered upon looking in the specified direction. Fourth, a description contributes to memories that are taken away from the situation, probably by both the listener who hears it and the speaker who produces it. Examples of this phenomenon are easy to find, ranging from Carmichael, Hogan, and Walter's (1932) work on ambiguous drawings to Loftus's (1979) work on eyewitness testimony. Each of these four functions, in which descriptions can become involved is psychologically complicated, plays an important role in determining the characteristics of cognition and the choice of action under given stimulus conditions and changes markedly in the course of development. For these reasons, studying the development of description opens a window onto the relations among several of the most fundamental social/cognitive processes.

GESTURE AS DESCRIPTION AND THE EARLY DEVELOPMENT OF DESCRIPTIVE ACTS

While the appearance of an infant's first words has long been regarded as a milestone by laymen and developmentalists alike, its status has more recently been undermined in the research community by the attention given to mother–child interactions and infants' behaviors *before* their first words. The title of Trevarthan's *New Scientist* (1974) paper, "Conversations with a Two-Month-Old," aptly condenses the position evolving in the last decade of research that young infants are both acutely responsive to the special manner in which their mothers speak to and play with them and active contributors to the content and form or direction of these interactions (Bateson, 1975; Stern, Jaffe, Beebe, & Bennett, 1975). Mothers carefully attend to prelinguistic vocalizations, facial expressions, and hand movements, replying with conversational comments, such as "You don't say," "Boy, that's a big story," and "What else happened?" (Snow, 1977; Sylvester-Bradley & Trevarthan, 1978), as though their infants were talking to them about the world and its events. Ultimately it is here, in the socialization of the neonate's speechlike acts, that a tracing of the ontogeny of description begins.

Descriptive acts per se on the part of the child begin to emerge in the second half of the first year. Both deictic gazing and pointing call attention to some area of an environment or an object within it, and at least potentially contribute to the participants' interpretations and memories of the situations they have shared. That infants one year of age or younger are able to follow the direction of their mother's gaze is suggested by the experimental findings of Lempers, Flavell, and Flavell (1977) and Scaife and Bruner (1975). More often in naturalistic situations, however, such deictic gazes are accompanied by explicit pointing gestures, which are followed by infants as young as nine months, depending on the location of the specific object in relation to the child and mother (Murphy & Messer, 1977).

It is unclear at what age the child moves from responding to these points and gazes merely as signs to responding to them as parts of a shared social signal system. However, the transition would appear to be accomplished by about one year, or alternatively, by about the time the child can be shown to have entered

Piaget's Stage 5 of sensorimotor development (Bates, 1976; Bates, Camaioni & Volterra, 1975; Leung & Rheingold, 1977; Snyder, 1978). By this time children use reaching, pointing, showing, and deictic gazing in spontaneous, flexible, and apparently intentional ways, monitoring the behavior of their listeners and persisting until mutual regard of a particular object is achieved. Bates refers to this gestural behavior pattern as the *protodeclarative*—a prelinguistic precursor of a statement, such as "There is a ball" (or "Look at that *beautiful* bird," perhaps). From our point of view, then, the protodeclarative, at least when accompanied by a facial expression or evaluative vocalization such as delight in the indicated object, qualifies as a beginning description.

The process by which vocalizations are added to gestures in ways that qualify as descriptions has been treated in detail by Carter (1978a, 1978b, 1979). She identified a period during the second year of life of a single middle-class male infant in which deictic morphemes, such as "this," "that," "there," and "look," as well as object names such as "dog," "duck," and "glass," gradually emerged out of generally alveolar vocalizations (/d/ and /l/ initial CV combinations) that consistently accompanied protodeclarative gestures much like those described by Bates: pointing toward an object not in the infant's possession. Carter called these gesture-vocalization combinations examples of a general Attention-to-Object schema whose goal was to draw another person's attention or regard to a specified object in the environment. Early in the first year an alveolar CV syllable co-occurred with some 70% of these pointing and showing gestures but only rarely with other kinds of gestures and physical activities. On the basis of co-occurrence, Carter attributed the pragmatic force of a deictic declarative to the vocalization as well as the gesture. Focusing on structural similarities in phonology and functional similarities in usage, Carter traced the evolution of these alveolar vocalizations into vocabulary items. As phonological differentiation progressed, the infant came more and more to use utterances deictically without the accompanying gesture, especially in situations where the infant's hands were otherwise occupied by holding toys or food.

It appears from Carter's analysis that when the utterances were referentially inadequate by themselves, communication depended primarily upon the gestures, but later in the development of the Attention-to-Object schema, as the utterances gained in referential adequacy, the burden of communication shifted away from the gesture and was born increasingly by the utterance. Bates offers a similar analysis of the transition from protodeclarative to deictic speech, arguing that the shift in reliance from a well-established gestural system toward a newly acquired verbal system constitutes an example of skill learning under conditions of limited information-processing capacity. A difficult, highly attention demanding, and therefore very fragile and easily disruptible skill—deictic vocalization—was first piggy-backed onto a functionally similar deictic skill over which the child already had cognitive control. The gestural system provided a foundation for learning and a protocol or template for performance until the verbal system was sufficiently well learned to begin to stand on its own. Such dependence of an emerging (and eventually more powerful) skill on an existing (though more rudimentary) skill has been used as a central concept in a variety of performance oriented developmental analyses and may be a very general characteristic of cognitive growth (Carr, in press; Case, 1977; Fischer, 1980; Piaget, 1952; Piaget & Inhelder, 1969; Siegler, 1981; Vygotsky, 1926/1962).

The developments discussed by Bates and Carter mark the beginning of profound change in communicative capacities. The rapid language acquisition, expanding cognitive abilities, and increasing talkativeness of children during early childhood drastically alter the form of their descriptions, continuing the direction of the development identified in the Attention-to-Object schema. Words appear to supplant pointing and showing gestures as a means of calling attention to objects and to events as well. Hence, it is perhaps not surprising that less research has been directed to the nonverbal components of children's messages after they have learned how to talk. What little developmental research there is on gestural behavior, however, has demonstrated the prevalence of hand gestures in older children's ongoing descriptions. In both a study by Jancovic, Devoe, and Wiener (1975), in which chidren age 4 to 18 talked about a movie they had seen, and a study by Evans and Rubin (1979), in which children aged 5 to 9 explained a board game that was present, the number of hand gestures increased with the age of the speaker. Evans and Rubin (1979) further noted that relative to the number of words spoken, the number of gestures used remained constant across ages 5 to 9, with one gesture occurring approximately every seven words. Far from dropping out with increasing age and verbal fluency, hand gestures become more frequent.

In spite of the frequency with which children use hand gestures, only cursory mention has been made within the extensive referential communication literature of children's pointing and tracing movements while describing abstract forms, games, or the actions of models. If anything, the use of hand gestures under the conditions of these studies in which speakers and listeners have been visually separated from one another has been interpreted as an indication of the child's egocentric manner of thinking, rather than as an integral part of the child's communicative repertoire. In contrast, the common occurrence of gestures in the conversation of adults has spawned a substantial literature on their frequency, form, and function (Birdwhistell, 1974; Ekman & Friesen, 1969; Knapp, 1972; Scheflen, 1973; Wiener, Devoe, Rubinow, & Geller, 1972).

While the terminology applied to hand gestures by the various theorists is not consistent, three basic types of gestures relevant to the act of describing may be delineated. Referencing signals or deictics denote or specify an object or aspect of an object (e.g., pointing to the location of an object, holding an object out, touching a part of an object). Pantomimics or demonstratives mimic, trace, or illustrate some attribute of an event or object (e.g., flicking the thumb to illustrate popping a cork). Semantic modifiers and relationals subtly amend the verbal content of a message or the relationship of the speaker to his message (e.g., moving the hand abruptly down when stating a point, hunching the shoulders when guessing an answer). Jancovic et al. (1975) view these types of gestures as being of increasing complexity in requiring that an increasing number of relationships be considered in interpreting the gesture. They noted an increase with age in the use of semantic modifiers and relationals and decrease with age in the use of pantomimics, while the least complex gestures, deictics, were rarely used by children aged 4 to 18. In contrast, Evans and Rubin (1979) observed no age differences in the frequency with which these forms of gestures were used, with pantomimics and deictics frequently used, and meta-communicative gestures only rarely used by children aged 5 to 9. These conflicting results are most likely due to the situation specificity of gestural usage, with more deictics and pantomimics occurring when the immediate situation provides support and a shared context for the topic of discourse (such as when explaining a board game that is physically present) than when it bears no relationship (such as when describing a movie). Hence, regardless of the age of the speaker, one may expect a greater number of gestures of a simple referential nature when the description concerns present objects and ongoing events, these topics being so much a part of early communicative acts. As Ochs (1979) has proposed, "Communicative strategies characteristic of any one stage are not replaced. Rather they are retained to be relied upon under certain communicative conditions" (p. 52).

Equally as important as the nature of gestures outlined above is the manner in which the information provided by gestures and words interlock, or the extent to which gestures supplement the discourse as opposed to being redundant with it. For example, cupping the hands out and upward while saying "It was sort of shaped like this" supplements and clarifies a vague and referentially inadequate spoken message, whereas the same gestures while saying "It was shaped like an 8-inch globe" parallels and reinforces a much more adequately spoken message and as such may be regarded as redundant. Evans and Rubin (1979) observed that if one ignored the gestures and demonstrations used by kindergarten children in explaining a board game and attended only to their verbal descriptions, the communications of these younger children were less adequate and more ambiguous than those of second graders. However, if hand gestures were taken into account, the combined information from the verbal and nonverbal channels rendered equally unambiguous statements of game rules at each grade level. In other words, information conveyed by the younger children in the verbal-symbolic modality was more dependent for its interpretation on the information supplied in the gestural-enactive modality. That younger children should point and trace in the air in referential communication studies may indicate not their egocentrism but rather the primary style of childish description, in which, as was in fact originally pointed out by Piaget (1926/1959), "gestures play as important a part as words." One may view gestures as providing a context for words, a context that becomes less obligatory as facility with words in describing events is achieved. (It might be noted here again, that under certain communicative conditions when the speaker is having difficulty with the topic matter, the developmentally earlier stage of a heavy reliance on gestures to convey information may be evidenced by older children and adults.)

Acknowledgement of the importance of gestures as carriers of additional—and critical—information in children's communications necessitates that both verbal and nonverbal channels be addressed in the study of communication development and that both channels be considered together. Given the tendency for preschool and primary-grade children to use pointing, tracing, and demonstration in lieu of explicit words, studies which visually separate listeners and speakers or allow for the use of only the verbal modality might better be called studies of referential *language* development rather than *communication* development.

SKILLED DESCRIPTION IN LATER CHILDHOOD

We have briefly addressed the form of children's descriptions but we have not yet considered what is it that gets described. Clark and Clark (1977) have suggested that the simple pointing and labeling of the one-word stage of speech are elaborated into two-word utterances commenting upon or asserting the presence, absence, locations, and attributes of objects ("See doggie," "All gone doggie," "There doggie," "Big doggie") as well as conveying the basic character of ongoing events ("Doggie eat"). Bates (1976) and Greenfield and Smith (1976) further suggest that children comment upon what is *new* for them—that is, what they have just noticed or to use Halliday's (1975a) terms, what objects or events have just impinged upon their experience. A more elaborate version of this hypothesis has been offered by Greenfield and Zukow (1978; see also Greenfield, 1979; Pea, 1979). This stage at which language is what Halliday calls "mathetic" in function serves as a transition to more adultlike language in which speech is more "informative" in function, serving less to document what is new in the environment for the speaker and more to communicate information to a listener who does not or may not already have it. While we know intuitively that children are eager to share and tell and that Halliday's proposal of a developmental trend from mathetic to informative is reasonable, there is nevertheless very little empirical research systematically documenting the topics of early informative speech.

Some indication of the incidence of descriptions during early childhood can be obtained from Schacter, Kirshner, Klips, Friedricks, and Sanders (1974). Here statements classified as "reporting"—that is, statements that functioned to share an observation, thought, or experience, such as "I went to the circus"—were the most frequent type of statement used by preschoolers in play. The incidence of reporting statements, which constitute descriptions of personal activities, was relatively high at age 2 and remained high across the preschool years. Tough (1977) found that about a quarter of the utterances of both socioeconomically advantaged and disadvantaged 3-year-olds involved reporting items or events from their recent past or immediate ongoing experience. Similarly, Umiker-Sebeok (1979) observed that slightly more than 34% of the conversations of 3- to 5-year-old children contained descriptions of one or more past events. Further, her data showed that the length of these descriptions increased with age and that by age 4 contained an average of 2.6 clauses, reflecting the child's increasing capacity for generating complex sentences and linking them together (cf. Case, 1977; Olson, 1973).

Unfortunately, just at the age of 4 or 5 when children regularly link several sentences together to comment upon some topic or event, the general research paradigm employed in studies of communication development shifts from naturalistic studies of ongoing discourse in preschool settings to structured laboratory tasks that do not call for an extended text. Hence, we know relatively little about the development of conversational description beyond early childhood. Moreover, as touched on earlier in the chapter, this shift in methodology has inadvertently contributed to incongruous conclusions regarding conversational *competence* in preschoolers but communicative *incompetence* in kindergartners and first graders. What is needed in order to gain some sense of continuity in children's descriptions are naturalistic observations of elementary-school children (Evans, in prep.; see also Flavell, 1977).

Some indication of the nature of school-aged children's descriptions may be gained from interview studies in which children have been asked to explain something, tell a personal narrative, or retell a story they have just been told, all of these tasks requiring several clauses or sentences linked together around a particular topic. It is commonly observed that such accounts continue to increase in length and quantity of information presented across middle childhood, but there is no clear account of what is added. Early observations by Piaget (1926/1959) suggest that explanations and stories as retold by children aged 5 to 7 are jumbled, ambiguous, and randomly incomplete, stemming from the child's inability to differentiate his or her own point of view from that of others—that is, from his or her egocentric mode of thinking. This interpretation has been questioned, however, both within the communication and the visual/social role-taking literature (see, for example, Cox, 1980).

Examination of the structure and content of children's narratives and explanations indicates that their accounts are normally more ordered than Piaget claimed. When asked to tell a simple story (Brown, 1975; Mandler & Johnson, 1977; Stein & Glenn, 1979), tell a personal narrative (Menig-Peterson & McCabe, 1978), explain a childhood game (Evans, 1981; Evans & Rubin, 1983), or describe common events (Nelson & Gruendel, 1979), children aged 4 to 7 have provided sequentially ordered accounts. It would appear that a common strategy in describing events even for young children is to proceed in a temporal fashion, a strategy that continues across childhood (Evans, 1981) and into adulthood (Linde & Labov, 1975).

The points in a temporal sequence of events at which the child chooses to initiate and to terminate his or her description directly influences the amount of information conveyed. It appears that younger children tend to omit orientation statements as defined by Labov and Waletsky (1967)—that is, they fail to orient the listener in respect to person, place, time, and behavioral situation in their descriptions of events, focusing immediately on what happened without establishing a context. For example, Menig-Peterson and McCabe (1978) noted an increase from 3.5 pieces of orienting information per narrative at age 4 to 7 pieces at age 9, and Kernan (1977) reported an increase in the proportion of orienting clauses to total clauses from 11% at age 7 to 22% at age 13. Similarly, Umiker-Sebeok (1979) found an increase in the percentage of narratives containing at least one orientation statement from 16%

at age 3, to 64% at age 4, to 100% at age 5. In addition, she observed an increase in the number containing at least one conclusion or resolution statement from 11% at age 3, to 17% at age 4, to 41% at age 5.

The above studies examined personal narratives, but their findings are mirrored in the manner in which children explain common games (Evans & Rubin, 1983). Here, kindergartners and first graders rarely mentioned how many players are required for a game, specified what materials are needed, or designated the roles of the various players, but all age groups from kindergarten to eighth grade knew these points of information equally well when specifically asked. In addition, the younger children less often described how the games came to a conclusion. Rather they concentrated their explanations on what the players *do* in the game and ended their explanations there. Older children, on the other hand, proceeded through the game's preparations and actions to terminate with the game's end rule. These findings held for two games played throughout middle childhood—Simon Says and Musical Chairs. Moreover, they also held for a third game—Doggie, Doggie, Who's Got the Bone. This game is played only in nursery school and was less familiar to the older children than to the kindergartners, but the younger children again provided less complete game descriptions.

The changing pattern of information relayed and omitted by children across the middle childhood range that has been observed in these studies demonstrates that the development of descriptive abilities in children is by no means complete by age 4, reinforcing the need for more studies of extended oral communication beyond the preschool years. It also suggests a second explanation of younger children's relatively poor referential communication skills that can be added to the explanation offered earlier involving the relation between information conveyed in the gestural and verbal modalities. Again, this explanation may serve as an alternative to the egocentrism hypothesis. Young children might well employ a different and less complete internal framework or schema to guide them in encoding and reporting events with which they are familiar, which focuses on the most salient features but makes for less complete though orderly descriptions.

This explanation is consistent with recall investigations of the development of story schemata which aid in the understanding and retelling of narratives. Such studies ordinarily find that a core of the central events of a story appears in the retellings of children from kindergarten to adolescence, but that the number and types of elaborations beyond the central core increase steadily with development. Stein (1979), using Stein and Glenn's (1979) story grammar (see Table 1) as a guide, summarize the trend as follows. Retellings by children of all ages above kindergarten are likely to include orientation or setting information, initiating events, and consequences. Internal responses of the characters are generally omitted by younger children, unless the internal responses specifies a goal that the protagonist wishes to accomplish. Young children recall goals relatively well. Other forms of internal responses, focusing on motivations and emotions, increase in relative likelihood with age, as do attempts. Even adults, however, continue to omit reactions (almost as if such end statements were anticlimactic after the consequence or resolution has been told). Thus, story recall tends toward increasingly elaborate and complete renditions, with the biggest developmental change occurring in the probability of including internal responses. This movement toward an emphasis on motivations can be found during the same age period in other areas of development as well, including social and moral cognition (Bigner, 1974; Flapan, 1968; Lickona, 1976; Scarlett, Press, & Crockett, 1971).

Beyond an increase in the extent and complexity of the framework that guides narrative descriptions, the level of generality of the framework also changes developmentally. Nelson & Gruendel (1979) asked preschoolers, kindergartners, and elementary-school children to describe what happens in common social situations such as a birthday party or a trip to a restaurant. As in the studies of story recall, a core of central events was supplied by even the youngest of the children, though descriptions became progressively more complex and complete with increasing age. Nelson and Gruendel analyzed these developments in terms of the acquisition of an internal script or schema that captures the stereotyped aspects of a situation's temporal and causal structure (see also Schank & Abelson, 1977; Day, Stein, Trabasso, & Shirey, 1979; Trabasso, 1981). The youngest children speak often in terms of a particular situation, usually the most recent example of the situation that they themselves have experienced. Older children tend more and more to speak in generalizations rather than particulars, describing the characteristics shared by all examples of the situation without necessarily recounting any specific occurrence or experience. This developmental trend probably results from a combination of many

TABLE 1
Category Analysis of the Content of a Simple, Well-formed Story Following Stein
(1979) Story Grammar[a]

Category	Story
Setting: Orienting statements, context for story.	Once there was a big grey fish named Albert who lived in a big icy pond near the edge of a forest.
Initiating Event: Critical occurrence that leads to goal-directed action.	One day, Albert was swimming around the pond when he spotted a big juicy worm on top of the water.
Internal Response: Emotional response to initiating event. Can include the setting of a goal.	Albert knew how delicious worms tasted and wanted to eat that one for his dinner.
Attempt: Overt actions in pursuit of the goal.	So he swam very close to the worm and bit into him.
Consequence: Outcome of attempt.	Suddenly, Albert was pulled through the water into a boat. He had been caught by a fisherman.
Reaction: Character's internal response to the consequence or a broader conclusion such as a moral.	Albert felt sad and wished he had been more careful.

[a] Table adapted from Stein, N. L. How children understand stories: A developmental analysis. In L. Katz (Ed.), *Current topics in early childhood education.* (Vol. 2). Norwood, NJ: Ablex, 1979.

factors, including larger numbers of personal experiences on which to draw, greater abstraction of the elements common to the experiences, and greater linguistic sophistication, such as a more mature grasp of the force carried by the indefinite article in a question, "What happens at *a* birthday party?" All of these factors, however, point toward the importance of the knowledge base, its size, strength, structure, and level of abstraction, in guiding descriptions.

THE CONSEQUENCES OF DESCRIPTION: ATTENTION, SET, AND MEMORY

In the foregoing sections of the chapter we have considered three factors underlying developmental increases in the quality of verbal descriptions: the modalities—verbal-symbolic or gestural-enactive—that are available for communication; the speaker's experience with the type of social situation and the content to be conveyed in that situation (see also Borke, 1975; Bruner, 1975; Donaldson, 1978; Maratsos, 1973; Menig-Peterson, 1975); and the acquisition of frameworks such as scripts and schemata to guide a description's formulation. So far, however, our discussion has emphasized the structural properties and propositional content of descriptions without taking any detailed account of their efficacy. If descriptions play an important role in social and communicative development, then their consequences are as important as their properties.

To illustrate just how fundamental the influence of a description can be, consider the ambiguous figures often used by textbook writers to illustrate perceptual set. One of the best known is a picture that can be interpreted either as a sophisticated young woman or a wizened old lady. It is clear from studies by Boring (1930) that presenting a series of unambiguous pictures of young women in advance of this figure will bias its interpretation in one direction, whereas a series of unambiguous pictures of old women will bias interpretation in the other direction. It seems equally clear, from the mere fact that the figure plus a caption will induce the phenomenon in students of introductory psychology, that verbal descriptions can play a biasing role much like that played by the series of pictures. The provision of a description can apparently influence memory in addition to initial interpretation, as shown by the work of Carmichael et al. (1932). They presented a drawing that objectively appeared to be about halfway between a pair of eye glasses and a barbell to one group of subjects, who were told that the drawing depicted glasses, and to another group of subjects, who were told that the drawing depicted a barbell. When asked later to draw the original figure from memory, subjects in the first group produced drawings that unambiguously resembled eyeglasses while subjects in the second group produced drawings that unambiguously resembled barbells.

Potter (1975, 1976) has provided a striking demonstration that a description sets up the perceptual processing and interpretation of a visual scene in the ways suggested by the ambiguous-figure phenomenon. Because this research is likely to be less familiar than the research discussed earlier in the chapter, we will treat it in considerable detail. Participants in Potter's experiments saw a series of simple pictures, such as a sailboat in the middle of a small lake or two men sitting at a table drinking mugs of beer. Each picture appeared for a very brief period of time and was immediately followed by the next picture. Under these conditions all but the last picture in the series was nearly impossible either to identify during presentation or to recognize in a subsequent test of recognition memory. Yet when participants received a description of a target picture in advance of viewing the series—"You are looking for two men drinking beer"—they were able to determine whether or not the target was present in the series with great accuracy. Thus the description, by telling the participant what to look for, facilitated the perception of visual information that was uninterpretable and unrememberable without such advance preparation. Remarkably, the facilitative effect of the description was nearly as great as that produced by showing a copy of the actual target picture in advance of the series. Descriptions, then, can exert a powerful influence on perceptual processing.

What is the nature of this influence? Intraub (1981) and Potter (1976) both argue that all scenes, however rapidly presented, are briefly identified—that is, that they make contact with stored knowledge in a way that activates information about their meanings—but that this semantic activation is fleeting and fragile, easily disrupted by subsequent perceptual input. If the perceiver does not attend to the information activated by a scene, it will be interrupted, fragmented, and finally replaced completely by activation from the next scene the perceiver sees. Descriptions prepare the perceiver to attend to particular information if it becomes activated, allowing the perceiver to tap into the flow of briefly activated meanings and save desired information from disruption by other information that is not desired. The result is that information that would have been lost without the advance description can be attended and processed sufficiently to support a detection decision.

This hypothesis is consistent with Olson's (1970) argument that descriptions foreground some of the information in a scene, drawing the listener's attention to that information at the expense of other potentially available information. Olson's position carries a further implication, however, that goes beyond Potter's: unforegrounded information may actually receive *less* processing than it would have if the description had not occurred. According to Olson, information emphasized by the description will be selected, as in Potter's theory, and unemphasized information will be actively ignored rather than being allowed simply to fade from activation by the ongoing process of perceptual interference.

To test this aspect of Olson's theory, Bacharach et al. (1976) presented a series of simple target scenes to first graders and fifth graders. Each scene consisted of two components that might naturally occur together, such as a bee near a flower or a horse hitched to a wagon. Different groups of children received either a description in advance of each picture that mentioned one component but not the other (e.g., "This is a picture of a horse"), the same kind of single-component description after, rather than before, the picture's presentation, or no description at all. The second condition was included in order to assess the purely memorial effects of relevant information that was provided at a time when it could *not* influence the initial encoding of the picture, and the third condition was included as a baseline to determine how well the contents of the pictures would be remembered with no extra verbal information of any kind. When the series of target scenes was completed, a recognition memory test was given to determine whether descriptions influenced memory for components of the target scene. This test presented single components, one at a time, and required the participants to indicate for each component whether it had been seen anywhere in the list of target pictures. Table 2 shows that descriptions provided after the picture had already been viewed improved memory for described or foregrounded components without affecting memory for unmentioned components relative to having no description at all. This is exactly what one would expect if the description gave the perceiver an additional, independent source of information about the contents of the scenes that could be utilized in making memory judgments. Advance descriptions had a very different effect. They improved memory for the foregrounded components, but they also reduced memory for unmentioned components relative to the other two conditions. Thus a description can act as Olson suggests, facilitating the perception and subsequent memory of foregrounded information and inhibiting the processing of unforegrounded information.

Table 2 does not separate the performances of first and fifth graders. That is because they did not differ. It would appear, then, that the kind of sensitivity to descriptions that was tapped in this experiment manifests itself to the fullest by age 6 or 7 in normally developing children. Subsequent work has indicated that mentally retarded children and adolescents are also sensitive to single-component descriptions, at least those who have attained a mental age of 6 or 7. An attempt was made to assess description sensitivity in mentally retarded individuals of mental age 3 to 4, but the attempt failed. Participants were quite comfortable with the idea of looking at pictures that had been described in advance, but had trouble grasping the requirements of a recognition memory test.

So far we have considered the developmental onset of sensitivity to descriptions that overtly identify one component of a scene and make absolutely no mention of anything else. Perhaps one should find it unsurprising that such a sledgehammer

TABLE 2
Correct Recognition Decisions about Single Components from Target Scenes in Bacharach, Carr, & Mehner's (1976) Study of the Effects of Descriptions on Picture Processing[a]

	Description was Provided		
Type of Component	After the Picture	No Description	Before the Picture
Mentioned (foregrounded)	95.5%	82.2%	93.0%
Unmentioned	85.5%	83.2%	74.0%
Difference	10.0%	−1.0%	19.0%

[a] Exposure duration of each target scene was 2 seconds; note the poor performance on unmentioned components when the description was provided before (that is, in advance of) the picture.

approach to describing the world affects perception and memory so strongly. However, subtler characteristics of a description can also modify perceptual processing and memory storage. In a followup study conducted with first graders, Carr et al. (1977) compared three different types of advance descriptions: single-component descriptions like those used in the previous study, conjunctive descriptions in which both components were overtly identified ("This is a picture of a horse and a wagon"), and interactive descriptions in which both components were identified and were also placed in an action-based relationship with one another ("This is a picture of horse pulling a wagon"). The components foregrounded in single-component descriptions were also the first components mentioned in the conjunctive descriptions and the agents of the actions described in the interactive descriptions. All of the descriptions were spoken in naturally occurring intonation patterns, with the result that conjunctive descriptions placed approximately equal prosodic stress on each component whereas interactive descriptions placed mild contrastive stress on the object of the interaction (as if to say, "Of all the things that this horse could be pulling, you will see it pulling a wagon"). The three types of descriptions exerted different influences on picture processing, again as assessed through performance on a recognition memory test. Single-component descriptions once again produced better memory for the foregrounded component than for the unmentioned component. Conjunctive descriptions produced equivalent memory for the two components. Interactive descriptions reversed the effect of the single-component descriptions in terms of which actual components were remembered better—where the single-component description had resulted in better memory for the horse, the interactive description resulted in better memory for the wagon. With respect to foregrounding cues provided within the description, however, the effect of the interactive descriptions was the same as that of the single-component descriptions: the objects, foregrounded by stress, were remembered better than the unstressed agents.

Since contrastive stress conveys strong cues about given-new distinctions (Clark & Clark, 1977; Halliday, 1975b; Halliday & Hasan, 1976; Wieman, 1976), one might conclude that descriptions act generally to facilitate the processing of environmental information that has been marked as new (and therefore as important or worthy of attention). This finding helps to elucidate the nature of the foregrounding effect proposed by Olson, and provides a listener-side complement to the developmental trends in description content discussed by Bates (1976) and by Greenfield and Zukow (1978; Greenfield, 1979). Listeners appear to be sensitive to much the same principles in comprehending a description that speakers utilize in constructing and producing one. We have already seen that speakers appear to allocate processing capacity and planning activities to ensure that the most salient or most important information receives priority in the communication. If limits on available capacity or planning and production time mean that not all relevant information can be mentioned, then the new information will be encoded and the old or given information will go unmentioned. If increases in available capacity, decreases in the capacity demands of processing, or increases in available time allowed, then both new and old information may be encoded linguistically, but the new information will be emphasized or highlighted. This may be accomplished syntactically, prosodically, or by a combination of both. In complementary fashion, listeners appear to use cues provided by a description to prioritize their processing of the described scene. They allocate processing capacity and time first to mentioned information, and if several pieces of information are mentioned, they allocate capacity and time according to the syntactic or prosodic highlights that they recognize within the description.

CONCLUSIONS

To restate the point we have just made, a striking similarity can be observed between the priorities by which speakers choose features for inclusion in a description and the priorities by which listeners allocate attention to those features in an environment to which the description applies. The basic rule seems to be that the most salient, central, or important features should receive first billing. This prioritization rule appears to hold in a number of different kinds of experimental paradigms used to study description and across a wide range of ages of experimental participants. Such prioritizing might imply that a resource or capacity-limited process of some kind is involved in the cognition under study, and we have already seen that capacity limitations figure prominently in explanations of the prioritizing observed in the production of descriptions by infants (Bates, 1976). Bock (1982) has applied a similar logic to similar prioritizing of production by adults. Bock argues that the formulation of a description taxes limited central processing capacity. Salient features—which by virtue of their very salience are more highly activated in the information-processing system at the time the description is being produced—are easier to think about and to encode linguistically. In order to ease the burden on the processes of speech production, then, salient features are encoded first and uttered first, getting them out of the way of the more difficult and time-consuming processing required by less salient features. Among infants, who are just learning language and who are always operating under severe capacity limitations, salience makes the difference between a feature being present or absent in an utterance that is simply not long enough to include all the relevant information. Among adults, whose capacity limitations for language production are not so severe, salience makes the difference between early versus late production within an utterance and the difference between production with an importance marking such as stress versus production without such a marking.

   Analysis of the properties of descriptions in terms of the capacity demands of the processes that produce them puts our discussion into the category of skill theories such as those proposed by Case (1977; Case, Kurland, & Daneman, 1979) and Fischer (1980). The implication of such an analysis is that descriptive ability can be understood in part as a skilled performance, and that the developmental trends we have examined can be understood in part as the acquisition of expertise in how to describe. The influence of communication modality on the quality of descriptions by young children becomes very transparent in such a framework—an ontogenetically prior and more highly practiced system consisting of gestures carries much of the communicative load during the early stages of the development of an ontogenetically later, less-practiced system consisting of verbalization. As the verbal system becomes better established, more overlearned, and more highly automated, it can carry a greater portion of the load.

Skill theories, however, need more than concepts of capacity limitation and skill learning or automatization to explain increasing expertise. They also need to consider the nature of the knowledge base that supports the processes of description (Carr, in press; Fischer, 1980). We have discussed the role that progressive schematization of the knowledge base plays in story retellings, event descriptions, game descriptions, and other forms of referential communication. In fact, study of the development of description during middle and late childhood has focused almost entirely on schematization in recent years. These studies have begun to illuminate the describer's knowledge of what he or she is trying to talk about in a description.

We would like to close by suggesting that successful description may also depend on acquiring a schema for the act of describing itself. This schema would be an integrated and overlearned framework that defines the temporal and causal structure of an adequate description *in general,* into which the particular content to be conveyed can be placed. Markman (1979) has reported that while young children can understand the content that is actually conveyed by a narrative description, they have difficulty deciding whether that content is *adequate,* whether it conveys all the information that is necessary to understand the referent supposedly captured by the description. Older children and adults are quite capable of making such judgments. Thus, in our view, the phenomenon reported in the referential communication literature that young children rarely ask for clarification of descriptions that are insufficient does not reflect their egocentrism, as some have speculated, but their lack of expertise. They are practicing the rudiments of a skill—description—about which they do not yet know enough to determine whether or not they are performing adequately (see also Halliday, 1975a). Such a view pulls together several lines of research that usually stand separate, allowing theories of language acquisition, communicative competence, knowledge acquisiton, and attention to speak to one another with the larger context of a developmental theory of skilled performance. Even if this type of theory proves wrong, its implications for an integration of concepts and research methods across the areas of investigation we have discussed are well worth pursuing.

REFERENCES

Asher, S. R. Referential communication. In G. J. Whitehurst & B. J. Zimmerman (Eds.), *The functions of language and cognition.* New York: Academic Press, 1978.

Bacharach, V. R., Carr, T. H., & Mehner, D. S. Interactive and independent contributions of verbal descriptions to children's picture memory. *Journal of Experimental Child Psychology,* 1976, 22, 492–498.

Bates, E. *Language and context: The acquisition of pragmatics.* New York: Academic Press, 1976.

Bates, E., Camaioni, L., & Volterra, V. The acquisition of performatives prior to speech. *Merrill-Palmer Quarterly,* 1975, *21,* 205–226.

Bateson, M. C. Mother-infant exchanges: The epigenesis of conversational interaction. In D. Aaronson & R. W. Rieber (Eds.), *Developmental psycholinguistics and communication disorders.* New York: New York Academy of Sciences, 1975.

Bigner, J. J. A Wernerian developmental analysis of children's descriptions of siblings. *Child Development,* 1974, *45,* 317–323.

Birdwhistell, R. L. Toward analyzing American movement. In S. Weitz (Ed.), *Nonverbal communication.* New York: Oxford University Press, 1974.

Bock, J. K. Toward a cognitive psychology of syntax: Information processing contributions to sentence formulation. *Psychological Review,* 1982, *89,* 1–47.

Borke, H. Piaget's mountain revistied: Changes in the egocentric landscape. *Developmental Psychology,* 1975, *11,* 240–243.

Boring, E. G. Apparatus notes: A new ambiguous figure. *American Journal of Psychology,* 1930, *42,* 444.

Brown, A. Recognition, reconstruction, and recall of narrative sequences by pre-operational children. *Child Development,* 1975, *46,* 156–166.

Bruner, J. The ontogenesis of speech acts. *Journal of Child Language,* 1975, *2,* 1–19.

Carmichael, L., Hogan, H. P., & Walter, A. A. An experimental study of the effect of language on the reproduction of visually perceived forms. *Journal of Experimental Psychology,* 1932, *15,* 73–86.

Carr, T. H. Attention, skill, and intelligence: Some speculations on extreme individual differences in human performance. In C. McCauley, R. D. Sperber, & P. Brook (Eds.), *Learning, cognition, and mental retardation.* Baltimore, MD: University Park Press, in press.

Carr, T. H., Bacharach, V. R., & Mehner, D. S. Preparing children to look at pictures: Advance descriptions direct attention and facilitate active processing. *Child Development,* 1977, *48,* 18–24.

Carter, A. L. From sensorimotor vocalizations to words: A case study of the evolution of attention-directing communication in the second year of life. In A. Lock (Ed.), *Action, gesture, and symbol: The emergence of language.* New York: Academic Press, 1978. (a)

Carter, A. L. The development of systematic vocalizations prior to words. In N. Waterson & C. Snow (Eds.), *The development of communication.* New York: Wiley, 1978. (b)

Carter, A. L. Prespeech meaning relations: An outline of one infant's sensorimotor morpheme development. In P. Fletcher & M. Garman (Eds.), *Language acquisiton.* London: Cambridge University Press, 1979.

Case, R. Intellectual development from birth to adulthood: A neo-Piagetian interpretation. In R. S. Siegler (Ed.), *Children's thinking: What develops?* Hillsdale, NJ: Erlbaum, 1977.

Case, R., Kurland, M., & Daneman, M. Operational efficiency and the growth of m-space. Paper presented at the biennial meeting of the Society for Research in Child Development, San Francisco, March 1979.

Clark, H. H., & Clark, E. V. *Psychology and language.* New York: Harcourt, 1977.

Cox, M. V. *Are young children egocentric?* London: Batsford Academic and Educational Ltd., 1980.

Day, J., Stein, N. L., Trabasso, T., & Shirey, L. A study of inferential comprehension: The use of story schema to remember picture sequences. Paper presented at the meeting of the Society for Research in Child Development, San Francisco, March 1979.

Dickson, W. P. Referential communication activities in research and in the curriculum: A meta-analysis. In W. P. Dickson (Ed.), *Children's oral communiciation skills. New York: Academic Press, 1980.*

Donaldson, M. *Children's minds.* Glasgow: Fontana, 1978.

Ekman, P. E., & Friesen, W. V. The repertoire of nonverbal behavior: Categories, origins, usage, and coding. *Semiotica,* 1969, *1,* 49–97.

Evans, M. A. What and how children show and tell. In preparation.

Evans, M. A. What you do is: Children's explanations of childhood games. Paper presented at the biennial meeting of the Society for Research in Child Development, Boston, March 1981.

Evans, M. A., & Rubin, K. H. Hand gestures as a communicative mode in school-age children. *Journal of Genetic Psychology,* 1979, *135,* 189–196.

Evans, M. A., & Rubin, K. H. Developmental differences in explanations of childhood games. *Child Development,* 1983, *54,* in press.

Fischer, K. W. A theory of cognitive development: The control and construction of hierarchies of skills. *Psychological Review,* 1980, *87,* 477–531.

Flapan, D. *Children's understanding of social interaction.* New York: Teachers College Press, 1968.

Flavell, J. H. *Cognitive Development.* Englewood Cliffs, NJ: Prentice-Hall, 1977.

Glucksberg, S., Krauss, A., & Higgins, E. T. The development of referential communication skills. In F. Horowitz (Ed.), *Review of child development research* (Vol. 4). Chicago: University of Chicago Press, 1975.

Greenfield, P. The role of perceptual uncertainty in the transition to language. Paper presented at the biennial meeting of the Society for Research in Child Development, San Francisco, March 1979.

Greenfield, P. N., & Smith, J. H. *The structure of communication in early language development.* New York: Academic Press, 1976.

Greenfield, P., & Zukow, P. Why do children say what they say when they say it?: An experimental approach to the psychogenesis of presupposition. In K. Nelson (Ed.), *Children's language* (Vol. 1). New York: Gardner Press, 1978.

Halliday, M. A. K. *Learning how to mean: Explorations in the development of language.* London: Edward Arnold, 1975. (a)

Halliday, M. A. K. *Intonation and grammar in British English.* The Hague: Mouton, 1975. (b)

Halliday, M. A. K., & Hasan, R. *Cohesion in English.* London: Longman, 1976.

Intraub, H. Rapid conceptual identification of sequentially presented pictures. *Journal of Experimental Psychology: Human Perception & Performance,* Special Issue on Reading and Related Processes, 1981, *7,* 604–610.

Jancovic, M., Devoe, S., & Wiener, M. Age related changes in hand and arm movements as nonverbal communication: Some conceptualizations and an empirical investigation. *Child Development,* 1975, *46,* 922–928.

Kernan, K. T. Semantic and expressive elaboration in children's narratives. In S. Ervin-Tripp & C. Mitchell-Kernan (Eds.), *Child discourse.* New York: Academic Press, 1977.

Knapp, M. *Nonverbal communication in human interaction.* New York: Holt, Rinehart & Winston, 1972.

Labov, W., & Waletsky, J. Narrative analysis: Oral versions of personal experience. In J. Helm (Ed.), *Essays on the verbal and visual arts.* Seattle: University of Washington Press, 1967.

Leung, E. H. L., & Rheingold, H. L. Development of pointing as social communication. Paper presented at the biennial meeting of the Society for Research in Child Development, New Orleans, 1977.

Lempers, J. D., Flavell, E. R., & Flavell, J. H. The development in very young children of tacit knowledge concerning visual perception. *Genetic Psychology Monographs,* 1977, *95,* 3–53.

Lickona, T. (Ed.). *Moral development and behavior.* New York: Holt, Rinehart & Winston, 1976.

Linde, C., & Labov, W. Spacial networks as a site for the study of language of languge and thought. *Language,* 1975, *51,* 924–939.

Loftus, E. F. *Eyewitness testimony.* Cambridge, MA: Harvard Univ. Press, 1979.

Mandler, J. M., & Johnson, N. S. Rememberance of things parsed: Story structure and recall. *Cognitive Psychology,* 1977, *9,* 111–151.

Maratsos, M. P. Nonegocentric communication abilities in preschool children. *Child Development,* 1973, *44,* 697–700.

Markman, E. Realizing that you don't understand: Elementary school children's awareness of inconsistencies. *Child Development,* 1979, *50,* 643–655.

Menig-Peterson, C. L. The modification of communicative behavior in preschool-aged children as a function of the listener's perspective. *Child Development,* 1975, *46,* 1015–1018.

Menig-Peterson, C. L., & McCabe, A. Children's orientation of a listener to the context of their narratives. *Developmental Psychology,* 1978, *14*(6), 582–592.

Murphy, C. M., & Messer, D. Mothers, infants and pointing: A study of a gesture. In H. R. Schaffer (Ed.), *Studies in mother–infant interaction.* New York: Academic Press, 1977.

Nelson, K., & Gruendel, J. M. From personal episode to social script: Two dimensions in the development of event knowledge. Paper presented at the biennial meeting of the Society for Research in Child Development, San Francisco, March 1979.

Ochs, E. Planned and unplanned discourse. In T. Givon (Ed.), *Syntax and semantics* (Vol. 12): *Discourse and syntax.* New York: Academic Press, 1979.

Olson, D. R. Language and thought: Aspects of a cognitive theory of semantics. *Psychological Review,* 1970, *77,* 257–273.

Olson, G. M. Developmental changes in memory and the acquisition of language. In T. E. Moore (Ed.), *Cognitive development and the acquisition of language.* New York: Academic Press, 1973.

Pea, R. Can information theory explain early word choice? *Journal of Child Language,* 1979, *6,* 397–410.

Pezdek, K. Life-span differences in semantic integration of pictures and sentences in memory. *Child Development,* 1980, *51,* 720–729.

Piaget, J. *The origins of intelligence in children.* New York: Norton, 1952.

Piaget, J. *[The language and thought of the child]* (M. Gabin & R. Gabin, trans.). London: Routledge & Kegan Paul, 1959. (Originally published, 1926).

Piaget, J. & Inhelder, B. *The psychology of the child.* New York: Basic Books, 1969.

Potter, M. C. Meaning in visual search. *Science,* 1975, *187,* 965–966.

Potter, M. C. Short term conceptual memory for pictures. *Journal of Experimental Psychology: Human Learning and Memory,* 1976, *2,* 509–522.

Scaife, M., & Bruner, J. S. The capacity for joint visual attention in the infant. *Nature,* 1975, *253,* 265–266.

Scarlett, H. H., Press, A. N., & Crockett, W. H. Children's descriptions of peers: A Wernerian developmental analysis. *Child Development,* 1971, *42,* 439–453.

Schacter, F. F., Kirshner, K., Klips, B., Friedricks, M., & Sanders, K. Everyday preschool interpersonal speech usage: Methodological, developmental and sociolinguistic studies. *Monographs of the Society for Research in Child Development,* 1974, *39*(3, Serial No. 156).

Schank, R. C., & Abelson, R. P. *Scripts, plans, goals and understanding.* Hillsdale, NJ: Erlbaum, 1977.

Scheflen, A. C. *How behavior means.* New York: Gordon & Breach, 1973.

Siegler, R. S. Developmental sequences within and between concepts. *Monographs of the Society for Research in Child Development,* 1981, *46*(2, Serial No. 189).

Snow, C. E. The development of conversation between mothers and babies. *Journal of Child Language,* 1977, *4,* 1–22.

Snyder, L. Communication and cognitive abilities and disabilities in the sensori-motor period. *Merrill-Palmer Quarterly,* 1978, *24,* 161–180.

Stein, N. L. How children understand stories: A developmental analysis. In L. Katz (Ed.), *Current topics in early childhood education* (Vol. 2). Norwood, NJ: Ablex, 1979.

Stein, N. L., & Glenn, C. G. An analysis of story comprehension in elementary school children. In R. O. Freedle (Ed.), *Discourse processing: Multidisciplinary perspectives.* Norwood, NJ: Ablex, 1979.

Stern, D., Jaffe, J., Beebe, B., & Bennett, S. L. Vocalizing in unison and in alteration: Two modes of communication within the mother–infant dyad. In D. Aaronson & R. W. Rieber (Eds.), *Developmental psycholinguistics and communication disorders.* New York: New York Academy of Sciences, 1975.

Sylvester-Bradley, & Trevarthan, C. Baby-talk as an adaptation to the infant's communication. In N. Waterson & C. E. Snow (Eds.), *The development of communication: Social and pragmatic factors in language acquisition.* Paper presented at the Third International Child Language Symposium. New York: Wiley, 1978.

Tough, J. *The development of meaning.* London: Allen & Unwin, 1977.

Trabasso, T. Causal cohesion in story comprehension. Paper presented at the annual meeting of the Psychonomic Society, Philadelphia, November 1981.

Trevarthan, C. Conversations with a two-month-old. *New Scientist,* 1974, *62,* 230–235.

Umiker-Sebeok, D. J. Preschool children's intraconversational narratives. *Journal of Child Language,* 1979, *6,* 91–109.

Wieman, L. A. Stress patterns of early child language. *Journal of Child Language,* 1976, *3,* 283–286.

Wiener, M., Devoe, S., Rubinow, S., & Geller, J. Nonverbal behavior and nonverbal communication. *Psychological Review,* 1972, *79,* 185–214.

Wilgosh, L. Effects of labels on memory for pictures in 4-year-old children. *Journal of Educational Psychology,* 1975, *67,* 375–379.

Vygotsky, L. S. [*Thought and Language*] (E. Hanfmann & G. Vakar, trans.). Cambridge, MA: MIT Press, 1962. (Originally published, 1926).

SECTION IV
AFTERWORD

Methodological Afterword: From Protoaskers to Panaskers

Roger Bakeman

No section or even chapter in this book is devoted exclusively to methodology, and this is perhaps as it should be. Like the mold in blue cheese, methodological considerations vein the reports and essays included here, just as they did discussions at the Institute on the Origins and Growth of Communication from which these chapters derive. The faculty and fellows at the Institute were a diverse lot and so, not very surprisingly, discussions of method were lively, usually friendly, and not likely to leave sacred stones unturned.

Oversimplifying greatly, such discussions often devolved into something of a debate between what could be called "counters" and "tellers." Tellers want only to tell the story they see, replete with its human meaning. Often they use film or videotape, viewed repeatedly until the last drop of "truth" is finally extracted. Frequently they suspect that counters tell a sterile tale, imposing "unnatural" metrics and prespecified behavior codes on others' experience. For their part, counters are skeptical of tellers' tales. After all, they might say, if two tales are told, how do we know which is better? Often counters use film or videotape, too, but they think it reasonable to count how often prespecified "behaviors" occurred and how many seconds each lasted. Probably the tellers would characterize their approach as "emic" and not "etic," while the counters would wonder what makes tellers so certain that they are revealing their subject's story and not just imposing their own construction on the events observed (see Hayes, Chap. 7).

Still, counters and tellers could meet around common themes. Two in particular stood out. First, both were concerned with time, that is, with the way events of interest unfolded in time, and both made frequent use of video technology. The second probably follows from the first because video (and film) provides a way to capture for subsequent reviewing events unfolding in time (Bakeman & Ginsburg, in press). And a concern with time is essentially preordained by the title of the Institute itself. Ignoring words such as "origins" and "growth," communication—even considering its many diverse definitions—can hardly be discussed without reference to a temporal dimension.

To suggest that all Institute participants could be neatly grouped into counters and tellers is, of course, false. These are only prototypes after all, seldom realized in fact. Yet somewhere between these two a third force seemed emergent, a "dialectic baby" whose influence is evident in some of the contributions to this volume.

Perhaps we could call practitioners of this third approach "askers," because many take Harre and Secord (1972) seriously when they suggest, if you want to account for human beings' behavior, "Why not ask them . . . ?" But it is not just a matter of listening and then telling the tale one believes one heard. Instead, a hallmark of askers' work is a concern with identifying "units of action," with cleaving the stream of behavior at the joints that seem correct and natural to the participants themselves (see Greenberg, Chap. 11; Lloyd, Baker, & Dunn, Chap. 15; Ninio & Wheeler, Chap. 10; also Collett, 1980; Lubin & Forbes, 1981; Newtson, 1973, 1976). In a broader sense, askers take seriously the sense humans have of their own agency as they act in and construct with others a social world (Shotter, 1978).

To many counters, to most "microanalysts" of the last decade, and to perhaps a majority of mid-twentieth century American psychologists, this may seem a regressive and regrettable methodological retreat, a return to the subjective sinning of the past. But one can also argue, I think, that askers—or perhaps I should call these new synthesizers "panaskers" to distinguish them from askers of the past—are attempting to combine the counters' concern with rigor and replicable science with the tellers' concern for getting at the meaning of things.

Consider time, for example. For traditional counters, time is a measured matter, flowing serenely from left to right and ticked off in unvarying units. It provides a metric and a frame for the description of behavior. Of course, such descriptions may wrench out of recognition individual human beings' experience (cf. Shotter, 1980). And when this wrenching occurs, tellers may feel somewhat smug and vindicated. Panaskers, too, understand the risks that follow when investigators impose their own "units" on "subjects." That is why they take such pains to identify how "actors" segment and structure time. But they do not usually leave the matter there as tellers might. Instead, having identified "action units" that make sense to participants (Ninio & Wheeler, Chap. 10), it is then possible to make use of the paraphernalia of normal science—including replicable measurement, which in this case means precise definitions of behavior codes and demonstrations of interobserver agreement (Greenberg, Chap. 11).

It is possible, I think, that we are seeing a new synthesis emerging around the theme of communication development, a combination of old concerns and methods into a quite new approach. Panaskers agree with tellers that human beings should be treated whole, in context, their experience respected, but panaskers—at least when on their best behavior and defined in my ideal way—also agree with counters that work must be replicable, else our understanding is likely to only change and not accumulate. Given current observational techniques and technology—especially inexpensive and readily available video—I see no reason why the panaskers' approach should not prove fruitful and multiply. Their approach may even contribute to a deeper understanding of what it means to communicate something called intentions, a topic which was vigorously discussed at the Institute and which remains unsettled still (see Scoville, Harding, Chaps. 5, 6). No new method, of course, will supplant all else—this is as undesirable as it is unlikely. Still, I think I discern a development. At the Institute many were what I would now call "protoaskers." Some have developed into panaskers, which is not to say that they have a panacea, but I think they do have an approach which is beginning to productively influence studies of communication development.

REFERENCES

Bakeman, R., & Ginsburg, G. P. The use of video in the study of human action. In M. Brenner & K. Knorr (Eds.), *Methods of social research: Developments and advances.* London: Academic Press, in press.

Collett, P. Segmenting the behaviour stream. In M. Brenner (Ed.), *The structue of action.* New York: St. Martin's Press, 1980.

Harre, R., & Secord, P. F. *The explanation of social behavior.* Oxford: Basil Blackwell, 1972.

Lubin, D., & Forbes, D. Understanding sequential aspects of children's social behavior: Conceptual issues in the development of coding schemes. Paper presented at the Biennial Meeting of the Society for Research in Child Development, Boston, April 1981.

Newtson, D. Attribution and the unit of perception of ongoing behavior. *Journal of Personality and Social Psychology,* 1973, *28,* 28–38.

Newtson, D. Foundations of attribution: The perception of ongoing behavior. In J. Harvey, W. Ickes, & R. Kidd (Eds.), *New directions in attribution research.* Hillsdale, NJ: Erlbaum, 1976.

Shotter, J. The cultural context of communication studies: Theoretical and methodological issues. In A. Lock (Ed.), *Action, gesture and symbol: The emergence of language.* London: Academic Press, 1978.

Shotter, J. Action, joint action, and intentionality. In M. Brenner (Ed.), *The structure of action.* New York: St. Martin's Press, 1980.

Rejoinder

Catherine Snow

One approach to the analysis of scientific contributions is to consider the sociology of their origins. While I do not propose to so indulge myself with reference to this volume, it should be pointed out that it emerged from a unique shared intellectual experience. The impact of the SRCD 1979 Summer Institute, "The Origins of Communication," on its participants, in terms of their areas of subsequent research, their subsequent producitivity, and their shared sense of connectedness and of being engaged in a joint enterprise, is striking to those who, like me, know many of the participants but did not share the original experience. The connectedness among the participants in that Institute is reflected, I think, in their writing as well as in their research, and is one reason why it is relatively hard to read through this set of papers and find major arguments or conflicts. Personal connectedness among these various authors has enabled them to achieve a degree of synthesis in their thinking which is refreshing in a field as laden with traditional controversies as communicative development.

For example, one hoary opposition in the field is that between biological and social explanations for development. There are chapters in this volume that emphasize the biological origins of communication (e.g., Baldwin, Miller, Miller & Byrnes), and those that emphasize the role of the child's social environment (e.g., Scoville, Zukow, Bohannon & Hirsh-Pasek). Yet, none of these papers sets up an opposition between the two positions. All seem to recognize that communicative development may be such a robust and buffered process precisely because the normally developing infant is both biologically well equipped and socially richly stimulated to achieve the status of competent communicator. Some chapters, such as Harding's, make explicit their positions that biological and social explanations must be combined. Others concentrate on one or the other kind of explanation without assuming that a correct explanation is a complete explanation.

Another opposition that seems endemic in studies of infant development (and of psychology in general) is that between cognition and emotion. Many studies of the development of communication have presupposed or attempted to demonstrate that an affective bond between infant and caregiver is crucial to normal communicative development. They have thus emphasized the primacy of emotional development in communicative development. Other researchers have seen communicative development as primarily a cognitive process, one dependent on the infant's ability to operate with crucial concepts such as the nature of cause and effect, and the agency of others, and to operate at a level of complexity sufficient to allow for decentration and for maintaining two modes of action at once. A novel and stimulating aspect of some of the papers presented here is the way in which affective development is seen also as a cognitive problem: the boundary between affective and cognitive development is dissolved. Thus, Miller's analysis of the development of voice and of face perception deals with an area central to affective development, but it is treated analogously to the way the development of linguistic discriminations (clearly a cognitive problem) has been treated. Miller and Byrne review data on the development of the infant abilities that underlie rhythmicity and perception of rhythmicity; they treat as a cognitive problem the rhythmic meshing of mother and child, a phenomenon long dealt with as a hallmark of a good affective relationship. Harding proposes that infants' cognitive advances occur as a result of perturbations in their emotional relations with their mothers. Greenberg presents several different methods of analyzing interaction between mothers and their hearing-impaired children. He found that ratings of dyadic enjoyment correlate highly with much more discrete measures of interaction, suggesting that the 'quality' of an interaction is both cognitive and affective in nature.

The themes that recur in these papers and that seem to me to be of special interest are:

1. that the adult is more important in determining the nature of an interaction than the child;
2. that metacognition has an important role in communicative development; and
3. that culture is as powerful as cognition in explaining advances in communicative ability.

I will discuss a few of the chapters that intrigued me particularly, in order to expand further on these themes.

Dunlea presents data on concept formation and language development in blind children. She points out that blind children cannot easily experience many of the attributes referred to in sighted children's early utterances (e.g., color, shape, location, class-membership, etc.), and puzzles over the fact that the blind children she studied did not develop vocabularies for discussing the salient aspects of their

own experiences, such as odors, textures, and sounds. This puzzle cannot be resolved on the basis of the data available, but it seems very likely to me that the blind
children failed to develop ways of talking about their own experiences because their
parents were doing a relatively poor job of identifying and providing linguistic
correlates to those experiences. Visual experiences are so much more salient than
other sensory events that it is relatively difficult for sighted people to talk about
sound or smells. The optimal linguistic environment for the child is obviously one
which matches the child's cognitive capacities. The match must occur for content as
well as for level (see Bohannon and Hirsh-Pasek, regarding level) if the consequences for the child are to be optimal.

Examples of very close matches between the child's cognitive level and maternal
speech are given by Ninio and Wheeler; in their examples, the match is ensured by
the ways in which the parents fit their utterances into the shared social context,
using them to model appropriate child utterances or to express presumed child
intentions. Although not discussed explicitly by Ninio and Wheeler, it is impressive
to see to what extent they are studying the acquisition of culture rather than simply
the acquisition of language. Their technique of asking caretakers to provide interpretations of their own actions and utterances accesses social–cultural meanings
directly and provides a rich technique for studying the child's acquisition of those
social-cultural meanings.

Culture plays a more explicit role in Zukow's reanalysis of milestones in symbolic development. She proposes, in essence, an analysis of the development of
play equivalent to that which has become standard in studies of the acquisition of
language—an analysis in which the input to the child is compared to the child's
output. Zukow argues that performing culturally appropriate actions within highly
determining contexts does not indicate symbolic capacities any more than saying
"Thank you" appropriately indicates control of the dative case. Some notion of
"productivity" and "creativity" must be brought to bear in assessing children's
development of symbolic capacities, as it is for language development.

Despite the fact that culture seems an important theme, this collection of papers
reflects a gap in the field of child development in that questions about children's
development are not seen as embedded in questions about caretakers' cultures.
There is little cross-cultural work presented here, the work by Ninio and Wheeler on
Israeli mothers being the only exception to the North American-Anglophone origins
of the subjects in the various studies. Child-rearing patterns and practices are an
intrinsic part of the system which is culture. Not just ideas about how infants and
young children should be treated, but also notions about what children are and about
what the ideal child of a given age is like, vary across cultures. Information about
these notions must be available as a context for understanding any data about child
development and the contribution of social interaction to child development.

Understanding cultural variation in beliefs about appropriate childhood behaviors
and milestones of development becomes even more crucial as researchers' attention
shifts to older children and to metalinguistics and metacognitive skills. The skills
referred to as metacognitive and metalinguistic can also be thought of as 'decontex-

tualized': using language for games or as a problem rather than for communication; thinking about thought processes rather than about problems to be solved. These are precisely the skills that some cultures value highly and other cultures do not value. We can only hope that the divisive and often misguided discussions about ''cultural deprivation'' carried out in the sixties with reference to language development will not be repeated in the eighties for metalinguistic development, simply because the field as a whole persists in its failure to deal in any substantial way with the notion of culture and cultural variation.

Author Index

Subject Index

Affect in communication, xiii
  development of meaning and, 23–6
  face perception by infant and, 63–5
  "motherese" and, 6, 18–26
  nonlinguistic, 33–5
  social competence and, 220–1
  voice perception by infant and, 67, 69
Alpern-Boll Communication subscale, 216, 217
Attachment behavior, social development and, 210–1
Attention, description and, 308–11
Attention-to-Object schema, 300–1
Auditory processing by infants:
  affect and, 18–23
  intersensory facilitation in, 16–7, 21–2
  intonation contours and, 13–6
  loudness and, 10–1
  pitch contours in, 11–3
  speech perception and, 59–61, 69–72
  voice perception and, 65–9

Birth, mother-infant interaction following, 36–8
Blindness, 224–41, 323–4
  analysis of language acquisition and, 229–41

word combination and, 228–9, 235–8
word meaning emergence and, 225–41

Cognitive development:
  cultural setting of, 168–9
  description in, 300–7
  ethological approach to, 32
  intent in communication and, 119–20, 128–33
  language acquisition and, xiii–xiv, 128–33, 164
  social interaction and, 39
Conversation:
  mother-child communication as basis for, 113, 139–53
  structure of, 138–9
Culture, cognitive development and, 168–9

Deafness, mother-child communication in, 212–21
Decentration in language acquisition, 227
Description, 297–312
  cognitive development and, 300–7
  consequences of, 307–11
  defined, 298–9
  gesture in early childhood as, 299–303